Overpayments and Recovery of Social Security Benefits:
A guide to advice and representation

PAUL STAGG is a barrister in private practice, practising general common law. He is a former tutor in law at the Universities of Essex and Buckingham, and at King's College, London. He has extensive experience of advising and representing social security claimants, both on a professional and voluntary basis.

Overpayments and Recovery of Social Security Benefits

A guide to advice and representation

Paul Stagg, BARRISTER

LAG Legal Action Group
1996

This edition published in Great Britain 1996
by LAG Education and Service Trust Limited
242 Pentonville Road, London N1 9UN

Reprinted 1997

© Paul Stagg 1996

All rights reserved. No part of this publication may be reproduced, stored in a retrieval system or transmitted in any form or by any means, without permission from the publisher.

The right of Paul Stagg to be identified as author of this work is hereby asserted in accordance with the Copyright, Patents and Designs Act 1988.

British Library Cataloguing in Publication Data
A CIP catalogue record for this book is available from the British Library

ISBN 0 905099 73 7

Typeset by Doyle & Co, Colchester
Printed in Great Britain by Bell & Bain Ltd, Glasgow

Foreword

by MARTIN PARTINGTON
Professor of Law and Pro-Vice Chancellor, University of Bristol

Overpayments of social security benefit can arise for a wide variety of reasons. Claimant error, administrative mistake, procedural defect, fraud: each can be a factor which results in the social security authorities – at both central and local government level – paying to claimants (or others) cash sums to which they are not entitled by law.

Government policy could be that *any* such incorrect payment is recoverable from those to whom it has been made; but it is not. Government recognises that there will be cases where recovery would be neither appropriate nor just. However, because the policy of the Department of Social Security is that not every overpayment of benefit should be recoverable, the circumstances in which overpayments are recoverable have to be distinguished from those where they are not. Setting that boundary has resulted in an extremely complex body of law, further glossed by decisions of the social security commissioners and the courts.

As well as being difficult to analyse, the law can be difficult to apply. Overpayments cases frequently involve disputes as to fact – did the claimant actually make the telephone call s/he says s/he made? did the claimant report a change of circumstances to the local office? – or disputes as to the amount of an alleged overpayment. And the stark social reality is that many to whom overpayments are made will have spent money so received, and will have few alternative resources, if any, from which repayments can be made without placing further stress on already limited means.

Thus, both as a matter of good administration, and to protect those who are entitled to the protection of the law, it is important that the rules should be applied properly. This will only happen if the rules are properly understood.

I am therefore delighted to welcome the publication of this book by Paul Stagg. Here, the law is analysed with exemplary clarity. The worked examples help to explain the detail and practical application of the provisions. The checklists provide invaluable reminders of the questions on which evidence needs to be obtained, or the issues to be determined. Further, the text is full of sound practical advice – I particularly welcome the consideration of the practices of the Benefits Agency, for example, in arranging terms for the repayment of a confirmed overpayment.

I am sure the book will be a most welcome and highly valued addition to the specialist literature on social security law. I anticipate that it will soon prove an essential source of independent analysis and guidance for all those who have the task of applying the rules, advising claimants, or determining apeals relating to the overpayment of social security benefits.

4 September 1996

Preface

The idea for this book arose from my work for the Free Representation Unit representing social security claimants at tribunals. Cases involving overpayments and recovery of benefit are some of the most complex that come before tribunals and review boards, and recovery of vast sums of money is frequently sought from impecunious clients who require the very best advice and representation to ensure they do not end up repaying money unnecessarily. The standard textbooks on social security law already contain useful summaries of the case-law, to which my debt will be obvious to the reader. However, there was a feeling amongst my colleagues at the FRU that a comprehensive work on the subject covering all the various aspects of overpayments and recovery, civil and criminal, would be a useful aid to those seeking to provide the required standard of advice and representation. This book is an attempt to live up to that aspiration.

In no small way, this book was also inspired by Professor Martin Partington's *Claim in Time* (3rd edn, LAG, 1994), a comprehensive survey of the complex law relating to claims for benefit. I felt that this book might compliment his well-established work and with that in mind I approached LAG, to the staff of which I am enormously grateful. Professor Partington has been generous enough to contribute the foreword.

Any book of this nature inevitably leads to a lengthy list of acknowlegements. I am grateful to past and present colleagues at the FRU who have discussed various issues with me and, indeed, first stimulated my interest in social security law: Simon Cox, Lee Humby (who made many useful suggestions in relation to Part III), Desmond Rutledge, Duran Seddon, Chandra Sekar and Jo Silcox (the present case-worker). I have received great help in recent months from attending meetings of the Social Security

Legal Challenges Group and the discussions of contemporary issues. I am indebted to the enormous collective wisdom of the members of the group. The staff at the Office of the Social Security and Child Support Commissioners have been tireless in assisting my attempts to locate increasingly obscure authority when they have had many other demands on their time, and I also owe thanks to Cleveland Welfare Rights Unit and to Carolyn George of CPAG in this connection. Thanks are also due to David Thomas of CPAG, Sally Robertson and Howard Levenson. The members of my chambers have been unfailingly helpful and supportive, and I would especially like to thank William Hunter and Julian Waters for taking the time to discuss specific points. A large number of friends have provided much-needed encouragement, and gratitude is particularly due to Sarah Jenkins, Rebecca Juste, Tyrone Smith and Janette Thomas. First among these is Melanie Lund. Without her support and understanding this project would have foundered.

I should not forget the clients, past and present, whose many and varied problems have led me to develop my interest in this subject. I hope that I have been as useful to them as the experience I gained from advising and representing them has been to me.

The book is dedicated to my parents with love and respect.

The law as reported is stated as at 1 August 1996.

Paul Stagg
No 1 Serjeants' Inn
29 August 1996

Contents

Table of cases and decisions xiv
Table of statutes xxvii
Table of statutory instruments xxxi
Abbreviations xxxvii

1 **Introduction** 1

PART I: STATUTORY RECOVERY OF GENERAL BENEFITS – SSAA S 71 AND ITS PREDECESSORS

2 **Structure and scope of SSAA s71** 7
 The applicability of the section 7
 Recovery from 'any person' 10
 '... whether fraudulently or otherwise ...' 15
 Time limits 15

3 **The 'review and revision' requirement** 17
 The nature of the requirement 18
 The process of review 19
 Exceptions to the requirement 20
 Failure to comply with the requirement 21

4 **Misrepresentation** 34
 Definition 35
 The content of the representation 37
 The relevance of personal factors 49

5 **Failure to disclose** 56
 The duty of disclosure 57

x Contents

    The nature of a disclosure 66
    The requirement of failure 79

6 The relevant material fact 92
    The need for a fact 93
    Primary and secondary fact 97
    Materiality 99

7 The requirement of a causal link 102
    Basic principles 105
    When is a breach of duty an operative cause? 109

8 Calculating the amount owed 124
    A method of calculating an amount 125
    Offsets allowed under statute 128
    Applying for extra-statutory offsets 140

9 Payments made and breaches of duty committed before 6 April 1987 142
    Non-retrospectivity of SSA 1986 s53 143
    Recovery of supplementary benefit: SSA 1975 s20 148
    Recovery of family income supplement: reg 10 149
    Recovery of benefits under the 'due care and diligence' test 149

10 Challenging DSS decisions 157
    The decision-making process 157
    Requests for review 161
    Appeals to a tribunal 162
    Challenging tribunal decisions 177
    Requests to waive recovery 178
    Recovery from third parties 181
    Application to the court for relief by personal representatives 184
    Judicial review 185

11 Enforcement of recovery 188
    Arrangements for payment 188
    Enforcement through the courts 190
    Deduction from benefits 191
    Bypassing SSAA s71 by recovery from third parties 196

Contents xi

PART II: STATUTORY RECOVERY OF GENERAL BENEFITS – OTHER RIGHTS

12 Recovery of income-related benefits after late receipt of income 201
Late payments of prescribed income 201
Prescribed payments from public funds 204
A third party receiving benefit in respect of the claimant 211
Enforcement 212
Challenging decisions 214

13 Payments under the severe hardship rule 215
The hardship direction 215
The content of the sections 216
Challenging SSAA s72 decisions 217
Enforcement 218

14 Overpayments by credit transfer 220
The four conditions 220
Challenging decisions 224
Enforcement 225

15 Miscellaneous rights of recovery 226
Recovery of social fund payments 226
Recovery of interim payments 229
Recovery on the grounds of failure to maintain 230
Recovery of income support paid after a trade dispute 231

16 Recovery from compensation payments 233
The Compensation Recovery Scheme 233
Recovery from compensation under employment protection legislation 248
Recovery from criminal injuries compensation 250

PART III: STATUTORY RECOVERY OF HOUSING BENEFIT AND COUNCIL TAX BENEFIT

17 The rules for recovery 253
Conditions for recovery 254
Calculating the amount 264

18 Challenging local authority decisions 268

xii *Contents*

The initial determination by the authority 269
Review by the local authority 273
Further review by a review board 276
Judicial review 278
Contribution proceedings 279

19 Enforcement of recovery 280
The system for repayment 280
Requests to waive recovery 280
Enforcements through the courts 281
Deductions from benefits 282

PART IV: RECOVERY UNDER COMMON LAW

20 Recovery through the courts 287
The basis of recovery: conversion 288
The basis of recovery: restitution 288

PART V: OVERPAYMENTS AND CRIMINAL LAW

21 The process of investigation 301
Mechanisms for detection of fraud 301
Interviews 303
Advising those under investigation 307

22 Prosecution of offences 309
Prosecution practice 309
The offences 310
Sentencing 316

APPENDICES

1 Extracts from legislation 323

2 Precedents 343
SSAA s71 343
Recovery of benefit paid before 1987 348
SSAA s74 349
Overpayments by credit transfer 350
Compensation recovery 350
Housing benefit and council tax benefit 351
Court proceedings 352

3 Checklist for conferences with defendants 357

4 Checklists for calculating amounts of overpayments 359
   SSAA s71 overpayments 359
   SSAA s74 overpayments 360
   Housing benefit and council tax benefit
   overpayments 361

5 Guide to decision-making by appellate bodies 362
   SSAA s71 appeals 362
   Housing benefit or council tax benefit review board 364

Index 366

Table of cases and decisions

Agromet Motoimport Ltd v Maulden Engineering Co (Beds) Ltd [1985] 1 WLR 702	190
Anglo-Scottish Beet Sugar Corporation Ltd v Spalding UDC [1937] 2 KB 607, CA	290
Associated Picture Houses Ltd v Wednesbury Corporation [1948] 1 KB 223, CA	187
Attorney-General of Hong Kong v Ng Yeun Shiu [1983] 2 AC 629	161
Avon County Council v Howlett [1983] 1 WLR 605	296
Barrass v Reeve [1981] 1 WLR 408	313
Beaney (deceased), Re [1978] 1 WLR 770	53, 55
Berriello v Felixstowe Dock and Railway Co [1989] 1 WLR 695	247
Bilbie v Lumley (1802) 2 East 469	291
Birkdale District Electricity Supply Co Ltd v Southport Corporation [1926] AC 355	159
Bissett v Wilkinson [1927] AC 177	95
Bogdal v Hall [1987] Crim LR 500	314
Brinkibon Ltd v Stahag Stahl [1983] 2 AC 34	67
Brown v Raphael [1958] Ch 636	96
C 1/89 (CB)	42
C 2/89 (WB)	42
CA 126/1989	144
CA 303/1992	84, 85, 89, 90
Caisse Regionale d'Assurance Maladie de Lille v Palermo (case 237/78) [1979] ECR 2729, ECJ	208
Caisse Regionale d'Assurance Maladie Rhone-Alpes v Gilletti (joined cases 379 to 381/85 and 93/86) [1987] ECR 955. ECJ	210
CCR 1/1993	236, 238, 240
CCR 2/1993	236, 240, 244
CCR 3/1993	240, 244
CCR 4/1993	239, 245, 246
CCR 5/1993	236, 238

xvi Table of cases and decisions

CCR 2/1994	240, 243, 245
CCR 158/1995	238
CCR 5336/1995	241
CF 26/1990	90
CF 13/1992	126, 173
CG 34/1988	155
CG 54/1988	67, 88, 114
CG 65/1989	10, 11, 176, 181
CG 1024/1992	238
CG 37/1994	115
CG 6140/1995	115
Chief Adjudication Officer v McKiernon (1993) unreported, 8 July, CA	143
Chief Adjudication Officer v Sherriff (1995) *Times*, 10 May, CA	14, 51–53, 87, 90, 293
Chief Supplementary Benefit Officer v Leary [1985] 1 All ER 1061, CA	138, 148
CIS 831/1985	81, 85
CIS 807/1992	28
CIS 1/1990	27, 29
CIS 35/1990	173, 175
CIS 159/1990	65, 110, 112
CIS 173/1990	86
CIS 219/1990	21
CIS 305/1990	57
CIS 352/1990	206
CIS 359/1990	41–44
CIS 360/1990	11
CIS 514/1990	175
CIS 616/1990	227
CIS 618/1990	86
CIS 222/1991	114
CIS 650/1991	96, 275
CIS 625/1991	206
CIS 137/1992	129, 130, 137, 174
CIS 173/1992	176
CIS 312/1992	24, 25, 26, 30, 175
CIS 395/1992	18, 21, 108, 110, 117
CIS 414/1992	129, 134, 176
CIS 522/1992	136
CIS 545/1992	13, 51, 53, 55, 59, 87, 176
CIS 695/1992	50, 51, 174, 175
CIS 726/1992	83
CIS 734/1992	11, 82, 176
CIS 759/1992	79
CIS 332/1993	11, 12, 13, 14, 25, 58, 82, 148, 181, 182

Table of cases and decisions   xvii

CIS 389/1993	70, 73, 74, 119, 121, 175
CIS 393/1993	34, 46, 50, 68, 173
CIS 501/1993	207, 208, 210
CIS 515/1993	118, 119, 121
CIS 645/1993	36, 114, 176
CIS 649/1993	10, 11, 58, 148
CIS 26/1994	16
CIS 145/1994	50
CIS 322/1994	81, 85
CIS 402/1994	95, 96, 97, 107, 111, 173
CIS 583/1994	40, 43, 50, 175, 176
CIS 584/1994	86, 173, 174, 176
CIS 668/1994	61
CIS 674/1994	40, 44, 45, 50, 57, 61, 83, 176
CIS 683/1994	139
CIS 451/1995	17, 18
CIS 627/1995	87
CIS 1209/1995	35, 36, 45, 107, 115, 121, 175
CIS 11230/1995	10, 49
CIS 12032/1996	90
CIS 13924/1996	122
Clayton's Case (1816) 1 Mer 572	132
Clear v Smith [1981] 1 WLR 399	313
Commock v Chief Adjudication Officer (1989) (Appendix to R(SB) 6/90), CA	124, 129, 131, 148
Cooper v Thomas [1988] 1 EGLR 257	119
Council of Civil Service Unions v Minister for the Civil Service [1985] AC 374	161, 186
CP 20/1990	125, 126, 141, 174
CP 34/1993	50, 155
CS 11/1976	152, 153
CS 42/1987	153
CS 106/1987	155
CS 18/1988	154
CS 155/1988	69
CS 30/1989	156
CS 130/1992	38, 88, 119, 120, 122
CS 102/1993	21, 38, 42, 44, 47, 85, 93, 99, 221, 222, 239, 292
CS 366/1993	176
CS 234/1994	57, 88, 123, 167, 173–175
CSB 53/1981	80, 81, 85, 138

xviii   Table of cases and decisions

CSB 681/1981	108
CSB 684/1981	113
CSB 14/1982	73
CSB 688/1982	67
CSB 759/1982	210
CSB 1158/1982	190
CSB 347/1983	67, 76
CSB 350/1983	166
CSB 360/1983	113
CSB 528/1983	206
CSB 114/1984	113
CSB 1195/1984	76–78, 173, 175, 176
CSB 296/1985	81, 82
CSB 392/1985	139, 166, 171
CSB 393/1985	65
CSB 403/1985	72
CSB 615/1985	167, 170
CSB 712/1985	68, 112, 167
CSB 903/1985	70, 73
CSB 906/1985	72, 74, 87
CSB 1006/1985	35, 45, 85, 138
CSB 1016/1985	121
CSB 1134/1985	175
CSB 1269/1985	166
CSB 1221/1985	110
CSB 1288/1985	66, 176, 253
CSB 1397/1985	61, 70
CSB 64/1986	75, 108, 113
CSB 677/1986	57, 62, 65, 68–70, 85, 86
CSB 699/1986	61, 62, 66, 67, 175, 176
CSB 1246/1986	65, 88
CSB 1325/1986	79
CSB 1341/1986	118, 121
CSB 510/1987	87, 156
CSB 727/1987	65, 70, 75, 86, 87, 88, 100, 112
CSB 957/1987	13, 57, 58, 90, 90
CSB 383/1988	205
CSB 790/1988	41, 43, 51, 68, 70, 174, 175
CSB 874/1988	112
CSB 1134/1988	68, 70, 253
CSB 942/1989	15, 119, 174
CSB 249/1989	35, 37, 99
CSB 1093/1989	28
CSB 1182/1989	164

Table of cases and decisions xix

CSB 1093/1989	21, 53–55, 93, 99
CSB 1272/1989	28, 30, 31, 131, 176
CSB 35/1990	29, 30, 31
CSB 89/1990	201
CSB 98/1990	118
CSB 99/1990	63, 64, 79, 125, 173, 176
CSB 274/1990	28, 31
CSB 329/1990	34, 42
CSB 348/1990	39, 102
CSB 83/1991	176
CSB 218/1991	53
CSB 18/1992	35, 44, 50, 129, 138, 148, 174
CSB 108/1992	86, 118
CSB 180/1992	119
CSB 389/1993	74
CSCR 1/1994	244–246
CSCR 1/1995	245, 246
CSIS 45/1990	19, 23
CSIS 118/1990	25, 175
CSIS 62/1991	28, 137, 174, 175
CSIS 48/1992	79
CSIS 50/1992	25, 61, 78, 173, 174
CSIS 64/1992	18, 22, 25, 28
CSIS 78/1993	19, 22, 26, 27, 28, 30, 31
CSIS 13/1994	26
CSIS 37/1994	139, 173
CSIS 51/1994	173
CSIS 8/1995	129, 176
CSP 11/1950	150
CSS 33/1990	76
CSSB 198/1984	138
CSSB 621/1988	28, 29, 64, 88, 175, 176
CSSB 105/1989	20, 22, 31
CSSB 316/1989	18, 25, 26, 28
CSSB 540/1989	22, 24, 25, 28
CSU 3/1991	39
CU 25/1988	155
CU 47/1993	112, 119, 174
CWSB 2/1985	39
CWSB 15/1985	69
Department of Health and Social Security v McKee (1995) 6 BNIL 17, CC(NI)	303
Department of Social Security v Barr [1996] 5 CL 674	313

Department of Social Security v Cooper (1994)
158 JPN 354   314
Department of Social Security v Lally [1989] Crim
LR 648   314
Diplock, Re [1948] Ch 465, CA   297
Donnelly v McCoy (1995) 9 BNIL 20, QBD (NI)   246, 247
DPP v Huskinson (1988) 20 HLR 562   255
Duggan v Chief Adjudication Officer (1988)
Times, 18 December   61, 65, 105–107, 109, 112
Edgington v Fitzmaurice (1885) 29 ChD 459   96
Etim v Hatfield [1975] Crim LR 234   314
Fossi v Bundesknappschaft (case 79/76) [1977]
ECR 667   209
Foster v Federal Commissioner of Taxation (1951)
82 CLR 606   65, 66
Foster v Green (1862) 7 H & N 881   288
Foster v Mackinnan (1869) LR 4CP 704, CCP   53
Franklin v Chief Adjudication Officer (1995)
Times, 29 December, CA   34, 43, 46–48, 50, 52
Frilli v Belgium (case 1/72) [1972] ECR 457, ECJ   208
Gaumont British Distributors Ltd v Henry [1939]
2 KB 711   311
Goya v Attorney-General (1984) Times, 27
December, CA   159
Hassall and Pether v Secretary of State for Social
Security [1995] 1 WLR 821   234, 236, 240, 241, 246, 247
Hodgson v Trapp [1989] AC 807   139, 247
Hoekstra (nee Unger) v Bestuur der
Bedrijfsvereniging voor Detailhandel en
Ambachten (case 75/63) [1964] 177, ECJ   209
Hulley v Thompson [1981] 1 WLR 519, CA   231
Hunter v Walters (1871) LR 7 Ch App 75, CA   53
Hydro-Electric Commission of the Township of
Nepean v Ontario Hydro (1982) 132 DLR
(3rd) 193   292
Insurance Officer v McCaffrey [1984] 1 WLR
1353   132
ITS President's Practice Direction No 2 (16 July
1993)   172
Jackson and Cresswell v Chief Adjudication Officer
(joined cases C-63/91 and C-64/91) [1992] ECR
1-4737, ECJ; CIS 501/1993   208
Jones v Chief Adjudication Officer; Sharples v
Same [1994] 1 WLR 62, CA   34, 38, 40–46, 49–52, 65, 87, 93, 99, 103, 292

Jones v Department of Employment [1989] QB 1, CA	294
Joy v Federation Against Copyright Theft Ltd [1993] Crim LR 588, CA	303
Kelly v Solari (1841) 9 M & W 54	291
L(AC) (an infant), Re [1971] 3 All ER 743, CA	160
Larner v London County Council [1949] 2 KB 683	296
Leslie, (R) Ltd v Sheill [1914] 3 KB 607	283
Lewis v Clay (1897) 67 LJ QB 224	54
Lipkin Gorman v Karpnale Ltd [1991] 2 AC 548	296, 297
Liverpool Corporation v Hope [1938] 1 KB 751, CA	293
Lloyd v McMahon [1987] AC 625	161
Maritime Electric Co v General Dairies Ltd [1937] AC 610	159
Mason v Wimpey Waste Management Ltd [1982] IRLR 454, EAT	248, 249
Mihalis Angelos, The [1971] 1 QB 164	96
Mitchell v Department of the Environment (1996) 3 BNIL 15	247
Moore v Branton (1974) 118 SJ 40	311, 313
Mulvey v Secretary of State for Social Security [1996] SLT 267	194, 228
National Assistance Board v Parkes [1955] 2 QB 506, CA	231
Norfolk County Council v Secretary of State for the Environment [1973] 1 WLR 1400, CA	160
Orakpo v Manson Investments Ltd [1978] AC 5	293
Orton v Butler (1882) 5 B & Ald 652	288
Padfield v Minister of Agriculture Fisheries and Food [1968] AC 997	295
Page and Davis v Chief Adjudication Officer (1991) *Times*, 4 July	15, 50, 80
Perrins v Bellamy [1898] 2 Ch 521	184
Plewa v Chief Adjudication Officer [1995] 1 AC 249	8, 12, 138, 142, 143, 145, 146, 149, 152, 194, 293
Puglia v C James & Sons [1996] IRLR 70, EAT	248
R v Adams (1985) 7 Cr App R(S) 411	318
R v Allardice (1988) 87 Cr App R 380, CA	307
R v Birshirgian [1936] 1 All ER 586, CCA	311
R v Breeze (1993) 15 Cr App R(S) 94, CA	317, 319
R v Canale [1990] 2 All ER 187. CA	307
R v Charambous (1984) 6 Cr App R(S) 389, CA	316
R v Curtis (1984) 6 Cr App R(S) 250, CA	316
R v Delaney (1989) 88 Cr App R 338	307

xxii Table of cases and decisions

R v Diggles (1988) Times, 6 July, CA	316
R v Enniskillen Supplementary Benefits Appeal Tribunal, ex p Department of Health and Social Security [1980] NI 95	178
R v Ghosh [1982] QB 1053, CA	315
R v Goldstraw [1981] Crim LR 728, CA	317
R v Gough [1993] AC 646, HL	178
R v Graham (1988) 10 Cr App R(S) 352, CA	319
R v Housing Benefit Review Board of the London Borough of Brent, ex p Connery (1989) 22 HLR 40	279
R v Housing Benefit Review Board of the London Borough of Islington, ex p de Grey and Hornby (1992) unreported, 11 February	258
R v Housing Benefit Review Board, ex p Thomas [1991] COD 335	272, 278
R v Inland Revenue Commissioners, ex p Preston [1985] AC 835	185
R v Inland Revenue Commissioners, ex p MFK [1990] 1 WLR 1545, CA	161
R v Jockey Club, ex p RAM Racecourses [1993] 2 All ER 225, CA	161
R v Keenan [1990] 2 QB 54, CA	307
R v Lambie [1982] AC 449	314
R v Liverpool City Council, ex p Griffiths (1990) 22 HLR 312	257, 261
R v London Borough of Brent, ex p Kalibala (1991) unreported, 17 June, CA	271
R v London Borough of Haringey, ex p Ayub (1992) 25 HLR 566	255, 278, 282
R v London Borough of Sutton Housing Benefit Review Board, ex p Keegan (1992) 27 HLR 92	278
R v McDonagh (1989) 11 Cr App R(S) 94	318
R v Medical Appeal Tribunal (North Midland Region), ex p Hubble [1958] 2 QB 228	81
R v Miah (1989) 11 Cr App R(S) 163, CA	319
R v Middlesborough Borough Council, ex p Holmes (1995) unreported, 15 February	274, 275
R v Mills (1987) 9 Cr App R(S) 3, CA	318
R v Olusoji (1993) 15 Cr App R(S) 356, CA	318
R v Parris (1989) 89 Cr App R 68, CA	307
R v Rae (1987) 9 Cr App R(S) 523	318
R v Samuel [1988] QB 621, CA	307
R v Secretary of State for Social Security, ex p Britnell [1991] 1 WLR 189; (1989) Times, 27 January	193, 293

Table of cases and decisions xxiii

R v Secretary of State for Social Security, *ex p* Golding (1996) *Times*, 13 March, QBD; (1996) unreported, 1 July, CA	197, 198, 290
R v Secretary of State for Social Security, *ex p* Chapman (1996) *Times*, 5 February	194
R v Solihull Metropolitan Borough Council Housing Benefit Review Board, *ex p* Simpson [1994] COD 225	277
R v Stewart [1987] 2 All ER 383, CA	309, 316–318
R v Stockton-on-Tees Borough Council, *ex p* Smith [1988] RVR 38	275
R v Tucker (1993) 15 Cr App R(S) 349, CA	318
R v Weild (1993) 15 Cr App R(S) 585, CA	318
R(A) 1/72	172, 177
R(A) 1/79	152
R(A) 2/86	16, 152, 190
R(FIS) 3/1985	81, 149
R(G) 7/51	150
R(G) 18/52	93
R(G) 2/71	94
R(G) 2/72	151, 155, 156
R(G) 1/79	153, 154
R(G) 4/91	144, 145, 156
R(I) 3/75	97, 100, 161
R(I) 14/75	177
R(IS) 5/91	59
R(IS) 5/92	133, 136
R(IS) 9/92	138
R(IS) 15/93	20, 130
R(IS) 5/94	57
R(IS) 14/94	201, 205, 212, 213
R(P) 1/70	153, 155, 156
R(S) 7/56	152
R(S) 2/70	152
R(S) 2/74	155
R(S) 2/80	166
R(S) 13/81	156
R(S) 4/86	47, 97
R(SB) 3/81	58, 67, 86, 176
R(SB) 21/82	10, 11, 59, 80–82, 84, 89, 105, 116
R(SB) 4/83	99
R(SB) 28/83	10, 11, 12, 13, 14, 60, 81, 82
R(SB) 34/83	165, 166
R(SB) 41/83	22
R(SB) 44/83	15, 80, 178

Table of cases and decisions

R(SB) 54/83	56, 61, 62, 69, 72, 73, 74, 75, 80, 81, 85, 87, 108, 158, 159, 173, 175
R(SB) 8/84	173
R(SB) 12/84	105
R(SB) 18/84	227
R(SB) 20/84	67, 137
R(SB) 36/84	73, 74
R(SB) 40/84	67, 81, 84, 89, 174–176
R(SB) 42/84	173
R(SB) 6/85	165, 166
R(SB) 9/85	15, 35, 38, 50, 80, 176
R(SB) 10/85	74, 76, 137, 148
R(SB) 15/85	138
R(SB) 18/85	35, 39, 67, 119, 120, 175
R(SB) 28/85	206, 210, 211
R(SB) 11/86	129, 131–133, 176
R(SB) 15/87	15, 61–63, 65–70, 75, 80, 85, 112, 117, 118, 120, 176
R(SB) 24/87	129, 138
R(SB) 13/89	61, 65, 67, 74, 75, 106, 110, 113
R(SB) 3/90	39, 42, 57, 119–121
R(SB) 5/90	12
R(SB) 1/91	208, 210
R(SB) 2/91	39, 73, 74, 89, 95, 173, 175
R(SB) 3/91	209, 210
R(SB) 5/91	16, 190
R(SB) 7/91	19, 20, 22, 28, 30–32, 173, 175, 221
R(SB) 2/92, CA	7, 15, 50, 80, 139, 182
R(U) 5/63	150
R(U) 7/64	152, 154
R(U) 6/70	154, 155
R(U) 10/72	153
R(U) 1/73	156
R(U) 7/75	151, 155
Redgrave v Hurd (1881) 20 ChD 1, CA	121
Rees v West Glamorgan County Council [1994] PIQR P37, CA	237
Riches v Secretary of State for Social Security [1994] SLT 731	63–65, 69, 113, 176

Roy v Kensington and Chelsea and Westminster Family Practitioner Committee [1992] 1 AC 624	294
Sadiq v Chief Adjudication Officer (1988) *Times*, 8 March, CA	154
Saker v Secretary of State for Social Security (1988) (appendix to R(I) 2/88), CA	99, 275
Saunders v Anglia Building Society [1971] AC 1004	53
Sawyer and Vincent v Window Brace Ltd [1943] 1 KB 32	292
Secretary of State for Social Security v Blackie [1975] CLY 3126	185
Secretary of State for Social Security v Solly [1974] 3 All ER 922, CA	10, 152
Secretary of State for Social Security v Tunnicliffe [1991] 2 All ER 712, CA	145, 146
Secretary of State for Social Services, *ex p* Taylor (1996) *Times*, 5 February	228
Sharp Brothers & Knight v Chant [1917] 1 KB 771	292
Smith v Land & House Property Corp (1884) 28 ChD 7	95
Smith v Littlewoods Organisation Ltd [1987] AC 241	110
Taylor's Central Garages (Exeter) Ltd v Roper (1951) 115 JP 445	312
Thomas v Chief Adjudication Officer (1987) (Appendix to R(SB) 17/87), CA	105
Tinelli v Berufsgenossenschaft der Chemischen Industrie (case 144/78) [1979] ECR 757, ECJ	209
Tolfreee v Florence [1971] 1 WLR 141	313
Vigier v Bundesversicherungsanstalt fur Angestellte (case 70/80) [1981] ECR 229, ECJ	209
Wandsworth Borough Council v Winder [1985] AC 461	227, 294
Warwick District Council v Freeman (1994) 27 HLR 616, CA	182, 227, 258, 260, 261, 272, 274, 281, 294
Western Fish Products Ltd v Penwith District Council [1981] 2 All ER 204, CA	159, 160
Westminster City Council, *In re* [1986] AC 668	187
William Whiteley v R (1909) 26 TLR 19	292
Yew Bon Tew v Kenderaan Bas Mara [1983] 1 AC 553	144

Table of statutes

Benefits Act 1976—
  s 20   128, 129
Child Benefit Act 1975—
  s 8   143, 150
Child Support Act 1991   203, 230
Civil Evidence Act 1968
  s 5   289
Civil Liability (Contribution) Act 1978   182, 183
  s 1(1)   182
  s 2(1)   183
  s 10   182
County Courts Act 1984—
  s 85, 111   191
Criminal Justice Act 1991—
  s 18(1)   316
Criminal Justice and Public Order Act 1994   303, 305
  s 34, (1), (3), (6)   304
  s 38(3)   304
Criminal Evidence Act 1984   195
Employment Protection (Consolidation) Act 1978   248
  s 132, (2)(a)   248
Fatal Accidents Act 1976   236
Insolvency Act 1986   228
  s 285   194
Interpretation Act 1978   144, 146
  s 7   79, 269
  s 16   138, 194
  s 16(1)   144
Jobseekers Act 1995
  s16(1)   215

Jobseekers Act 1995—*contd*
  s16(3)(a)   215
  s16(3)(c)   216
  s34(1)   310
Limitation Act 1980   15
  s 2   191, 281
  s 5   298
  s 7   190
  s 9(1)   16
  s 10   183
Magistrates' Court Act 1980—
  s 17   315
  Sched 1, para 28   315
Police and Criminal Evidence Act 1984   304, 306
  s 67(9)   303
  ss 76, 78   307
Powers of the Criminal Courts Act 1973—
  s 33   316
  s 35   139
Prescription and Limitation (Scotland) Act 1973   190
  s 6   191, 281, 298
  Sch 1 para 1   191
  Sch 1 para 1(b)   298
  Sch 1 para 1(d)   281
  Sch 1 para 2(a)   190
Social Security Act 1975—
  s 20   146, 148, 149
  s 20(1)   148
  s 119   143, 145, 146, 151,

Table of statutes

Social Security Act 1975—contd	
	152, 154
s 119(1), (b)	150
s 119(2)	151
s 119(2A)	150
Social Security Act 1986	144, 148, 151, 193, 194
s 53	8, 142, 143, 144–151, 154, 156
s 89(1)	193
Social Security Act 1989	233, 235
Social Security Administration Act 1992	281
s 21(2)	29
s 22(1)	29
s 22(1)(b)	162
s 22(5)	163
s 23(7)	31
s 25	27, 215, 275
s 25(1)(a)	19, 97
s 25(2)	19, 31, 143
s 25(2)(b)	19
s 25(2)(c)	96
s 26	241
s 28	162
s 30	162
s 30(5)(a), (b)	19
s 33(1)	162
s 33(1)(b)	162, 163
s 36	27, 30, 131
s 36(1)	27, 28
s 60	294
s 60(1)	32
Pt III	293, 294
s 71	2, 7, 8, 10, 11, 13–17, 18, 20–22, 24, 28–30, 34–36, 48–51, 56, 57, 59, 65, 79, 80, 92–95, 97, 99, 100, 102, 103, 105, 116, 118, 124, 129–131, 139, 140, 142, 143, 148, 149, 156, 157, 161–163, 165, 166, 171, 173, 174,

Social Security Administration Act 1992 —contd	
s 71—contd	180–182, 184, 188, 192, 196, 198, 201, 213, 216–218, 220, 221, 223–225, 227, 229, 230, 239, 246, 253, 256, 258, 259, 262, 264, 268–270, 273, 274, 279, 291, 293–295, 311, 313
s 71(1)	9, 17, 23, 27, 102, 221
s 71(2)	9, 18, 24, 124, 134
s 71(3)	216
s 71(4)	220
s 71(5)	17, 20, 22–24, 26, 27, 29, 30, 92, 220, 221
s 71(5)(a)	27, 30
s 71(5)(b)	27
s 71(5A)	20
s 71(5A)	18, 27
s 71(6)	128, 217, 223
s 71(8)	192, 194, 219
s 71(8)(b)	225
s 71(8)(c)	213
s 71(9)	192
s 71(10)	218, 225, 281
s 71(10)(a), (b)	191
s 71(11)(e)	227
s 71A	8, 216, 219
s 71A(3)	216
s 71A(4)(a)	216
s 71A(4)(b)	217
s 71A(5)	217
s 71A(6)	216
s 71A(7)	217, 218
s 72	8, 216–219
s 72(2)(b)	217
s 72(3), (4)(a)	216
s 72(5)	217
s 72(6)	216
s 72(7)	216–218

Social Security Administration Act 1992 —contd	
s 74	188, 201–204, 206, 208, 210, 213, 214, 231
s 74(1)	201, 207
s 74(2)	201, 204–207, 210, 212, 213
s 74(2)(a)	205, 214
s 74(2)(b)	213
s 74(3)	211–214
s 74(4)	213
s 74(4)(a), (b)	212, 213
s 74(5)	210
ss 75, 76	253
s 78	226, 228
s 78(2)	228
s 78(3)	226
s 78(6)	231
s 81(1), (3)(c)	236
s 81(4)	238
s 81(50	247
ss 81(7), 82(1)(a), 83, 84, (1)	235
ss 85, 86, 87	237
s 87(4)	234
s 88	237
s 91	139
s 93	237
s 94	234
s 95(1)(a)	235
s 96	235
s 96(4)	235
s 97	239, 243
s 98(1)	243
s 98(2), (3), (5), (6)	244
s 98(8), (9), (11)	246
s 98(12)	244
ss 99, 100	246
ss 106, 108	231
s 110	310
s 110(2), (d)	302
s 111(1)	302

Social Security Administration Act 1992 —contd	
s 112(1)	310
s 112(1)(a), (b)	311
s 115	311
s 122(2)	314
s 125	219
s 126	60
s 126(1), (2)	14
s 134(5)	255
s 134(8)	254
s 139(5)	255
s 139(6)	254
Social Security Contributions and Benefits Act 1992	283
s 122	8
s 125(1), (3)	215
s 125(4)	216
s 126	231
s 127	232
s 138(1)(a), (b)	227
s 139(1)	227
s 139(3)	226
s 139(4)	227
s 140(2)	226
Social Security (Overpayments) Act 1996	15, 18, 20, 22–24, 42, 294
Supplementary Benefits Act 1976—	
s 12	210
s 20	143
Sch 1, para 27	138
Supreme Court Act 1981—	
s 31(3)	186
s 109	11
Theft Act 1968—	
s 4(1)	314
s 15	314
s 28	317
s 34	314
Trustee Act 1925—	
s 61	184

Table of Statutory Instruments

Child Benefit (Determination of Claims and
   Questions) Regulations 1976 (SI No 962)
reg 21	153
reg 22	151

Compensation Recovery Unit Council Tax
   Benefit (General) Regulations 1992 (SI No 1814)—
reg 28	264
Pt XI	253
reg 59(8)	275
reg 59(9)	274
reg 65	256
reg 67(1)	272
reg 68(1), (2)	269
reg 68(3), (4), (5)	268
reg 69(1)(c)	276
reg 69(2)	273
reg 69(3)(a)	274
reg 70, (1)	276
reg 72	277
reg 74	269
reg 75	278
reg 83	254, 270
reg 83(a), (b)	254
reg 84(1)	256
reg 84(2)	257, 259, 261
reg 84(3), (5)	257
regs 85, 86(1)	255
reg 86(2)	283
reg 87(2)(b)	282
reg 88	281
reg 89(1)	264
reg 89(2)	265
reg 90(a)	266
reg 90(b)	267
reg 91(1)(a), (b)	283

Compensation Recovery Unit Council Tax Benefit
(General) Regulations 1992 (SI No 1814)—*contd*
    Sch 6, para 16   272
    Sch 7   276
Council Tax (Deductions from Income Support)
Regulations 1993 (SI No 494)   198
County Court Rules—
    Ord 25, r 12   191
Criminal Justice and Public Order Act 1994
(Commencement No 6) Order 1995 (SI No 721)   304
Employment Protection (Recoupment of
Unemployment Benefit and Supplementary
Benefit) Regulations 1997 (SI No 674)—
    reg 3(1), (a), (b)   248
    reg 5(1), (2), (3), (5)   249
    reg 5(8)   248
    regs 6, 7   348
    reg 9(1), (2), (6), (9)   249
    reg 11(1), (2)   250
    reg 12(2)   250
Family Income Supplement (General) Regulations
1980 (SI No 1437)—
    reg 10   143, 149
Fines (Deductions from Income Support)
Regulations 1992 (SI No 2182)   198
Housing Benefit and Council Tax (Amendment)
Regulations 1995 (SI No 511)   274
    reg 4   274
Income Support (General) Regulations 1987
(SI No 1967)—
    reg 13A   215
    reg 37   264
    Pt XIII   253
    reg 68(6)   275
    reg 68(7)   274
    reg 74   269
    reg 77(1)   272
    reg 78(1), (2)   269
    reg 78(3), (4), (5)   268
    reg 79(1)(c)   276
    reg 79(2)   273
    reg 79(3)(a)   274
    regs 81, 82(1)   276
    reg 83   277
    reg 86   278
    reg 98   254
    reg 98(1)   270
    reg 99(1)   256

Table of Statutory Instruments xxxiii

Income Support (General) Regulations 1987
(SI No 1967)—*contd*
reg 99(2)	257, 259, 261
reg 99(3)	257
reg 99(4)	256
reg 100	255
reg 101(1)(a)	256
reg 101(1)(b)	255
reg 101(2)	283
reg 102	282
reg 103(1)	264
reg 103(2)	265
reg 104(a)	266
reg 104(b)	267
reg 105(1)(a), (c)	283
Sch 1A	215
Sch 2, para 13(3ZA)	206
Sch 6, para 14	272
Sch 7	276
Sch 9	203

Non-Contentious Probate Rules 1987 (SI No 2024)—
r 47	11

Rules of the Supreme Court—
Ord 53, r 3	186
Ord 53, r 4(1)	186

Social Fund (Recovery by Deduction from Benefits) Regulations 1988 (SI No 35)   228

Social Security Act 1986 (Commencement No 4) Order 1986 (SI No 1959)   143

Social Security (Adjudication) Regulations 1995 (SI No 1801)   163
reg 1(3)(b)	163
reg 3(3), (3A)–(3D)	163
reg 3(3F), (5)	164
reg 18	22
reg 25(1)	172
regs 55–57	131
reg 55	133
reg 55(1)	22
Sch 2, para 4	163
Sch 2, para 5	163, 177

Social Security (Adjudication) and Child Support Amendment Regulations 1996 (SI No 182)   163

Social Security (Mobility Allowance) Regulations 1975 (SI No 1573)—
reg 23	143

xxxiv *Table of Statutory Instruments*

Social Security (Claims and Payments) Regulations
1987 (SI No 1968)—

reg 4(8)	115
reg 5(1), (2)	130
reg 9(1)	134
reg 13, (a)	130
reg 13(1)	96
reg 17(4)	241
reg 32	49
reg 32(1)	35, 48, 57, 67, 85, 87, 207
reg 33	12
reg 37	308
reg 37(1)	192
Sch 1	134
Sch 9	198
Sch 9A, para 11(1)	198
Sch 9A, para 11(2)(b), (3)	197

Social Security (Determination of Claims and
Questions) Regulations 1975 (SI No 558)—

reg 38	151

Social Security (General Benefits) Regulations 1982.
(SI No 1408)—

reg 7	153

Social Security (Payments on Account,
Overpayments and Recovery)
Regulations 1987 (SI No 491)—

reg 20(2)	193

Social Security (Payments on Account, Overpayments
and Recovery) Regulations 1988 (SI No 664)

	18, 129, 130, 138, 148, 192
reg 2(2), (3), (4)	229
reg 3(b)	229
reg 4(2), (3), (a)(i), (ii), (c)	230
reg 5	133, 134, 136, 138
reg 5(2)	134, 135
reg 5(4)	135
reg 6	133, 134
reg 7(1)	202
reg 7(1)(b)	203
reg 7(2)(a), (b)	202
reg 7(3), (4)	204
reg 8(1)	205
reg 8(1)(g)	208
reg 8(2)	206
reg 9	211
reg 10	149, 210

Social Security (Payments on Account, Overpayments
    and Recovery) Regulations 1988 (SI No 664)—*contd*
        reg 11   220–225
        reg 11(2)(a)   220
        reg 11(2)(b)   223
        reg 11(3)   224
        reg 12   20, 22, 28, 221
        reg 13   129
        reg 13(b)(i)   135
        reg 13(b)(ii)   136
        reg 14   88, 137
        reg 13, (1)   138
        reg 15, (2)   192
        reg 16   196
        reg 16(3)   192
        reg 16(5), (7), (8)   195
        reg 17   192
        regs 18–29   232
Social Security (Recoupment) Regulations 1990
    (SI No 322)—
        reg 2(1), (2)   238
        reg 3   237
        reg 4   238
        reg 5   234
        reg 8(1)(a)   234
        reg 10   235
        reg 11, (7)   244
        reg 13   243
Social Security (Recoupment) (Prolongation of Period
    for Furnishing of Certificate of Total Benefit)
    Order 1995 (SI No 1152)   235

Abbreviations

Adjudication Regs	Social Security (Adjudication) Regulations 1995 SI No 1801
AO Guide	*Adjudication Officers' Guide* (looseleaf, HMSO, 1988)
Bonner	Bonner, Hooker and White, *Non-Means Tested Benefits: The Legislation* (Annual, Sweet & Maxwell, 1995)
Claims and Payments Regs	Social Security (Claims and Payments) Regulations 1987 SI No 1968
commissioner(s)	Social Security Commissioner(s)
CRG	Central Recovery Group
CRU	Compensation Recovery Unit
CTB Regs	Council Tax Benefit (General) Regulations 1992 SI No 1814
DSS	Department of Social Security (though see p3)
EP Recoupment Regs	Employment Protection (Recoupment of Unemployment Benefit and Supplementary Benefit) Regulations 1977 SI No 674
EU	European Union
HB Regs	Housing Benefits (General) Regulations 1987 SI No 1971 (as amended)
Mesher	Mesher and Wood, *Income Related Benefits: The Legislation* (Annual, Sweet & Maxwell, 1995)

Overpayments Act	Social Security (Overpayments) Act 1996
Overpayments Regs	Social Security (Payments on Account, Overpayments and Recovery) Regulations 1988 SI No 664
Recoupment Regs	Social Security (Recoupment) Regulations 1990 SI No 322
Rowland	Rowland, *Medical and Disability Appeal Tribunals: the legislation* (2nd edn, Sweet and Maxwell, 1995)
SSA	Social Security Act (followed by relevant year of Act)
SSAA	Social Security Administration Act 1992
SSCBA	Social Security Contributions and Benefits Act 1992
UBO	unemployment benefit office

CHAPTER 1
Introduction

The Department of Social Security (DSS) now has a larger budget than any other ministry. The Treasury has allowed for £89.4 billion to be spent in the budget year 1996/97 on social security benefits and administration.[1] In the continuous drive for economies, the DSS has made vigorous efforts to identify cases where claimants have been receiving more benefits than they should have been, and to combat what is seen by the government and its supporters as a continuous plague of fraud.[2]

In 1993/94 a total of £80m in overpaid benefits administered by the DSS was recovered.[3] It seems likely from the piecemeal information supplied that the total amount of overpaid benefit which was not recovered, be it because claimants are paying back by instalments, because recovery has not commenced or due to the overpayment not being legally recoverable, will have been substantially in excess of that figure. Overpayments of housing benefit, which is administered by local authorities, are also huge: for 1989/90 a figure of £213m was given.[4]

So much for the financial impact of overpayments. Excess payments of benefit can cause problems and anxiety for the recipients and their families. For every seasoned fraudster caught by the DSS's investigators, there are many more claimants genuinely bewildered by the extreme and excessive complexity of the rules and regulations that govern their entitlement to benefit and those who are simply forgetful or ignorant of their obligations. There will also be those who are victims of the DSS's mistakes or over-zealous attempts to enforce its rights of recovery.

1 Department of Social Security, *Press Release 95/35*, 9 March 1995.
2 See, eg, A Neill, 'The poor may be richer but the underclass is growing' (1995) *Sunday Times*, 25 May, p3.5.
3 HC Written Answers, vol 252, col 541.
4 HC Written Answers, vol 177, col 736

2 Overpayments and Recovery Ch 1

Advisers in benefit matters, lay and professional, will need to assist clients in all these situations and in an infinite spectrum of others. The five substantive sections of this book aim to cover all the information needed to deal with clients who have been paid too much benefit and others who are required to compensate the DSS for overpayments:

a) Part II of the book contains a detailed consideration of s71 of the Social Security Administration Act 1992 (SSAA), which gives the DSS a right to recover benefit where there has been some breach of duty by the client. The law prior to 1987 is also considered in chapter 9, and detailed discussion of the mechanisms of challenging decisions and of enforcement appears in chapters 10 and 11.
b) Part III deals with various other rights of recovery under statute which are less significant than s71 but nevertheless need to be known by advisers. The various systems for recovery of benefit following a compensation payment are also considered in chapter 16.
c) Part IV considers the totally distinct law dealing with recovery of benefits administered by the local authority.
d) Part V discusses whether the DSS or local authorities have any rights to recover benefit outside the relevant statutory procedures.
e) Part VI gives a brief outline of how the criminal law affects those who are overpaid benefit and how offences are investigated by the DSS.

The five appendices aim to place practical information and guidance at the hands of those that need it:

a) Appendix 1 sets out the main statutory provisions, to minimise the need for cross-referencing to other books or original statutory material.
b) Appendix 2 contains a selection of precedents which can be used in challenging decisions in commonly arising cases.
c) Appendices 3 and 4 give checklists to assist advisers respectively in obtaining the information which needs to be asked of the client and in considering whether the amount sought to be recovered has been correctly calculated.
d) Appendix 5 seeks to lay out in an easy format all the issues that tribunals and review boards must consider when determining a case.

The legislation in this area of the law is complex, as are some of the concepts involved. In an attempt to simplify the language used, certain abbreviations have been used. For example, 'the DSS' has been used in a generic sense, to cover both the remaining sections which are still under the direct control of the Secretary of State for Social Security and the government agencies, such as the Benefits Agency, which now carry out the bulk of its work. Others are referred to in the table of abbreviations at page xxxvii above. The subject-matter of this book does not always lend itself well to division into distinct topics and so readers are advised to make full use of all cross-references and of the tables and index.

Finally, it should not be assumed that a claimant only requires help with one problem concerning an overpayment of benefit. For example, where there is an overpayment of income support, there will often be an accompanying overpayment of housing benefit which needs separate consideration. There may also be criminal proceedings. Advisers should attempt to co-ordinate the response to these different lines of attack to ensure that a coherent picture is put forward.

Part I

Statutory recovery of general benefits: SSAA s71 and its predecessors

CHAPTER 2
Structure and scope of SSAA s71

The right to recover under the Social Security Administration Act 1992 (SSAA) s71 is by far the most frequently used of the powers of the DSS to secure recovery of benefit. The intricacies of its interpretation mean that the largest section of this book is devoted to discussing the section in detail. A good working knowledge of the operation of s71 is required by advisers to ensure that all relevant information is obtained from a client.

The objective of s71 is to compensate the DSS for the loss caused to it by the overpayment. It is not in the nature of a fine for a criminal offence or of a civil penalty.[1] The view taken by the courts and commissioners is that it is in the public interest that the state should recover the money that it has wrongfully paid over.[2] It is recognised that the section can operate harshly in many contexts but that is not a reason to disapply the section. The correct course to take in such circumstances is to ask the Secretary of State to exercise his/her discretion and not enforce the right to recover.

The applicability of the section

Before a detailed examination of the section is made, it is necessary to deal with a number of general matters about the scope of the section and when it can be invoked by the DSS.

1 R(SB) 2/92 para 13.
2 It has been held that the section does not breach the right to enjoy possessions in the European Convention of Human Rights Protocol 1 art 1: R(SB) 2/92 para 14.

The benefits covered

The vast majority of benefits can be recovered under s71. The full list is as follows:

a) contributory benefits: unemployment benefit, sickness benefit, invalidity pension and allowance, incapacity benefit, widow's payment, widow's pension, widowed mother's allowance, retirement pension, child's special allowance, graduated retirement benefit;
b) non-contributory benefits: attendance allowance, mobility allowance, severe disablement allowance, invalid care allowance, disability living allowance, guardian's allowance, age addition to retirement pensions;
c) increases to the above benefits;
d) industrial injuries benefits: disablement pension, reduced earnings allowance, retirement allowance;
e) child benefit and one parent benefit;
f) means-tested benefits: income support,[3] family credit, disability working allowance;
g) social fund payments: funeral expenses, maternity expenses and cold weather payment;
h) jobseekers' allowance (of both types);
i) abolished benefits.[4]

The section does not apply to statutory maternity pay, statutory sick pay or health benefits, eg, free prescriptions, nor does it apply to housing and council tax benefit, which are dealt with under a separate system discussed in Part IV of this book.

The time at which benefit was paid

It is established that s71 and its previous incarnation in the Social Security Act 1986 s53 do not have retrospective effect.[5] This means that payments of benefit before 6 April 1987 must be recovered under the old legislation. This is discussed in detail in chapter 9.

---

3 Though not where the overpayment was to a claimant under the age of 18. Such situations are dealt with by SSAA ss71A and 72: see chapter 12 below.
4 These are defined by the Social Security Contributions and Benefits Act 1992 (SSCBA) s122. Note that this does not affect the principle that SSAA s71 does not operate retrospectively.
5 *Plewa v Chief Adjudication Officer* [1995] 1 AC 249 at p260C, HL.

The conditions for recovery

Section 71(1) contains the basic definition of what must be shown to make an overpayment recoverable:

> Where it is determined that, whether fraudulently or otherwise, any person has misrepresented, or failed to disclose, any material fact and in consequence of the misrepresentation or failure –
> a) a payment has been made in respect of a benefit to which this section applies, or
> b) any sum recoverable by or on behalf of the Secretary of State in connection with any such payment has not been recovered,
> the Secretary of State shall be entitled to recover the amount of any payment which he would not have made or any sum which he would have received but for the misrepresentation or failure to disclose.

The subsection must be broken down into its constituent parts to ensure that every element of recoverability exists in the particular case. Part I of the book has been structured in this way to allow detailed consideration of each element set out below:

a) 'Where it has been determined that ...' This imports, in virtually all cases, the requirement that the decisions awarding benefit be reviewed and revised (see chapter 3). In addition, s71(2) requires that at the time of the determination to recover, the amount of the overpayment is calculated (see chapter 8).
b) '... whether fraudulently or otherwise ...' The significance of this phrase is discussed at p15 below.
c) '... any person ...' The implications of this are that other people besides the claimant can be made to repay the benefit sought. See further at pp10–14 below.
d) '... has misrepresented, or failed to disclose ...' This makes it clear that there is no absolute right to recover and that it is dependent on showing some shortcoming on the part of the defendant. The concepts of misrepresentation and failure to disclose are dealt with in chapters 4 and 5 respectively, and are given the umbrella term 'breach of duty' in this book.
e) '... any material fact ...' The question of what is a material fact is discussed in chapter 6.
f) '... and in consequence of the misrepresentation or failure a payment has been made ...' etc. This imports the concept of causation, discussed in chapter 7 below.

Recovery from 'any person'

It is a common misconception that s71 only allows recovery from claimants. The use of the words 'any person' apparently make it clear that there can be recovery from any person who commits a breach of duty. Recent developments have made this rather less straightforward where appointees are concerned, but the general rule remains. It should be noted that in cases of failure to disclose, there can only be recovery from a person if s/he is under a duty to disclose (see pp57–61 below).

It follows that there may be more than one person from whom there can be recovery. For example, in *CG 65/1989*, the adjudication officer decided that there could be recovery from the claimant and from two firms of solicitors who had allegedly become the claimant's appointees. Adjudication officers are instructed to issue decisions against all defendants from whom there can be s71 recovery in a particular case.[6] This requirement, however, is honoured more in the breach than the observance and there will be many cases in which advisers feel that there could be recovery from other persons besides the client. It does not seem likely that the mere fact that the adjudication officer has failed to consider the question of recoverability from other persons could affect the validity of the decision issued against the defendant.[7] The question of whether it is possible for a defendant to take action against third parties is discussed at pp181–183 below.

The various parties from whom there can be recovery are discussed below.

Claimants

Although s71 permits recovery from other parties, the vast majority of cases still concern recovery from claimants.

It has been clear for a long time that s71 permits recovery from the estate of a deceased claimant.[8] However, before this can be

---

6 *Adjudication Officers' Guide* (looseleaf, HMSO, 1988) (hereafter referred to as '*AO Guide*') para 12110.
7 This issue is being raised in *CIS 11230/1995*, currently before the commissioner.
8 *Secretary of State for Social Security v Solly* [1974] 3 All ER 922 at p926, CA; *R(SB) 21/82* para 3; *R(SB) 28/83* paras 7 and 12; *CIS 649/1993* para 28.

Ch 2 Structure and scope of s71

done, the estate must have a personal representative.[9] It will not be possible to evade recovery by declining to take out a grant of probate or letters of administration, since as a creditor the Secretary of State will be able to force the hand of the prospective personal representative by citing him/her as administrator or, in the last resort, by asking the Official Solicitor to administer the estate.[10]

Where someone has been appointed to act for a claimant, and in that capacity commits a breach of duty, the better view is that the claimant will be fixed with liability under s71 for the appointee's actions.[11] The same principle applies where a personal representative commits a breach of duty.[12] However, if the appointee's actions amount to a breach of trust, it is arguable that the claimant is not bound by the consequences of the appointee. Certainly, where there is fraud by the appointee, this ought to mean that there can be no recovery from the claimant. Claimants in such case ought not to be put to the trouble of suing appointees in order to indemnify themselves for their liability to the DSS.

Appointees

Although the position cannot be regarded as finally settled, the better view is now that, outside the circumstances set out in the previous paragraph, the DSS cannot recover from an appointee personally.

In *CG 65/1989*, it was assumed by the commissioner that there could be recovery from the solicitors. In *CIS 734/1992* the claimant's mental incapacity, it was said, prevented the claimant being fixed with the actions of the appointee. These decisions, and others concerning the implications of an appointee's actions in different contexts, were reviewed in *CIS 332/1993*. After much deliberation, Commissioner Mesher declined to follow the two earlier decisions and preferred the conclusion in *R(SB) 28/83*[13]

---

9 *R(SB) 21/82* para 9.
10 See Non-Contentious Probate Rules 1987 SI No 2024 r47 and Supreme Court Act 1981 s109 respectively.
11 *CIS 332/1993* paras 19-20 and *CIS 649/1993* paras 39-40, rejecting the approach in *CIS 734/1992* paras 4 and 8.
12 *R(SB) 28/83* para 12. Se the next section for more details.
13 Para 12.

that the claimant was fixed with the actions of the receiver appointed by the Court of Protection.

There is no obligation on a tribunal to follow the decision of Commissioner Mesher, but it does contain a full review of the authorities, including the decision of the House of Lords in *Plewa v Chief Adjudication Officer*[14] and it is suggested that it is correct. However, it is clear from the commissioner's reference to 'a person who acts on behalf of a claimant without a formal appointment, whose acts are not attributed to the claimant',[15] that the decision only applies to cases where a formal appointment of the appointee has been made under Social Security (Claims and Payments) Regulations 1987[16] reg 33 (hereafter referred to as the Claims and Payments Regs). It will not protect those who help claimants on an informal basis. However, it should be noted that an appointment can have retrospective effect over any period prior to the appointment when the claimant was unable to act,[17] so it follows that a subsequently appointed person must be protected by the principle of *CIS 332/1993* over that period. There appears to be no reason why an appointment should not be made after the overpayment decision is issued.

EXAMPLE 2.1

A is a social worker who has been helping B, who is blind, with her entitlement to benefits since 1986. In 1988 B claimed income support. B is suffering from senile dementia and there is medical evidence that from 1990 she was incapable of managing her affairs following a head injury sustained in a bad fall. Unknown to A, in 1989 B's brother died and left her a large capital sum which puts her over the capital limit. That same year, a visiting officer from the DSS calls and A signs a statement on B's behalf certifying that she has no capital resources. In 1992 the DSS discovers that B has possession of the capital sum and issues an overpayment decision against A. Simultaneously, A is formally appointed to look after B's affairs. The overpayment will only be recoverable from A until 1990, because the appointment will have retrospective effect back to the time when B was incapable of looking after her affairs. From 1990 the overpayment is recoverable from B.

---

14 [1995] 1 AC 249, HL.
15 *R(SB) 28/83* para 15.
16 SI No 1968.
17 *R(SB) 5/90* para 6.

Court of Protection receivers

It is suggested that the same principle will apply to receivers appointed by the Court of Protection to manage a claimant's affairs. It seems to have been envisaged in *CIS 545/1992* that there could, in principle, be recovery from a receiver. In *R(SB) 28/83* recovery was being sought from the claimant's estate and the commissioner added the following words at the end of his decision, as to the liability of the claimant's brother who had been a receiver during the claimant's lifetime and the personal representative after his death:

> The personal representative, in failing to disclose the deceased's assets, was acting as receiver (or agent) on the deceased's behalf. The personal representative is acting in a representative capacity only in this appeal and, if there is any question as to his liability to the estate or to the Court of Protection in connection with the repayment, those are not matters within my jurisdiction.[18]

The latter sentence could mean either that the commissioner could not decide whether the overpayment was recoverable from the brother because the decision under appeal was one that the claimant's estate should make repayment, or it could mean that he felt that there was no jurisdiction under s71 to order that an overpayment was recoverable from the receiver. In *CIS 332/1993* it was argued for the defendant and by the DSS that the commissioner was taking the latter view.[19] The commissioner appears, by expressing his 'surprise' that no mention was made by Commissioner Watson in *R(SB) 28/83* of the receiver's personal liability 'if such a liability existed', to accede to the defendant's submission.[20] If that is correct, *R(SB) 28/83* is to be regarded as authority that an overpayment cannot be recovered from a receiver personally. This would be consistent with Commissioner Watson's observation that the receiver is the agent of the claimant in this context. As with appointees, however, this analysis probably does not apply where there is some abuse by the receiver of his/her position.

---

18 Para 12.
19 Paras 15 and 17.
20 Ibid para 24. But see *CSB 957/1987* para 10.

Personal representatives

As stated above, the receiver in *R (SB) 28/83* had been the personal representative of a claimant's estate after his death. However, it does not follow from the non-liability of a receiver that a personal representative can never be liable personally. The legislation imposes a specific duty on those managing the estates of certain claimants to disclose the contents of the estate to the DSS.[21] This is enforceable by an order of the county court (sheriff court in Scotland) and the personal representative may be made to pay the costs of such an application.[22] A failure to comply with this obligation will, it is suggested, give rise to a personal liability under s71 if the DSS fails to recover any overpayment as a result of that failure to disclose (see pp60–61 below). Personal liability may also arise if a personal representative fails to inform the DSS of a claimant's death.

As an alternative, the DSS may have an action in devastavit[23] available if the personal representative distributes the estate when there is a recoverable overpayment. There is, however, the possibility of the representative applying to the court for relief against the breach of duty (see pp184–185 below).

Other third parties

Recovery is rarely sought from other third parties. As discussed at p61 below, the circumstances where there is an obligation to disclose on such a third party will be rare. However, it is clear that there can be recovery from all third parties committing breaches of duty, whether the third party is a fraudster or a kindly neighbour trying to help a claimant who finds it difficult to conduct his/her affairs. The analysis in *CIS 332/1993* is specifically stated not to assist an '"ordinary" third party'.[24]

Cases where friends and relatives assist with filling in claim forms, which are then signed by the claimant, are very common. It is clear that provided the form is signed by the claimant, there is no breach of duty by the assisting person.[25]

21 SSAA s126(1).
22 Ibid s126(2).
23 The mismanagement of the estate of a decesased person by his/her legal representatives.
24 Para 23. See also p13 above.
25 *Chief Adjudication Officer v Sherriff* (1995) *Times* 10 May, CA (official transcript pp9 and 11).

'... whether fraudulently or otherwise ...'

Probably the most controversial aspect of s71, and certainly that which aggrieves a very large number of defendants, is the principle that an overpayment is recoverable whether the breach of duty was committed fraudulently, negligently, or even innocently.[26]

The principle is now beyond doubt, following ingenious attempts in *Page and Davis v Chief Adjudication Officer*[27] and *CSB 942/1989*[28] to apply various rules of statutory construction to s71(1) to interpret it as requiring that an innocent breach of duty does not give rise to recovery. The Court of Appeal was unimpressed. Dillon LJ decided that the meaning of the words was 'plain and unambiguous' and, therefore, the rules of construction were unnecessary:

> 'The whole burden of the phrase "whether fraudulently or otherwise" must be ... that it is to apply even if the misrepresentation is not fraudulent, in other words, if it is innocent. No other construction makes any sense, in my view, of this particular subsection.'[29]

Time limits

There have been many attempts in the past to argue that the limitations legislation applies to decisions by the adjudicating authorities so that overpayments occurring more than six years previously are not recoverable. These arguments are based on a misunderstanding of the nature of limitation. It does not act as an automatic and complete bar to taking action against a defendant. It is a defence to an action brought in a court of law. However, the issuing of a s71 decision is not an action, and the adjudicating authorities are not courts of law, and so the expiry of the limitation period cannot be a defence to recoverability.

---

26 A proposed amendment to the Social Security (Overpayments) Act 1996 (hereafter referred to as the 'Overpayments Act') which would have restricted recovery to 12 months' benefit where the defendant breached the duty innocently was withdrawn: HC Debates, vol 280, cols 1019 to 1020.
27 (1991) *Times* 4 July (appendix to *R(SB)* 2/92), CA, confirming *R(SB)* 44/83 para 7; *R(SB)* 9/85 para 7; *R(SB)* 15/87 (T) para 14 and countless unreported decisions.
28 Para 5.
29 *Page and Davis v Chief Adjudication Officer* (n27 above) (appendix to *R(SB)* 2/92 at para 17).

The plain fact is that s9(1) of the Limitation Act 1980 simply has no application to proceedings before the adjudication authorities.[30]

Further, the expiry of the limitation period is not a change of circumstances, and so a claimant cannot obtain a review of an overpayment decision on the basis that the period has expired.[31]

It follows that there is no time limit beyond which a s71 decision cannot be issued. However, once the final decision has been made by the adjudicating authorities that an overpayment is recoverable, time then starts to run against the DSS as regards enforcement of recovery (see pp190–191 below). In addition, vigilance will be necessary to ensure that adequate proof has been provided in cases where recovery is sought over a long period.

30 R(SB) 5/91 para 7. See also R(A)2/86 para 11.
31 CIS 26/1994 para 4.

CHAPTER 3
The 'review and revision' requirement

Before a SSAA s71(1) decision can be issued providing that an overpayment is recoverable, s71(5) requires that the decision awarding benefit must be altered to reflect the correct award of benefit, whether the new amount is part of that which was paid to the claimant or nil.

This requirement can be met in two ways. The first and most simple is for the decision(s) awarding benefit to be 'reversed or varied on an appeal'. Neither the Secretary of State nor an adjudication officer can appeal against an award of benefit and so such cases will be rare, but they can occur.

> EXAMPLE 3.1
> A is in receipt of income support. There are two mortgages on the property, one of which was taken out for the use by B, A's estranged partner, for business purposes. It does not, therefore, form part of eligible housing costs and is refused by the adjudication officer. A appeals, claiming that B no longer lives with her and she can only stay in the home if the non-eligible mortgage is met. During the hearing of the appeal it becomes clear to the tribunal that A is in fact still living as husband and wife with B. The tribunal therefore reverses the adjudication officer's decision to award benefit and can then go on to find that the amount of benefit paid is liable to s71 recovery.

A tribunal might prefer in a case like EXAMPLE 3.1 to draw the potential s71 liability to the attention of the adjudication officer and leave the DSS to deal with the situation, as this will reduce the risk of the tribunal breaching natural justice by not giving the claimant an adequate chance to deal with the overpayment question. Following the decision in *CIS 451/1995*, however, this was not permissible as the recoverability decision had to be made at the same time as the decision on the appeal or not at all, and then only if the adjudication officer submitted that there should be recovery.[1] The substitution of the new SSAA s71(2) and (5A) by the Overpayments Act 1996 reverses the situation. A review decision may be made first, and that may be followed by a recoverability decision, where the recoverability decision was made after 25 July 1996.

If a review decision is issued and the claimant appeals against that review decision, the tribunal must consider whether there can be recovery. This only applies, however, where the adjudication officer submits to the tribunal that a recoverability decision should be made. The tribunal cannot decide to do this of its own volition.[2]

In the vast majority of cases, however, the condition will be fulfilled in the second way, which is for the decision awarding benefit to be 'revised on a review'. The rest of the chapter covers what this involves.

The nature of the requirement

The requirement of review and revision might appear to be a technicality but there are valid reasons for making it a precondition of recovery. First, it is illogical to have two decisions in place at once, one awarding benefit and another holding that it is recoverable. This may not always be merely something that offends against a sense of neatness and order. There are situations in the benefits system where entitlement to benefit at one time depends on entitlement to benefit at another, so that a non-entitlement at one time might have a knock-on effect to periods of benefit outside the scope of the overpayment period. Secondly and more importantly, the Social Security (Payments on Account, Overpayments and Recovery) Regulations 1988 SI No 664 (hereafter referred to as the Overpayments Regs) provide for any entitlement on the review decision to be offset

---

1 Paras 10 and 16; CIS 395/1992 para 8. Section 71(2) was introduced on 6 April 1990; before then the recovery decision could be made after the review decision: CSSB 316/1989 para 9; CSIS 64/1992 para 6.
2 CIS 451/1995 paras 13 to 16. This part of the decision appears to survive the Overpayments Act, as the tribunal still has no power to create its own recoverability decision.

against the amount of the overpayment (see pp128–133 below). It will often be impossible for a claimant or a tribunal to understand an adjudication officer's calculation unless a proper review has been carried out.

Whatever the reason for the requirement of review and revision, it is a mandatory preparatory step in making a s71 decision. The requirement cannot simply be ignored[3] and a failure to meet the requirement causes a very uncertain state of affairs (see pp21–33 below). Some of the concepts involved in the review process are difficult to grasp, but familiarity with them is important, because surveys have shown that over half of review decisions in income support overpayment cases are defective in some way.[4]

It should be noted that for overpayments before 6 April 1987, the requirements of review are different (see chapter 9). The analysis presented here relates to overpayments after that date.

The process of review

There are four stages to carrying out a review:

a) *Determine the decision(s) to be reviewed.* In order to comply with the requirement *all* the decisions within the overpayment period must be identified and reviewed.[5]

b) *Decide the grounds for review.* In s71 cases it is likely that only two of the possible grounds for review will be relevant.[6] Where the material fact which gave rise to the overpayment existed at the time of the decision, this will be ignorance of or mistake as to a material fact.[7] Where the subject-matter arose after the decision, the correct ground will be a relevant change of circumstances.[8] It will also be necessary at this stage to identify the relevant material fact which gives rise to the review, which may not be the same material fact as that

---

3 R(SB) 7/91 para 4; CSIS 78/1993 para 14.
4 *Report of the Chief Adjudication Officer 1994-5*, HMSO, 1995, p44. Fifty-seven per cent of all income support overpayment appeals required some comment about the review carried out.
5 CSIS 45/1990 para 6. See p23 below for the consequences if this is not done.
6 The others being error of law and that the claimant no longer fulfils the conditions of entitlement: SSAA s25(2); Claims and Payments Regs reg 17(4).
7 SSAA ss25(1)(a) and 30(5)(a).
8 Ibid ss25(2)(b) and 30(5)(b).

which is the subject-matter of the breach of duty (see chapter 6 below for a definition of 'material fact').
c) *Determine the period within which the grounds for review take effect.* There may be more than one ground for review and separate grounds have to be shown for each.[9] This will be particularly relevant where a claimant wishes to claim that an adjudication officer should have taken some additional entitlement into account on the review (see pp130–133 below).
d) *Decide the amount of benefit which is payable on the review.* This will have to be offset against the amount of the overpayment of benefit (see p129 below).

Exceptions to the requirement

Section 71(5) states that the requirement of review and revision must be met 'except where regulations otherwise prescribe'. The only relevant provision is Overpayments Regs reg 12:

> [Section 71(5)] of the Act (recoverability dependent on reversal, variation or revision of determination) shall not apply where the fact and circumstances of the misrepresentation or non-disclosure do not provide a basis for reviewing and revising the determination under which payment was made.[10]

What is clear is that reg 12, by its reference to a breach of duty, clearly only applies to s71 recovery and not to those absolute rights of recovery which require a review of the decisions awarding benefit. It is also clear that if it is possible to carry out a review, reg 12 cannot be used to excuse a failure to carry out such a review.[11] Apart from that, this rather delphic formulation gives no clue as to what 'circumstances' might be appropriate for its use. The *Adjudication Officers' Guide* suggests three possible uses:[12]

a) Decisions relating to retirement pension before 1 October 1986 due to the different decision-making system in force at that stage.
b) 'For the correction of accidental errors': the kind of situation envisaged by this is unclear. It may be intended to allow an

---

9 *R(IS) 15/93* para 9.
10 This regulation will have to be amended after the commencement of the Overpayments Act 1996 to refer to s71(5A) as well.
11 *R(SB) 7/91* para 4; *CSSB 105/1989* para 12.
12 Para 12021.

Ch 3 The 'review and revision' requirement

adjudication officer to change review and recoverability decisions where a slip has been made in the wording used.
c) Irregular encashments: by far the most frequent use of the provision and, although the wording does not make it clear, foremost in the mind of the draftsman. It was applied by the commissioner in *CS 102/1993*, where the claimant was sent a letter informing him that he was not entitled to invalidity benefit and asked him to return his order book. He cashed the slip for the following week before returning it. The commissioner held that even though the award of invalidity benefit had already been reviewed, it could still be said that the payment of benefit was made 'under' the award and so reg 12 removed the need for review and revision.[13] It will also be applicable in cases where order books have been stolen or where a breach of trust has been committed.[14]

Failure to comply with the requirement

One of the greatest areas of uncertainty in the law relating to s71 recovery concerns the status of an overpayment decision where the requirement that the existing awards of benefit should be reviewed and revised has not been properly met. There are over 20 commissioners' decisions on the subject and extracting coherent principles from the mass of case-law is extremely problematic. Scottish commissioners have tended to be more exacting than those in England and Wales, but all unreported decisions carry equal weight and the subject urgently needs examination by the Court of Appeal or by a tribunal of commissioners.

One thing that is reasonably clear is that if a claimant requires the adjudication officer to prove the validity of the review, specific proof that the review was carried out must be produced before a tribunal. The documents showing the process of the review will be an invaluable aid to seeing how the amount said to be recoverable has been calculated. For that reason, proof of the review process should always be required as part of the grounds of appeal.

---

13 Para 16. If *CIS 219/1990* para 4 holds otherwise, it is wrongly decided.
14 So the provision could be used to recover from the claimant's husband in *CIS 395/1992* and the claimant's mother in *CSB 1093/1989*, though it is referred to in neither of those cases.

Five issues arise when considering the effect of a failure to comply with the requirements of s71(5) (in this chapter, 'the requirement' is used as shorthand for the need for review and revision):

a) what happens when there is no evidence at all of the requirement being met;
b) whether the requirement is met when a review decision is defective;
c) whether secondary evidence of compliance is acceptable and, if so, what type of evidence will suffice;
d) whether a tribunal or a Commissioner is able to remedy the absence of compliance with the requirement;
e) the consequences of a recovery decision being held to be invalid.

There is an obligation on the adjudication officer to notify all decisions relating to income support to a claimant in writing.[15] This will include a review decision for the purposes of s71. However, if the decision was never forwarded to the claimant, it appears that the decision will be not be rendered invalid.[16]

No review

If there is no evidence available whatsoever that the requirement had been met, then any decision to recover an overpayment will, initially at least, be invalid and of no effect.

This is clear from *R(SB) 7/91*, which is the only reported commissioner's decision in this area. An argument on behalf of the adjudication officer that the requirement was merely a technical one and was not an essential pre-condition of recovery was rejected. The Overpayments Act does not affect this fundamental principle. Moreover, Commissioner Reith decided that Overpayments Regs reg 12 (see pp20–21 above) could not be used to obviate the need for the requirement being met where it was possible to review the award had the proper procedure been complied with.[17] Unless 'the fact and circumstances' of the breach of duty 'do not provide a basis' for review and revision, reg 12 has no application.

---

15 Social Security (Adjudication) Regulations 1995 SI No 1801 (hereafter the Adjudication Regs) regs 18 and 55(1).
16 *R(SB) 41/83* para 5; *CSSB 540/1989* para 11. *CSIS 78/1993* para 11 therefore seems incorrect on this point.
17 Para 4. See also *CSSB 105/1989* para 13, followed in *CIS 360/1990* para 3; *CSIS 64/1992* para 6; *CSIS 78/1993* para 14.

> EXAMPLE 3.2
> C claims income support in February and does not disclose the fact that he starts work in May. The DSS discovers the situation in October. A decision is issued claiming recovery of the benefit, but there is no review of the award made in February, and no decision revising it to remove entitlement from May to October is made. Review on the grounds of a change in circumstances would clearly have been possible and so reg 12 cannot be relied on.

It is also clear that where the overpayment period contains more than one decision awarding benefit, they must all be reviewed and revised. Where there is a single recovery decision, a failure to revise any decision will render the whole recovery decision, and not just that part covering the decision not reviewed, invalid.[18] This is because s71(5A) requires that 'the determination in pursuance of which it was paid' to be revised prior to a decision under s71(1).

> EXAMPLE 3.3
> D is in receipt of income support from January to November. The award made in January is reviewed and revised in April and June following changes in D's mortgage interest rate. When the DSS discovers that D has been working, a review decision is issued in which the adjudication officer states, 'I have reviewed the decisions dated January and June ...' A single recovery decision for the whole period accompanies it. This recovery decision is prima facie invalid. Had there been separate recovery decisions for January, April and June, only that for April would be prima facie invalid.

Defective review

In other cases the situation may be that a review decision has been issued but that decision is defective in some way. In such cases, the validity of the recoverability decision depends on two factors.

The first factor is when the decision regarding recoverability was made. If it was made after the Overpayments Act 1996 came

18 CSIS 45/1990 para 6.

24 Overpayments and Recovery Ch 3

into force,[19] then the recovery decision will be valid and any defects in the review decision can be corrected by a tribunal on appeal.[20] This is because the new s71(2) does not make any specific requirements in relation to the review decision other than its existence prior to the recoverability decision.

If the overpayment was held to be recoverable before the Act substituted the new s71(2), the situation is more complex. The old version provided that the award must be expressed to be revised, the amount recoverable must be stated in the review decision, and the fact that it is recoverable must also be specifically mentioned.[21]

In *CIS 312/1992* the submission to the tribunal referred to a review decision having been made. The grounds for that review were made clear in a separate document. Commissioner Hoolahan accepted a submission that no valid review had been shown because the three specific requirements of s71 as to the review had not been met.[22] It is therefore suggested that where a review decision which fails to comply with one of these three elements (called a 'fundamental defect'), the recovery decision will be prima facie invalid. However, if some other deficiency is apparent, then the recovery decision is valid and the fault can be corrected by a tribunal on appeal.[23]

EXAMPLE 3.4

E is receiving income support along with child benefit in respect of F, her 18-year-old son who leaves school on 1 July and starts work. E does not disclose this to the DSS. When attempting to recover the benefits before the Overpayments Act 1996 came into force, the two review decisions read in part as follows:

I have reviewed the decision awarding child benefit. From 1 July E is not entitled to child benefit. As a result of E's failure to disclose the material fact that F had left school, an overpayment of child benefit of £100 has been made which is recoverable from E.

I have reviewed the decision dated 1 February awarding income support from that date. I am satisfied that there has

---

19 The commencement date for the Act was 24 July 1996.
20 *CSSB 540/1989* paras 13 and 14.
21 SSAA s71(2) and (5).
22 Para 17; *CSSB 540/1989* para 14.
23 *CSSB 540/1989* paras 13 and 14.

> been a change of circumstances. On 1 July F left school. As a result of E's failure to disclose the material fact that F had left school, an overpayment of income support has been made.
>
> E appeals. The recovery decision in respect of child benefit is valid, because the facts of review and recovery and the amount recoverable are expressly stated. The tribunal can insert the missing details such as the date of the decision and the grounds of review. The recovery decision relating to income support is however invalid, as the fact of recoverability and the amount recoverable have not been clearly stated. These are fundamental defects.

Secondary evidence

Where no review decision has been produced, or on the face of the text of a review decision, it is invalid through the presence of a fundamental defect, the invalidity may be cured by the production of other evidence as to what was decided by the adjudication officer. It is permissible to construct the review decision through secondary evidence.[24] However, the secondary evidence must be comprehensible and reliable. Where such evidence is relied on to validate an otherwise defective review decision, the evidence must be examined 'very critically'[25] to ensure that it really does demonstrate that a review has been carried out and the requirement met.

The level of evidence necessary depends on whether the validity of the review is in issue. Where there is no dispute, a reference in the form AT2 containing the adjudication officer's submission to the tribunal will suffice.[26] Provided there is some reference to a review decision, a tribunal can find that there is a valid review where the question is not in issue. Mere proof that the case was referred to an adjudication officer for a decision will not, however, suffice.[27] Nor is a statement that a review decision was made on a certain date adequate, without proof of the contents of the decision.[28]

---

24 *CSSB 316/1989* para 11; *CSB 540/1989* para 12.
25 *CSSB 316/1989* para 11.
26 *CSIS 50/1992* para 7(a); *CIS 332/1992* para 5.
27 *CSIS 118/1990* para 4; *CIS 312/1992* para 17.
28 *CSIS 64/1992* para 5.

26 *Overpayments and Recovery Ch 3*

Where the defendant puts the existence of the review decision in issue, the requirements of evidence are substantially more exacting. If a review decision can only be extrapolated from an analysis of numerous documents, that is insufficient.[29] A failure to prove the dates of the decisions revised will mean that the review decisions are invalid.[30] A presenting officer at a tribunal cannot give oral evidence of the terms of the review unless it was carried out by him/her personally.[31]

Where evidence is not immediately comprehensible, it may be acceptable to show the terms of a review decision but only if it is explained by oral evidence. In particular, if a computer print-out does not clearly show that a review was carried out and the terms of the resulting decision, oral evidence will be required to explain specifically why and how the print-out reveals the information contended for.[32]

Rectification on appeal

The most uncertain area relating to the requirement is whether a tribunal or a commissioner can deal with the situation where the review decision is defective or totally absent.

Undoubtedly there are strong policy reasons why it should be possible to correct the adjudication officer's omission, particularly where it is crystal-clear what the result of an appeal would be were it not for the failure to meet the requirement. To require the DSS to start the whole process again costs a great deal of public money and will mean that the claimant has to appeal against the fresh decision, which means a greater period of uncertainty for him/her. On the other hand, as suggested above at p18–19, the real purpose behind s71(5) is to require the adjudication officer to go through a logical process when making a recovery decision and to help the claimant and his/her representative see how the amount claimed has been calculated. The policy arguments as well as the legal ones are far from clear-cut.

At least six decisions of the commissioners say that either a tribunal or one of them has the power to rectify a failure to

---

29 *CSSB 316/1989* para 11.
30 *CIS 312/1992* para 20.
31 *CSIS 78/1993* para 8.
32 *CSIS 78/1993* paras 9 and 10; *CSIS 13/1994* para 4.

comply with the requirement; seven decisions say that this is not possible. In order to make sense of this mass of confused case-law, it is necessary to look at the wording of s71(5) or (5A), for overpayment decisions made before and after 24 July 1996 respectively.

Section 71(1) obviously cannot operate until there is compliance with requirements of s71(5)(a) and (b), or s71(5A), as the case may be. The fact of review and revision is a 'condition precedent'[33] of the operation of s71(1). Not only can the Secretary of State not start to enforce a right of recovery under s71(1), but no decision can be made under s71(1) until the requirement is met. Hence a recovery decision is prima facie invalid if no review decision is made.

A tribunal cannot itself carry out a review under SSAA s25 when considering an appeal by a defendant. Powers under that provision can only be exercised by the adjudication officer. It cannot therefore circumvent the problem by declaring the adjudication officer's decision invalid and then acting as if it were in the adjudication officer's shoes. It has no jurisdiction to do this.[34]

With that in mind, it is necessary to examine the ways in which it has been said that a tribunal or a commissioner can cure the absence of a review or rectify a review decision containing a fundamental defect.

SSAA s36

SSAA s36 (1) states:

> Where a question which but for this section would fall to be determined by an adjudication officer first arises in the course of an appeal to a social security appeal tribunal ... or a Commissioner, the tribunal ... or the Commissioner may, if they or he think fit, proceed to determine the question notwithstanding that it has not been considered by an adjudication officer.'

In *CSB 1272/1989* the commissioner held that this provision could be used by a tribunal or by him to carry out a review decision. He had taken it for the first time when the matter had

---

33 *CSIS 78/1993* para 14.
34 *CIS 1/1990* para 7.

not been considered by the adjudication officer or the tribunal.[35] However, the commissioner made no reference to previous authorities which had already decided that a recovery decision was totally invalid if the requirement was not met.[36] In addition, the approach of the commissioner has been rejected in a number of more recent decisions.[37]

The problem with this approach is whether the question about the requirement having been met 'first arises' in the course of an appeal. It is suggested that this is inconsistent with the structure of s71. Reviewing and revising is not merely something that ought to be done in parallel to making a recovery decision. Provided that Overpayment Regs reg 12 does not apply, it is a necessary precondition of the adjudication officer having any jurisdiction to make a recovery decision.[38] The first thing that the adjudication officer must consider is whether reg 12 applies or whether review and revision is necessary. That question arises before the adjudication officer and it cannot therefore be said that the question of review and revision 'first arises in the course of an appeal'. Section 36(1) does not refer to a question which 'is first disputed' or 'is first raised' in the course of the appeal. If the question forms part of what had to be decided by the adjudication officer, the section cannot be used.[38A]

The fundamental mistake made by the commissioner in *CSB 1272/1989*, it is suggested, is the notion that the recovery decision was 'undoubtedly an effective decision'.[39] If the argument in the preceding paragraph is correct, then it is an invalid decision, being made without jurisdiction. The actual decision in *CSB 1272/1989*, to remit the case to the tribunal, may have been correct because there was a reference in the adjudication officer's submission to the tribunal about a review having been

---

35   Para 14; followed in *CSB 1093/1989* para 23.
36   *R(SB) 7/91* para 4; *CSSB 621/1988* paras 5 and 6; *CSSB 316/1989* para 11; *CSSB 540/1989* para 12.
37   *CSB 274/1990* para 18; *CSIS 62/1991* para 12; *CSIS 64/1992* para 6; *CSIS 78/1993* para 14 (at least a partial rejection). See Mesher and Wood, *Income Related Benefits: The Legislation* (Annual, Sweet & Maxwell, 1995) (hereafter referred to as Mesher), p707.
38   *CSSB 621/1988* para 5.
38A *CIS 807/1992* paras 13 and 14.
39   Para 10.

carried out,[40] which could have been secondary evidence on which basis the tribunal could have concluded that there was a review and, hence, that there was jurisdiction to make the recovery decision. The reasoning is defective, however, and ought not to be followed.

Appellate body seised of the issue
Commissioner Sanders adopted a slightly different approach to the problem in *CSB 35/1990*. In that case there seems to have been no mention of review at all in the evidence before the tribunal.

> In the present case, according to [the] record, the adjudication officer decided that income support "... has been overpaid and is recoverable by the Secretary of State as the claimant failed to disclose a material fact to the Department". Now both questions were before the adjudication officer for his decision and the terms of his decision suggest that he dealt, as required by [SSAA s21(2)] with both questions or at least attempted to; by deciding as he did that the amount overpaid was "recoverable" he dealt, as it seems to me, however imperfectly with the recoverability question that arises under [SSAA s71(5)]. The claimant's appeal necessarily related to both questions ...[41]

He had earlier noted that s71 requires two separate decisions concerning review and recovery. Given that, the reasoning set out above cannot be correct. The terms of the adjudication officer's decision quoted by the commissioner do not even disclose an attempt to produce a review decision. All that was made was a recovery decision. That decision did not put the review question in issue before the tribunal at all. This distinction is supported by the fact that SSAA s22(1) gives a right to appeal to a tribunal 'where the adjudication officer has decided a claim or question'. If a question has not been addressed by the adjudication officer, then it cannot form part of the subject-matter of an appeal to a tribunal and the tribunal has no power to deal with it, subject to the power under s36 discussed above. A tribunal has no 'originating jurisdiction'[42] and can only deal with those matters which, as a result of its statutory powers, are properly before it. The commissioner's reasoning blurs the

---

40 Paras 8 and 9.
41 Para 8.
42 *CSSB 621/1988* para 6; *CIS 1/1990* para 7.

distinction envisaged by s71(5) between review and recovery decisions.[43]

Reversing or varying award on appeal

An argument was put to the commissioner in CSB 35/1990 based on the fact that the jurisdiction conferred by s71(5)(a) does not necessarily come from a review but can also come from the decision awarding benefit being 'reversed or varied on an appeal'. It was said that on an appeal against the recovery decision, a tribunal could itself reverse or vary the decision to award benefit and give itself jurisdiction to make a s71 decision in that way.

Commissioner Sanders, without saying why, indicated that he would have rejected the argument.[44] It is suggested that it is unsound. For the reasons given above, apart from its limited jurisdiction under SSAA s36 (see pp27-29 above), a tribunal only has a power to reverse or vary a decision on an appeal if that decision is the subject-matter of the appeal. When a claimant appeals against a recovery decision, the only decision before the tribunal is that recovery decision. The decision to award benefit is not the subject-matter of the appeal and the tribunal has no power to alter it. Where there is a review decision in conformity with the requirement, the tribunal can indirectly alter the decision to award benefit by changing the terms of the review decision. Where there is no review decision, it cannot do this.

The position of the commissioner

If the above analysis is correct and tribunals have no power to remedy a failure to meet the requirement, it must follow that commissioners do not have any such power either. Commissioners no more have an originating jurisdiction than tribunals do.

On the other hand, if the conclusions above are wrong and tribunals do have power to deal with an omission themselves, then it must still be questioned whether a commissioner has the same power. In CSIS 78/1993, the commissioner stated that although he accepted that tribunals could use s36 to carry out a review of their own motion (see pp27-29 above), he did not agree with the decision in CSB 1272/1989 that the commissioner

---

43 CSB 35/1990 was not followed in CIS 312/1992 para 20, where the commissioner appeared to be sceptical about the reasoning and followed R(SB) 7/91 instead.
44 Para 9.

Ch 3 The 'review and revision' requirement

had the same power.[45] This is clearly wrong, as s36 explicitly gives the commissioner the same power as the tribunal to deal with matters 'first arising' on an appeal. It may be that the commissioner does not have sufficient material to make the review decision and may choose to remit the case to the tribunal for convenience,[46] but the commissioner could equally use the power to make further findings of fact and give the decision that the tribunal should have given.[47]

Consequences of invalidity

If a recovery decision is declared to be invalid on an appeal, can the adjudication officer then take further action to recover the overpayment? The answer to this seems to depend on the wording of the final decision of the tribunal or commissioner that the previous recovery decision is invalid. There appear to be three possibilities:

a) *A decision that no valid recovery decision has been made.*[48] In this case the effect of the tribunal's decision is that there is no adjudication officer's decision about the overpayment extant. The adjudication officer can simply issue fresh review and recovery decisions and the claimant then has a fresh right of appeal.

b) *A decision that the specific recovery decision is of no effect.*[49] Strictly speaking, this leaves the decision in existence (although of no effect) and so the appropriate course will be to review the decision to award benefit as appropriate and then review the recovery decision on the grounds that it is erroneous in point of law under SSAA s25(2). Again, the claimant then has a fresh right of appeal against the review.

c) *A decision that the overpayment is not recoverable.* In *CSIS 78/1993* Commissioner Walker, clearly exasperated with the number of cases that had come before him where the requirement had not been properly met, decided that the failures of the DSS after repeated commissioners' decisions about the consequences of such a failure meant that its

---

45 Para 14.
46 As happened in both *CSB 1272/1989* and *CSB 35/1990*.
47 SSAA s23(7). See *CSB 274/1990* para 18 for an example of this approach.
48 *R(SB) 7/91* para 5.
49 See *CSSB 105/1989* para 13.

omission should 'rebound to their loss rather than the claimant's' and held that the overpayment was not recoverable.⁵⁰ The basis for this seems rather dubious, but it may be possible to try to convince a tribunal to adopt the same course, perhaps by adopting the commissioner's policy arguments on the cost of allowing the process to begin again. If the tribunal does this, then it will not be possible for the DSS to make another attempt to recover that benefit for the same period because a final decision has been made as to the recoverability of that benefit, and there is no power to alter that decision unless it is appealed.⁵¹ This provision does not apply in the above cases, because the final decision on appeal is simply that the particular recovery decision is invalid, not that there is no right to recover.

Conclusions

It seems that as a matter of principle a failure to comply with the requirement cannot be dealt with on appeal. Although the point cannot be regarded as finally resolved, the greater weight of the authorities supports this suggested principle. If any tribunal is in doubt about this, it ought to be urged that the only reported decision, *R(SB) 7/91*, should be followed in preference to the unreported cases.

Moreover, although it has been suggested that a tribunal should deal with a failure to meet the requirement itself where the merits of the case are clear,⁵² strictly speaking the principle ought to be applied universally. If a tribunal would have decided a case in favour of the claimant were it not for the failure to meet the requirement, it ought to express that view in its decision. The result in practice will be that the adjudication officer will probably not then issue a fresh decision and there will be no need for the claimant to appeal again.

The five principles below clarify the position:

a) to comply with the requirement, there must be *either* a review decision which states the facts of revision of the decision awarding benefit and recoverability, and states the amount which is found to be recoverable *or* secondary evidence

50 Para 15.
51 SSAA s60(1).
52 Mesher, p707.

which clearly shows that the adjudication officer has reached the above conclusions;
b) if one of the two things above is demonstrated, then the recovery decision is valid and a tribunal or commissioner on appeal can (and must: see p175 below) remedy any other defects or omissions in the review decision;
c) if the requirement is not complied with, the recovery decision is invalid and of no effect;
d) a tribunal or commissioner cannot remedy a failure to comply with the requirement;
e) if a recovery decision is found to be invalid, the adjudication officer can issue fresh review and recovery decisions.

CHAPTER 4
Misrepresentation

The first breach of duty which can give rise to recovery from a defendant under SSAA s71 is that s/he has misrepresented a material fact. It is a more straightforward concept than that of failure to disclose, being easier to prove[1] than the latter ground and offering fewer bases for challenge by a claimant.

For these reasons, there has been a noticeable trend in recent years for the DSS to base recoverability decisions on misrepresentation wherever possible. Crucial to this has been reliance on the declarations signed by claimants at the end of various forms. A legal battle has raged over the precise effect of such declarations, which has revealed deep divisions of opinion not only among commissioners but also in the Court of Appeal. *Jones v Chief Adjudication Officer*[2] appears to give a partial victory to the DSS, in that these declarations can be relied upon as founding a misrepresentation but only within certain limits which have now been confirmed in *Franklin v Chief Adjudication Officer*.[3]

The declarations have been widened in scope in recent years and reliance on them by the DSS has meant that many cases which are truly cases of failure to disclose can be dealt with on the basis of misrepresentation. However, it is clear that there can be no argument that cases of this nature should be dealt with on the basis of failure to disclose, unfair though this may be.[4] But following tantalising dicta in *Franklin*, it may yet be the case that

---

1 *Jones v Chief Adjudication Officer* [1994] 1 WLR 62 at p65G, CA; *Franklin v Chief Adjudication Officer* (1995) *Times* 29 December (official transcript p11F), CA.
2 [1994] 1 WLR 62, CA.
3 (1995) *Times* 29 December, CA.
4 *Jones* (n2 above) at pp69A-B; *CSB 329/1990* para 6; *CIS 393/1993* para 5.

Ch 4 Misrepresentation 35

the DSS's attempts to widen the scope of s71 by use of the declarations will be defeated.

Because these declarations are of crucial importance in view of the frequency of reliance on them by the DSS, they are discussed in more detail below (see pp40–49). The declarations will be given the umbrella term 'general representations' and representations of specific fact will be called 'specific representations'.

Definition

For there to be a misrepresentation, there must be an 'actual statement which is untrue'.[5] There must be some 'positive and deliberate action', though there need be no intention to make a misrepresentation, or even an intention to make a representation at all,[6] since an innocent breach of duty is still a ground for recovery (see p15 above).

Usually, the DSS will rely on a written representation. However, just as disclosures may be made orally or by conduct (see p16 below), representations may be so made. In *R(SB) 18/85*, the claimant produced his war pension book at an interview with the DSS, which omitted this fact from a statement of circumstances compiled by an officer and which was later signed by the claimant. It was decided that the claimant had represented that the implications of the book should be taken into account.[7] In *CSB 249/1989* the adjudication officer successfully argued that when the claimant continued to cash his order book after receiving a letter from the DSS asking him to return it, he misrepresented by his conduct that he believed that he had a current entitlement.[8]

It should, however, be noted that the practice of the DSS is to require significant statements as to changes of circumstances to be made in writing.[9] Specific proof is required of any misrepresentation alleged,[10] and this can be used against the DSS when there is a dispute over what was said or done by the defendant.

5 *CSB 1006/1985* para 5; *CIS 1209/1995* para 24.
6 *R(SB) 9/85* para 7.
7 Para 10.
8 Para 4.
9 Claims and Payments Regs reg 32(1).
10 *CSB 18/1992* para 18.

EXAMPLE 4.1
A receives unemployment benefit. The DSS claims that when A signed on as unemployed, he told the officer in the unemployment benefit office that his wife had also become unemployed, making him eligible for an increase in respect of her as a dependant. The adjudication officer awards this increase without seeking confirmation of the situation from A or his wife. No statement is available from the officer in question, but the manager of the office claims to remember the officer in question getting authorisation to take the necessary steps. A disputes the alleged statement. In support of his case, A can rely on: (a) the fact that proper procedure was not followed; (b) the fact that the DSS's account of the misrepresentation is second-hand hearsay; and (c) the unlikelihood of a manager remembering such a transaction.

The definition of misrepresentation was widened still further in *CIS 645/1993*. In that case, the claimant had not filled in a part of his income support claim form at all. Had he filled it in correctly, he would have disclosed that he had a certain resource. If there was a misrepresentation in this case, it would have been the general representation in the signing of the declaration at the end of the form that the 'information that I have given on this form is correct and complete'. However, the commissioner held that the claimant's silence in not completing the relevant part of the claim form was itself a misrepresentation, as the claimant was under a duty to ensure that the information he gave was complete.[11]

It is suggested that the commissioner in this case confused the content of the declaration with the claimant's duty. The decision ignores the requirement for an 'actual statement' and blurs the distinction between misrepresentation and failure to disclose to an unacceptable degree. In *CIS 1209/1995*, where the same part of the claim form was left incomplete, the commissioner neither rejected the analysis nor followed it. The case was remitted to the tribunal for consideration of whether 'the absence of an answer [could] indicate or carry the implication that there was no money coming in'.[12]

Section 71 does not require that a misrepresentation be made to the DSS. Provided that as a result of the misrepresentation, an

11 Para 6.
12 Para 14.

overpayment is made, the misrepresentation could be made to anybody. Thus, the argument of the claimant in *CSB 249/1989* that he had made no misrepresentation to the DSS but only to the post office in presenting his order book was rejected.[13]

EXAMPLE 4.2
B is in receipt of income support for himself, his partner C and their children. C is working eight hours per week. C controls the family finances. Unknown to B, C increases her hours to 16 per week. C tells B that she is visiting her friends. She keeps the extra money for her own use. One day, B asks C whether she is still only working eight hours a week and she says, 'Yes'. In principle the DSS could recover the overpayment from C on the grounds of her misrepresentations to B, though there may be arguments over causation.

The content of the representation

Having established that there has been a representation, the next step is to consider precisely *what* has been represented by the defendant.

Has a material fact been represented?

It must be carefully considered whether the claimant has represented a material fact, as opposed to a secondary fact or a view of law, opinion or intention. This question is dealt with fully in chapter 6 below. However, it must always be borne in mind that where the main representation (called a 'primary representation' in this chapter and chapter 6) is not one of a material fact, there may be other representations (called 'secondary representations') implicit in the primary representation. This possibility is addressed at p97–99 below.

Construing a representation

It is suggested that when determining exactly what has been represented by the claimant, two basic rules must be followed.

13 Para 6.

The precise wording of the representation

Normally, the meaning of the words of a representation will present no difficulty, but they must always be examined to ensure that they mean exactly what the DSS contends that they mean. So if a claimant added some words to or crossed out part of a declaration, then it would be the amended rather than the original form which had been represented.[14]

There may be cases in which the grammar of the representation becomes important. Thus in *CS 102/1993*, an argument that the part of the order book declaration, which is quoted at p42 below, that 'I am entitled to the above sum' added nothing to the preceding part of the declaration was rejected.[15] It has also been held that where there is a list of representations, each may be considered individually, though the meaning of each must be considered in light of the other representations.[16]

It is also suggested that where there is ambiguity in the meaning of a representation, the claimant is entitled to the benefit of the doubt.[17] This follows from the doctrine of *contra proferentem*, which provides that where a party relies on a document, any ambiguities are to be construed against him/her. Where claimants who may not be particularly literate or articulate do not express themselves with exemplary clarity, this should not be held against them.

EXAMPLE 4.3
D is in receipt of invalid care allowance and works a few hours per week in a library. An issue arises over whether D is earning more than the earnings limit and a form is sent to D asking her to list her weekly expenses for laundering clothes and so on. D misunderstands this to mean her total living expenses and not merely those connected with the job. She therefore overstates the relevant amounts. This is not a misrepresentation because she was responding literally to the question she was asked.

---

14 *R(SB) 9/85* para 7.
15 Para 10.
16 *CS 130/1992* paras 13 and 15.
17 *Jones v Chief Adjudication Officer* and *Sharples v Chief Adjudication Officer* [1994] 1 WLR 62, CA. The fact that the majority limited the scope of the declarations would tend to support the proposition.

The representation must be seen in context

The tribunal in *R(SB) 18/85*, discussed above, erred in law because it failed to consider the circumstances surrounding the representation. The general principle that the plain words of a representation may be coloured by the circumstances in which it is made has been applied in a number of different ways.

First, as was held in *R(SB) 18/85* itself,[18] if a claimant makes a representation orally or by conduct which is inconsistent with a written misrepresentation before the adjudication officer, then the latter representation should be regarded as qualified by the former. This can also give rise to particular problems in considering whether a misrepresentation caused an overpayment (see pp118–123 below).

Secondly, a representation must be interpreted in the light of any documents which the adjudication officer had, or ought to have had, before him/her at the time that the representation was being considered. In *R(SB) 2/91* the nature of the claimant's course of study had been misrepresented on a literal reading of one letter sent to the DSS, but what the claimant had meant became clear on viewing a second letter.[19] Likewise, the claimant in *CSU 3/1991* put the correct figure for his occupational pension on a claim form and an incorrect one on a form for details about the pension. The commissioner decided that the DSS should have had both documents and queried the discrepancy. In *CSB 348/1990* it was held that a sheet of paper that had allegedly been attached to a claim form should have been taken into account.[20] A claim form must be seen as a whole, so information put in the wrong place on a form is not misrepresented by a contradictory answer in the correct place.[20A]

This principle cannot be extended to include all documents that the DSS has had before it in relation to previous claims. So, in *R(SB) 3/90* the contents of a previous claim form submitted by the claimant were not required to be taken into account.[21] However, provided reference is made to a specific document in

---

18 Para 10.
19 Para 13.
20 Para 4.
20A *CWSB 2/1985* para 2(b).
21 Para 12.

relation to previous claims, it is suggested that the principle would apply as it would put the adjudication officer on notice.[22]

Thirdly, a representation may be coloured by advice from the DSS. Guidance notes that accompany any document on which the defendant has made a representation should be considered.[23] *CIS 583/1994* takes this principle further. The claimant asserted that she had been advised by an officer that working for 17½ hours per week would not affect her entitlement to income support. The commissioner held that if this evidence was accepted, then the general representation that all material facts had been reported was qualified and the claimant did not warrant that she had reported her increase in hours correctly, even where the guidance notes clearly contradicted the advice given.[24]

A final point is that a written representation, or the absence of one, may be affected by a general representation. A general representation generally qualifies the whole of the relevant document to which it is appended.[25]

Analysis of general representations

Because of their importance, a detailed analysis of the four common types of general representation upon which the DSS relies is presented below, but first the wider context of general representations must be discussed.

The importance of *Jones v Chief Adjudication Officer*[26] has already been alluded to. Mr Jones was in receipt of concurrent awards of unemployment benefit and income support. He had disclosed a claim for the former on his income support form, but did not disclose its subsequent receipt. The DSS's procedure for taking account of subsequent awards of unemployment benefit broke down and recovery was sought on the basis that Mr Jones

---

22 In *R(SB) 3/90* itself, the commissioner relied heavily at para 11 on the fact that the claimant stated, wrongly, that he had not previously made a claim.
23 *Jones v Chief Adjudication Officer* [1994] 1 WLR 62 at p67H, CA; *CIS 583/1994* para 14.
24 Para 15. This seems questionable in view of the decision in *Jones v Chief Adjudication Officer* [1994] 1 WLR 62 at p73A, CA that the declaration could not be qualified to read as a declaration that all facts which the claimant believed were material. The decision must, however, be applied by tribunals.
25 *Sharples v Chief Adjudication Officer* [1994] 1 WLR 62 at p70G, CA; *CIS 674/1994* para 14.
26 [1994] 1 WLR 62, CA.

Ch 4 Misrepresentation 41

misrepresented the material fact that he had disclosed all material facts when he signed the order book declaration (quoted below) each week.

It was argued before the commissioner in Mr Jones' case, *CIS 359/1990*, that the declaration had to be qualified to one that Mr Jones had disclosed all facts of which he knew (and it was not disputed that he knew about the award of unemployment benefit) and thought ought to be disclosed. This submission had been accepted in *CSB 790/1988*. The commissioner decided that:

> I regret that I have to disagree with that restricted interpretation. I do not see how it could be said that the declaration was qualified and limited to what the claimant believed she had to disclose. Such a construction, it seems to me, is wholly artificial and at variance with the plain words of the declaration. A claimant ... specifically warrants that the factual position is as he has reported it.[27]

Before the Court of Appeal, counsel for Mr Jones sought to raise a new argument, namely, that the misrepresentation on the order book slip was not a misrepresentation of a material fact. The court was substantially divided in its view of this contention, and it is worth setting out its conclusions in detail.

Evans LJ agreed with the submission on behalf of Mr Jones. The statement that he had 'correctly reported all material facts' only represented that there had been a disclosure and that the disclosure had been of all material facts. But the calculation of Mr Jones' benefit was not affected by the non-disclosure of facts. It was the facts themselves that were relevant to the calculation of benefit. Accordingly, that general representation was not a representation of a material fact.[28]

Stuart-Smith LJ appears to have decided that the general representation contained within it secondary, specific representations of all the material facts. He then went on to say that the claimant was not entitled if the general representation was untrue, so a material fact had been misrepresented.[29] This is a leap in logic and does not address the point made by Evans LJ that the mere fact of non-disclosure has nothing to do with entitlement in itself. For Dillon LJ, the mere fact that the general representation was false seems to have been sufficient.

---

27 Para 7.
28 *Jones* (n23 above) at p67A to 68C.
29 Ibid p72A-B.

It is suggested that the reasoning of the majority is not satisfactory.[30] A more logical way to reach the same result is to rely on Stuart-Smith LJ's first point, that the general representation contains secondary representations of the material facts, and that these material facts were misrepresented by the signing of the declaration. This analysis is similar to the fundamentalist view taken in *CIS 359/1990*, though the commissioner does not address the point. There are three problems with this way of addressing Evans LJ's objections. First, there are the general arguments about the fairness of forcing a claimant to warrant facts and depriving him/her of the defences available when a failure to disclose is alleged . Secondly, it is difficult to reconcile this reasoning with the view taken by the majority that the declaration was limited to one that all material facts known to the claimant had been disclosed.[31] Finally, it is questionable whether a declaration that, 'I have correctly reported any facts which could affect the amount of my benefit', can be said, as a matter of language, to contain representations that '... I have not worked, that I have not started to receive any other benefits ...', and so on. It seems unlikely that the average claimant would view his/her statement that way.

The judgments in the Court of Appeal are a clear attempt to balance the interests of the public purse against fairness to claimants, though at the expense of coherent reasoning in the case of the majority. Whatever the academic criticism that might be made, until such time as the House of Lords examines the problem,[32] the reasoning of the majority must be applied, with the result that general representations are clearly representations of material fact.[33]

The order book declaration

> I declare that I have read and understood all the instructions in this order book, that I have correctly reported any facts which could affect the amount of my payment and that I am entitled to the above sum.

---

30 A view held by other commentators. See Mesher, p698; Rowe, 'Misrepresentation or failure to disclose' [1994] 2 JSSL 85.
31 *Jones* (n23 above) at p71H and 72F. See p43 below.
32 A petition for leave to appeal was dismissed in *Jones* (n23 above): see [1994] 1 WLR 73.
33 Following *R(SB) 3/90* para 6 and *CSB 329/1990* para 5; overruling the Northern Ireland cases *C 1/89 (CB)* and *C 2/89 (WB)*. A proposed amendment to the Overpayments Act 1996 to reverse *Jones* was withdrawn: HC Debates, vol 280, cols 1016 to 1020.

This declaration amounts to three separate general representations.[34] The first part cannot be a representation of a material fact because it has nothing to do with entitlement or payment. The only effect it might have is as evidence which would tend to suggest that a reasonable person would follow the instructions, notwithstanding any advice to the contrary.

The second limb of the declaration, that all facts have been correctly reported, must now be read in the light of *Jones*. Although, as discussed above, the Court of Appeal held that this was a material fact and could trigger recovery based on misrepresentation, it then decided that the declaration had to be read as a declaration that, 'I have correctly reported any facts known to me.'[35] This interpretation of the declaration was unanimously endorsed by the Court of Appeal in *Franklin v Chief Adjudication Officer*,[36] where the claimant had not known of a decrease in the rate of interest on one of her mortgages. Evans LJ explained the view taken of the declaration in this way:

> In a case which rests essentially upon non-disclosure, the words "I have correctly reported any facts" cannot be read literally, because there has been no relevant report. In such a case, it seems to me that the representation has to be taken as meaning something to the effect of "I have not failed to disclose any material fact". Since you cannot disclose what you do not know and there is no duty to do so, I would hold that the representation is not false in a case where the claimant had no knowledge of the relevant facts. Conversely, the Minister cannot recover under section 71 either for non-disclosure or by relying on the representation contained in the declaration, as *Jones* permits him to do, in a case where the claimant did not know the material facts which were not disclosed.[37]

The Court of Appeal in *Jones* went on to consider whether the declaration could be qualified so that only those facts which a reasonable person would report had been reported. Dillon LJ concluded 'regretfully' that this was too wide an extension of the words of the declaration.[38]

---

34 *CS 102/1993* para 11.
35 *Jones v Chief Adjudication Officer* [1994] 1 WLR 62 at pp71H and 72F, CA. *CIS 359/1990* para 7 is therefore overruled.
36 (1995) *Times* 29 December (official transcript pp7C-D, 12A-D and 15A-B), CA.
37 Ibid (official transcript p12A-D).
38 *Jones v Chief Adjudication Officer* [1994] 1 WLR 62 at p73A-B, CA. *CSB 790/1988* para 10, which decided that this was possible, should therefore be regarded as overruled: *CIS 583/1994* para 17.

The final general representation, that the claimant is entitled to the sum in question, cannot be relied upon because it is a representation of law, not of fact.[39] However, this general representation contains secondary representations.

The claim form declaration

> I declare that the information I have given on this form is correct and complete.

The above is the standard declaration which has been used on all claim forms for several years. Old claim forms should be checked to see whether the declaration matches the one above. The effect of *Jones* on attempts to rely on this declaration was subjected to a detailed analysis by Commissioner Rowland in *CIS 674/1994*. The claimant in that case asserted that he knew nothing of two large sums of money held in bank accounts by his wife. He had only disclosed £6,000 of savings on his claim form. The commissioner decided that the answer he had given was qualified by the declaration, as had been held in *Sharples*.[40] Although the declaration that the information was 'complete' was identical in effect to the order book declaration at issue in *Jones*, this was not what the claim form declaration said.

> ... the declaration on the claim form does not refer simply to the information being "complete" but to it being "correct and complete". In my view, the issue is whether the declaration that "The information I have given on this form is correct and complete" is to be construed as meaning that the information is "complete in so far as I have knowledge of the material facts and correct to that extent" or as meaning that it is "correct in all respects where I have answered specific questions and otherwise complete in so far as I have knowledge of the material facts". I take the view that the latter construction is to be preferred ... Where a claimant is asked specific questions he guarantees the accuracy of the answers by his declaration and lack of knowledge on his part is no bar to recovery on the ground of misrepresentation if any of the answers is wrong.[41]

The claimant's appeal in the case was therefore dismissed, since he had given a specific answer that he and his wife had capital

---

39 *Jones v Chief Adjudication Officer* [1994] 1 WLR 62 at p69C, CA; *CS 102/ 1993* para 11; *CSB 18/1992* para 9. *CIS 359/1990* para 8 must be regarded as overruled.
40 Para 14.
41 Para 15.

resources of £6,000 and had warranted that the answer was correct. If *CIS 674/1994* is correct, where specific answers are given by the defendant, the fact that s/he was unaware that the answers given were false is no defence. If the answer is omitted from the claim form and the defendant does not know the material fact, there is a defence to a charge of misrepresentation relying on the claim form.

In *CIS 1209/1995* it was argued that this interpretation was too wide and that Commissioner Rowland had focused too narrowly on the words 'correct and complete'. The declaration refers to 'the information that I have given ...' and so the declaration can only attach to actual answers that have been given on the form and will not found a claim of misrepresentation where no answer has been given. The commissioner did not accept the argument and adopted Commissioner Rowland's formulation.[42]

> As far as I know, the information on this form is true and complete.

The above form of the declaration was used on the now defunct supplementary benefit forms. It was held by Evans LJ in *Sharples v Chief Adjudication Officer*[43] that the words 'as far as I know' qualified all the answers on the claim form, so that provided that the claimant did not know that the representation was false, there was no misrepresentation.

The UB 24 declaration

Only the relevant parts of the long declaration on form UB 24, which is signed fortnightly by those claimants who are required to register as unemployed, are produced below:

> 2. On each day since the first date I claimed (other than any day for which I have made a separate declaration).
> – I was unemployed and I did no work, paid or unpaid ...
> – The circumstances of myself and my dependant(s) are and have remained as last stated in writing (if there has been any change do not sign this form tell the clerk about the change) ...
> 3. Each day since the last day I claimed falls in a week in which I have actively sought work.
>
> I declare that the information I have given on this form is correct and complete.
>
> I have reported everything I am required to report ...

---

42 Paras 15 and 16.
43 [1994] 1 WLR 62 at p70G, CA; upholding *CSB 1006/1985* para 5.

In *CIS 393/1993* the effect of the declaration was described as 'somewhat similar'[44] to the order book declaration considered in *Jones* and *Franklin*. It is therefore suggested that there is no misrepresentation of the matters in paragraph 2 of the declaration where the claimant is not aware of the true state of affairs. The first of the final two paragraphs, about the information being 'correct and complete' must be interpreted in the same way as the claim form declaration, discussed above. The final paragraph represents that there has been no failure to disclose. In *CIS 393/1993* the commissioner decided that as a reasonable man would have reported receipt of child benefit, there had been a misrepresentation by signing to the last paragraph.[45] If the DSS relies on the last paragraph, the claimant will have available all the defences to a failure to disclose. In addition, unless there is some specific requirement (usually in the guidance notes in form UBL 18) on the claimant to report the fact, there can be no misrepresentation under the last paragraph.

If the DSS is to rely on a change of circumstances from the last written statement, it must produce the statement relied on. Mere assertion of its contents will not be sufficient. If there is an oral disclosure to the clerk which is not acted on in the interim, then the overpayment may not have been caused by the misrepresentation on the UB 24. Moreover, following *Sharples*, the final paragraph of the declaration must qualify those parts going before. So if there has been no failure to disclose the change of circumstances, there has been no misrepresentation on the UB 24.

EXAMPLE 4.4

E is in receipt of income support, including unemployment benefit with an increase for her husband, F. Unknown to her, F has started working for a friend of his for a few hours each week. They have also taken in a lodger who pays rent every week, but when E had told an officer at the unemployment benefit office about this the last time that they took a lodger in, he said that it did not matter, not realising that the family was receiving income support as well. There has been no failure to disclose either item and so there has been no misrepresentation under the last paragraph of the UB 24 declaration. Furthermore, although there have been

---

44 Para 7.
45 Ibid.

> changes of circumstances, E did not know about F working and a reasonable person in her position would not have thought it necessary to report the income from the lodger. She has made no misrepresentation that there have been no changes of circumstances.

It will be rare for the DSS to rely on the representation that a claimant has been actively seeking work. If this occurs, it is suggested that whether a claimant is actively seeking work is an inference from primary facts rather than a primary fact itself. The adjudication officer will therefore need to point to some underlying change as the material fact, such as the claimant unreasonably restricting his/her availability for work or failing to attend interviews.

The Med 3 declaration

> I declare that because of incapacity I have not worked since the date of my last claim. I also declare that my circumstances and those of my dependants are and have been as last stated. (If there has been a change cross out this declaration and attach a signed and dated statement of new facts).
> The information given by me is true and complete ...

The first part of the declaration certainly represents that the claimant has not worked since last claiming[46] but there is no clear representation that the claimant is incapable of work. Even if there is such a representation, the DSS could not rely on it because the fact of incapacity is not a material fact but an inference from primary facts.[47] It would have to show a secondary representation 'that the claimant's underlying condition had not changed'.[48]

The second paragraph will be interpreted in a similar way to the corresponding part of the UB 24 form declaration.

The power to rely on general representations

A second argument was put to the Court of Appeal in *Franklin v Chief Adjudication Officer*[49] quite apart from the main issue

---
46 *CS 102/1993* para 11.
47 *R(S) 4/86* para 8.
48 Mesher, p697.
49 (1995) *Times* 29 December, CA.

48 *Overpayments and Recovery* Ch 4

in the case, discussed in the next section. It was submitted that the DSS has no power to require the claimant to sign general representations as a pre-condition to the receipt of benefit and then rely on such declarations as being representations of material fact. The sole basis for the DSS's power to require information to be furnished lies in the following regulation:

> Every beneficiary and every person acting by whom and on whose behalf sums payable by way of benefit are receivable shall furnish in such time and such manner and at such times as the Secretary of State may determine such certificates and other documents and such information or facts affecting the right to benefit or to its receipt as the Secretary of State may require (either as a condition on which any sum or sums shall be receivable or otherwise), and in particular shall notify the Secretary of State of any change of circumstances which he might reasonably be expected to know might affect the right to benefit, or to its receipt, as soon as is reasonably practicable after its occurrence, by giving notice in writing (unless the Secretary of State determines in any particular case to accept notice given otherwise than in writing) of any such change to the appropriate office.[50]

Staughton and Evans LJJ both expressed obiter views on the subject, it not being necessary for their decision due to the unanimous decision in favour of the claimant on the primary point. Staughton LJ stated that the regulation does not give the Secretary of State the right to provide for the consequences of a breach of duty. He also pointed out, however, that this is immaterial as SSAA s71 itself provides for such consequences, before then adding the following statement:

> It is not open to the Secretary of State to provide – as the declaration seeks to provide – that non-disclosure shall count as misrepresentation and therefore attract a sanction which is not available in the case of non-disclosure under section 71 of the Act.[51]

Evans LJ focused on the requirement to 'notify' the Secretary of State of any changes. That, he suggested, connoted a degree of knowledge on the part of the claimant of the fact that there had been a change of circumstances.[52] It seems to follow that the Secretary of State has no power to require a claimant to make representations that s/he has notified facts which s/he does not

---

50 Claims and Payments Regs reg 32(1).
51 *Franklin v Chief Adjudication Officer* (1995) *Times* 29 December (official transcript p9A-D), CA.
52 Ibid p12E-G.

know. It is true that this is a misrepresentation of a material fact within the meaning of s71 following *Jones* (see p43 above), and Staughton LJ is correct when he points out that s71 provides for the fate of a claimant guilty of a breach of duty and that reg 32 purports to do nothing of the kind. However, it is arguable that if the Secretary of State has no power to require a claimant to sign a statement, the DSS has no right to rely on it in making payment. It would follow that benefit was not paid 'in consequence' of the claimant's misrepresentation.

The Court of Appeal ignored the first part of the regulation. The declarations signed by a claimant probably come within the phrase 'such certificates and other documents and such information or facts affecting the right to benefit or to its receipt' in the regulation. It seems to be arguable that the claimant does not 'furnish' the forms on which the declarations are signed, because they are produced by the DSS and not by the claimant. The stumbling block in this line of argument is that, again following *Jones*, the claimant must be furnishing a fact when s/he states that s/he has disclosed all material facts, because that is a statement of material fact. On the other hand, if one cannot disclose what one does not know, it is difficult to see how one can 'furnish' something which one does not have. The effect of the declaration is to require claimants to furnish information which they are not in possession of, and it is highly arguable that it is *ultra vires* the powers of the Secretary of State to require the claimant to sign such declarations. This is an argument which requires further investigation in future cases.[53]

The relevance of personal factors

Consideration is now given to whether the personal circumstances of the defendant can provide a defence to recovery based on misrepresentation. Generally, as will be seen, there is much less scope for taking such factors into account than with failure to disclose.

---

53 The argument will be raised in *CIS 11230/1995*, currently before the commissioner.

Lack of knowledge of the material fact

With specific representations, it is clear that whether or not the claimant knew the true facts is immaterial.[54] Such a misrepresentation may be innocent, but it can found recovery under SSAA s71 nonetheless.

In the case of general misrepresentations, however, the situation is different. As has already been stated, the majority of the Court of Appeal in *Jones v Chief Adjudication Officer*[55] held that Mr Jones only represented that he had reported all facts known to him. However, in *Jones*, the claimant's knowledge of the material fact was not disputed. This was seized upon by Commissioner Henty in *CP 34/1993*. It was held that the effect of *Jones* was to prevent recovery simply on the basis that the misrepresentation was innocent, which was contrary to the unanimous decision in *Page and Davis v Chief Adjudication Officer*.[56] It was decided that the observations of the majority on this point were obiter and not necessary for its decision. The commissioner therefore declined to follow the majority in *Jones*.[57]

However, the approach in *Jones* was applied in no less than five commissioners' decisions and, notwithstanding Stuart-Smith LJ's apparent desire to contain the decision to the particular case,[58] was applied to different types of general misrepresentation.[59] Only one commissioner was minded to follow Commissioner Henty's analysis, and the Court of Appeal unanimously allowed that claimant's appeal in *Franklin v Chief Adjudication Officer*,[60] in which *Jones* was unanimously followed. *CP 34/1993* has therefore clearly been overruled.

It is suggested that the claimant will not be able to rely on the principle in *Jones* if s/he had known the fact but had then forgotten it. This reflects the law in relation to failure to disclose (see pp80–81 below).

54 *R(SB) 9/85* para 7; *CIS 674/1994* para 16.
55 [1994] 1 WLR 62 at pp71H and 72F, CA.
56 (1991) *Times* 4 July (appendix to *R(SB) 2/92*). See p15 above.
57 Paras 7 to 10.
58 [1994] 1 WLR 62 at p71H, CA.
59 *CIS 695/1992* para 15; *CSB 18/1992* para 18; *CIS 583/1994* para 14 (all dealing with the order book declaration which was the subject of *Jones*); *CIS 393/1993* para 7 (UB 24 declaration); *CIS 674/1994* para 18 (claim form declaration). The latter case contains a convincing critique of *CP 34/1993* in paras 9 to 13.
60 (1995) *Times* 29 December, CA; the appeal from *CIS 145/1994*.

Lack of understanding of materiality

It is clear that whether the misrepresentation in question is general or specific, it is no answer to an alleged SSAA s71 liability to assert that the defendant or a reasonable person would not have thought that the true state of affairs was a material matter.[61] However, a representation can be qualified by advice received from the DSS (see pp39–40 above) in certain circumstances and this needs to be borne in mind.

EXAMPLE 4.6

G is disabled and depends on her neighbour, H, who works for the local DSS office, for help. She receives the care and mobility components of disability living allowance. She has an operation on her hip which is successful and significantly increases her ability to walk. H says that under DSS policy she need not worry about informing it but should wait until her next examination. She continues to sign the declaration that there has been no change of circumstances. If a tribunal is satisfied that H's advice can be viewed as being given in his capacity as a DSS officer, G makes no misrepresentation on her order book slips.

Incapacity and incapability

Another difficult question concerns whether a claimant may be bound by a misrepresentation when s/he has some deficiency in his/her mental capacity to make such a representation. At first glance it appears from the decision of the Court of Appeal in *Chief Adjudication Officer v Sherriff* [62] that such a claimant cannot raise his/her incapacity as a defence. The matter is, it is suggested, not that simple and detailed consideration of two arguments put forward on behalf of claimants is necessary.

No knowledge of representation

Sherriff was the adjudication officer's appeal from *CIS 545/ 1992*. The claimant was elderly and incapable of looking after her affairs. She was subject to the Court of Protection and later a claim for income support to cover her nursing home fees was

---

61 *Jones v Chief Adjudication Officer* [1994] 1 WLR 62 at pp72H to 73B, CA; CIS 695/1992 para 15. CSB 790/1988 para 10 is therefore overruled.
62 (1995) *Times* 10 May, CA.

made. The existence of a large amount of capital was not disclosed. Having decided that the claimant's son was not liable for failing to disclose the existence of the capital, the commissioner then decided that as there was evidence that the claimant would be incapable of being negligent at the time the representation had been made, she was mentally incapable of any representation.

The Court of Appeal disagreed. But the claimant's case seems to have been argued on a very narrow basis. The submission was that, while a defendant need not have knowledge of the material fact represented, it was necessary for him/her to know that a representation had actually been made. This was clearly rejected by the court,[63] so the mere fact that a claimant does not know that a representation is being made cannot absolve him/her. However, Nourse LJ pointed out that if a claimant had capacity to make a claim, she had capacity to make a misrepresentation. So the decision in *Sherriff* does not deal with situations where the claimant's mental capacity deteriorates during the currency of a claim and the DSS seeks to establish a misrepresentation through declarations signed by the claimant. Those declarations are not separate claims. The Court of Appeal suggests that where the claimant does not have the mental capacity to make a claim, there can be recovery from the claimant in restitution.[64] For the reasons given in chapter 20, this is probably not correct.

No reference seems to have been made to the decision of the majority in *Jones* (see above) that a general misrepresentation requires knowledge of the relevant fact on the part of the defendant. *Sherriff* does not affect this principle. It would not have availed the claimant in any case, since the DSS was relying on a specific misrepresentation as to the amount of capital which the claimant possessed.[65] It therefore seems that a claimant who was not aware of the true state of affairs due to mental incapacity will be in the same position as any other claimant and so will not make a misrepresentation through signing the declaration.

Non est factum

Non est factum (translated as 'it is not my deed') is a common law doctrine under which a person can in very restricted

---

63 Ibid official transcript p8.
64 Ibid pp9 and 11.
65 A point specifically made by Staughton LJ in *Franklin v Chief Adjudication Officer* (1995) *Times* 29 December (official transcript p6E-F), CA.

circumstances be treated as though s/he had never signed or written a document. In *CIS 545/1992* the commissioner rejected an attempt to argue that the doctrine applied to a claim form, describing it as 'exclusively a contractual consideration'.[66] This is incorrect. The doctrine is applicable to formal documents of all kinds.[66A]

In addition, Commissioner Johnson did not refer to *CSB 1093/ 1989*, in which the commissioner entered into a detailed analysis of the doctrine and concluded that it did apply where the claimant had signed her order book slips and her mother had taken them to be cashed. It is suggested that the commissioner's reasoning is sound and should be preferred to *CIS 545/1992*. In addition, the decision in *CSB 218/1991* that a claimant could not escape the consequences of misrepresentation does not refer to any authority and so the doctrine cannot be said to have been convincingly rejected there.

The argument that *non est factum* was relevant does not appear to have been specifically put to the Court of Appeal in *Sherriff*. Millett LJ cited *CSB 1093/1989* but did not disapprove it, apparently taking the view that if there were cases where the commissioner's analysis was correct, there could then be recovery in restitution.[67] Accordingly, it appears that it is still open to a claimant to argue that the doctrine applies.

Although all the cases cited above concerned claimants who were mentally incapacitated, the doctrine of *non est factum* is of wider application. It applies to 'those who are permanently or temporarily unable through no fault of their own to have without explanation any real understanding of the purport of a particular document, whether that be from defective education, illness or innate incapacity',[68] and whose incapacity causes them to make a mistake as to the consequences of their signature. The claimant's mistake must be as to the 'practical result' of signing the form rather than its legal significance.[69] So it will not be enough for the claimant not to understand the meaning of the representation, or that s/he has made a representation which the DSS will rely on to pay him/her benefit, or that s/he has made a

---

66 Para 16.
66A See, eg, *Foster v Mackinnan* (1869) LR 4 CP 704, CCP (bill of exchange); *Re Beaney (dec'd)* [1978] 1 WLR 770, HC (will); *Saunders* (n68 below) (assignment of land).
67 *Sherriff* (n62 above, official transcript p12).
68 *Saunders v Anglia Building Society* [1971] AC 1004 at p1016, HL.
69 Ibid at pp1017, 1019, 1021, 1026 and 1034.

representation, or if s/he thinks that s/he is 'only signing a form'.[70] If claimants understand that money is paid to them as a result of the signature, they cannot rely on *non est factum* as a defence.

Practically speaking, this will mean that the defence is not open to those who are poorly educated or those who speak little English, as they will understand that they receive money as a result of their signature. The doctrine is only likely to be applicable in two classes of case:

a) where the claimant is so mentally incapacitated as to be incapable of appreciating that money is being paid to him/her as a result of his/her signature;
b) where the claimant is being given forms to sign to further some fraud committed by a third party.[71]

EXAMPLE 4.7

I is blind and relies on her nephew, J, for assistance with official documents. He places a claim form for income support before her and tells her that it contains the relevant details for her council tax. She signs and J pockets the resulting benefit before disappearing. As I did not appreciate that money would be paid as a result of her signature, she can rely on the defence of *non est factum*.

Proof of incapacity

If it is proposed to argue *non est factum* on the basis of the claimant's medical condition, then it will be necessary to obtain adequate medical evidence of the claimant's condition. The commissioner states in *CSB 1093/1989* that other, non-expert evidence of the claimant's condition will be less useful.[72] This is certainly true, but evidence should be sought from such people as friends and relatives or carers of the claimant. Tribunals are often ready to listen to such people testify about the changes observed in their loved ones and such evidence may place a valuable human perspective on the cold facts of the medical evidence. The combination of the two types of evidence ought to be particularly persuasive.

---

70 On the latter point see *Hunter v Walters* (1871) LR 7 Ch App 75, CA.
71 *Lewis v Clay* (1897) 67 LJQB 224, QBD.
72 Para 20.

Understanding the fact that money will be paid as a result of signing a claim form or a declaration requires a relatively low level of mental capacity.[73] In *CSB 1093/1989* tribunals are exhorted to analyse the claimant's condition throughout the relevant period. If they are satisfied that at the time that any particular representation was made the claimant showed a sufficient degree of understanding of what s/he was doing, then that particular misrepresentation can be relied upon by the DSS and all overpayments flowing from that representation can be recovered.[74] The commissioner in *CIS 545/1992* suggests that there must be a presumption in the case of a Court of Protection patient that s/he is incapable of understanding the nature of what s/he is doing.[75] It will be for the DSS to rebut this presumption. It is suggested that there must be fairly specific proof relating to a particular period that the claimant's condition had improved. Evidence that the claimant's condition fluctuates will not be sufficient.

EXAMPLE 4.8

K, who is receiving income support, is suffering from advanced Alzheimers disease. In 1990 K inherits a large capital sum which is invested for him. He continues to sign the Med 3 certificates provided for him, certifying that there has been no change in his circumstances. When the DSS attempts to recover the overpayment, K raises the issue of *non est factum*. There is medical evidence, supported by the observations of K's family, that his condition varied from day to day but is slowly worsening and that he has been incapable throughout the relevant period of managing his affairs. There is reference to a period in 1994 when K recovered some lucidity due to an experimental drug. The adjudication officer attempts to argue that as the condition is variable, it is likely that at some point the claimant must have had sufficient understanding of what he was signing. This evidence should only be accepted in relation to the 1994 period, because that is the only specific proof available. All overpayments from the first Med 3 signed within the 1994 period are recoverable.

---

73 *CSB 1093/1989* paras 18 and 19, applying *Re Beaney (deceased)* [1978] 1 WLR 770, HC.
74 Paras 16 and 19.
75 Para 18.

CHAPTER 5
Failure to disclose

The second ground for recovery under SSAA s71, a failure to disclose, has rightly been described as a 'much more troublesome concept'[1] than that of misrepresentation. It involves greater consideration of the facts of individual cases and of the circumstances of individual defendants than is the case with misrepresentation. The legal meaning of the phrase is much more vague, and there is therefore considerably greater scope for challenging decisions based on failure to disclose.

In order to establish a failure to disclose by a defendant, it will be necessary for the DSS to meet three conditions:

a) throughout the period over which the benefit of which recovery is sought was paid, the defendant was under a duty to disclose to the DSS;
b) during that period, the defendant did not make an effective disclosure to the DSS at any stage;
c) there was a 'failure' on the defendant's part because s/he did not take the steps that could reasonably be expected of him/her towards alerting the DSS to the situation.

In appeals where recovery is based on a failure to disclose, adjudication officers usually cite the six-point test outlined in *R(SB) 54/83* for the assistance of the tribunal.[2] This analysis does not distinguish between the first and third elements above. However, separating the issues of whether the defendant is obliged to do anything and whether his/her actions are sufficient will be useful in cases where the defendant is not a claimant and a duty to disclose does not arise automatically. The three elements are now considered in turn.

1 Mesher, p700.
2 Para 13.

The duty of disclosure

If a defendant was never under a duty to disclose, then consideration of the other two elements will not be necessary as there can never be recovery from such a defendant under SSAA s71. A fresh duty to disclose arises in relation to each claim. In *R(SB) 3/90* it was held that a claimant who omits information from the claim form for the latest claim could not rely on a disclosure made on a previous form.[3] So people who are not claimants but may be under an obligation to disclose must exercise care when a new claim is made to ensure that the DSS is kept fully informed of relevant circumstances.

While it is possible to make an advance disclosure,[4] the obligation to disclose a change of circumstances only arises at the time when that change affects the claimant's benefit entitlement. So when an income support claimant's mortgage interest rate decreases, there is only an obligation to disclose at the time that his/her liability to pay that interest arises.[5]

Claimants

Unsurprisingly, in most cases the person with the primary duty to disclose is the claimant. The claimant's obligation to disclose is based on a statutory requirement[6] which is very widely drawn. The reason for the duty is that:

> in the ordinary case the claimant is the person with the most immediate and direct knowledge of his circumstances. He is, accordingly, the obvious person upon whom to lay the duty of keeping the authorities appropriately informed. In the ordinary case he omits so to do at his peril.[7]

It seems very unlikely that a claimant could ever successfully claim that the duty rested on somebody else. An obligation on a third party to disclose is additional to and does not replace the claimant's duty.[8] In *CIS 674/1994* the claimant claimed that he

---

3 Para 12.
4 *CS 234/1994* para 5.
5 *R 5/94 (IS)* paras 9 and 10 (a Northern Ireland case); *CIS 305/1990* paras 5 and 6.
6 Claims and Payments Regs reg 32(1).
7 *CSB 677/1986* para 14.
8 *CSB 957/1987* para 10.

did not know about his wife's savings. The commissioner suggested that it was 'at least arguable'[9] that she was under a duty to disclose but it is clear that this did not mean that the claimant was under no duty.

The position is the same where the claimant relies on somebody else to inform the DSS. At the very least, the claimant will be under a continuing duty to disclose with all the attendant consequences (see pp61–65 below).

EXAMPLE 5.1

A is claiming income support after breaking up with his wife, B. Their children are living with A and the estranged couple make an informal arrangement through their solicitors by which B will pay A £50 per week towards the maintenance of the children. A's solicitor promises A that he will inform the DSS but fails to do so. The DSS will be entitled to recover from both A and the solicitor.

The only exception to this principle is where an appointee or receiver has taken over the claimant's affairs in relation to benefit due to the claimant's incapacity. In such a situation, the third party is acting 'in the claimant's shoes' and s/he takes over the claimant's duty to disclose.[10] The question of who is liable to make repayment if such a duty is breached is discussed at pp11–13 above.

It is clear that the extent of the claimant's obligation can be affected by past dealings between the DSS and the claimant.[11] There may therefore be an exception to the general principle where a practice has grown up between the claimant and the DSS for somebody else to disclose changes in circumstances, but where the claimant has never been formally appointed for the purpose. The DSS would only have the right to recover from the third party.

EXAMPLE 5.2

C is elderly and receiving income support. He is housebound and does not have a telephone. He receives regular visits from a social

---

9 Para 17.
10 *CSB 957/1987* para 10; *CIS 649/1993* para 39; *CIS 332/1993* para 23.
11 *R(SB) 3/81* para 7.

> worker, D. For several years, D has handled C's affairs with the DSS, dealing with various benefits and keeping the DSS informed of its levels for income support purposes. D has never been made an appointee. C reaches the age of 65 and starts to receive retirement pension, but D forgets to tell the DSS. C can argue that the duty to disclose rests on D rather than on him.

Other defendants

In *R(SB) 21/82* it was held that there must be a 'moral or legal' obligation on a person before there was a duty to disclose.[12] In relation to defendants who are not claimants, this means that liability under SSAA s71 will not be restricted to cases where there is some specific legal obligation on the defendant to disclose. A 'moral' obligation is one which a reasonable person would see as existing in normal circumstances, and will arise in situations other than those specifically referred to in the legislation.

Appointees, receivers and other people assisting claimants

Where appointees have been given power to act on the claimant's behalf, they are usually required to sign an undertaking 'to give ... all the information required' by the DSS and to let it know 'at once' about any change of circumstances. While it now seems that there is no personal liability on the appointee or receiver (see pp11–13 above) the issue is still important to determine the claimant's liability. The duty passes to the appointee or receiver at the date the appropriate appointment is made.[13]

The terms of appointment are usually restricted. Appointees are not normally given general powers but rather oversee only specified matters or benefits.[14] Therefore, if the relevant benefit is outside the scope of the appointment, it is unlikely that there is any duty to disclose and the duty in relation to that benefit will still rest on the claimant.

> EXAMPLE 5.3
> E is a disability adviser and has been appointed by the Secretary of State to assist with F's claim for severe disablement allowance.

12 Para 4(2).
13 *CIS 545/1992* para 15. Note however that an appointment can be made retrospectively: see p12 above.
14 *R(IS) 5/91* para 6.

> F is also in receipt of income support. E knows this but does not disclose the award of severe disablement allowance to the local office. E is not under a duty to disclose in relation to income support and so it must be considered whether F is guilty of a failure to disclose.

Likewise, in *R(SB) 28/83* a receiver appointed by the Court of Protection was held to have a duty to disclose, because his terms of reference specifically included claiming any benefits due to the claimant.[15] Other officials who take similar wide control over the claimant's affairs, such as a mental health custodian in Scotland, will be in a similar position, particularly if dealing with benefits is specifically included within their remit.

Personal representatives

Personal representatives[16] of an estate can be required by the DSS to give information about the contents of the estate where a claimant has been receiving income support or supplementary benefit.[17] Where such disclosure has been required, there is no doubt that the personal representatives will be under a duty to disclose such information.

A personal duty giving rise to recovery from the individual personal representative is probably limited to those circumstances, although in other cases the DSS would still be able to recover from the estate of the deceased (see pp10–11 above). Certainly, there should be no duty where the representative was unaware that the claimant was receiving benefit.

> EXAMPLE 5.4
> G and his wife, H, die in a car crash. They were in receipt of family credit. I, who is G's brother and the executor of his will, discovers that the couple had a substantial amount of capital. G and H never kept any of the correspondence from the DSS and there is nothing to indicate to I that they were receiving family credit. He accordingly disposes of the assets of the estate according to the will and is only later informed that the couple were in

---

15 Para 8. The DSS was seeking to recover from the claimant and so the case is not inconsistent with the analysis presented here. See p13 above.
16 That is, executors of a will or administrators of an estate where the claimant died intestate.
17 SSAA s126.

Ch 5 Failure to disclose 61

> receipt of benefit. The DSS will not be able to recover from I personally.

Other third parties

In certain circumstances other people can also come under a duty to disclose. In *CIS 674/1994* it was suggested that a claimant's partner will be under a duty where s/he 'is aware of facts that are unknown to the claimant and knows that they are unknown to the claimant and that they are material to the claim'.[18] It is suggested that duties on persons other than the claimant's partner will be similarly restricted to those circumstances.

A continuing duty?

It used to be thought that a duty to disclose was always a continuing duty, so that if it became clear to the defendant that the disclosure had not been effective, s/he was obliged to disclose again until such time as action was taken.[19] However, it is now clear from *R(SB) 15/87 (T)* that the general rule is that once a defendant has made an effective disclosure, 'it is difficult ... to visualise any circumstances in which a further disclosure of the same matter can arise'.[20] There is no inconsistency between this principle and the observations of Croom-Johnson LJ in *Duggan v Chief Adjudication Officer*[21] that a claimant's duty of disclosure is a continuing one. The judge was dealing with a case in which no disclosure was made at all. In those circumstances, the duty to disclose continues throughout the claim. Once disclosure is made, the obligation is discharged.

It has been held that the reference to 'the same matter' by the Tribunal of Commissioners can include matters that occur once and an event repeated at regular intervals.[22] So if a claimant discloses an award of sickness benefit to the income support office in the week in which the latter is awarded, s/he does not

---

18 Para 17.
19 *R(SB) 54/83* para 18.
20 Para 28. This was succinctly put in *CSB 1397/1985* paras 9 and 10 as 'disclosure is disclosure'. See also *CSIS 50/1992* para 8(b); *CIS 668/1994* para 6.
21 (1988) *Times* 18 December (appendix to *R(SB) 13/89* at p607B-E), CA.
22 *CSB 699/1986* para 5.

have to disclose the award every week. However, there are limits to what a single disclosure would cover. It has been held, for example, that even where receipt of sickness benefit has been disclosed, an award of invalidity benefit requires a separate disclosure because it amounts to a change in circumstances in itself.[23]

It follows that there will only be a continuing duty to disclose in certain situations and the general rule is that there is no such duty. There is a continuing duty where a defendant 'subsequently becomes aware, or should have become aware, that the information has not been transmitted to the proper person or place and ... is then under a duty to make disclosure to that person or place.'[24] This general statement has been applied to a number of situations.

Circumstances where there is a continuing duty

In *R(SB) 15/87 (T)* the Tribunal of Commissioners decided that the reference in *R(SB) 54/83* to a continuing duty referred to cases where:

> an officer in another office of the Department of Health and Social Security or local Unemployment Benefit Office accepts information in circumstances which make it reasonable for the claimant to think the matters disclosed will be passed on to the local office in question.[25]

This statement must be read subject to the qualification that where the unemployment benefit office is acting as an agent for the DSS for income support purposes, there appears to be no continuing duty to disclose, because disclosure to the unemployment benefit office is seen as equivalent to disclosure to the income support local office. None of the cases on the point mention the issue.

EXAMPLE 5.5
J is awarded child benefit following the birth of her son. She asks the Child Benefit Centre in Newcastle what to do about her income support, and she is told that it will tell the local office (though not that she need not disclose the receipt of child benefit herself to the local office). A few weeks later, J wonders why no money has been deducted from her income support. She is under a continuing obligation and must now make disclosure herself.

---

23 *CSB 677/1986* para 14; *CSB 699/1986* para 5.
24 *R(SB) 15/87 (T)* para 28.
25 Para 28.

In *Riches v Secretary of State for Social Security* the claimant was receiving invalidity benefit with a dependency addition for his wife. His wife claimed sickness benefit in her own right twice. On the first occasion she made it clear on her claim form that he was receiving benefit for her; on the second occasion she failed to do this. The commissioner held that even if it was reasonable for the claimant to assume that his wife had disclosed his benefit on the second occasion, he should have realised that the DSS had failed to make the connection and there was therefore a continuing duty. The Court of Session upheld this conclusion.[26]

Finally, in *CSB 99/1990* it was held that where the claimant had sent a letter to the local office containing the relevant information, which never arrived, a continuing duty arose because the claimant should have realised that the letter had not been acted upon.[27]

The concept of a continuing duty is not restricted to cases of these types. It is a question of fact, based upon the test in *R(SB) 15/87 (T)* set out above, as to whether there is a continuing duty in any given case. Receivers and appointees can come under a continuing duty as claimants can, but it seems unlikely that other third parties could ever come under a continuing duty to disclose, unless they receive specific information from the DSS which ought to lead them to believe that they still have an obligation.

It must also be borne in mind that a continuing duty will not necessarily exist in the above circumstances. The crucial requirement is that the claimant 'becomes aware, or should have become aware' that the disclosure has not been effective.

EXAMPLE 5.6

K is receiving income support. She takes in a lodger, her niece L, who pays a small rent every week, and starts a part-time job at the same time. She discloses her work to the local office. L claims income support in her own right and tells K that she has disclosed the fact that she is paying rent to K and that K is also receiving income support on her claim form. K thinks that there is no need to disclose her receipt of rent. In due course her income support is reduced. The letter from the DSS attributes this to 'a change in money coming in'. K thinks that both changes of circumstances

---

26 [1994] SLT 731 at p734F, Court of Session.
27 Para 14. This is rather doubtful in view of the applicability of the presumption of posting: see p79 below.

> have been taken into account, but only her work has been. Her belief is reasonable and there is no continuing duty.

The consequence of a continuing duty

The existence of a continuing duty means that the claimant has done all that s/he is required to do for a certain period of time and that for that period of time the overpayment will not be recoverable.[28] The period of time should be that period within which the individual claimant ought to have realised that the initial disclosure had been ineffective. If this was actually realised by the claimant on a particular date, then his/her continuing duty runs from that date. However, it will be far more common for the claimant never to have realised that his/her actions were insufficient for the discharge of his/her obligations.

The case-law offers little guidance on the length of the period of time in such cases. In *Riches v Secretary of State for Social Security* one month was allowed.[29] In *CSB 99/1990* it was merely said that four days was insufficient for the claimant to realise that the letter had not been received.[30] The *AO Guide* suggests that the claimant should realise that s/he must disclose again at the time of the second payment after the first disclosure which gives rise to the continuing duty.[31] This cannot be a universal rule regardless of the circumstances. How long the period of time is will be a question of fact, differing from case to case.

To determine the period, it will be essential to look at the claimant's past dealings with the DSS. If there have been previous disclosures of similar information, the period should be however long it took the DSS to act on the information plus some extra time to allow the claimant to realise that the disclosure was ineffective. If there is statistical evidence available about how long the DSS takes to process information, this will also be a good indication.

Also of importance may be how the claimant is paid. A claimant receiving regular giro cheques is more likely to notice that there have been no changes in the amount that s/he is receiving than someone receiving benefit by credit transfer into a bank account.

---

28 *CSSB 621/1988* para 8.
29 [1994] SLT 731 at p734D.
30 Para 14.
31 Para 12093.

Likewise, a claimant who has an order book ought to expect a letter telling him/her to return it.

Thirdly, the more unlikely it is that the DSS has not acted on the disclosure, the longer the period should be. A claimant such as in *Riches* (see above) has a right to rely on his/her partner's word to some extent and to expect the office to make the connection, as Mr Riches thought it had with Mrs Riches' first period of claim. By contrast, if a letter is sent to the DSS informing it that the claimant has started a full-time job, and no action is taken, the claimant should quickly realise that something is wrong.[31A]

Knowledge of the material fact by the DSS

If the DSS acquires knowledge of the relevant fact from an official source, the defendant's obligation to disclose automatically ceases. This is because 'it is not possible, according to the ordinary use of the language, to "disclose" to a person a fact of which he is, to the knowledge of the person making a statement, already aware'.[32]

With one modification, this principle has been applied to disclosure of material facts for the purpose of SSAA s71.[33] The modification is that it does not appear to be necessary for the defendant to be aware that the DSS has acquired the relevant knowledge.[34] The relevance of the DSS's knowledge is usually considered with reference to whether an overpayment is caused by a failure to disclose,[35] but it can also be said that there is no failure to disclose in the first place.

It seems clear, however, that the principle cannot be extended to cover facts which the DSS ought to know, as opposed to those which it actually knows.[36] There may, however, be circumstances in which there is an effect on causation (see pp114–115 below).

31A Cf, *CSB 393/1985* para 5 (claimant moving in with parents): 'may not be a very long time'.
32 *Foster v Federal Commissioner of Taxation* (1951) 82 CLR 606 at pp614 and 615, HC of Aust.
33 *Jones v Chief Adjudication Officer* [1994] 1 WLR 62 at p66D, CA; *CSB 677/1986* para 6; *CSB 1246/1986* para 7; *CSB 727/1987* para 7.
34 *R(SB) 15/87 (T)* para 30.
35 *R(SB) 15/87 (T)* para 30; *CIS 159/1990* para 4. See pp112–113 below.
36 *CSB 677/1986* para 14. The argument was not put before the commissioner or the Court of Appeal in *Duggan v Chief Adjudication Officer* (1988) Times 19 March (appendix to *R(SB) 13/89*) but the tenor of the decision is clearly against an extension of the proposition. The suggestion to the contrary in *Jones v Chief Adjudication Officer* [1994] 1 WLR 62 at p66E, CA, cannot yet be seen as representing the law.

> **EXAMPLE 5.7**
> M is receiving invalid care allowance for caring for his elderly mother. The allowance is not payable if the claimant is working more than a certain number of hours or earning more than a certain amount every week. In fact, M has been working for an employer part-time since 1986 and is over both limits. He does not disclose this. Every year the Contributions Agency sends a list of those paying contributions from employed earnings to the invalid care allowance unit so that checks can be made. For the first two years, M's name is missing from the list due to a computer fault. In 1989, however, the Contributions Agency lists M as one of those paying contributions, and it is clear from the level of contributions that M no longer satisfies the conditions for the allowance. The unit fails to take any action until 1991. The overpayment is recoverable until 1989 only.

The nature of a disclosure

Once it is clear that there is a duty to disclose, the next question is whether the defendant has in fact made a proper disclosure.

The definition of disclosure

> ... disclosure consists in the statement of a fact so as to reveal that which is so far as the discloser knows was previously unknown to the person to whom the statement was made.[37]

There are a number of points to be made in relation to this definition. First, the 'statement' must be sufficiently clear, both in its content[38] and in its reference to the claim so that it is placed before the correct person.[39] This does not mean that the wording of the disclosure has to be a model of clarity. Provided it is 'adequate to ... put the DSS on notice that a change had been reported which might have an effect on the claimant's benefit entitlement',[40] the defendant's duty will be discharged.

---

37 R(SB) 15/87 (T) para 25. The definition is based on that in *Foster v Federal Commissioner of Taxation* (1951) 82 CLR 606, HC of Aust.
38 CSB 1288/1985 para 5; CSB 699/1986 para 4.
39 R(SB) 15/87 (T) para 28.
40 CG 54/1988 para 5.

Secondly, even though the statutory provision[41] relating to information supplied by claimants requires 'notice in writing' unless the Secretary of State decides otherwise, it is clear that a disclosure does not have to be written to be sufficient. An oral disclosure has always been considered adequate.[42]

In addition, it is possible to make a disclosure by conduct. There are a number of cases where documents have been produced to a clerk in different circumstances and the production of the documents has been held to be sufficient disclosure.[43] On the other hand, there was no disclosure by conduct of the fact that benefit received by the claimant's wife should be taken into account by the mere fact that the claimant's wife attended the office with him.[44]

Fourthly, the extent of what is expected of the claimant can be altered by the practice of the DSS in dealing with the claimant's affairs. So in *R(SB) 3/81* the fact that the local office had adopted the practice of assessing the claimant's yearly income on the basis of a P60 from the previous tax year meant that it could not recover an overpayment for the period between the end of the tax year and the receipt of the P60, when the claimant's income had increased over the previous year.[45]

Finally, it is insufficient simply to 'state' the information. It is necessary to 'reveal' it to the recipient. So if a fax was sent which did not transmit properly, this will not be sufficient disclosure, but will give rise to a continuing obligation to disclose.[46] If the fax was received but not read, then there has been good disclosure of the contents.

---

41 Claims and Payments Regs reg 32(1).
42 *CSB 688/1982* para 5; *CSB 347/1983* para 5; *R(SB) 20/84* para 5; *R(SB) 40/84* para 10; *R(SB) 15/87 (T)* para 13.
43 *R(SB) 20/84* para 4 (documents produced while a claim form was being filled in); *R(SB) 18/85* para 10 (while statement of circumstances being taken); *CSB 688/1982* para 5 (while signing on); *CSB 699/1986* para 4 (while making inquiry).
44 *R(SB) 13/89* para 7.
45 Para 8.
46 *Brinkibon Ltd v Stahag Stahl* [1983] 2 AC 34 at p41, HL. This analysis does not, it is submitted, apply to disclosure by post: see p79 below.

Who can make disclosure?

Obviously, the person who normally makes disclosure will be the claimant. Where an appointee or receiver is acting on the claimant's behalf, the burden for making disclosure will fall on him/her. The difficult question is whether a third party can fulfil the defendant's duty to disclose in other circumstances. In *R(SB) 15/87 (T)* the Tribunal of Commissioners decided that it was necessary to fulfil three conditions for a valid disclosure to be made on behalf of a claimant:[47]

a) '... *the information was given to the relevant benefit office* ...'. As with a disclosure by a claimant, disclosing to a different part of the DSS in itself will be insufficient. Disclosure within the same local office of matters concerning different benefits, however, would be sufficient.[48]

b) '... *the claimant was aware that the information had been so given* ...'. The reasoning behind this requirement is the claimant should only be permitted to rely on a third party disclosure when it is the subject of agreement between the claimant and the third party and not based on some assumption by the claimant. In *R(SB) 15/87 (T)* the claimant's daughter disclosed the fact that he was receiving supplementary benefit when making a claim in her own right. It appears that this was done without his knowledge and it was held that 'casual or incidental disclosure by some other person'[49] would not discharge the claimant's duty. The mere fact that a third party has made a claim which affects the claimant's entitlement will not suffice of itself.[50] However, the Tribunal of Commissioners does specifically say that it is possible for a disclosure to take place in the third party's claim.[51] This must mean that if specific reference is made in the claim form to the claimant's entitlement so as to draw the adjudication officer's attention to the fact that an award to the third party may affect the claimant's entitlement, then the claimant's duty is discharged.

c) '... *in the circumstances it was reasonable for the claimant to believe that it was unnecessary for him to take any action*

---

47 Para 28.
48 *CSB 677/1986* para 6; *CSB 1134/1988* para 5; *CSB 790/1988* para 10.
49 Para 29.
50 *CSB 712/1985* para 10; *CIS 393/1993* para 5.
51 Para 29.

himself. In *CSB 677/1986* it was held[52] that if the claimant's wife made a disclosure to an officer during the course of a query about her own benefit while he was present, then it would be reasonable for the claimant not to take any further action.

EXAMPLE 5.8

N's daughter, O, is 18 years old. She leaves school and claims income support in her own right before going to university. N is receiving child benefit and has always dealt with the claim through the local office. N, who is very busy with his work, knows that child benefit continues up to the age of 19 as long as O is in full-time education and lives at home, but does not know that she is not a qualifying child if she receives benefit. He asks her to tell the local office about her claim. After signing on at the unemployment benefit office, O goes to the local office and tells it that she has claimed income support and that her father is receiving child benefit. In these circumstances, the disclosure by O has fulfilled N's obligation.

Where these criteria are not shown, it must be borne in mind that if it is reasonable for the claimant to think that the disclosure was valid initially, even if s/he should have realised at a later stage that it was ineffective, then there is a continuing duty to disclose.[53]

Where is disclosure made?

Disclosure to the relevant office

R(SB) 15/87 (T) decides that the defendant's duty of disclosure 'is best fulfilled by disclosure to the local office where his claim is being handled either in the claim form or otherwise in terms that make sufficient reference to [the claimant's] claim to enable the matter disclosed to be referred to the proper person.'[54] It is not necessary for the claimant to disclose to the officer responsible for dealing with his claim.[55] So long as the actual person to

---

52 Para 13; *CWSB 15/1985* para 4 holds otherwise.
53 *Riches v Secretary of State for Social Security* [1994] SLT 731, Ct Sess (Inner House). See pp61–65 above.
54 Para 28.
55 *R(SB) 15/87 (T)* para 28, overruling *R(SB) 54/83* para 16. *CS 155/1988* para 8 is therefore wrong.

whom disclosure is made is associated with the appropriate office, disclosure will be sufficient. So disclosure to a visiting officer[56] or to a counter clerk at the local office[57] will both discharge the obligation.

The question then becomes what is meant by the 'local office' in the above definition. The analysis in *R(SB) 15/87 (T)* may be somewhat outdated. In the mid-1980s when many of the cases defining failure to disclose were decided, the usual practice was for an integrated local office to liaise with claimants relating to the whole range of benefits. It was consistently held that it was not necessary for a claimant to identify the particular part of the local office dealing with the benefit which s/he was receiving[58] unless s/he had been told to refer to a specific part of the office.[59] This is particularly true where a claimant is instructed in the order book to make a disclosure to 'the issuing office' and that office is the local office.[60]

In light of the modern way in which the DSS's work is structured, things will not be so simple. There has been an ongoing trend towards centralisation of initial adjudication of claims at large offices dealing solely with one or a group of benefits.[61] So income support claims are adjudicated centrally and management of the claims is then passed to local offices. Moreover, centralisation of at least some day-to-day handling of benefits has occurred on a regional basis, so it is no longer safe to assume that claimants have been dealing with the office closest to them. The creation of the Benefits Agency has, if anything, accelerated this trend. However, it may be that this development will be reversed in years to come, with the government considering the introduction of 'one stop' services at which claimants can deal with all their benefit matters. If this proposal comes to fruition, then disclosure to an officer offering such a service would be sufficient disclosure in relation to all benefits received by the claimant.

The implication of these changes for advisers where disclosure to the DSS is alleged is that it is essential to examine the whole

---

56 *CSB 903/1985* para 8.
57 *CSB 1397/1985* para 11; *CIS 389/1993* para 7.
58 *CSB 677/1986* para 6; *CSB 790/1988* para 10; *CSB 1134/1988* para 5.
59 *CSB 790/1988* para 10.
60 *CSB 727/1987* para 13; *CSB 790/1988* para 10.
61 For example, the two major benefit directorates at Newcastle and Fylde. The *AO Guide* para 12088 gives a list of those offices which the DSS feels are the proper offices at which disclosure should be made.

Ch 5 Failure to disclose 71

history of the claim. The potential for confusion caused by a claimant dealing with a profusion of different people is high. If the claimant is unable to give a history, then presenting officers can often give valuable help at tribunal hearings in how claims are adjudicated and questions dealt with. One must also look at advice that the claimant may have received, both official and unofficial. A claimant following the notes attached to a claim form or order book should be held to have disclosed in the right office. But the right office may no longer be the local office for all benefits or in all situations.

Questions which must be considered will include the following:

- Where was the claimant instructed by the documentation to make disclosure?
- Did the claimant make initial inquiries at the local office or simply apply directly to the centralised office with a form obtained from the post office?
- Where was the claim form sent?
- Has the claimant ever sought help or advice from the local office in relation to changes of circumstances?
- Has the DSS ever sought further information from the claimant and, if so, which office was seeking this information?
- Where did the claimant think disclosure had to be made and why?

This final question may be the most significant. If a good reason can be given for disclosing at the office where disclosure was made, that should mean that the duty has been discharged.

EXAMPLE 5.9

P has been in receipt of widowed mothers' allowance since the death of her husband. She claimed at the local office. There was an issue over whether her late husband was the father of her child or not and so she attended more than one interview at the local office and was involved in a considerable amount of correspondence with it. Once the benefit was awarded, the local office was the office that issued the order books until P's claim was transferred to a centralised office and the notes in her order book altered to require her to disclose to the centralised office. P marries. P has not read the new notes in the order book and there has been no letter telling her of the change in the arrangements, although she is aware that the books are posted from a different place. She discloses the marriage to the local office, because she

> is not sure whether her re-marriage disqualifies her from benefit or not (it does). She recalls that all her previous dealings have been with the local office. The local office does not inform the centralised office. P has discharged her duty of disclosure.

The unemployment benefit office (UBO)

An unemployment benefit office is part of the Department of Employment and so it might be thought that disclosure to an officer there could not fulfil the defendant's duty. However, when a claimant is required to be available for work as a condition of receiving income support, s/he will be required to sign on at the UBO and account for his/her efforts to find work there, and will be offered a range of assistance at the job centre which is usually in the same building. Accordingly, all the claimant's dealings with the DSS may be carried out through the UBO.

In this situation two arguments have been used by claimants who have disclosed to the UBO but have made no separate disclosure to the DSS. First, it has been suggested that the UBO is the agent of the DSS in law and therefore that all disclosures made to the UBO must be deemed to be made to the DSS. Secondly, there is the contention that even if there is no agency relationship in law, it would not be reasonable to expect the claimant to make further disclosure to the DSS.

It is important to recognise that these are distinct arguments. In *CSB 403/1985* the commissioner referred to the argument with regard to the claimant's behaviour as the 'subjective' aspect and to the agency argument as the 'objective' aspect.[62]

Taking the subjective aspect first, similar questions must be asked as in the situation where the claimant has disclosed to the local office instead of the centralised office or vice versa (see pp71 above). A claimant who has had no dealings at all with the DSS and who has dealt with the UBO throughout will have a strong case. So will the claimant who believes that it was not necessary to disclose to the DSS or, which is far more commonplace, simply does not understand the distinction between the UBO and Benefits Agency offices.[63] In addition, if an officer

---

62 Paras 8 to 11; *R(SB) 54/83* para 17.
63 This point is put graphically by Commissioner Mitchell in *CSB 906/1985* para 6.

in the UBO takes down information and promises to forward it to the DSS, it is 'unquestionable'[64] that the claimant has discharged his/her duty.

It should also be noted that in *R(SB) 36/84 (T)* the Tribunal of Commissioners considered the agency question in another context and made the point that form UBL 18, which is issued to claimants signing on at the UBO, requires the claimant to 'tell us' about relevant information. It considered it 'scarcely surprising'[65] that claimants reading that form could think that disclosure to the UBO was sufficient. A comparison between the current edition and the version described by the tribunal suggests that little has been done to remedy this.

It may also be that this argument can be used outside the limited context in which agency exists, which is discussed below. Even where the UBO cannot be the agent of the DSS for receipt of the information, it may still be possible to argue that the claimant made sufficient disclosure.[66]

EXAMPLE 5.10
Q is a single parent with young children. Accordingly she is not required to sign on as available for work as a condition for receipt of income support. Nevertheless she decides to look for work. She registers at the job centre as seeking work and attends regularly. She obtains a part-time job for six hours a week and seeks advice from an officer in the UBO, which is attached to the job centre, on the implications for her benefit. The officer does not realise that she is not signing on and notes down what she tells him. She says that she is in a rush to return to her children and the officer tells her that the UBO will inform the DSS. Q has probably discharged her duty, though it is possible that there is a continuing duty in these circumstances.

Turning to the objective aspect, it now appears settled that where the claimant is signing on at the UBO and made a claim for unemployment benefit along with a claim for income support, then the UBO is acting as agent for the DSS.[67] It must be

64 *R(SB) 54/83* para 17.
65 Appendix para 17.
66 *CSB 903/1985* para 8.
67 *R(SB) 2/91* para 11; *CIS 389/1993* para 7. *CSB 14/1982* para 6 cannot now be sustained.

remembered that all income support claimants who sign on are required to claim unemployment benefit, even if they know that it is futile because they do not fulfil the contribution conditions. Agency is not dependent on the claimant receiving unemployment benefit. Only a claim is required.

The older authorities treat the existence of agency in this situation as a question of fact for a tribunal.[68] The practices and procedures for dealing with claims and passing information between the UBO and the DSS for claimants in this situation are the same regardless of geographical location. It would be most unsatisfactory for tribunals to take different views of whether or not there is agency. Whether that relationship amounts to agency ought to be treated as determined by the commissioners and applied universally, and that is what has happened in more recent cases. It is therefore suggested that the approach in *R(SB) 2/91* and *CIS 389/1993* is the correct one.

The consequence of the agency relationship is that an officer of the UBO is regarded as if s/he were an officer of the DSS. Accordingly, provided the disclosure is sufficiently clear, it does not matter that a reasonable claimant would also have proceeded to inform the DSS separately.

EXAMPLE 5.11

R loses his job. He claims unemployment benefit, which is refused because he has not made sufficient contributions. He claims and is awarded income support and is required to sign on every two weeks as available for work. Eventually R finds work and speaks to an officer in the UBO, handing in his completed UB 40 form with details of his new job. R takes the view that the officer is clearly inexperienced and does not understand the procedures. He is told that he ought to disclose the matter to the DSS, just to be safe. R does not bother and the officer fails to inform the DSS of R's work. The overpayment is not recoverable because R effectively disclosed to the DSS.

It is essential to recognise, however, that the agency relationship seems to only apply to claimants in the position outlined above. In *R(SB) 13/89* it was held[69] that the UBO was not an agent for the

---

68 *R(SB) 54/83* para 17; *R(SB) 36/84 (T)* Appendix II paras 31 and 35; *CSB 906/1985* para 11; *R(SB) 10/85 (T)* para 7.
69 Para 7.

disclosure of receipt of unemployment benefit *by the claimant's wife* to the DSS. It might be possible to argue that agency exists where the claimant has registered for work even though s/he is not required to do so. In such a case it would probably be necessary to show that some practice had grown up of the claimant acting through the UBO. Such a claimant will be more likely to succeed on the grounds that s/he had made sufficient disclosure in the circumstances.

Disclosure to other offices

It is clear that a disclosure made to a different office of the DSS will not suffice of itself to discharge the obligation.[70] In particular, it cannot be argued that because all offices are part of one large body, disclosure to one part of the body will constitute implied disclosure to another part.[71]

There may, however, be sufficient disclosure where the defendant is assured by the office to which disclosure is made that the information will be forwarded.[72] At most there will be a continuing duty to disclose.

EXAMPLE 5.12
S receives child benefit and one parent benefit for his two children. He is also receiving income support. The eldest leaves school and starts work. S telephones the Child Benefit Centre which tells him that it will send the information on to the local office, but it does not do so. There is no request from the local office for the return of the income support book. After a reasonable time, S ought to realise that the Child Benefit Centre has not passed on the information and he comes under a continuing obligation to disclose.

Disclosure to the Child Support Agency will come within this category where the carer of the child relies on the Agency informing the relevant office dealing with his/her income support about an increase in maintenance. Neither can a defendant rely on a disclosure to the local authority's housing benefit office, even though there are procedures for passing information between the DSS and the local authority.

70 *R(SB) 54/83* para 16; *R(SB) 15/87* para 25.
71 *CSB 64/1986* paras 6 to 8; *CSB 727/1987* para 7; *R(SB) 13/89* para 7.
72 *R(SB) 15/87 (T)* para 28.

There is probably one exception to this rule, which is where the claimant is receiving disability premium as part of his/her income support and the benefit is paid through the incapacity benefit office because the incapacity is long-term. If the claimant then makes disclosure to the office, perhaps when sending in one of his/her medical certificates, but makes no disclosure to the income support authorities, it would seem that the office dealing with sickness benefit would be regarded as the agent of the local office for income support purposes, in a similar way to the UBO (see pp72–75 above).

It must also be remembered that where it is not reasonable to expect the claimant to do more than s/he has, it is possible to argue that there is no failure on his/her part, even though s/he has not disclosed to the correct office.

Post offices

The claimant cannot fulfil his/her obligation by disclosing to a counter clerk in a post office when cashing his/her order book or giro cheque.[73] Post offices only act for the DSS in relation to the payment of benefits, and their employees are instructed not to advise claimants on matters of entitlement.

Proving disclosure

As with all matters concerned with recovery, generally speaking the DSS must prove that no disclosure was made (see pp87–89 above). This has important implications which are frequently overlooked.

Once a defendant has asserted that disclosure was made, the DSS must prove that it is more likely than not that no such disclosure was made. In *CSB 347/1983* it was held that it is not sufficient for an adjudication officer merely to state that there was record of disclosure or that a search for one had been conducted without success.[74] The commissioner states that the DSS must put forward evidence of what instructions are given to officers who are having a disclosure of the kind alleged made to them. In addition, there should be a statement from a 'responsible officer' giving details of steps taken to discover whether there was a disclosure.[75] In *CSB*

---

73 *CSS 33/1990* para 6.
74 Para 10(3); *R(SB) 10/85* para 7; *CSB 1195/1984* para 10.
75 Para 10(4).

1195/1984 it was held[76] that if specific officers are identified by the defendant and they deny disclosure then they must be produced at the hearing and tendered for cross-examination if their denials are to be of evidential value.

These cases appear to still be good law, though their requirements are honoured more in the breach than in the observance. The practice of the DSS is to provide a certificate by the Secretary of State that no record is held of the alleged disclosure. If these cases are correct, this is clearly insufficient.

A tribunal is unlikely to allow an appeal on the basis that the DSS has failed to comply with the requirements of proof. It is more likely to adjourn so that the necessary documents can be produced. However, the contents of the document can be utilised in the defendant's favour. If there is no procedure for recording disclosures of the type alleged, then the point can be made that it is no wonder there is no record of the disclosure. If there is such a procedure, then the likelihood of it being consistently followed can be questioned. It might be possible to show that it was not followed on a previous occasion.

Once the DSS has discharged its burden of proof, then the defendant's evidence must be considered. If the DSS cannot show it is more likely than not that there would be a record of the disclosure if such disclosure was made, then it must follow that the defendant's evidence must be accepted unless it is inherently unreliable. It is essential to make this point to the tribunal.

Tribunals have a tendency to be sceptical about the evidence of defendants who claim that they have disclosed a matter of which the DSS has no record, often taking the view that disclosure is something that is easy to allege and difficult to disprove. They will therefore seize upon any inconsistencies and vagueness in the defendant's evidence and regard it as damaging. In any case of disputed disclosure, therefore, it is vital that the maximum amount of detail regarding the disclosure be given and that a clear account of events is given by the defendant.

The best way to convince a tribunal that a disclosure was made is to produce corroborating evidence. Therefore, anyone advising a defendant on how or whether to make a disclosure to the DSS must advise him/her to ensure that s/he will have solid documentary evidence or a witness, preferably independent, if things go wrong. If no such evidence is available, it should be

---

76 Para 10.

emphasised to the tribunal that most defendants do not keep records of their dealings with the DSS, and that there is no requirement that a defendant's oral evidence be corroborated.[77] It should be borne in mind that indirect corroboration is better than no corroboration at all.

> EXAMPLE 5.13
> T has a low-paid job as a waiter. He and his wife are in receipt of family credit. T is promoted to assistant manager and receives a pay rise. The DSS claims that he failed to disclose this fact. T's employer, U, distinctly remembers T telling her about his visit to the DSS shortly after he claims that he went and that he was told that an officer would write to her about his earnings. Although U cannot give evidence that the disclosure was made, her evidence will be important to bolster the credibility of T's assertion.

Oral disclosure

In the case of a face-to-face disclosure at a DSS office, the defendant should provide details of date, time of day, the office attended and whether the attendance was for a specific appointment (as the DSS might have a record of this). Claimants are unlikely to recall the name of the officer spoken to, but another visit to the office may help to jog their memory and enable them to take a name. If there is uncertainty about whether the officer has been correctly identified, s/he should not be named. A tribunal would take a dim view of an officer being named who did not start work at the office until a year after the alleged disclosure. Failing this, if the defendant has any memory of what the officer looked like, a description should be given.

Where the disclosure is by telephone, again date, time and the office telephoned will be useful information. The number telephoned may give a clue as to who the officer was, particularly if the defendant rang a number on a letter from the DSS. The defendant may be able to describe the officer's accent.

In either case, the defendant should describe the conversation in as much detail as possible, though it would be unrealistic to expect a verbatim or particularly lengthy account.[78]

---

77 *CSB 1195/1984* para 10.
78 A point made by the commissioner in *CSIS 50/1992* para 8(a).

Ch 5 Failure to disclose 79

Disclosure by post

Cases where the DSS claims not to have received letters are common. The defendant will have to prove two things. It will first be necessary to prove that the letter was written. Few defendants seem to keep copies of their correspondence with the DSS. If there is no copy of the letter, tribunals often take an unduly harsh view of this. This reaction can be blunted by evidence that the defendant had few previous dealings with the DSS or that the defendant has never previously had problems with sending correspondence.

The second step is to give evidence of the posting of the letter. Details such as date, time, and place of posting should be put before the tribunal. Most important of all is the address to which the letter was sent. A certificate of posting, if available, will be irrefutable evidence.

If these two points are proven, it is probably not then necessary for the defendant to convince the tribunal that the DSS received the letter. There is a rule of law called the presumption of posting by which a document, the posting of which is authorised, is deemed to have been received a few days after posting, unless the contrary is proved. It is now established that this presumption applies to claim forms.[79] It is suggested that the same will apply to letters posted to the DSS. Claimants are provided with pre-paid envelopes when they are awarded many benefits (certainly income support) which they are told they can use to report changes of circumstances. This must mean that posting a letter is an authorised method of disclosure.[80] It will be for the DSS to prove non-receipt of the letter, which it is extremely unlikely to be able to do.

The requirement of failure

The mere fact that the defendant has not disclosed the relevant fact will not suffice to ground recovery. SSAA s71 refers to

---

79 Interpretation Act 1978 s7; *CSIS 48/1992* para 8; *CIS 759/1992* para 5. See Appendix 2, precedent 9 for the full argument.
80 The suggestion to this effect in Bonner, Hooker and White, *Non-Means Tested Benefits: The Legislation* (Annual, Sweet & Maxwell, 1995) (hereafter referred to as Bonner), p62. No reference was made in *CSB 1325/1986* para 6 or *CSB 99/1990* para 16 to the presumption of posting and it is suggested that these cases were wrongly decided on this point.

failure to disclose, not non-disclosure. The use of the word 'failure' introduces an extra element:

> I consider that "failure" to disclose necessarily imports the concept of some breach of obligation, legal or moral - ie, the non-disclosure must have occurred in circumstances in which, at lowest, disclosure by the person in question was reasonably to be expected ...[81]

An innocent failure to disclose still renders the overpayment recoverable.[82] There is no inconsistency between the concept of 'innocence' and the need for a 'failure'. 'Innocence' in relation to s71 is connected to the fact that the overpayment is recoverable regardless of whether the defendant's breach of duty is 'fraudulent or otherwise'. An 'innocent' breach of duty is one that does not involve an attempt to defraud the DSS, but is a breach of duty nevertheless. If a defendant has an honest but unreasonable belief that a fact does not have to be disclosed, there is an innocent failure to disclose and the overpayment is recoverable. This is also true if the claimant forgets the material fact, or forgets to disclose it. The concept of 'failure' does not consider the defendant's intention, but rather the defendant's conduct and whether that course of conduct was reasonable.

In order to demonstrate a 'failure', the DSS will have to prove that:

a) the defendant had knowledge of the material fact; and
b) disclosure was reasonably to be expected of the claimant in all the circumstances of the case.

Lack of knowledge of the material fact

It is clear that if the defendant had no knowledge of the material fact, there cannot be said to be any kind of failure to disclose.[83] Two qualifications must be placed on this statement. First, a distinction must be drawn between a defendant who has never known the material fact and a defendant who knew about the fact but at all material times had forgotten about it. A defendant who forgot about the fact is in the same situation as one who

---

81 *R(SB) 21/82* para 4(2).
82 *Page and Davis v Chief Adjudication Officer* (1991) *Times* 4 July (appendix to *R(SB) 2/92*), CA; *CSB 53/1981 (T)* para 7; *R(SB) 44/83* para 7; *R(SB) 15/87 (T)* para 14.
83 *R(SB) 21/82* para 19(2) and (3); *R(SB) 54/83* para 13(2); *R(SB) 9/85* para 7.

knew of the fact, unless perhaps the forgetfulness is the result of mental incapacity (see pp89–91 below). Forgetfulness will not excuse non-disclosure.[84]

The second qualification is that the type of knowledge required will vary with different types of defendant. In particular, for some defendants actual knowledge of the fact will have to be shown and others may be caught if they ought to have known the fact.

The level of knowledge required

It seems probable that a defendant's non-disclosure of a fact that s/he ought to have known can amount to a failure. In *R(SB) 28/83* it was stated that if the defendant could with 'reasonable diligence'[85] have known of a capital resource, then s/he would be treated as knowing the material fact. Commissioner Watson claimed that *R(SB) 21/82* supported this conclusion, but this does not appear to be correct. Commissioner Edward-Jones, in the latter case, was considering the effect of a lapse of memory, which does not excuse a failure to disclose provided that the defendant 'once knew of' the existence of the asset.[86] The language of the case clearly militates against imputed knowledge, as do several other authorities. There must be a 'fact known to the person who does not disclose it'.[87] In *CSB 296/1985*, however, Commissioner Goodman explicitly held that constructive knowledge would suffice, and several other cases make passing reference by stating that it is enough if a claimant 'ought to have known' a fact.[88]

In relation to cases involving non-disclosure of resources, a further complication is whether it can be assumed in law that the claimant knew of their existence. This is suggested in *CSB 53/1981 (T)*[89] but knowledge was not in issue in that case, so that conclusion does not bind tribunals. The commissioner in *R(SB) 28/83* states that no such assumption can be made.[90]

---

84 *R(SB) 21/82* para 4(3).
85 Para 10.
86 Para 20(4).
87 *R v Medical Appeal Tribunal (North Midland Region) ex p Hubble* [1958] 2 QB 228 at p242, DC; *CSB 53/1981 (T)* para 7; *R(SB) 54/83* para 13(2).
88 Para 11. See *R(SB) 40/84* para 9; *R(FIS) 3/1985* paras 18 and 20; *CIS 831/1985* para 10; *CIS 322/1994* para 7.
89 Para 7.
90 Para 10. The fact that tribunals are enjoined to consider the question of the claimant's knowledge in *R(SB) 54/83* para 13(2) also supports this conclusion.

There are particular complications with regard to recovery from a claimant's estate when it is found that the claimant had a resource available while s/he was alive. By definition, the claimant will not be available to give evidence. *R(SB) 21/82* sets out principles for dealing with cases like this. The DSS must prove that the claimant knew or had known about the asset.[91] This burden of proof can be discharged by circumstantial evidence. If the estate can prove that it is more likely than not that the claimant did not know of the asset for the first part of the period of claim, then the overpayment in respect of that part will be recoverable.

EXAMPLE 5.14

V died in 1995 and following disclosure of the contents of his estate by his executor, it is found that he had a savings account. On inspection, it appears that the account was opened in the name of his wife in 1975. On her death in 1983 all transactions in the account appear to cease. V claimed supplementary benefit in 1985. In 1990 it is clear that V transferred the account into his own name and drew sums from it. The DSS can recover the overpayment after 1990 but it seems to be a fair inference from the evidence that V did not know about the account until then. No overpayment from 1985 to 1990 would therefore be recoverable.

In *R(SB) 28/83* it is held that in the case of receivers and those in a similar position who take complete charge of a claimant's financial affairs, it will be enough that they ought to have known about an asset.[92] The justification for this is that receivers are not discharging their duty if they do not take care to obtain precise information about the claimant's assets.[93]

By contrast, in *CIS 734/1992* it was pointed out that appointees are limited to dealing with benefit and will often not know every detail of a claimant's affairs. It is doubtful whether this decision remains good law in view of its disapproval in *CIS 332/1993* (see p11 above). Where an agent of a claimant has knowledge but the claimant does not, the claimant is fixed with that knowledge, provided that dealing with benefits is within the scope of the agent's duties.[94]

91 Paras 19(3) and 20(4).
92 Para 10.
93 Para 11; *CIS 734/1992* para 9.
94 *CSB 296/1985* paras 13 and 14.

Where other third parties are concerned, it is difficult to envisage any circumstances where anything other than actual knowledge of the fact would be required.[95]

Proving lack of knowledge

It can be difficult for a claimant to rely on lack of knowledge of a material fact. Tribunals will often look at a case with the benefit of hindsight and think that the existence of the material fact is so obvious that no-one could possibly be unaware of it.

Two points follow from this. First, thought should be given as to why the existence of the fact might seem obvious in retrospect and an explicit explanation made for why it did not seem so at the time. Secondly, external proof of the claimant's belief will be important to bolster the claimant's evidence about the state of his/her mind at the material time. This evidence will depend on the type of case under consideration.

A common type of case is where a claimant disclaims knowledge of a partner's earnings, assets or activities due to estrangement between them. A significant lack of communication will have to be shown in such a case. This can be provided by friends or relatives, and by detailed evidence of the souring of the relationship. It must be borne in mind that if the estrangement amounts to separation of households, this may raise the question of whether the couple are still partners at all.[96] It will also be helpful if there was little discussion of the relevant circumstances when the relationship was still healthy.

EXAMPLE 5.15

W has always jealously guarded the running of the family finances. His wife, X, finally rebels against his attitude and takes a low-paid job, claiming family credit to top up the family income. She discloses all the savings of which she is aware, leaving her just below the capital limit. W is furious and the couple move into separate bedrooms and eat meals apart. W has an insurance policy which matures and he banks the resulting payment without telling his wife. X leaves him and eventually the payment to W is discovered. W's general attitude and the total lack of communication between the couple will both help to prove X's assertion that she was unaware of the payment.

---

95 As was the case in *CIS 674/1994* para 17.
96 *CIS 726/1992* para 9.

Personal characteristics of the defendant

It is clear that the question of the claimant's mental capacity must be taken into account when deciding whether the claimant knew the material fact.[97] The adjudicating authorities are considering the 'person in question'.[98] Complete incapability to look after one's affairs will not be necessary. Any illness affecting the claimant's ability to deal with his/her finances will be relevant.

EXAMPLE 5.16

Y is suffering from an inactive thyroid and severe depression. There is medical evidence that he is unable to concentrate on complex documents as a result. He receives a long letter from his mortgage company explaining that the mortgage rate has decreased. This information is hidden among a number of items regarding changes in mortgage policy. When the DSS seeks recovery of the overpaid income support mortgage interest, Y claims that he was unaware of the decrease. Even if the tribunal thinks that any healthy person would have read and understood the letter, it must take account of Y's illness.

There does not seem to be any reason why regard cannot be had to other characteristics of the claimant when assessing whether they have sufficient knowledge of the fact. Matters such as educational difficulties and illiteracy can be taken into account. It must, however, be borne in mind that these matters are only evidence which may reduce the likelihood of the claimant having known the relevant fact. Once it is shown that the claimant had such knowledge, then the second consideration with regard to 'failure' comes into play.

Whether disclosure was reasonably to be expected

In *R(SB) 21/82* the commissioner made clear that the fact that a claimant knows the relevant material fact does not mean that

---

97 *R(SB) 21/82* para 19(5); *R(SB) 40/84* Appendix para 1; *CA 303/1992* para 6.
98 *R(SB) 21/82* para 19(5).

there is a 'failure' to disclose the fact.⁹⁹ It seems that this requirement will apply to all defendants.¹⁰⁰

In relation to claimants, this is reinforced by the fact that the statutory provision regarding the provision of information by the claimant requires notification of a fact that 'he might reasonably be expected to know might affect the right to benefit ...'¹⁰¹ Once the knowledge of the defendant has been established, a tribunal must then consider whether a reasonable person in the defendant's position would have disclosed. It is not sufficient that the defendant did not realise that disclosure was necessary, if a reasonable person would have done so.¹⁰²

The general principle has been applied in a number of cases, which can be subdivided into groups. However, a case outside these categories can still come within the scope of the general principle.

DSS advice and specified requirements

> Unless there is a question as to the claimant's knowledge of the material fact, an adjudication officer or tribunal considering whether disclosure by the claimant was reasonably to be expected will usually focus on the clarity and circumstances surrounding the instructions or requests for information which the adjudication officer claims gave rise to the claimant's obligation to disclose. Those matters are relevant to the question whether "a reasonable man would have thought that it was material to disclose the knowledge in question".¹⁰³⁻¹⁰⁴

If the DSS gives unequivocal advice in an accessible way that disclosure of a fact is required and how this is achieved, it will be extremely difficult to argue that a reasonable defendant would not disclose the fact.

However, where the advice given is vague and it can be shown that a reasonable person could have acted as the claimant did,

---

99 Para 4(2).
100 This follows from the approval of the test in *R(SB) 54/83* para 13(3) and *R(SB) 15/87 (T)* para 26. See also *CSB 831/1985* paras 11 and 13; *CSB 677/1986* para 7 ('well settled'). *CSB 53/1981 (T)* para 7, which seems to suggest that only knowledge is relevant, and *CSB 1006/1985* para 10, which suggests it only applies to defendants who are not claimants, must be regarded as overruled. The latter suggestion was also made in *CIS 322/1994* para 7, where the commissioner overlooked *R(SB) 15/87(T)*.
101 Claims and Payments Regs reg 32(1).
102 *CS 102/1993* para 20.
103-104 *CA 303/1992* para 6.

there will be no failure to disclose. In *CSB 677/1986* the claimant was told that he had to disclose changes of circumstances to the 'issuing office' of his order books. He received a letter from the same office concerning an award of invalidity benefit. The commissioner held that a reasonable person would not think that it was necessary to disclose to the office the contents of a letter from that same office.[105] In *CSB 727/1987* the order book requested the reporting of all facts 'not already reported'. The commissioner held that as the claimant had already reported the fact that she had made a claim, the claimant could reasonably think that she had already reported the fact.[106]

Where the advice misleads a claimant into thinking that there is no need to disclose, then this will mean that there is no failure to disclose.[107] This is so even if oral advice given by a DSS officer contradicts the contents of an order book.[108] It seems likely, however, that a reasonable claimant will regard advice given some time previously as being potentially out of date and may seek further advice.[109]

EXAMPLE 5.17

A works for 15 hours a week. Her husband, Z, is receiving income support, having disclosed A's work on his claim form. One day he asks a DSS officer what will happen 'if A's hours change'. The officer replies that provided she is not earning more money it will make no difference. Some time later, A's employer forces her to work an extra hour for the same weekly wage and Z does not disclose this, relying on the officer's advice. The extra hour worked disqualifies the couple from benefit altogether, but any resulting overpayment will not be recoverable, even though the income support order book requires Z to report any changes to working hours.

A claimant is only under a duty to provide such information 'as the Secretary of State may require'.[109A] There may be cases in

105 Paras 7 and 8; *CIS 618/1990* para 6.
106 Para 13.
107 *R(SB) 3/81* para 7; *CSB 108/1992* para 5; *CIS 584/1994* para 11; *CIS 173/1990* paras 5 and 6.
108 *CIS 584/1994* para 15.
109 *CSB 108/1992* para 8(1).
109A Claims and Payments Regs reg 32(1).

which those changes of circumstances that have to be notified will be determined by the Secretary of State. In *CIS 627/1995* the claimant disclosed receipt of a Canadian pension and the fact that its standing value fluctuated with the exchange rate. When the pound weakened, an overpayment resulted. Commissioner Rice held that if the DSS required details of the fluctuations, 'they should have asked'.[109B] In all these cases, the touchstone will be the contents of leaflets and order books sent to the claimant.

Finally, where an officer in a different office of the DSS gives an explicit promise that information will be forwarded to the correct office, this may mean that further disclosure is not reasonably to be expected.[110] It is important to bear in mind the possibility of a continuing obligation in this type of case (see pp61–65 above).

Reliance on advice from other experts

In *CSB 510/1987* the claimant was advised by her barrister and solicitor that disclosure was not required. In the circumstances of that case it was held that a tribunal could conclude that disclosure was not reasonably to be expected, but there would also have to be consideration of the notes in the claimant's order book.[111]

The category of 'experts' may not be confined to practising lawyers, but it is likely that highly cogent reasons will need to be given for following their advice without checking the situation with the DSS. Given the widespread reliance by claimants on lay advisers in relation to benefit matters, firm indication from such an adviser that disclosure was not necessary ought to come within this principle. In *CIS 545/1992* Commissioner Johnson decided that a receiver could rely on a letter from a local health authority stating that the DSS was to continue to pay the claimant's nursing home fees to show that disclosure of the claimant's capital resources was not reasonably required.[112]

Reliance on advice from friends, no matter how experienced in social security matters, could not be regarded as reasonable, unless the friend was in fact an expert adviser.

109B   Para 7.
110   *R(SB) 54/83* para 17.
111   Para 7(3).
112   Para 14. This aspect of the case was not addressed by the Court of Appeal in overturning the commissioner's decision: *Chief Adjudication Officer v Sherriff* (1995) *Times* 10 May, CA.

Disclosure of intention

If a claimant discloses that a claim has been made for a benefit but does not go on to report the award of that benefit, in some circumstances expecting further disclosure of the award may not be reasonable.[113] However, a very clear statement will be required of the fact that benefit will be forthcoming. In *CSB 727/1987* the claimant had claimed child benefit. She stated on her claim form for supplementary benefit that she was owed 'family allowance', that she had applied for child benefit, and that she had applied for one parent benefit but had yet to receive any money. The commissioner stated that this made it 'abundantly clear'[114] that the claimant was to receive child benefit. In *CSSB 621/1988* a claimant in a similar position merely wrote that she had 'not yet' applied for child benefit. While disapproving of *CSB 727/1987*, the commissioner also noted that the decision was distinguishable because the claimant had not made it clear that the benefit would be forthcoming.[115]

In *CS 130/1992* the claimant tried to argue that disclosure of his intention to start work was sufficient disclosure of the fact that he had in fact started work. The commissioner held that disclosure of future intention may be sufficient provided that intention is 'sufficiently settled'.[116]

EXAMPLE 5.18

B is receiving income support and does not come within those categories of persons entitled to receive it while abroad. She is paid by credit transfer into her bank account. She decides to use her savings to take a long trip abroad. She writes to the DSS in March telling them that she is planning to leave the country in June, enclosing a photocopy of her air ticket. B forgets to return her UB 40 before she leaves. The DSS continues to pay income support while she is abroad. As she made her commitment to going abroad clear, the overpayment is not recoverable under SSAA s71, though it may be possible for the DSS to use Overpayments Regs reg 14 in relation to some of the benefit at least (see chapter 14 below).

---

113 *CSB 906/1985* para 11; *CSB 727/1987* para 10. In *Jones v Chief Adjudication Officer* [1994] 1 WLR 62 at p71D-F, CA, Stuart-Smith LJ suggests that disclosing a claim rather than receipt of benefit will be insufficient. This was not necessary for his decision and should not be regarded as setting down any general rule.
114 Para 10.
115 Para 10.
116 Para 18; *CG 54/1988* para 8; *CS 234/1994* para 4.

Matters of public knowledge

In *CSB 1246/1986* the DSS sought to argue that an overpayment was recoverable because the claimant failed to disclose the fact that his unemployment benefit had been increased. The commissioner held that as the annual uprating of benefits was public knowledge, there could be no failure to disclose.[117]

It is doubtful whether this category of case could be extended too widely. It is probably linked solely with matters of public knowledge relating to the social security system.

Disclosure by the claimant is irrelevant

In *R(SB) 2/91* the DSS sought recovery on the grounds that a student had misrepresented the fact that his course was part-time. It was held that as the decision on whether a course is full-time or part-time is one for the DSS in light of information supplied by the college, disclosure was not reasonably to be expected.[118]

Another example might be where a claimant represented that s/he had sufficient contributions to qualify for benefit and that there was some lapse of procedure following which benefit was wrongly awarded. However, the comment that 'it is expecting too much for a claimant to assess whether a matter is relevant or not, and this case would have been better dealt with on the basis that what was being disclosed was not a material fact'[119] seems correct.

Personal characteristics of the defendant

In *CA 303/1992* the claimant's child had been taken into care and placed in a residential home, meaning that attendance allowance was no longer payable. The claimant suffered a nervous breakdown and spent time in hospital. He sought to argue that his mental state meant that he could not be expected to realise that he had to report that his son had left home. In *R(SB) 21/82*, Commissioner Edwards-Jones had made it clear that the mental capacity of the claimant's wife could be relevant to the issue of whether there was a 'failure' to disclose on her part.[120]

Commissioner Rowland decided that mental capacity was only relevant to whether or not the claimant knew the fact and that 'once knowledge has been established, the claimant's mental

---

117 Para 7.
118 Para 8.
119 Mesher, p701.
120 Para 19(2).

capacity ceases to be relevant'.[121] However, in *R(SB) 40/84*, Commissioner Edwards-Jones specifically instructed a tribunal to have regard to the mental capacity of the claimant in relation to both knowledge and whether a reasonable person would disclose the facts.[122] It would seem therefore that it is possible to argue that *CA 303/1992* is inconsistent with reported commissioners' decisions and should not be followed by a tribunal. In addition, *CSB 957/1987* was not referred to. Commissioner Penny there decided that medical evidence could be relevant in ascertaining the claimant's awareness of his responsibility for disclosing facts.[123]

However, no other factors relating to the individual defendant will be relevant. In *CF 26/1990* an argument that the tribunal should take into account the family's educational difficulties and the claimant's illiteracy failed. It was decided that the test for whether the defendant's conduct amounts to a 'failure' is objective and that personal characteristics are not relevant.[124]

There is no inconsistency between that test for other characteristics and the relevance of mental capacity. Mental capacity is in a category all of its own, and by the system of appointees, the system has facility for dealing with the situation. If a defendant is mentally incapable of understanding that s/he has obligations under the benefit scheme, or of forming any kind of view as to the extent of that duty, it is hard to see how s/he can have breached that duty by being guilty of a 'failure'.[125] By contrast, a defendant such as the claimant in *CF 26/1990* will be able to understand, however imperfectly, that s/he has duties and will have formed a view of the extent of those duties. Incorrectly assessing the extent of those duties will amount to a 'failure' to disclose, albeit an innocent one. There is no inconsistency between this suggested distinction and the decision in *Chief Adjudication Officer v Sherriff*[126] because no concept of 'failure' is involved where a misrepresentation is made.

121 *CA 303/1992* para 6.
122 Appendix para 1.
123 Para 10. The conflict ought to be resolved in *CIS 12032/1996*, currently pending before the commissioner.
124 Para 11.
125 This was the basis of the decision in *CSB 957/1987* para 10. In debating the Overpayments Act 1996, the government appeared to accept the logic of this position: R Evans MP, HC Debates, vol 280, col 1018.
126 (1995) *Times* 10 May, CA. See pp51–53 above.

Example 5.19

C suffers from ME, and is also illiterate, which rend[ers him] incapable of reading and understanding his income supp[ort] book. He is under the mistaken impression that he is receiving sickness benefit. His wife starts work and he fails to disclose this fact. The tribunal must consider whether a reasonable claimant with ME would have understood that this fact had to be disclosed. They cannot take account of his illiteracy.

CHAPTER 6
The relevant material fact

An often overlooked facet of SSAA s71 is the requirement that the subject-matter of the misrepresentation or failure to disclose must be a *material fact*. The mere fact of a breach of duty is insufficient. Adjudication officers often seek to base their decisions on matters which are not factual nor material to the decision to award benefit, and defendants have a right to require that s71 is properly complied with.

By demanding that the breach of duty relates to a material fact, s71 associates itself with the law relating to misrepresentation in a contractual context; some commissioners have made explicit references to contract and insurance law cases. There are, however, few commissioners' decisions on the nature of a material fact and so this chapter embraces other principles established by contract law. These will be equally applicable where the DSS is proceeding on the basis of a failure to disclose.

The matter which is alleged to have been misrepresented or not disclosed is always explicitly stated within the terms of the adjudication officer's decision. Even if this subject-matter is not itself a material fact, then by his/her representations the claimant may well have implied the existence or non-existence of other material facts (termed 'implied facts' in this chapter). Implied facts arise particularly frequently in cases of misrepresentations. However, caution should be exercised before imputing representations of implied fact to the defendant. The rule should be that no such representation will be implied unless it would be a matter of common sense to the reasonable claimant. A failure to exercise such caution could result in an unjust relaxation of the conditions for recovery under s71.

Remember that the material fact which is the subject-matter of the breach of duty need not be the same material fact as is used to review the decision to award benefit under s71(5), where the ground for review is ignorance of a material fact. For example, in *Jones v Chief Adjudication Officer*[1] the ground for review was ignorance of the material fact that the claimant was in receipt of unemployment benefit, whereas the material fact misrepresented was that the claimant had reported all facts relevant to his claim for income support.

In order to demonstrate that the subject-matter of the breach of duty is a material fact, the DSS will have to show that the subject-matter is:

a) a fact;
b) a primary fact; and
c) material to the decision in question.

The need for a fact

Fact not law

There is a long-established distinction under the law relating to reviews between matters of law and matters of fact.[2] This is equally applicable to the requirement for a material fact in SSAA s71.

The main matter where this has been relevant to date has been in relation to a representation by a claimant that s/he is entitled to the sum paid. It is now clear that this is a representation of law (see p44 above). However, when claimants state that they are entitled to a payment, there are representations of implied fact that they believe that there is such an entitlement and that there is a current award in their favour.[3] In addition, a third party presenting a pre-signed payment order represents that the signature is genuine and that the signatory understood what s/he was signing.[4] These facts are all clearly material.

Other possible applications of the distinction could relate to entitlement in law to certain resources or the legal status of a marriage. As to the former category, the assets of income support claimants come in an infinite variety of forms and difficult questions of property and trust law may arise. If benefit is awarded due to the claimant representing that s/he does not

1 [1994] 1 WLR 62, CA.
2 *R(G) 18/52 (T)* para 8.
3 *CS 102/1993* para 12.
4 *CSB 1093/1989* paras 12 and 13.

have any interest in a piece of property, and that view is accepted by the adjudication officer, then the fact that the claimant and the adjudication officer have been acting under a mistaken view of the law does not give rise to liability under s71. If, however, there has been some primary fact misrepresented or not disclosed by the claimant, as a result of which the adjudication officer comes to an erroneous view of the law, then there can be recovery.

EXAMPLE 6.1

A's marriage to B breaks up after A loses his job. He moves into a small flat and claims income support and housing benefit. He asserts that he has no interest in the matrimonial home on the basis that it is registered in B's sole name. He does not disclose to the DSS that he has paid half the mortgage payments during the currency of the marriage and has been advised by his solicitors that he has therefore acquired an interest in the house. He also states that he gave money to his son C to enable him to start a business some time previously. C had died before anything was done about this and the money was in C's bank account awaiting administration of C's estate. He claims that he is not entitled to receive the money back. The adjudication officer awards income support on the basis that C does not have either asset available as a resource.

A misrepresented that he is not entitled to receive the monies given to C but this is a representation of law, not fact, as it is only the operation of a resulting trust that allows A to be entitled to the money. However, the non-disclosure of his contribution to the mortgage is a material fact, since it could be expected to give rise to a question of ownership of the property. In view of the solicitor's advice, this is probably also a matter that a reasonable person would have disclosed.

Finally, it must be noted that where a question of foreign law is involved, it is treated by English law as a question of fact[5] and so could conceivably give rise to s71 liability, which would be extremely harsh.

EXAMPLE 6.2

D goes through what she believes to be a marriage ceremony with E in Pakistan. In fact the marriage is not valid under Islamic law.

---

5   R(G) 2/71 para 4.

> The couple live and work in Britain until E's death. D then claims and receives widows' benefit. Later the DSS discovers the invalidity of the marriage. This is a material fact and could give rise to recovery of the widows' benefit under s71.

Opinions and beliefs are not facts

A second distinction that must be drawn is between facts, which have an objective existence, and opinions and beliefs as to the existence of facts which are subjective to the person holding them.[6] The latter will not ground SSAA s71 recovery. Where the ground for recovery is misrepresentation, it will be worth looking for some element of subjectivity in what the defendant has allegedly asserted. Where s/he is responding to a question, then if the question asks him/her what s/he thinks or believes, the answer is arguably a matter of opinion or belief. It will be a matter of degree in each case.

In *CIS 402/1994* the claimant made a misrepresentation that she was not living with a partner and it was argued that this was a matter of opinion of both the claimant and the adjudication officer and was not a material fact. The commissioner clearly accepted the distinction between opinion and fact, because he held that there were implied representations of material fact by the claimant, namely that she had grounds for this opinion. As she had no such grounds, she misrepresented a material fact.[7] However, it was made clear that, in common with the law in contractual misrepresentation, this implied representation will only be made where the defendant is in a better position to know the true facts than the adjudication officer.

This will not always be the case. In *R(SB) 2/91* the claimant was alleged to have misrepresented the fact that his course of study was part-time rather than full-time. The commissioner implicitly held that as the view taken of his course by the college was the primary determining factor, the claimant's opinion as to the nature of the course will not be a material fact.[8]

---

6   *Bisset v Wilkinson* [1927] AC 177, PC.
7   Para 5(i), applying *Smith v Land & House Property Corp* (1884) 28 Ch D 7 at p15, CA.
8   Para 8.

> EXAMPLE 6.3
> F claims invalidity benefit with an increase for his wife, G. G has always controlled the family finances and F gives her all his benefit each week. There is little communication between them. G is doing some work, a fact of which F is unaware. The DSS writes to F asking him if G is working and if she is receiving any benefit. F replies, 'I do not think so', before explaining the problems in their relationship. Because of this, F has only represented his belief and is not in a better position to know the facts than the DSS, which should write to or interview G to check the situation.

Where the claimant is in a better position to know the true facts, an adjudication officer is entitled to rely on a claimant's belief. If such a belief is not actually held, the representation that the belief is held is one of material fact.[9]

Intentions and expectations are not facts

Defendants frequently make statements to the DSS about what they intend or expect to happen. Indeed, there is specific provision for a claim to be made in advance of the claimant being entitled and for a review to be made in anticipation of a change of circumstances.[10]

Such statements should be distinguished from representations of fact because a fact, by definition, must exist.[11] For there to be a representation of fact, the fact must be in existence at the time of the representation. However, in making such a representation, there may well be implied representations that the claimant actually does believe the change will occur,[12] that the claimant has a basis for the view s/he takes,[13] and that the claimant believes s/he will be able to bring about the change.

Moreover, if the intention or expectation of the defendant does not happen and there has been an award on the basis that it would, then the fact that matters have not turned out as

---

9 *CIS 402/1994* para 5(iii); *Brown v Raphael* [1958] Ch 636 at p641, CA.
10 Claims and Payments Regs reg 13(1); SSAA s25(2)(c).
11 *CIS 650/1991* paras 13 to 16.
12 *Edgington v Fitzmaurice* (1885) 29 Ch D 459 at p482, CA.
13 *The Mihalis Angelos* [1971] 1 QB 164 at pp194 and 205, CA.

anticipated must itself be a material fact. It would have to be clear that the true situation is not as anticipated before s71 liability arises on this basis.

Primary and secondary fact

Once it has been determined that the subject-matter of the breach of duty is a fact, then consideration must be given to the nature of the fact. For the purposes of review, a clear distinction is drawn between facts (called 'secondary facts') which only exist by virtue of inference or reasoning, and more basic facts which can give rise to such inferences (termed 'primary facts' in this chapter). Only primary facts can be material facts. The reason for the distinction is set out below:

> In all such cases the duty of the determining authority is to consider the evidence and reach a conclusion. That conclusion is an inference of fact – that the claimant was or was not incapable of work; that she was or was not cohabiting with a man as his wife. [Section 25(1)(a)] does not authorise a review of a decision founded on such an inference merely because the [adjudication] officer is satisfied that in the light of the evidence before the determining authority, the inference was faulty or mistaken. He must go further and assert and prove that the inference might not have been drawn, if the determining authority had not been ignorant of some specific fact of which it could have been aware, or had not been mistaken as to some specific fact which it took into consideration.[14]

Incapacity for work

It has been explicitly held that whether or not a claimant is incapable of work is a secondary fact.[15] A representation to that effect or a failure to disclose that a claimant was capable could not of itself give rise to SSAA s71 liability.

It has been suggested[16] that the claimant may be caught by an implied fact that his/her underlying condition has not changed. The better view is that this should not be the case except where it would be clear to a reasonable claimant that s/he is clearly not incapable of work. Where a Med 3 certificate has been issued,

---

14 *R(I) 3/75* para 9.
15 *R(S) 4/86* para 4.
16 Mesher, p697.

a claimant is entitled to rely on the doctor's judgement. Such a fact would be implied by a claimant in only two circumstances:

a) when the claimant makes a complete recovery during the currency of a Med 3 certificate and there is no reason for him/her to think that s/he is still incapable of work (eg, through being infectious);
b) where the claimant has misled his/her doctor to obtain the medical certificate.

Cohabitation

The vexed question of whether two people are cohabiting depends on whether the following six criteria are present:

- a common household;
- stability in the relationship;
- financial support;
- a sexual relationship;
- children; and
- public acknowledgement of the relationship.[17]

Clearly, therefore, a representation that a couple are cohabiting is not in itself a primary fact.

However, in *CIS 402/1994* it was made clear that a claimant representing that there is no cohabitation, without providing more information, represents the implied material fact that the claimant knows facts which justify that conclusion and the adjudication officer is entitled to believe the claimant in the absence of anything that may warrant investigation.[18]

Things will not be so straightforward in cases where there has been an investigation into the claimant's circumstances and an adjudication officer has concluded that there is no cohabitation and benefit has been awarded accordingly. In this situation the fact cannot be implied because the adjudication officer has examined the full situation without accepting the claimant's word. In this case reliance must be placed on a primary fact that has changed, and this may cause difficulties. This is discussed further below.

---

17 See Bonner, pp173 to 176 and Mesher, pp23 to 26 for detailed analyses of the criteria.
18 Para 5(i) and (iii).

Household

Whether a married couple are living in the same household is also a secondary fact, which will depend on all the circumstances of the case.[19] Similar considerations to those under the cohabitation test will apply.

Other secondary facts

The varieties of secondary fact discussed above are those well-known to the law, but there may well be others. For example, whether or not a claimant is habitually resident in the United Kingdom, and whether a particular loan is for the purpose of acquiring an interest in the home and is therefore an eligible housing cost for income support purposes may also be secondary facts and must be broken down into their components.

Materiality

In *Saker v Secretary of State for Social Security*[20] the Court of Appeal held that for a fact to be material and to be capable of triggering a review, it was not necessary that knowledge of it would have altered the decision in question. It was sufficient if 'serious consideration' would have been given to it.

However, this cannot be the correct test for SSAA s71 purposes. It is essential to show, on the balance of probabilities, that the fact relied on would have certainly altered the decision. This is because if the decision may not have been different then the breach of duty cannot have caused the overpayment (see chapter 7 below).

In addition, under the test in *Saker* (above) a fact is only material if it affects the claimant's entitlement. There is clear authority that under s71 a fact affecting the payment of benefit will also be material.[21] The definition of a material fact as 'information we need to work out your benefit'[22] is therefore incomplete. In determining whether a fact is material or not, a

---

19 *R(SB) 4/83*.
20 (1988) (appendix to *R(I) 2/88*), CA.
21 *CSB 249/1989* para 5; *CSB 1093/1989* paras 12 and 13; *CS 102/1993* paras 10 and 12.
22 *Jones v Chief Adjudication Officer* [1994] 1 WLR 62 at p65F-H (Evans LJ), CA.

tribunal must take an objective view. The views or beliefs of the defendant as to whether or not a fact was material are irrelevant.[23]

The question of materiality will often rear its head in relation to implied facts. Implied facts must be material as well as false if they are to be relied on. There will be instances where the adjudication officer is not relying on inferences from the claimant's representation.

EXAMPLE 6.4

H is receiving income support including mortgage interest. He reads in the newspaper that base rates may rise by 1 per cent after the budget next month. He tells the DSS that base rates will rise. Due to an error, the rise is not checked with H's mortgage lender. Without such a check, the adjudication officer cannot argue that credence is being given to H's word alone.

The mere fact that an adjudication officer considers that the decision of a previous adjudication officer was wrong does not justify a review[24] and it certainly does not justify s71 recovery. The adjudication officer must identify a primary fact that has changed and is the subject of a breach of duty, and it may not be easy to show that the adjudication officer's decision would definitely have been different.

EXAMPLE 6.5

I is awarded family credit on the basis that she is living with her husband, J, and their children. At the time of the claim, she discloses that the couple are living in separate bedrooms and there is no sexual relationship. The couple go on outings with the children and cook for the whole family. J earns £80 per week from his job and gives some of this to I. On the basis of this information, the adjudication officer decides that the couple are living in the same household. Benefit is awarded in January. Over the months, there is less contact between the couple. J becomes a vegetarian and cooks only for himself, buying food separately from the family. I starts working, earning a similar sum to J and so there is no mutual support. In June J moves into a different flat in the same building, though he continues to use the flat to

---

23 CSB 727/1987 para 8.
24 R(I) 3/75 para 9

participate in activities with the children. In October I is interviewed again by the adjudication officer, who decides that at some time between January and June the couple ceased to be living in the same household. There is no single primary fact that would have given rise to a review had the adjudication officer been informed of this, until June. An overpayment is only recoverable from June, relying on the non-disclosure of J's departure from the flat.

CHAPTER 7
The requirement of a causal link

An aspect of SSAA s71 often neglected by advisers and tribunals is the need for the breach of duty to cause the overpayment of which recovery is sought. In many cases the issue will not arise, because the dispute will be over whether there has been a breach of duty. Once that has been demonstrated, it is clear that the DSS paid benefit as a result of that failing. However, there are a number of situations where the overpayment occurred as a result of a series of unfortunate events, often involving failings by the DSS and sometimes the actions of third parties.

The requirement of such a causal link arises from two parts of s71(1). First, the payment or failure to recover must be 'in consequence of' the breach of duty. Precisely when an overpayment is a consequence of a breach of duty is the main focus for arguments on causation; most of this chapter deals with the meaning of the word 'consequence'.

Secondly, it must be shown that the payment would not have been made 'but for' the breach of duty. This underlines the fact that if the DSS would have paid the money even had the breach of duty not occurred, then there can be no recovery of that amount. It does not at all follow that just because a breach of duty has caused some overpayment, that the full amount overpaid is recoverable. The DSS must prove that every penny of the overpayment claimed is a result of the breach of duty. Those parts of the overpayment which have some other cause are not recoverable.[1]

---

1 CSB 348/1990 para 5. See further pp127–128 below concerning the effect on the calculation of the amount of the overpayment.

> EXAMPLE 7.1
> A receives income support. As a single person, £5 of any earnings are disregarded. In period 1, he takes a part-time job for five hours per week, earning £20. He forgets to disclose this to the DSS. At the beginning of period 2, his hours and earnings double and he informs the DSS, which fails to adjust his benefit. In period 3, he works for 15 hours and earns £80. This is not disclosed. During period 4, his earnings are reduced to £60 for a further ten weeks. For period 1, the overpayment is £15 per week. No overpayment is recoverable during period 2, because A has disclosed his earnings and their amount. In period 3 the full £75 overpayment is recoverable and not just the additional earnings, because disclosure of the full earnings and not merely the increase is required. In the period 4, only £55 is recoverable, because A would have been entitled to more benefit for that period.

Causation is a difficult legal concept. In areas of the law such as marine insurance, where the test for avoiding a contract of insurance is much like the test for a breach of duty under s71, analysis of what caused a certain event can reach the levels of philosophical debate. Evans LJ stated in *Jones v Chief Adjudication Officer*[2] that he hoped that such complexities would not be allowed to enter consideration of s71. Few would disagree with this sentiment, and yet it is necessary to understand some of the concepts of the general law if any broad principles are to be drawn from the case-law on s71.

In analysing the causation of an occurrence, a chain of events can be seen, each of which is a consequence of the preceding event. For example, a woman is driving her car along the road with her partner in the passenger seat. A wasp flies into the car and lands on the woman's neck. Her partner tries to swat the wasp and accidentally hits the woman. She is distracted and the car veers into the opposite lane and collides with an oncoming vehicle. The chain of causation of the accident is: the presence of the wasp, the attempt to swat it, the pain felt by the driver, her inability to keep her concentration, and her incorrect steering of the car. The terminology of the law of causation divides the events in the chain into two categories:

---

2 [1994] 1 WLR 62 at p66G, CA.

a) The *causa sine qua non* or originating cause. These are the links in the chain without which the accident would not have occurred. The presence of the wasp and the distraction of the driver are examples of this category of cause.
b) The *causa causans* or operative cause. These are the links in the chain which can truly be said to have a firm connection with the accident. They are not necessarily the last link in the chain and there may be more than one of them in a chain. In the example, these will be the action of the partner in swatting the wasp and the woman's failure to steer the car.

Into which category an event falls will depend largely on the concept of remoteness. In deciding whether an event is too remote to be an operative cause, two questions must be considered. First, was the event insignificant compared with how other events in the chain affected the situation? Secondly, were there many links in the chain between the event in question and the result? The more interpolating occurrences and the less significant the event, the more remote the event is and the less likely it is to be an operative cause.

There may be more than one series of events causing the accident in question. The presence of the other car on the road has nothing to do with the unfortunate events in the woman's car. The decision of the driver to use that road and his/her presence at that particular stretch of road is another chain of events leading to the consequence. But the mere presence of the car could only be an originating cause, because nothing the driver did contributed to the accident in any way. It would be different if that driver had taken a risk in overtaking while the woman was approaching, and the distraction meant that the woman did not apply the brakes. In that case, the actions of the woman, her partner and the other driver would all be operative causes.

EXAMPLE 7.2

B is elderly and lives with her son, C. She begins to receive retirement pension but, on claiming income support, fails to complete the part of the form dealing with other benefit. She had asked C to inform the DSS for her but he forgot. On her claim form she made it clear that she was 60 years old and retired. There are four operative causes of the overpayment: (a) B's failure to complete the claim form; (b) C's failure to inform the DSS; (c) the

> adjudication officer's error in not making the appropriate inquiries; and (d) the Secretary of State's error in not returning the form for completion.

The above analysis may seem rather convoluted and it may seem difficult to decide in which category an event belongs. At this point a healthy dose of common sense is called for from tribunals charged with determining appeals. Deciding whether event A or event B or both are operative causes of event C will largely be a matter of instinct, considering all the facts of the case in detail.

With these concepts in mind, it is now necessary to look at the basic principles of causation in s71 and their application in common types of case.

Basic principles

Tribunals have been constantly reminded by commissioners that causation of the overpayment is a pre-condition of recoverability, and that they should analyse the chain of events leading up to the overpayment to decide whether the breach of duty was truly the cause. A tribunal must demonstrate a 'clearly stipulated causal basis'[3] for its findings.

There are cases where it will be easy to decide whether the breach of duty caused the overpayment. Obviously, only amounts paid after the breach of duty can be recoverable.[4] All payments prior to the breach could not be related in any way to that breach. On the other hand, it is equally clear that in examining the question of causation, the adjudicating authorities must examine the facts as they actually transpired and not speculate on the actions of the defendant in different circumstances.[5]

There has, however, been precious little analysis in the case-law of exactly what it means for an overpayment to be 'in consequence' of a breach of duty. The reason for this is probably that causation is basically a question of fact for the tribunal and the commissioners are only entitled to overturn a tribunal's findings on causation if there has been some error of law in the way the question has been considered. In *Duggan v Chief*

---

3   *R(SB) 21/82* para 18.
4   *R(SB) 12/84* para 6.
5   *Thomas v Chief Adjudication Officer* (1987) (appendix to *R(SB) 17/87*), CA.

Adjudication Officer the Court of Appeal felt able to do this on the basis that the tribunal's decision had been irrational.⁶ The comments made by May and Croom-Johnson LJJ in that case must be the starting-point in ascertaining the basic test for causation.

The analysis in Duggan

The facts in *Duggan* are significant. Mr Duggan claimed supplementary benefit on the basis that the only income he and his wife had was the maternity allowance she was receiving following the birth of a child. When maternity allowance expired the adjudication officer reviewed the award of supplementary benefit and increased the rate to reflect the reduction in income. However, Mrs Duggan wished to return to work and was eligible for unemployment benefit, which she claimed and received. This was not disclosed to the local office administering supplementary benefit and an overpayment resulted.

On appeal, the tribunal accepted a submission that the overpayment was not 'in consequence' of Mr Duggan's failure to disclose. The adjudication officer appealed. Commissioner Morcom decided that for the tribunal to 'put the onus on the adjudication officer to establish the facts is ... turning matters upon their head'. Even if the adjudication officer had been negligent, that of itself did not mean that there was no causation.⁷

The Court of Appeal unanimously dismissed Mr Duggan's appeal, but there were important differences in approach in the two substantial judgments. May LJ pointed out that in the case the adjudication officer was entitled

> to make the assumption that this mother with a young child was neither going back to work nor becoming available for work ... He was under no duty to make that enquiry, but if the assumption which he made turned out, as it did, to have been wrong, that may well have been a cause of the overpayment as well as the failure to disclose. The wrong assumption by the adjudication officer may in certain circumstances have been a cause of the overpayment, but it does not follow that it was the sole cause. As a matter of common sense, which questions of causation always are, if one poses the question: did the failure of the

6 (1988) *Times* 18 December (appendix to *R(SB) 13/89*), CA.
7 *R(SB) 13/89* para 7.

Ch 7 The requirement of a causal link 107

claimant to disclose the fact that his wife was in receipt of unemployment benefit have as at least one of its consequences the overpayment of the supplementary benefit?, the only reasonable answer that one can give is "yes".[8]

As one of the causes of the overpayment was Mr Duggan's failure to disclose, the overpayment was 'in consequence' of the breach of duty. In response to the claimant's submission that the adjudication officer was under a duty to inform himself of the relevant facts, May LJ responded that:

> ... it may be in particular circumstances that the obligation on the adjudication officer will be wider than that, in order that he may be fully apprised of the situation and claim with which he has to deal. But I would deprecate any suggestion that when any claim is made for social security benefit there then necessarily arises an obligation on the adjudication officer investigating it effectively to investigate the full financial position of the claimant.[9]

Croom-Johnson LJ, on the other hand, focused on the fact that there was a continuing duty on Mr Duggan to disclose the receipt by his wife of unemployment benefit. The tribunal had ignored this fact and whatever the adjudication officer had failed to do, the 'other and real' cause of the overpayment was Mr Duggan's breach of statutory duty in failing to disclose the material fact.

Glidewell LJ agreed with both the judgments given. There is a significant difference of approach, however, and in the absence of any preference by the third judge, tribunals may choose which analysis is preferable. It is suggested that the approach of May LJ should be applied. The problem with Croom-Johnson LJ's approach is its relevance to cases of misrepresentation. Where the DSS seeks to rely on a misrepresentation, the overpayment must be made 'in consequence' of the misrepresentation on which the DSS relied. The fact that the defendant is under a duty of disclosure becomes irrelevant. May LJ's criterion, on the other hand, is of universal application. In *CIS 1209/1995* the commissioner posed May LJ's question as the appropriate one for the tribunal to which the case was remitted to consider.[10]

---

8   *Duggan v Chief Adjudication Officer* (1988) *Times* 18 December (appendix to *R(SB) 13/89* at p603A-D), CA.
9   Ibid at p604F.
10 Para 21. See also *CIS 402/1994* para 5(ii).

When is a breach of duty one of the causes?

May LJ's test begs a further question, however, which is whether the breach of duty must be an operative cause or whether it is sufficient for it to be an originating cause. The formulation of Commissioner Rice in *CSB 64/1986* clearly contemplates that provided the breach of duty forms part of the chain of causation, that will suffice:

> If, irrespective of the intervention of any other party or event, the claimant's compliance with his duty to disclose would have prevented an overpayment, then the failure to disclose is ... the cause of the unnecessary expenditure.[11]

Other authorities, however, do not support this approach. The requirement of causation has been described as a need for a 'direct causal connection'[12] or a 'proximate cause'.[13] If there is an intervention of the type described by Commissioner Rice, and that intervention is significant in the effect on the situation, the breach of duty cannot be said to be direct or proximate. In *CIS 395/1992*, Commissioner Rowland explicitly adopted the language of the general law of causation:

> If the claimant intended to stop claiming and her order book was then stolen by her husband who cashed the orders without her knowledge, it cannot be said that payments made when the stolen orders were cashed were in consequence of the claimant's failure to disclose a material fact. It might possibly be argued that there would have been no overpayment if there had been disclosure of the material facts because it could be suggested that a "stop notice" would then have been issued. However, the failure to disclose would still not have been an *effective* cause of the overpayment; it would have been *causa sine qua non* but not *causa causans*.[14]

The weight of authority clearly leans towards the correct approach, which is to require that the breach of duty is an operative cause. Commissioner Rice's approach fails to take proper account of the concept of remoteness. At some point the connection between the breach of duty and the payment becomes so remote that it cannot truly be said to be a cause.

---

11 Para 11.
12 *R(SB) 54/83* para 15.
13 *CSB 681/1981* para 7.
14 Para 10. The emphasis is the commissioner's.

> **EXAMPLE 7.3**
> D writes a letter notifying the DSS that she is leaving the country for six months. Shortly after she posts her letter, there is a postal strike and the letter remains in the letterbox for two weeks. The letter is then stolen on the way to the DSS's offices. During a police raid on the thief's house, coffee is spilt on the discarded letter, rendering the contents illegible but not the address or claimant's details which D has written on the cover of the envelope. When the DSS receives the letter, the local office does not contact D to ask what the contents of the letter were. An overpayment results which Deborah knew nothing about. Her failure to disclose is not an operative cause of the overpayment.

When is a breach of duty an operative cause?

Having considered what the breach of duty must amount to in order for the overpayment to be 'in consequence' of the breach, it is now necessary to consider what other events can prevent it being an operative cause.

In *Duggan* (see p100), it had been argued that the adjudication officer's failure to carry out the necessary investigations was the only cause of the overpayment. Several of the observations made in the case provide important pointers. First, Commissioner Morcom was critical of the attempt to place the burden on the adjudication officer to establish the facts. The policy reason for this can be well understood. It cannot be right that every time an adjudication officer carries out a review there must be a fresh appraisal of a claimant's circumstances. The administrative burden caused would be intolerable. Where there is something before the adjudication officer to call for such investigation, however, this policy ground for the decision disappears. It is suggested that this was recognised by May LJ, when he accepted a submission that there will be situations where the adjudication officer has a wider duty.

Secondly, May LJ emphasised the fact that the adjudication officer was entitled to make the assumption that s/he did. There will be situations, however, where this is not the case. Similarly, there are cases, discussed below, where the conduct of a third party makes it more likely that such actions will not merely be a second operative cause, but will be effective to prevent the breach of duty being an operative cause at all. It will not be possible to say that one of the causes of the overpayment was the breach of duty. The conduct of the third party will be an intervening event. In deciding whether the link between the breach and the overpayment has been broken in this way, it is suggested that three factors must be examined:

a) *Whether the defendant could anticipate the intervening event.* The defendant has a right to expect that normal DSS procedure will be followed. As will appear at pp113–114 below, a breach of procedure does not of itself break the link. It is suggested, however, that it is a factor to be taken into account. Some support for this appears in *CIS 159/1990*, where the commissioner emphasised the DSS's failures to act on information received.[15] Clearly, this is something that the claimant is entitled to expect the DSS to do.

b) *Whether the actions of the third party in causing the intervening event were reasonable.* In *Duggan*, as already pointed out, the adjudication officer acted in an entirely reasonable way. It is clear from the commissioner's decision in that case that negligence by an adjudication officer will not suffice to break the link. However, by stating that it could not break the chain 'of itself', the commissioner clearly envisaged that it may be relevant.[16] It is suggested that it is another factor to be considered. *CIS 395/1992* shows that criminal conduct will be especially likely to prevent causation being proven.

c) *Whether the behaviour in question is an act or omission.* It will often be very difficult to tell which it was. If, however, the flavour of what was done was some deliberate, positive act, then it will be more likely to affect the causation of the overpayment.[17]

It is necessary to sound a note of caution at this point. Tribunals will not lightly find that an intervening act has affected the causation of an overpayment in this way. Following May LJ's test from *Duggan*, even if a tribunal thinks that most of the blame must rest on the intervening event, it must still find that one of

---

15 Para 4.
16 *R(SB) 13/89* para 7, approving *CSB 1221/1985* para 7.
17 See, from the general law of causation, *Smith v Littlewoods Organisation Ltd* [1987] AC 241 at pp270 and 271, HL.

the causes of the overpayment is the breach of duty. The impact of the intervening event will have to be 'overwhelming'[18] before the link can be found to have been broken.

Moreover, in cases of failure to disclose, the point made by Croom-Johnson LJ needs to be borne in mind. It might be that initially the intervening event complained of has a sufficiently profound effect on the situation to mean that the defendant's failure is not an operative cause of the overpayment. However, as time passes and the claimant continues to fail to make a disclosure, the influence of the intervening event must diminish and eventually, one of the operative causes of the overpayment is the defendant's continuing failure to make a disclosure. If the intervening event is to prevent the breach of duty being an operative cause for the whole period of the overpayment, it must either itself be a continuing state of affairs, just as the breach of duty is, or its influence must be so significant that it has altered the entire course of events throughout the period of the overpayment.

> EXAMPLE 7.4
> E is in receipt of income support. She gives birth to a child and takes in a lodger, F. She writes to the DSS alluding to F moving in but does not mention the rent she will pay. Neither does she confirm her receipt of child benefit. The Child Benefit Centre informs the local office in accordance with procedure. The local office fails to ask for details of the rent paid by F and does not take action on the information from the Child Benefit Centre. The fact that the DSS knows about the child benefit is a continuing state of affairs and so that part of the overpayment will not be recoverable. The local office knows about the presence of F and her status as a lodger. Its failure to enquire whether rent is being paid is a highly significant cause of that part of the overpayment and so it will probably not be recoverable either.

Acts and omissions of the DSS

The effect that some error by the DSS has on the causation of an overpayment has correctly been described as 'the most controversial issue' relating to causation.[19] Most of the cases on

---

18 *CIS 402/1994* para 5(ii).
19 Mesher, p704.

the issue concern the internal DSS procedures for informing other sections about changes in a claimant's benefit entitlement. The effect of these depends on whether the procedures successfully work or not.

Failure to act on knowledge of the material facts

If the procedures work and the local office is informed of the material fact, then it seems clear that the overpayment cannot possibly be 'in consequence' of any breach of duty by the claimant. The Tribunal of Commissioners in *R(SB) 15/87 (T)* said that 'there could be circumstances' where this would be the case.[20] However, other decisions take a more robust view. At least where passing of information from other sections of the DSS is concerned, the general principle is that 'overpayments of benefit made after the facts had come to the notice of the DSS could not be in any circumstances recoverable from the claimant'.[21]

As the Tribunal of Commissioners noted, DSS procedure should be followed, and so local offices notified by other sections of the DSS of information will be expected to act upon it. Moreover, the possession of information is a continuing state of affairs, so there is no inconsistency with what Croom-Johnson LJ said in *Duggan* (see p107) about the claimant's duty being a continuing one. Once the DSS has acquired information, it has the means and the power to act on that information at any time. The significance of its possession of the information far outweighs the defendant's failure to disclose. The reason is given by Commissioner Sanders in *CIS 159/1990*:

> How can the local office complain that the claimant did not tell them something of which they had officially been notified? The payments in question would not have been made had they acted on the information they already had and which had been supplied to them so that they could adjust the amount of benefit. How can one be sure they would any the more have acted on information given to them by the claimant?[22]

The explanation is clearly that the payments would or might have been made 'but for' the failure to disclose.

20 Para 30.
21 *CSB 712/1985* para 6. See also *CSB 727/1987* para 7; *CSB 874/1988* paras 4 and 5; *CU 47/1993* para 14.
22 Para 4.

The DSS are currently implementing reforms that will enable claimants to be paid single girocheques for each benefit entitlements. Presumably a single agency will make these payments. If this is the case, it would seem to follow that the agency will have full knowledge of the facts of entitlement to each benefit. If there is an obvious inconsistency in the amounts being paid, then the paying agency should be fixed with notice of the error and the overpayment will not be caused by the claimant's breach of duty.

Failures of communication
Many of the current procedures for sharing information appear to honoured more in the breach than in the observance. A particular weak point, judging by the number of cases stemming from it, is communication between the Child Benefit Centre and local offices administering income support. What happens is that a claimant has a new child and claims and receives child benefit in respect of that child. The claimant does not inform the local office separately and so income support is not adjusted to reflect the increased child benefit.

Current developments in the administration of benefits will hopefully render such cases less common. In particular, it is known that the Child Benefit Centre is establishing a system of cross-checks by computer on whether claimants are also receiving income support. These are unlikely to completely solve the problems, however, and claimants will continue to be caught out in this way.

The DSS is not, for these purposes, to be seen as one entity.[23] Except in the limited situations where there is an agency relationship (see pp72–76 above), there is no imputed notice to another office when one office is informed of a material fact.[24] It follows that there is no disclosure to the local office for income support claims just because the Child Benefit Centre knows that the claimant is receiving extra child benefit.[25] The same result has been reached where other failures in communication have occurred.[26] The procedures are only a 'back-up' to prevent

---

23 *CSB 684/1981* para 7; *CSB 360/1983* para 12; *CSB 114/1984* para 11.
24 *R(SB) 13/89* para 7.
25 *CSB 64/1986* para 11.
26 *Riches v Secretary of State for Social Security* [1994] SLT 731 at p734, Ct Sess (invalidity benefit increases); *CSB 360/1983* para 12 (special hardship allowance).

overpayment where the claimant fails to report receipt of other benefits.[27] If the procedures fail, the causal link between the breach of duty and the overpayment is not affected.

> **EXAMPLE 7.6**
> G gives birth to a child, suffering severe complications which make her unfit for her job. She is dismissed from her job at the same time. She claims income support, incapacity benefit and child benefit. She does not disclose receipt of the latter two benefits. The Child Benefit Centre fails to inform the local office, but the office dealing with incapacity benefit does. Only an amount of income support equivalent to the amount of child benefit being received is recoverable.

Failure to carry out investigations

As stated above at p110, the mere fact that the DSS has been negligent will not suffice to sever the causal link. However, there is authority that where the information before the DSS is 'plainly ambiguous'[28] it is put on notice to investigate the true facts. In *CIS 222/1991*, the claimant had written on her claim form that she paid £32.50 ground rent per month (presumably mistaking this for rent payable under a short-term tenancy) and that she did not have a lease. She did not fill in the part of the form asking whether she held her house on a long lease. She was awarded the £32.50 as part of her housing costs. The commissioner decided that it was inherently improbable that ground rent on a long lease would be so high and that she had said that the house was not leasehold in any case. The cause of the overpayment was the DSS's failure to clarify the situation rather than the claimant's misrepresentation.

How uncertain does the information before the adjudication officer have to be before s/he is put on inquiry? The test must be that the ambiguity would be clear to an adjudication officer under normal working conditions, without him/her having to trawl through a lot of documents or go through a detailed process of reasoning. Again, there is no inconsistency with *Duggan* since in that case there was absolutely nothing before

---

27 *CIS 645/1993* para 6, citing Mesher, p704.
28 *CIS 222/1991* paras 4 and 5; *CG 54/1988* para 5.

the adjudication officer to suggest that the claimant's wife had any income.

> EXAMPLE 7.6
> G claims unemployment benefit. He is in receipt of a small occupational pension from his former employer. G finds it difficult to fill in the form and does not fill in the section regarding compensation from his former employer. He visits his employer to ask him how much money he is getting from the pension scheme. The employer scribbles '£120 per month' on a sheet of headed notepaper and G gives this to the DSS with the claim form. The DSS are put on notice to enquire about this money.

In *CIS 1209/1995* the claimant had failed to complete a part of his claim form in which other income was listed. Had the form been properly completed, the claimant would have disclosed his wife's receipt of maternity pay. It was argued that by referring the form to the adjudication officer rather than requiring the claimant to complete the form, the Secretary of State ran the risk of some material fact being missed. The commissioner found that the minister had a discretion in determining whether the form was defective and that there was 'nothing improper' about the procedure followed.[29] The answer to this ought to be that if the Secretary of State decides not to take a certain course of action, the DSS runs the risk of any loss resulting from that failure. What is the point of painstakingly devising claim forms to elicit the relevant information, when a failure to provide it is not corrected?

It may also be possible to argue that the breach of duty does not cause the overpayment where the DSS either had sufficient information to enable a review of the claimant's entitlement or for the suspension of benefit pending further investigation into the claimant's affairs.[30]

Acts and omissions of third parties

Actions of third parties may have a decisive influence on events and may well break the chain of causation between the defendant's

---

29 Paras 22 and 23. See Claims and Payments Regs reg 4(8).
30 These arguments are being raised in *CG 37/1994* and *CG 6140/1995*, currently before the commissioner.

breach of duty and the overpayment. In many such cases, the third party will be liable under SSAA s71. This point should always be made to a tribunal which may be reluctant to write off a large amount of money.

Where a third party makes a misrepresentation to the DSS which is material to the continuation of benefit, a previous misrepresentation by the defendant will probably not cause a subsequent overpayment. In *R(SB) 21/82* the claimant's husband had claimed supplementary benefit for them as a couple. The claimant had signed a statement that there had been no changes of circumstances. The husband had later done the same before he died and the wife claimed in her own right. Large capital resources had been held throughout. The commissioner considered that there was a 'tenable argument' that the overpayment could only be recovered from the claimant, as distinct from the husband's estate, for the period after she signed the statement until her husband signed the next statement.[31] It is suggested that the argument is sound. The reason why long-term claimants are asked to sign such forms is to confirm that there has been no change over the period and benefit only continues once such a form is signed. Clearly benefit is paid 'in consequence' of the form rather than the initial claim.

EXAMPLE 7.7

H is claiming income support for himself and his partner, I, who is working ten hours a week. H receives £5 per week child care allowance from I's employer. I knows that they will find it hard to make ends meet and does not tell H that she has been given a pay rise. H does not disclose the allowance on the claim form. Three months into the claim, the DSS requires I to sign a form confirming that there has been no change in her wages and asking for her recent payslips. I returns only the form, but benefit continues in payment. When I's true wages are discovered, H and I split up. The DSS pursues H for the overpayment on the basis of misrepresentation. Before I signed the form, the whole overpayment is recoverable because H specifically misrepresented the level of I's earnings on the claim form. After I signed the form, the overpayment relating to I's wages increase was caused by her misrepresentation and not H's. But H's receipt of the allowance was not dealt with by the form and remains recoverable from H.

---

31 Para 21.

Ch 7 *The requirement of a causal link*

When the third party makes a disclosure, this may be sufficient to satisfy the claimant's obligation of itself in certain circumstances (see pp68–69 above). Even where this is not the case, the Tribunal of Commissioners in *R(SB) 15/87 (T)* clearly envisages that such a disclosure could break the chain of causation.[32] This will only be the case where the third party's disclosure would have been sufficient to discharge the obligation of disclosure if made by the claimant.

EXAMPLE 7.8
J is elderly and receives income support and retirement pension. She does not understand the distinction between the two. K is a neighbour who often helps out with household tasks but is not an appointee for benefit purposes. One day, J mentions that she has inherited a large sum of money from her brother. Later, K realises that this will affect J's entitlement and so goes into the local office. A clerk makes a note and assures her that the information will be acted on. The DSS takes no action. Recovery of the resulting overpayment is not possible because although J did not know that K was giving the information to the local office on her behalf, had she made the disclosure herself it would have satisfied her obligation. The overpayment is not caused by her failure to disclose.

Where there is some criminal action by a third party after the claimant's breach of duty, this will break the chain of causation. In *CIS 395/1992* the claimant had returned to the matrimonial home from a women's refuge hostel. She asked her husband to return her order book but some giros were cashed. She claimed that her husband had retained the book and cashed it. The commissioner held that if this was correct, her failure to inform the DSS about her change in circumstances would not be an effective cause of the overpayment.[33]

It may be possible in some cases to extend this principle beyond criminal conduct to careless or negligent conduct. Bearing in mind the claimant's continuing duty to disclose, there would have to be some degree of reliance on the third party and a reasonable belief that the third party had acted in a proper manner.

32 Para 30. *CIS 395/1992* para 9 is therefore wrong on this point, confusing satisfaction of the claimant's obligation of disclosure by a third party with the effect such a disclosure has on the causation of the overpayment.
33 Para 10.

> EXAMPLE 7.9
> As in EXAMPLE 7.8 above, except that J asked K to pass the information to the local office. K forgets, and in her embarrassment tells J that she had done as she was requested when J next sees her. A tribunal would be justified in holding that J's failure to disclose did not cause the overpayment.

Misrepresentations and previous disclosures

The discussion above is concerned with the effects of events occurring between the breach of duty and the payment. Generally speaking, no event before the breach of duty could break the chain of causation. There is, however, one disputed exception to this rule, which is where a claimant makes a sufficient disclosure but later makes a misrepresentation, usually on a standard form.

Can a previous disclosure have any effect?

In considering this question, there is a clash between two of the basic principles of SSAA s71. First, there is the principle stemming from *R(SB) 15/87 (T)* that once a sufficient disclosure has been made, it need not be repeated (see pp61–62 above). On the other hand, a claimant is expected to bear responsibility for the contents of all written material placed before the DSS and must accept the consequences of any misrepresentation.

There has been substantial disagreement between commissioners on this question and there appear to be three main lines of authority:

a) Only a contemporaneous disclosure can qualify a misrepresentation. Most of the cases that take this line were cases in which the disclosure was in relation to a previous claim.[34] In *CIS 515/1993* the claimant disclosed the relevant income to an officer at the local office on the same day that she completed the claim form, in which she stated she had no other income. The commissioner decided that as the disclosure was not contemporaneous with the claim and so was not effective to nullify the misrepresentation on the claim form, as it would not be possible to link the disclosure with the claim, an 'intolerable burden' would be put on the system to ensure consistency.[35]

---

34 *CSB 98/1990* para 4; *CSB 108/1992* para 5 (the same case).
35 Para 17. See also *CSB 1341/1986* para 7.

b) A disclosure may nullify a misrepresentation if the claimant could reasonably think that it had not been overlooked and was before the relevant person processing his/her claim. In *CS 130/1992* the claimant stated that he had been told that it was possible for him to work for up to 24 hours per week before his invalidity benefit was affected. He started work, but continued to sign the declaration on his Med 3 certificates that he had done no work. Commissioner Rowland held that there were circumstances where such a disclosure could be sufficient.
c) Any disclosure will qualify a subsequent misrepresentation, because the DSS cannot be misled by a misrepresentation once it knows the correct facts.[36]

In *CIS 515/1993*, Commissioner Heggs relied on three authorities. She cited *CSB 180/1992* and *R(SB) 3/90*, both of which dealt with a situation where the disclosure had been in relation to a previous claim. *R(SB) 18/85* does state that a written representation can be qualified by a representation made orally or by conduct at the same time as making the claim, but says nothing about whether this can be true where the latter representation is not made contemporaneously. The authorities do not provide solid support for the finding. In *CIS 389/1993*, where the facts were virtually identical to those in *CIS 515/1993*, the commissioner, while not explicitly considering the causation point, remitted the case to the tribunal for proper findings of fact about the earlier disclosure and therefore clearly considered that, if established, the earlier disclosure could qualify the later representation.

On the other hand, the powerful policy argument invoked by Commissioner Heggs and put forward in the decisions cited by her cannot be ignored. There will be many situations in which an officer to whom a disclosure is made is not involved in the adjudication process and so cannot be expected to pass information on to the correct person. Neither of the commissioners who have decided that any previous disclosure nullifies a misrepresentation considered the question at any length. Commissioner Rowland's reasoning in *CS 130/1992* provides the best balance between the two competing principles

---

36 *Cooper v Tomans* [1988] 1 EGLR 257 at p261H, HC; *CSB 942/1989* para 6; *CU 47/1993* para 11.

and ought to be followed. The relevant part of his decision in CS 130/1992 deserves to be set out in full:

15. In *R(SB) 18/85* it was held that a written representation might be qualified by a contemporaneous disclosure. I take the view that contemporaneity may not be essential in all circumstances. It seems to me to be relevant that the representation as to not having worked was accompanied by one to the effect that there had been no change of circumstances and it is also relevant that the form, which must be signed as a matter of routine procedure if an existing award of invalidity benefit is to be continued, makes no provision for a person to sign it after working. It is specifically indicated that the declaration of the change of circumstances may be crossed out if appropriate; there is no such indication in respect of the declaration as to not having worked. Therefore, I would accept that in *some* circumstances a representation on form Med 3 can be read as having been qualified by an earlier disclosure. The circumstances in which that is so must in my view be limited because one purpose of requiring a person to sign a declaration when claiming benefit or seeking its continuation is to provide an opportunity for the Department to check the accuracy of information held on file.

16. In particular, it seems to me that a claimant can only rely on a prior qualification of a misrepresentation if the earlier disclosure was in sufficiently clear terms that the claimant could reasonably have believed that it had not been overlooked. A disclosure made in the course of a general enquiry by telephone is unlikely to fall into that category unless, perhaps, the claimant knew that the officer answering the telephone had already had dealings with his or her case and so could be expected to be familiar with it and to act on the disclosure.

When does an earlier disclosure suffice?

An important point made in the commissioner's analysis in CS 130/1992 is that the mere fact that there was an earlier disclosure is not enough; the disclosure must be sufficient. It must be 'in terms that make sufficient reference to his claim to enable the matter disclosed to be referred to the proper person'.[37] There are three separate factual situations that call for discussion.

Disclosure made on an earlier claim form. In cases of this nature, the disclosure can never vitiate the later misrepresentation. *R(SB) 3/90* concerned four supplementary benefit claims made in succession. In the second claim form the claimant disclosed receipt of retirement pension but failed to do so on the fourth, as

---

37 *R(SB) 15/87* (T) para 28. See pp66–67 above.

a result of which an overpayment occurred. It was held that the fact that the DSS had the means of knowledge at its disposal was irrelevant, as it could not be expected to trawl through past files to ascertain whether the information provided was correct.[38]

The only possible exception to this principle will be where specific reference is made on the claim form to the earlier claim. In *R(SB) 3/90* itself, the commissioner referred to the fact that there was no mention of the fourth claim form to the existence of the second claim. This would suggest that if such reference was made, the previous disclosure might then affect the misrepresentation. Indeed, it may be possible to argue that the claimant is asking the adjudication officer to take account of the contents of the old claim form, and so there is no misrepresentation at all (see p39 above).

Disclosure made prior to claim. Cases where a defendant discloses facts to an officer of whom s/he is making enquiries but fails to repeat the disclosure on the claim form are legion.[39] In income support cases, the principle that disclosure to the unemployment benefit office is effectively disclosure to the local office must be borne in mind (see pp71–75 above).

It is in such cases that the policy argument relied on by Commissioner Heggs is most compelling. If a claimant is making general enquiries about benefit, and tells the officer helping him/her a relevant fact, that officer is not expected to take notes. His/her function is to advise the claimant. Some cases will not be so clear-cut, however, and it is suggested that the fundamentalist approach of Commissioner Heggs is not justified. Applying Commissioner Rowland's approach, the claimant will need good reasons to think that the disclosure had not been overlooked. Certainly, if the officer tells the claimant that the information must be put in the claim form, the disclosure to the officer will not suffice. Neither will it be sufficient if the officer records the information, unless the claimant has some reason to think that the record will be forwarded to the proper officer.[40] It also seems likely that a general misrepresentation, such as a declaration on a form, will be more readily nullified than will a specific representation of fact. The reason for this is that adjudication

---

38 Para 11, citing *Redgrave v Hurd* (1881) 20 Ch D 1, CA. See also *CSB 1016/1985* para 13.
39 *CSB 1341/1986, CIS 389/1993, CIS 515/1993* and *CIS 1209/1995* were all cases of this type.
40 *CSB 1341/1986* para 7.

officers must be entitled to rely on specific facts stated by the claimant on a form, except where a clear indication is given that the facts are to be qualified by some other statement.

> EXAMPLE 7.10
> L is certified as unfit to work. She goes to the local office to request an incapacity benefit claim form. She speaks to a clerk and shows her the Med 3 certificate that she has been given. She refers to the work that she does for a charity shop for three hours per week and that it is the only thing keeping her sane. The clerk writes down what she says and states that she will 'pass it on to whoever is dealing with your case'. L takes the claim form home. She does not fill in the parts of the claim form relating to work but benefit is awarded anyway. Her previous disclosure renders her failure to complete the claim form of no effect.

Disclosure made during currency of claim. This category of cases arises where a disclosure is made to the DSS but a misrepresentation is made by signing a declaration. In the first place, careful analysis of the contents of the form will be necessary to ascertain whether it really amounts to a misrepresentation at all.

CS 130/1992 is a case in this category. Reference was made to a problem common to several of the standard form declarations made by claimants. A claimant may not understand even some of the basic rules of entitlement to the benefit being claimed. S/he will simply sign the declaration as a matter of routine. The wording of the declaration may be defective for someone who remains entitled to benefit but who is technically misrepresenting every time s/he signs the standard form. There was an argument that the claimant in *CS 130/1992* might have remained entitled to invalidity benefit even though he was working, because it was not work that he could reasonably be expected to do. However, to maintain the claim for invalidity benefit he was required to sign the Med 3 declaration that he had done no work.

This problem also arises in relation to income support claimants who are required to make themselves available for work and sign form UB 24 every fortnight.[41] A claimant might start a part-time job for five hours a week, earning £20. S/he will remain entitled

---

41 This situation arose in *CIS 13924/1996*, currently under appeal to the commissioner.

Ch 7 The requirement of a causal link 123

to benefit and will be required to make themselves available for full-time employment. S/he continues to sign form UB 24, and so represent that, 'On each day since the first date I claimed (other than any day for which I have made a separate declaration) ... I was unemployed and did no work, paid or unpaid'. S/he will be making a misrepresentation, unless s/he discloses the work s/he has done every time s/he signs on. This is inconsistent with the general principles that an oral disclosure is sufficient, that disclosure need only be made once and also that it is possible to make a disclosure in advance.[42]

It is therefore suggested that these representations made during the claim will be readily qualified by an earlier disclosure. A written disclosure will always vitiate a later misrepresentation. As to oral disclosures, if the officer spoken to promises to take action on the disclosure, then that will operate to qualify the misrepresentation, whether or not the officer had experience of dealing with the claimant. Again, if the claimant is told that s/he must put the disclosure in writing, then s/he is not entitled to rely on the oral disclosure. Commissioner Rowland's additional requirement, that the officer is familiar with the claimant's case, is probably relevant only where the officer neither asks the claimant to confirm the disclosure in writing nor promises to act on the disclosure.

EXAMPLE 7.11
M is claiming income support. He starts a part-time job for ten hours per week, earning £60. He sees a clerk at the local unemployment benefit office and tells him about the work. The clerk says nothing, but merely takes a note. M's disclosure is sufficient and the DSS cannot rely on a misrepresentation on form UB 24.

---

42 The latter point is emphasised by Commissioner Rowland in *CS 234/1994* para 4.

CHAPTER 8
Calculating the amount owed

When adjudication officers issue a SSAA s71 decision that an overpayment is recoverable, they are under an obligation to state the amount which the Secretary of State is entitled to recover.[1] It must also be shown how that amount is calculated. The practice is for adjudication officers to provide a schedule illustrating how their calculation has been performed.

The calculation of the amount of an overpayment is often a difficult task, and studies have shown that it is very common for mistakes to be made.[2] Furthermore, it seems that tribunals rarely bother to satisfy themselves that the calculation is correct unless the issue is raised by the defendant, so it is dangerous to rely on them to carry out the necessary checks. It is therefore essential that the amount of the overpayment is carefully examined in even the most apparently simple case. A simple error by the adjudication officer, if not spotted and corrected, can result in a much larger amount being sought by the Secretary of State than has in fact been overpaid.

When considering authorities on the amount of an overpayment, it is important to remember that many of them were decided on the law prior to the introduction of regulations setting out specifically what offsets can be made from the amount of an overpayment. Under the supplementary benefits legislation, there was no specific statutory authority to make offsets.[3] Regulations to this effect were first introduced in 1987. These are generally more generous to the defendant than the old

---

1 SSAA s71(2).
2 One survey of a sample of income support overpayments found that less than half of the amounts had been correctly calculated: *Report of the Chief Adjudication Officer 1994-5* (HMSO, 1995), p44.
3 *Commock v Chief Adjudication Officer* (1989) (appendix to *R(SB) 6/90*), CA.

law and they will apply to any decision made now regarding a period before the introduction of the Regulations.

A method of calculating an amount

Checklists to aid the calculation of amounts are set out in Appendix 4 to this book. One way to go about the task of calculating an overpayment is to follow a three-stage process:

a) calculate the total benefit paid to the claimant under the original decision;
b) deduct any parts of that total benefit which are not recoverable, giving what will be called the 'gross overpayment';
c) deduct any offsets allowable, giving the 'net overpayment', which is the amount properly recoverable.

Calculate the benefit paid

The first step is to calculate the total amount of benefit paid to the claimant under the original decision. Usually this will simply be a matter of adding up the amount of money paid under the various determinations that make up the award. Adjudication officers usually get this part of the calculation correct at least, but their arithmetic should always be examined. When carrying out the calculation, it is important to remember changes in the benefit paid due to annual uprating.

There may be some cases, however, where the claimant wishes to challenge the fact that an amount of benefit has in fact been paid. There is authority that there is no need for the DSS to adduce evidence of the amount of the overpayment where this is not put in dispute by the defendant.[4] However, once an issue has been raised as to payment, the normal rule that the burden of proof is on the DSS to prove all parts of a recoverable overpayment will apply. If the DSS's intended introduction of 'smart cards' which claimants are required to produce when claiming benefit goes ahead, it should enable the DSS to produce this information much more readily than is the case at present.

In the normal case the DSS's record of payment will suffice to show the amount of payment made to the claimant.[5] This will

4 *CSB 99/1990* para 17.
5 *CP 20/1990* para 30.

usually be in the form of a computer record. However, the DSS's computer information is only as reliable as the information held by those entering the data. If the claimant can give cogent reasons why the computer record may be inaccurate, then *CF 13/ 1992* decides that the tribunal should be slow to favour the computer printout. If there is corroboration of the claimant's assertions, then the claimant's evidence should be accepted unless there are 'special reasons' to the contrary.[6]

EXAMPLE 8.1

A is alleged to have been paid income support from the late 1980s on the basis that he misrepresented the fact that he had a partner. The DSS's handwritten and computerised records seem to confirm this. A is baffled. He maintains that he was only ever paid as a single person. He has kept the original handwritten form A14N, which sets out the elements from the initial award, and shows him being paid as a single person. The tribunal ought to accept A's evidence.

This corroboration could come from a number of sources. If the claimant's benefit is paid directly into a bank account, then bank statements should show how much was being paid in. In *CF 13/ 1992*, the corroboration was oral evidence from another. Some claimants keep their old order books, which will show the amount they were receiving. All correspondence with the DSS that claimants have kept should also be examined carefully for clues as to the amount of the payment.

Where, as in *CP 20/1990*, the DSS's records do not make it clear that the correct amount was paid under the original award, then it must provide further clear proof of the actual amount received.[7] In such cases, producing a sample order book will not suffice.[8] In *CP 20/1990* itself, the DSS claimed that the claimant had received an increase of retirement pension for his wife. The evidence showed that the increase had been awarded by an adjudication officer, but there was a procedure by which the payments section was ordered not to pay the increase because the claimant's wife's earnings were too high. The DSS asserted that

6   Para 10.
7   Para 26.
8   Para 31.

the payments section had nevertheless paid the amount. It was held that as the documentation relating to the award was ambiguous, specific proof would have to be provided as to the level of the payments.[9] In such cases, it is unlikely that actual proof will be forthcoming, especially as it is the practice of the DSS not to keep old order books surrendered at the post office on expiry.

Deduct any elements which are not recoverable

Where the original award of benefit can be divided into component parts, careful consideration must be given to each as to whether it is recoverable. Every penny of benefit of which recovery is sought must have been paid 'in consequence' of the defendant's breach of duty. This principle will be relevant in cases where part of the benefit is paid by official error. A common example is the case of a dependency increase where the award should never have been made and the fact that it was made is not the consequence of some breach of duty by the defendant. In cases like this, the relevant component should be deducted from the amount received under the original award.

EXAMPLE 8.2

B and his wife, C, have run a corner shop for many years. B is awarded sickness benefit and then invalidity benefit on the basis that he is unfit to help in the running of the shop and that C will run it. The adjudication officer awards a dependency addition for C. Several years later, it is found that B has been helping out with the business to the extent that he is no longer eligible for benefit. The basic amount of benefit will be recoverable from B, but the increase for C must be deducted from the amount, because C's work in the business is such that most of the profits of the business are attributable to her work and it cannot be said that B was contributing to her maintenance.

EXAMPLE 8.3

D is receiving income support. He has disclosed that his partner, E, is earning £40 from her part-time job from April. In fact the

---

9 Para 31.

true figure is £45, and so D is receiving £5 overpaid income support. In June, E, unknown to D, increases her earnings to £60 per week. No specific representation that E's earnings are still £40 per week is ever made by D. There is no breach of duty by D causing the extra £15 per week overpaid as a result. In calculating the amount recoverable, £15 per week from June must be deducted from the benefit paid to give the gross overpayment.

Deduct any allowable offsets

The final step is to apply the complex rules set out in this chapter (see below) for deducting allowable offsets from the overpayment to give the 'net overpayment'. When applying the offsets, it will be important not to allow a further reduction in respect of any part of the benefit found not to be recoverable in calculating the gross overpayment, as this would result in a double deduction.

Offsets allowed under statute

SSAA s71(6) gives the Secretary of State powers to make regulations in relation to the calculation of the amount of an overpayment. The Overpayments Regs comprise a complete code for allowable deductions from an amount, and seem to resolve most of the disputes under the old law on whether certain types of deductions are permissible.

Offsets in the course of review

One remaining potential area of confusion results from the distinction between the two decisions now required in overpayments cases: the review decision and the recoverability decision.

An inherent power?

Under the old law of recovery in Supplementary Benefits Act 1976 s20, it was frequently argued that any extra amount found to be payable on a review carried out in conjunction with a recoverability decision should be deducted from the amount of the overpayment.[10] This argument was rejected in *Commock v Chief Adjudication Officer*.[11]

In *CIS 137/1992*, Commissioner Rowland considered whether there was a power under the new legislation to make allowances for benefit awarded following the review decision. The claimant was working while claiming income support and the adjudication officer decided that the full amount of benefit was recoverable because her work rendered her unavailable for employment. The commissioner decided that if she could not be exempted from that requirement, then it was necessary to decide whether she might be entitled to income support on hardship grounds. It was argued that such entitlement could not be deducted from the amount of the overpayment because it was not authorised by the legislation. This argument was rejected.

> I do not accept that regulation 13 of the 1988 Regulations has any bearing on a case such as the present. It is concerned with deductions from an overpayment and so only comes into play after the overpayment has been calculated. The review which results in a decision as to the amount of benefit that ought to be paid is therefore to be carried out without any fetter being imposed by regulation 13.[12]

In principle, there is no conflict between what Commissioner Rowland said and the Court of Appeal decision in *Commock*. The reason for this is that under s20, it was not necessary to review the existing decisions to award benefit as a pre-condition to issuing a decision that benefit was recoverable.[13] Any review of the existing decisions was a quite separate process, and so was extraneous to the calculation of the amount recoverable. However, under SSAA s71 the recoverability decision is parasitic on the review decision and so benefit awarded on a review must be taken into account in calculating the amount.

Other commissioners have expressed the view that the application of the Overpayments Regs is part of the process of the calculation and not some separate operation.[14] It appears

---

10 Commissioner Mitchell argued particularly strongly for this interpretation. In *R(SB) 24/87* para 15 he states that it 'would be little short of monstrous to allow the adjudication officer to reopen one side of the balance sheet without allowing the claimant to open the other side'. See also *R(SB) 11/86* paras 13 and 14.
11 (1989) (appendix to *R(SB) 6/90*), CA, overruling *R(SB) 24/87* para 13.
12 Para 10.
13 *CSB 18/1992* para 10. See chapter 3 for the position under the new legislation.
14 *CIS 414/1992* para 10; *CSIS 8/1995* para 10.

that the fact that there is a specific power to offset an award on review under the Overpayments Regs was overlooked in *CIS 137/1992*.

Offset of the review award under the Overpayments Regs

Overpayments Regs reg 13 provides for 'any amount which has been offset under Part III'[15] of the regulations to be offset. The review carried out under SSAA s71 is a 'subsequent determination'[16] and will result in the award being varied. The arrears awarded on the review must therefore be offset against the amount of the overpayment.[17]

EXAMPLE 8.4

F is receiving income support for himself, his wife, G, and their two children. G and the children leave, but F does not inform the DSS. He receives a disability premium, but he has in fact gone back to work and the DSS has been told about this. When his failure to disclose is discovered, the amount of overpayment is calculated as follows. First, the relevant period is from the time that G left up until the review of the award and the total benefit must be calculated for that period. Secondly, payment of the disability premium was not the result of a breach of duty and so it must be deducted from the total benefit received up until the time G left to give the gross overpayment. Finally, on the review F is entitled to income support as a single person throughout the relevant period. The arrears must be deducted from the gross overpayment to give the net overpayment.

Scope of the review

Two issues arise in relation to the review. The first is what matters can be taken into account by the adjudication officer in considering the review. Grounds for review in relation to one aspect of a benefit do not allow the entire award to be reconsidered.[18] It will be necessary to show separate grounds for a review which will take into account matters other than those identified by the adjudication officer in the review

---

15 Overpayments Regs 1988 reg 13(a).
16 Ibid reg 5(1).
17 Ibid reg 5(2), Case 1.
18 *R(IS) 15/93* para 7.

decision.[19] This can be dealt with by the tribunal as first arising on the appeal.[20] There is no conflict between this statement and the *Commock* principle that only offsets inherent in the decision-making process under s71 can be made. If a tribunal considers grounds for review other than those considered by the adjudication officer, it can incorporate those grounds in the review decision and substitute the amended review decision for that given by the adjudication officer.

EXAMPLE 8.5
H's 16-year-old granddaughter, I, has come to England to study. She is living with him in his flat. H is receiving income support and knows little about the rules of disclosure. He takes a part-time job to help pay the bills. Neither I's arrival nor H's job are disclosed to the DSS. Eventually the DSS discovers that H is working. The award of income support is reviewed and reduced on the grounds of a change of circumstances, and overpayment of the excess amount is sought. H must show separate grounds for a review before the tribunal in order to have I's requirements taken into account as an offset. This would be the DSS's ignorance of the material fact that I was H's dependant. The tribunal can then incorporate those grounds in the review decision of the adjudication officer and offset the monies payable for I.

Secondly, it must be asked whether there is any time limit on how far back arrears can be awarded on the review. The precise rules differ according to the benefit in question but the time limit is 12 months for means-tested benefits.[21]

This might suggest that when an offset to an overpayment is awarded on review, the offset can only be applied for up to a year before the date of review. However, in *R(SB) 11/86*, Commissioner Mitchell pointed out that the time limits only apply to reviews which 'make income support payable or ... increase the amount of income support payable'.[22] In the

---

19 For consideration of the grounds of review, see p19 above.
20 SSAA s36; *CSB 1272/1989* para 11.
21 The relevant rules appear in the Social Security (Adjudication) Regulations 1995 SI No 1801 (the Adjudication Regs) regs 55 to 67.
22 The provisions considered in the case, the predecessor of the Adjudication Regs, were identical with the words 'Supplementary Benefit' substituted for 'income support'.

overpayment context, the review will increase the claimant's *entitlement* over the relevant period, but it will not increase the *amount payable* because the entitlement will be deducted from the amount of the overpayment. There is a clear distinction between the concepts of entitlement and payability of benefit[23] and so this decision should still be regarded as good law. If anything, its correctness is even more clear under the new legislation, because the Overpayments Regs specifically link the review awarding the offset to the question of the amount of the overpayment.

In summary, R(SB) 11/86 means that the 12-month time limit will not be applicable to reviews awarding an offset. The 12-month limit only applies if the offset exceeds the overpayment, in which case the remaining amount will only be payable for the year before the review. It seems logical to offset the arrears from the start of the overpayment period first, so as to give the claimant the maximum advantage from his/her benefit entitlement.[23A] This will have the effect that the whole of the remaining amount will be payable when it is up to 12 months of benefit.

EXAMPLE 8.6

J is a single parent with a one-year-old son. She is receiving income support of £60 per week, including premiums of £15 per week after deduction of child benefit of £10 per week. Her estranged husband obtains a residence order in respect of the child and, in her distress, J forgets to tell the DSS. Six months later, J's boyfriend, K, moves in with her. The DSS is not informed about this either and J's income support is not reviewed to treat her as being one of a couple, which would have increased the income support award by £25. The couple do not realise this. Eighteen months later the DSS finds out about J's son leaving and issues two overpayment decisions in relation to income support and child benefit. Six months later, J's appeals are dismissed but the tribunal is asked to consider a review of income support to reflect K moving in. The income support overpayment is calculated as follows:

Total benefit paid over the two year period is £60 × 52 × 2 = £6,240. (A)

---

23 *Insurance Officer v McCaffrey* [1984] 1 WLR 1353, HL.
23A *Clayton's Case* (1816) 1 Mer 572 at pp608 and 609, Ch D.

The amount of benefit which is not overpaid is her single person's entitlement, which is £45 × 52 × 2 = £4,680. **(B)**

Deducting B from A gives a gross overpayment of £1,560. **(C)**

The amount to be offset is the entitlement for 18 months as a couple minus J's single person entitlement during that time (to avoid double counting). The offset is (£70 - £45) × 52 × 1.5 = £1,950. **(D)**

As D exceeds C the income support overpayment becomes nil. Deducting C from D leaves a figure of £390 **(E)**. As this is less than 12 months of income support, this will be treated as payable within the last year. The full amount will be payable.

It is possible to remove the 12-month limit to paying of benefit on review in certain cases.[24] In that case, any surplus offset will be payable even prior to the 12-month period. This means that where the offset exceeds the gross amount of the overpayment by an amount equivalent to more than 12 months' benefit, it may still be necessary to invoke this possibility in addition to *R(SB) 11/86*.

Furthermore, when considering whether an offset will be allowed on the review, it is possible to extend the review back to the date of claim, not merely back to the period where the overpayment commenced.[25]

EXAMPLE 8.7

As with EXAMPLE 8.6 above, except that K moves in six months before J's son leaves and writes to the DSS informing it that he has moved in. His letter is mislaid and so no award is made. The fact that the DSS had the information lifts the 12-month time limit. Had figure E exceeded 12 months of income support, the full amount of figure E would be payable to J and K.

Other offsets under reg 5

At a glance it might be thought that Overpayments Regs reg 6 prevents any offset from an overpayment under reg 5. However,

---

24 Adjudication Regs reg 55.
25 *R(IS) 5/92* para 6.

reg 6 prevents the offsetting of the amount under the later determination if it is itself a recoverable overpayment. It does not prevent an offset of that amount from an overpayment. It appears that this may have confused the commissioner in *CIS 414/1992*.[26]

Besides the statutory authority to offset amounts of benefit awarded on review, Overpayments Regs reg 5 contains a number of other provisions for the offsetting of arrears of entitlement under a subsequent determination. These amounts of benefit are as follows:

a) *Subsequent benefits paid 'in lieu' of the original award.*[27] Exactly what this refers to is a little obscure but it seems likely, in the present context, that it principally concerns cases where a claim for one benefit is treated as if it were for another benefit on the review under SSAA s71(2). A claim cannot be treated as being for any other benefit; only certain combinations are possible.[28] It is important to bear in mind that the Secretary of State must decide to accept the claim form as being a claim for the second benefit,[29] so a tribunal cannot award the new benefit on review until this has been done. This will necessitate an adjournment, so all efforts should be made to obtain the Secretary of State's decision before the hearing. When such a review is made, the whole sum awarded from the date of claim can be offset against the overpayment.

EXAMPLE 8.8

L is disabled. She is receiving family credit in respect of her 16-year-old daughter, M. M leaves home. L fails to inform the DSS. When her failure to disclose is discovered, repayment is sought. L's representatives immediately write to the Secretary of State and ask him to treat the original family credit claim as a claim for disability working allowance. The Secretary of State agrees and the adjudication officer, on review, awards the allowance. The amount of the allowance that would have been paid since M left home will be deducted from the family credit overpayment.

---

26 Para 11.
27 Overpayments Regs reg 5(2), Case 2.
28 Claims and Payments Regs Sch 1 gives a list of benefits claimed and which benefits can be treated as claimed on the same claim form.
29 Ibid reg 9(1).

b) *Increases to benefits where the family member is entitled to benefit in his/her own right.* Where a dependant is subsequently awarded benefit in his/her own right or it is decided that somebody else should receive the increase, then arrears of the benefit or increase can be offset against any overpayment to the person initially receiving the increase.[30] This also applies where an increase is paid for a partner, who subsequently receives benefit in his/her own right.[31]

c) *Child benefit paid to the wrong person.* Where there is an overpayment of child benefit, the amount can be reduced by 'treating as properly paid' the benefit for any week when it was handed over to someone other than the claimant who 'either had the child living with him or was contributing towards the cost of providing for the child at a weekly rate' equal to or greater than the award of benefit, and who would have been entitled to child benefit had s/he claimed.[32]

> EXAMPLE 8.9
> N is receiving child benefit in respect of his daughter, O. She goes to live with her aunt, P, as N's job involves a lot of travelling. He pays P £50 per week towards O's living expenses. N is rather forgetful and in five weeks he forgets to send the money and does not pay it later. The DSS seeks recovery when it finds out about the arrangements. As N was paying more than the award of child benefit every week, and P would have been awarded child benefit had she claimed, benefit for all the weeks except those five where no money was paid can be offset against the amount of the overpayment.

Offsets based on the original claim

In the case of income support recovery, the third possibility for an offset stems from the contents of the claim form. If an extra component of income support should have been paid on the basis of the claim form,[33] or 'as it would have appeared had the misrepresentation or failure or non-disclosure been remedied

---

30 Overpayments Regs reg 5(2), Case 4.
31 Ibid reg 5(2), Case 5.
32 Ibid reg 5(4).
33 Ibid reg 13(b)(i).

before the determination',[34] then that can be offset against the award. In considering this provision, it is important not to double count any offset already performed under the auspices of Overpayments Regs reg 5.

This provision relating to the form itself is not to be too narrowly interpreted. In *R(IS) 5/92* the claimant had been in receipt of supplementary benefit and income support since 1985. In 1989 it was discovered that she had been working part-time since 1987. On appeal against the overpayment decision, it was contended that she should have been awarded a heating addition when she was receiving supplementary benefit. Although on the facts it was held that she was not entitled to an addition, the commissioner decided that 'the claim as presented' could include facts which would have been elicited by 'any reasonable inquiry ... prompted by the claim form'.[35] Furthermore, the offset is to be considered right back to the date of claim, not to the beginning of the period of the overpayment.[36] New evidence can be adduced to support assertions made on a claim form and originally rejected or ignored by the adjudication officer.[37]

EXAMPLE 8.10
Q failed to disclose the fact that his wife had left him, resulting in an income support overpayment. On his claim form he did not answer the question, 'Are you sick?' However, he did write the following in the 'Other Information' box: 'I would appreciate it if you would speed up this claim because I cannot afford to pay for my medicines for my heart and back any more'. Q can argue that this statement should have led the adjudication officer to investigate whether he was incapable of work and to consider an award of a disability premium. If this argument is accepted, the amount of disability premium since the date of claim will be deducted from the overpayment (assuming constant evidence of incapacity is available).

Applying this approach, where a claimant receiving income support has his/her medical evidence of incapacity rejected by the adjudication officer and cannot be exempted from the

34 Ibid reg 13(b)(ii).
35 Para 8.
36 Para 6.
37 *CIS 522/1992* para 10.

requirement to be available for employment on any other grounds, the adjudication officer must consider exemption on hardship grounds, because there is 'always the possibility of hardship where a person is left on income less than that which is usually guaranteed by a reduced amount of income support'.[38]

In relation to the other limb of this regulation, the reference is to 'the' misrepresentation or non-disclosure. This must refer to that breach of duty relied on by the adjudication officer. In *CSIS 62/1991* the claimant was found to have been living with her husband while claiming as a single person, at a time when there would have been entitlement as a couple. The entitlement as a couple was to be offset against the amount.[39] However, if other information was not put on the claim form, that cannot form the basis of an offset under this limb.

The diminishing capital rule

Where a defendant has misrepresented or failed to disclose capital resources which exceed the limits in relation to a means-tested benefit, Overpayments Regs reg 14 seeks to avoid an injustice that might occur where the capital is not far above the limit. The injustice is that if refused benefit, the claimant would have had to use his/her capital resources for living expenses until it fell below the capital limit, whereupon s/he would have become entitled to benefit.

Reg 14 seeks to avoid this by requiring the capital resources to be reduced every 13 weeks by the amount of the relevant benefit and entitlement to benefit to be reassessed following the reduction.

EXAMPLE 8.11
R fails to disclose the fact that he has £10,000 capital and received five years of income support. At all material times the capital limit was £8,000. R was paid income support of £100 per week, or £1,300 per quarter. After one quarter, his capital is deemed to be £8,700; after two quarters it is £7,600. The adjudication officer calculates a tariff income of £18 per week from this

---

38 *CIS 137/1992* para 11. Note that this cannot be applied to an urgent case application under supplementary benefit: *R(SB) 10/85 (T)* para 13, overruling *R(SB) 20/84* para 7.
39 Para 10.

> capital. The overpayment for the third quarter is £18 per week and so his capital is deemed to be £7,366. This process will continue until the capital is deemed to fall below £3,000.

Although there was no statutory authority for applying a diminishing capital rule to overpayments prior to 1987, a similar effect was achieved by exploitation of a discretion to disregard capital resources in the Supplementary Benefits Act 1976[40] up until 1980. Between 1980 and 1987, however, the rule was applied without statutory authorisation.[41]

This may not be of merely historical interest because until the introduction of the Overpayments Regs, the capital resources were deemed to be reduced weekly rather than every quarter.[42] While considerably more troublesome, this method will produce slightly higher offsets. There appears to be no provision in the Overpayments Regs which could make them apply retrospectively.[43] It can be argued that the Overpayments Regs are not merely procedural but alter the defendant's rights substantially,[44] and are therefore only applied from the date that their predecessor came into force. If the argument is right, then until 6 April 1987 the diminishing capital rule must be applied on a weekly basis and only thereafter every quarter. The commissioner adopted this approach in *CSB 18/1992*.[45]

Offsets of other benefits

Apart from the circumstances in reg 5, it is not possible to have regard to a different benefit which the claimant ought to have received or a benefit which would have been received by a different person.[46]

---

40 Sch 1 para 27. The provision was applied in *Chief Supplementary Benefit Officer v Leary* [1985] 1 All ER 1061, CA and *CSB 53/1981 (T)* para 12.
41 *R(SB) 15/85* para 14(5); *CSB 1006/1985* para 4.
42 *R(SB) 15/85* para 14(1).
43 Reg 31(1) may aim to have this effect but does not appear to be specific enough to permit retroactive effect.
44 Interpretation Act 1978 s16; *Plewa v Chief Adjudication Officer* [1995] 1 AC 249 at pp259 and 260, HL, per Lord Woolf.
45 Para 20. See also the discussion about the new rules for notional capital in *R(IS) 9/92* para 11.
46 Overpayments Regs reg 13; *CSSB 198/1984* para 6; *R(SB) 24/87* para 16.

Prevention of double recovery

It is a general principle of the law relating to damages that no-one should recover twice for the same loss.[47] This has been applied to the recovery of overpayments in relation to two other possible ways of extracting payment from a claimant.

a) *Recovery from compensation payments.* In *CSIS 37/1994* the claimant had been overpaid benefit but the whole amount in question had already been recovered by the DSS's Compensation Recovery Unit. The commissioner held that the tribunal to which he remitted the case should make clear that the Secretary of State was not entitled to the benefit which had already been recouped.[48] Although the commissioner based his decision on the general principle, there is in fact a statutory provision to this effect in SSAA s91.

b) *Compensation orders made by a criminal court.* The courts have power to order a convicted defendant to pay compensation for 'any personal injury loss or damage resulting from the offence'.[49] In *CIS 683/1994* no such order had been made but the commissioner decided that if such an order was made, then 'the right to repayment or recovery would *pro tanto* [to that extent] have abated'.[50] A compensation order does not determine the amount recoverable by the Secretary of State and the DSS is entitled to issue a SSAA s71 decision,[51] but any amount awarded by the court must be deducted from the s71 overpayment.

The purpose of recovery under s71 is to compensate the Secretary of State for loss incurred due to the defendant's breach of duty.[52] It is therefore suggested that, notwithstanding reg 6, any payments received from the defendant which are designed to compensate the Secretary of State should be deducted from the amount of the overpayment, because such sums cannot sensibly be said to be owing to the DSS. So if the DSS recovers from a claimant under the

---

47 See, eg, *Hodgson v Trapp* [1989] AC 807 at p823A-B, HL.
48 Para 6.
49 Powers of Criminal Courts Act 1973 s35. See p316 below.
50 Para 5. In *CSB 392/1985* para 20(2) the commissioner declined to express an opinion, considering it 'most unlikely' that the DSS would recover twice. Such confidence seems misplaced and such demands could easily arise through the local office being unaware that there was a concurrent obligation imposed by the criminal courts.
51 *CSB 392/1985* para 20(2).
52 *R(SB) 2/92* para 13.

common law (see chapter 20 below) then the sum awarded by the court should be deducted from the amount recoverable under s71. On the other hand, fines imposed by criminal courts, even though they are paid to the state, are not compensatory but punitive, and no allowance should be made for them in the calculation of the amount.

Neither of the commissioners in the above two cases makes it explicitly clear how a tribunal should deal with this situation, though Commissioner Henty states that a deduction should be made 'if and in so far as that order had been satisfied'. That statement is clearly obiter and does not bind tribunals. It is suggested that this is the wrong approach and that the whole amount which is to be recovered from the other source of compensation should be deducted from the overpayment. This is because the statutory recovery and enforcement of the other compensation may occur in parallel and there will either be double recovery through lack of liaison between the two enforcement agencies, or a need for continually reviewing the amount recoverable by the Secretary of State under s71.

EXAMPLE 8.12

S fraudulently fails to disclose the fact that he is working while in receipt of income support. He is convicted and the magistrates impose a compensation order of £1,500. S is ordered to pay at the rate of £25 per week. He has been overpaid £3,000 and by the time his appeal comes before a tribunal, he has paid £250 towards the compensation order. The tribunal find that the Secretary of State has the right to recover the full amount and deduct the £250 already paid from the amount recoverable, leaving £2,750. S agrees with the Central Recovery Unit to pay £25 per week, but fails to make all the payments due and loses track of what has been paid to which creditor. In this situation S will be forced to apply for a review every time he makes a payment to the magistrates' court, or there will come a time when he is paying an amount in excess of the amount of the overpayment. Had the tribunal deducted the full £1,500 owing under the compensation order, this problem would not arise.

Applying for extra-statutory offsets

Once the adjudicating authorities have decided that an amount is recoverable by the Secretary of State under SSAA s71, it is for the Secretary of State to decide whether or not to enforce repayment and in some cases the right of recovery is not pursued. If the Secretary of State, acting through a local officer, has promised not to enforce part of the overpayment, this cannot be taken into account when determining the amount recoverable.[53]

Tactics for persuading the DSS not to enforce the award are outlined at pp178–181 and these will be equally applicable where the Secretary of State is being asked to forgo only part of his/her entitlement.

---

53 *CP 20/1990* para 33. Note however that it may be possible to argue that such a promise prevents actual recovery of the benefit: see pp158–161 below.

CHAPTER 9

Payments made and breaches of duty committed before 6 April 1987

On 7 July 1994, the House of Lords gave judgment in *Plewa v Chief Adjudication Officer*.[1] The case decided that SSAA s71 only applies to overpayments made after 6 April 1987, the day that s71 was brought into force as Social Security Act 1986 (SSA) s53. For overpayments before that time, the correct test applicable under the old legislation must be applied to determine whether the benefit is recoverable.

Some discussion of the pre-1987 law is therefore necessary, and this chapter attempts to provide a comprehensive outline. Because it is now nine years since s71 was introduced, new cases of overpayments in which the old test is relevant will be rare, but not non-existent. Furthermore, the amounts involved in such cases can be very large,[2] and so familiarity with the old law will be important for those advising.

Perhaps more importantly, as the decision in *Plewa* overturned what had been the settled view of the law for four years, it may be that advisers will know of old cases decided on the basis that SSA 1986 s53 did have effect before 1987. In many of those cases, the DSS will have been repaid large amounts of money or will still be in the process of being reimbursed under s53 when it is questionable whether it would be so entitled under the old law.

These cases will need reconsideration to see whether steps can be taken to challenge the decisions in the light of *Plewa* by either

1 [1995] 1 AC 248, HL.
2 In one case in which the author represented the claimant, the DSS sought recovery of £36,000 of invalidity benefit paid since 1977. Had records from 1971 not been destroyed, the figure would have been over £50,000.

appeal or review. Where there has been no previous challenge to a decision, a review can be sought on the ground that the existing adjudication officer's decision is erroneous in law.[3] It will be difficult to seek review in cases which have been previously determined by a tribunal or commissioner, because an adjudication officer has no power to review decisions of higher bodies on this ground. In addition, it has been held that a decision of a court overturning the previous understanding of the law, as *Plewa* did, is probably not a relevant change of circumstances,[4] and so that ground of review cannot be employed. In these cases, the only solution will be a late appeal to the next appellate body, be it the commissioner or the Court of Appeal.

Non-retrospectivity of SSA 1986 s53

Before SSA 1986 s53 was enacted, there were three different statutory requirements for the recovery of overpayments, depending on the benefit concerned.

a) Supplementary Benefits Act 1976 s20, which applied to supplementary benefit. It was very similar to, and formed the model for, SSAA s71 as originally enacted.

b) Family Income Supplements (General) Regulations 1980 SI No 1437 reg 10, which allowed for recovery of family income supplement. This was a more severe test than provided for by s20.

c) The test of due care and diligence, which applied to other types of benefit. For most benefits the relevant legislation appeared in Social Security Act 1975 s119.[5] As will be seen, this test is significantly different to s71.

Social Security Act 1986 s53 was brought into force on 6 April 1987.[6] The government's aim was laudable enough: to produce a single test for recoverability across the whole range of benefits. There was some controversy about s53 being based on the more

---

3   SSAA s25(2).
4   *Chief Adjudication Officer v McKiernon* (1993) unreported, 8 July, CA.
5   The test also appears in Child Benefit Act 1975 s8 for child benefit and in a modified form for certain claims for mobility allowance: Social Security (Mobility Allowance) Regulations 1975 SI No 1573 reg 23.
6   Social Security Act 1986 (Commencement No 4) Order 1986 SI No 1959 ('the 1986 Order').

rigorous test applicable to supplementary benefit rather than the test of due care and diligence. The government, during the Commons debate on the 1986 Act, refused to countenance a suggestion by the opposition that the latter criterion should be used.[7]

No indication was given during the debate on whether s53 was intended to have retrospective effect. The words of the section itself were and are ambivalent. A junior social security minister, one John Major MP, suggested that the government had not intended that the section should apply to overpayments before 6 April 1987.[8] By then, however, great confusion had been caused by judicial differences of opinion on the subject.

English law has always frowned on the notion of legislation having retrospective effect. The Interpretation Act 1978 provides, in broad terms, that a statute cannot affect the legal situation before it was passed 'unless the contrary intention appears'.[9] This reflects the rule of the common law. One important exception arises in the case of purely procedural matters, 'because no person has a vested right in any particular course of procedure'.[10] Where recovery of non means-tested benefits was sought, defendants argued at tribunals that the due care and diligence test should still apply, because there was no 'contrary intention' apparent from s53. In addition, the section created a new obligation or new duty on the defendant by removing the defence of due care and diligence.

In *R(G) 4/91* Commissioner Johnson accepted these two submissions and also decided that the change in the law created a new substantive obligation and did not just change the applicable procedure.[11] By a majority, a tribunal of commissioners agreed in *CA 126/1989 (T)* that the section did not have retrospective effect. Commissioners Mitchell and Hoolahan decided that there was nothing in s53 or in the secondary legislation bringing it into force which explicitly made it retrospective, and so therefore the presumption applied against the new test being applicable to overpayments occurring before 6 April 1987.[12]

7 HC Debs, vol 98, cols 238 to 249.
8 HC Written Answers, vol 148, col 452.
9 Section 16(1).
10 *Yew Bon Tew v Kenderaan Bas Mara* [1983] 1 AC 553 at p558, HL.
11 Paras 13 to 15.
12 Paras 21 to 26.

Commissioner Rice, however, focused on the opening words of s53 as 'crucial and decisive'.[13] 'Where it is determined that' means that the crucial date to decide which section applies must be the date of the decision that the overpayment is recoverable, and where that decision is made after 6 April 1987, regardless of when payment was made to the claimant, s53 was to be applied. The language was sufficiently clear to rebut the presumption against retrospectivity.

The DSS appealed *R(G) 4/91* to the Court of Appeal. In *Secretary of State for Social Security v Tunnicliffe*[14] it was unanimously held that s53 did have retrospective effect. They adopted and expanded the reasoning of Commissioner Rice. The opening words of the section 'spoke of a future determination in relation to past events'.[15] The presumption against retrospectivity had to be a weak one in the case of recoverability of overpayments, bearing in mind that the claimant wished to keep money to which s/he was not entitled.[16]

There things remained until the decision in *Plewa* (see above). An important point had not been taken on behalf of the claimant in *Tunnicliffe*, namely that although both SSA 1975 s119 and SSA 1986 s53 could make claimants liable to repay, third parties committing a breach of duty could only be liable under s53. Under s119 a person acting on the claimant's behalf was required to exercise due care and diligence, but if s/he failed to do so the claimant was liable and not that person. *Plewa* centred on whether an executrix and wife of a deceased claimant could be liable for an overpayment of retirement pension before 6 April 1987. A tribunal, following *Tunnicliffe*, had held that s53 applied to that period and that Mr Plewa had innocently failed to disclose his wife's earnings, but that it might have found that there was due care and diligence had that been the applicable test.

The House of Lords unanimously held that s53 should not have retrospective effect. Lord Woolf, who gave the only substantial judgement, decided that 'it was obvious' that the obligation on a third party to repay was an 'entirely new obligation' created by s53. In view of that, the presumption

---

13 Para 39.
14 [1991] 2 All ER 712, CA.
15 Ibid at pp722d-e and 723f.
16 Ibid at 721f and 724f-g.

against retrospectivity would apply 'with full effect'.[17] He disagreed with the view taken by the Court of Appeal in *Tunnicliffe* that retrospective effect was not unfair, in view of the effect on third parties such as Mrs Plewa. Lord Woolf also disagreed with the views of the Court of Appeal on the importance of the removal of the defence of due care and diligence in relation to claimants as well as third parties who might therefore be placed under a liability that did not previously exist. In addition, because the effect of the Interpretation Act 1978 was that s119 remained in force in relation to overpayments occurring before the commencement of s53, there were no gaps created by the House of Lords' decision. Lord Woolf concluded his judgment by giving a useful summary of the effect of the decision:

> 1. An overpayment is only recoverable from a *third party* under the new regime (section 53) where the overpayment is made after 6 April 1987 in consequence of a misrepresentation or failure to disclose made by the *third party* after that date. In other cases the overpayment would be recoverable from a *third party*, if at all, under section 20.
> 2. Similarly, an overpayment is only recoverable from a person to whom it is made under the new regime (section 53) when payment has been made to the claimant after 6 April 1987 in consequence of a misrepresentation or failure to disclose any material fact made by him or with his authority after that date. In determining whether there has been non-disclosure after 6 April 1987, the fact that there may be a continuing obligation to make disclosure would need to be taken into account.
> 3. Where an overpayment is not recoverable under the new regime, because section 53 does not apply, then it may be recovered from the claimant in accordance with section 119 or section 20 if the Secretary of State is in a position to comply with the requirements of those sections, which will still be effective after 6 April 1987 in respect of payments to which the new regime does not apply.[18]

An important point to emphasise is that SSA 1986 s53 only applies where *both* the breach of duty is committed *and* the payment is made after 6 April 1987. If the breach of duty is committed before that date, then the old law applies. The reason for this is that a breach of duty is a condition precedent for s53 liability, and if the breach of duty was committed before s53 was introduced, 'then from the practical point of view [the defendant was] being placed under a liability which did not previously exist

---

17 *Plewa v Chief Adjudication Officer* (n1 above) at p257D.
18 Ibid at p260C-F. The emphasis is Lord Woolf's.

Ch 9 Payments and breaches of duty before 6 April 1987 147

by the change in the law'.[19] It will be noticed that Lord Woolf qualifies his statement by referring to a continuing duty to disclose. Where there has been no disclosure at all to the DSS, there will be a failure to disclose as from 6 April 1987. Where there has been a disclosure, however, there is only a continuing obligation to disclose in very limited circumstances (see pp61–65 below).

EXAMPLE 9.1

A receives invalidity benefit from February 1985. Due to the nature of his condition, he is required to submit Med 3 certificates every six months. In January 1987 he is offered five hours' voluntary financial work for a charity. He thinks that this will do him good and asks the DSS whether it will affect his benefit. The officer tells him that therapeutic work is permissible but neglects to tell him that there must be a medical opinion supporting the fact that the work is therapeutic. A tells the officer that he will do the work. A submits the Med 3 signed with the representation that he has done no work in February 1987, and does so again in August. He continues to do this until the DSS discovers that he is doing the work. A's doctor says the work has no therapeutic value. Even though A was overpaid benefit due to a misrepresentation from 6 April 1987, the misrepresentation causing that overpayment took place before SSA 1986 s53 was brought into effect, and since there has been no failure to disclose there can be no recovery under s53 of the benefit paid between April and August 1987. The benefit from February 1985 to April 1987 is only recoverable if A fails to show that he used due care and diligence.

A second point that needs to be made concerns paragraph 3 of Lord Woolf's summary. On first impression it might be thought that he is saying that any overpayment since 6 April 1987 which is not recoverable under s53 may also be recoverable under the old tests. This, of course, is not the case. When he talks of an overpayment to which 'section 53 does not apply' he is not referring to an overpayment where the s53 criteria are not met, but rather one where s53 is not operational because the conditions in the first two paragraphs are not met.

19 Ibid at p258C-D.

Recovery of supplementary benefit: SSA 1975 s20

Plewa explicitly states that SSA 1975 s20 is the proper section to apply when considering recoverability of supplementary benefit prior to 6 April 1987. Recent commissioners' decisions have confirmed that it will be an error of law for tribunals to apply SSA 1986 s53, even if there is no material difference.[20] Section 20(1), in its form immediately prior to its repeal by the 1986 Act, reads as follows:

> If, whether fraudulently or otherwise, any person misrepresents, or fails to disclose, any material fact, and in consequence of the misrepresentation or failure – (a) the Secretary of State incurs any expenditure under this Act; or (b) any sum recoverable under this Act by or on behalf of the Secretary of State is not recovered; the Secretary of State shall be entitled to recover the amount thereof from that person.

It will be seen that s20 was clearly the model for s53. There are only two differences of any substance which will need to be borne in mind by a tribunal applying s20:

a) There is no need for the decision awarding benefit to be reversed or varied on appeal or revised on a review as a condition precedent to recovery. In *CSB 18/1992* the overpayment period extended both sides of 6 April 1987. There was no evidence of a proper review by the adjudication officer. Commissioner Mesher decided that the recovery decision could be valid for recovery of supplementary benefit prior to that date, but the decision was invalid with regard to the later period.[21]

b) The Overpayment Regs have no application for the purpose of calculating the amount of the overpayment and so the old rules must be applied. This means that the diminishing capital rule must be applied on a weekly basis rather than every 13 weeks[22] and the circumstances in which an offset is allowable will be restricted.[23]

---

20 *CSB 18/1992* para 10; *CIS 332/1993* para 12; *CIS 649/1993* para 23.
21 Para 10. See chapter 3 above for discussion of the requirement of review in SSAA s71 cases.
22 *CSB 18/1992* para 20, applying *Chief Supplementary Benefit Officer v Leary* [1985] 1 All ER 1061 at p1063g, CA. See pp137–138 above for an account of the rule.
23 See *Commock v Chief Adjudication Officer* (1989) (appendix to *R(SB) 6/90*), CA; *R(SB) 10/85* paras 9 and 10.

Ch 9 Payments and breaches of duty before 6 April 1987 149

Recovery of family income supplement: reg 10

Although Lord Woolf did not mention the test for recovery of family income supplement in *Plewa*, it must follow from that decision that the old test for recoverability must apply before 6 April 1987. Cases where Family Income Supplements (General) Regulations 1980 SI No 1437 reg 10 are applicable will, however, be extremely rare. The regulation reads as follows:

> Where it is found by the determining authority that sums paid by way of benefit were not due and the persons by whom the sums were receivable cannot satisfy that authority that they had disclosed all material facts, the Secretary of State shall be entitled to recover the sums from the persons by whom they were receivable.

The regulation has similarities to SSA 1975 s20 and SSAA s71. In *R(FIS) 3/85* Commissioner Heggs held that the meaning of the words appearing in both those sections and the regulation is the same. Authorities relating to 'failure to disclose' under s71 will therefore also apply to recovery of family income supplement.[24] However, there are two important differences:

a) Whether or not the claimant has made a misrepresentation is irrelevant. The wording of the regulation exclusively centres on disclosure.
b) The claimant must show that s/he has disclosed all material facts. This effectively reverses the burden of proof from that under SSA 1986 s53.[25]

Recovery of benefits under the 'due care and diligence' test

There are likely to be hardly any cases where there is any material difference between SSA 1986 s53 and the old tests for recovery of supplementary benefit and family income supplement. It is a different matter where the test of due care and diligence must be applied. This test is fundamentally distinct in almost every way from s53.

It has been said that the criteria in s53 are much more onerous on defendants. This is probably an exaggeration. Indeed, there are some overpayments which will be recoverable on the due care and

24 Para 18; see chapter 5 above.
25 *R(FIS) 3/85* para 18.

diligence test but not under s53. What is clear is that there are a multiplicity of situations where an overpayment may not be recoverable under both tests and careful consideration needs to be given to whether this is the case.

The decision-making process

Unlike SSA 1986 s53, a decision under the due care and diligence test 'shall require repayment' to the Secretary of State, rather than simply finding that the overpayment is recoverable. There is no practical difference, however, since the Secretary of State's discretion to waive recovery is unaffected. As with s53, the adjudicating authorities have no such discretion.[26] The adjudicating authorities do not specify the method of repayment, which is a matter for the DSS to decide.[27]

Before a decision is issued under the test, the Secretary of State usually seeks the claimant's explanation as to how the overpayment occurred.[28] A decision may be issued on review or appeal.[29] In addition, repayment may be required by a subsequent decision in relation to the same benefit, where facts have come to light which mean that there was an overpayment.[30] Calculation of the amount recoverable under the test is a four-stage process:

a) Calculate the gross amount of benefit paid under the decision(s) which will be varied to require repayment.
b) Deduct the amount of benefit which would have been paid under the revised decision(s).
c) Deduct any amount which is 'directed to be treated as paid on account of the benefit awarded' by the revised decision(s).[31] Benefit is 'awarded' if the tribunal decides that the claimant is entitled to it. It is not necessary that the benefit should be payable after all the restrictions on payment of benefit after review for it to be deductible from the gross overpayment.

---

26 *R(U) 5/63* paras 6 and 7.
27 *R(G) 7/51* paras 3 and 5.
28 *AO Guide*, para 12282.
29 SSA 1975 s119(1); Child Benefit Act 1975 s8.
30 SSA 1975 s119(2A); Child Benefit Act 1975 s8. The requirement specified in *CSP 11/1950*, that the decision on repayment be included in the review decision, therefore no longer applies.
31 SSA 1975 s119(1)(b); Child Benefit Act 1975 s8.

Ch 9 Payments and breaches of duty before 6 April 1987

> **EXAMPLE 9.2**
> B left his partner, C, who is in receipt of child benefit for their three children, in 1986. The eldest child, D, is B's child by his first marriage and he goes to live with his father. B does not claim child benefit and C does not tell the DSS about the change until the second child leaves school years later. On appeal, the tribunal decides that C must repay the child benefit but that one parent benefit which was not paid to her must be treated as having been paid on account. The amount of one parent benefit, notwithstanding that it would not have been payable had C simply claimed it, is deducted from the amount to be repaid.

d) Where the lower amount of benefit payable under the revised decision would have meant that the claimant would have been entitled to extra supplementary benefit, the DSS is not entitled to repayment of that amount.[32]

The nature of the test

SSA 1975 s119(2), as it appeared at the time it was repealed by SSA 1986, read as follows:

> A decision given on appeal or review shall not require repayment of benefit paid in pursuance of the original decision in any case where it is shown to the satisfaction of the person or tribunal determining the appeal or review that in the obtaining and receipt of the benefit the beneficiary, and any person acting for him, has throughout used due care and diligence to avoid overpayment.

Peripheral matters

The language of the subsection gives rise to a number of points, which need to be discussed before consideration of the test itself.

a) '... *where it is shown to the satisfaction of the person or tribunal ...*'. Unlike SSA 1986 s53, SSA 1975 s119 places the burden of proving due care and diligence on the claimant.[33] There is some suggestion that where there is delay by the DSS

---

32 Social Security (Determination of Claims and Questions) Regulations 1975 SI No 558 reg 38; Child Benefit (Determination of Claims and Questions) Regulations 1976 SI No 962 reg 22.
33 *R(G) 2/72* para 8; *R(U) 7/75* para 7.

in seeking recovery, the Scottish doctrine of mora (delay of the party causing prejudice to an opponent affecting a right to bring a claim) may apply to reduce the standard of proof expected of the claimant.[34] There is no English equivalent of this doctrine, but it is suggested that tribunals should apply it as a matter of common sense.

> **EXAMPLE 9.3**
> E has a poor memory and is in the habit of keeping records of his dealings with the DSS. A question arises over whether there has been an overpayment of sickness benefit. E claims he disclosed the relevant material and that his documents demonstrate this. The DSS fails to issue a decision requiring repayment for some five years due to an oversight. In this time E has lost the relevant records while moving house and can remember little about the relevant period. The tribunal should make the appropriate allowances.

b) '... *in the obtaining and receipt of the benefit* ...'. The test must be fulfilled in relation to the claim as a whole or not at all. But where the overpayment has two distinct components and the claimant has shown due care and diligence in relation to one of them, the portion of the overpayment referable to that component will not be recoverable.[34A]

c) '... *the beneficiary and any person acting for him* ...'. Where a person forges someone's signature and claims in his/her name, the latter person is not a 'beneficiary' and so there can be no recovery from him/her.[35] There can be recovery from a claimant's estate after his/her death.[36] As is noted in *Plewa* (see above), the other person is not liable. Where the claimant has had help from somebody, due care and diligence on the part of both must be shown. In *R(U) 7/64* the claimant was illiterate and disclosed the true level of his wife's earnings as soon as he was aware of this. However, she had originally

---

34 *R(A) 2/86* para 15.
34A *CS 11/1976* para 8(3).
35 *R(S) 2/70* para 23.
36 *R(S) 7/56* is not authority to the contrary, as the case was dismissed on the undertaking of the insurance officer not to enforce recovery. There seems no reason why the reasoning of *Secretary of State for Social Security v Solly* [1974] 3 All ER 922, CA cannot be applied to recovery under SSA 1975 s119.

made the mistaken declaration on the claim form and while the claimant had shown due care and diligence, she had not and so repayment was required.[37] This principle applies whether the assistance is from a formal appointee or is given on a casual basis.

This element of the defence is modified by two obscure pieces of secondary legislation. Where benefit is paid to someone other than the claimant, that person and not the claimant is required to make repayment if the defence is not made out.[38] In relation to child benefit, where the benefit is paid to someone other than the claimant (be it the claimant's partner or someone else) and the claimant uses due care and diligence but the recipient does not, repayment can only be required of the latter.[39]

d) '... throughout ...'. This word only requires the showing of due care and diligence in relation to the whole of the period for which a payment of benefit was made, not throughout the period of the overpayment.[40] So if a claimant shows due care and diligence in week 1 but not in week 2, only benefit paid in week 2 is recoverable.

Due care and diligence

At the heart of the test is the criterion of due care and diligence. 'Care' and 'diligence' mean much the same, although perhaps 'care' emphasises not doing something to initiate an overpayment, while 'diligence' means that the claimant must be watchful as to whether s/he is receiving the correct amount. This fits in with the requirement to show due care and diligence in relation to both obtaining and receiving benefit. However, the criterion is wide and imposes a general duty of care in all aspects of the claimant's dealings. Mere honesty is not sufficient.[41] The best general definition of the defence is that given in *R(G) 1/79*:

> The statutory language does not necessarily import considerations of good faith but a standard of care and diligence which it is expected will be exercised. It involves not merely refraining from carelessness, neglect, inattention or indolence in regard to the conditions and

---

37 Para 8; *R(A) 1/79* para 8.
38 Social Security (General Benefit) Regulations 1982 SI No 1408 reg 7.
39 Child Benefit (Determination of Claims and Questions) Regulations 1975 SI No 962 reg 21.
40 *CS 11/1976* para 8(2); *CS 42/1987* para 5.
41 *R(P) 1/70* para 8; *R(U) 10/72* para 15.

circumstances of entitlement to benefit. It signifies also positive action such as furnishing full information to enable entitlement to benefits to be correctly ascertained and finding out by inquiry the conditions and circumstances of such entitlement.[42]

Whether the claimant has shown due care and diligence is a question of fact to be decided on the basis of all the evidence in the case. Perhaps the most important difference between SSA 1986 s53 and SSA 1975 s119 is that the test is subjective; the claimant is only required to show 'due' or reasonable care and diligence for a person with his/her characteristics. Illiteracy[43] and the claimant's experience of the benefits system[44] are both matters which must be taken into account. Other matters may include the health[45] and age[46] of the claimant, his/her ability to make inquiries, and any circumstances in his/her life at the time which affected the claimant's ability to understand the circumstances which led to the overpayment.

There is a substantial body of case-law on the test. As the test is a factual one, it is difficult to distil any firm principles from the authorities. For cases where the overpayment results from some fact not known to the DSS, however, it is suggested that three principles can be gleaned from the passage in *R(G) 1/79* cited above and the other case-law:

a) All forms and documents supplied by the claimant must have been accurate and, where relevant, filled in correctly as far as the claimant's knowledge allowed. Failing to answer a question on a claim form, as well as giving a wrong answer, will usually mean that there is no due care and diligence.[47] But the making of a misrepresentation in the s53 sense may not be fatal. In *R(U) 6/70* the claimant signed a form completed by a clerk in the local employment exchange. The commissioner stated that this was 'not decisive against him' because it was common for claimants to sign forms given to them by clerks without having an opportunity to read them.[48] A claimant is entitled to assume that a clerk has filled in such a form correctly according to his/her directions. In addition,

---

42 Para 11.
43 *R(U) 7/64* para 7.
44 *R(U) 6/70* para 13.
45 CS 18/1988 para 5.
46 *AO Guide*, para 12279.
47 *Sadiq v Chief Adjudication Officer* (1988) *Times* 8 March, CA.
48 Para 13.

Ch 9 Payments and breaches of duty before 6 April 1987   155

where a claimant makes a mistake and could not be expected to discover that mistake, there should not be liability.
b) A claimant must have disclosed all facts which s/he ought to realise may affect his/her benefit.[49] It appears that it may not be necessary to disclose to the correct office, provided that there has been some disclosure to the DSS.[50] The subjective factors will be relevant here in an investigation as to what the claimant ought to have been able to understand. In addition, the claimant is expected to take reasonable steps to check relevant facts.[51]

EXAMPLE 9.4

F is illiterate and is receiving invalid care allowance in respect of the care of his elderly blind mother. He does not know that there are limits on the amount of work which can be done in order for there to be entitlement for the benefit. He does not have the assistance of social services and has no friends to ask about the relevance of the benefit. He visits the local office of the DSS several times but is unable to obtain any information. Eventually he gives up and starts his part-time job. Although a literate person would read the order book and understand the need to disclose work, the circumstances mean that F has done everything that can reasonably be expected and has shown due care and diligence.

---

c) A claimant must have taken reasonable steps to discover the true extent of his/her obligations. There will be no due care and diligence where a claimant does not read instructions,[52] fails to ask for assistance if instructions are not understood,[53] or does not follow instructions which have been read and understood. On the other hand, the test is fulfilled where the claimant follows advice whether received from the DSS[54] or elsewhere. So an employee who followed his employer's

---

49 *R(P) 1/70* para 8; *R(U) 6/70* para 9; *R(S) 2/74* para 14.
50 *CP 34/1993* para 4. This part of the case is not affected by the implied overruling of the main part of the decision relating to misrepresentation (see p50 above). See also *CS106/1987* para 9.
51 *R(U) 7/75* para 9.
52 *CG 34/1988* para 9.
53 *R(G) 2/72* para 9.
54 *CU 25/1988* para 4.

suggestion not to withdraw his claim fulfilled the test.[55] The same will apply to skilled legal advisers, whether from professional lawyers or lay advisers, or 'anyone who might reasonably have been expected to understand the benefit rules'.[56] Where advice from the DSS contradicts that given by an adviser, the claimant may be entitled to follow the latter, particularly if the adviser is a professional or has been asked to comment on the DSS's advice.[57] A claimant is not entitled to make assumptions, even where s/he is sure that the DSS's advice does not apply in his/her situation[58] and even where there is a 'common misconception'.[59] Guidance must be sought.

Where the overpayment results from official error rather than some omitted information, the claimant must show that s/he has taken all reasonable steps to check that s/he is being paid the correct amount. It is clear that the mere fact that there has been an official error is no defence.[60] Not too much can be expected of most claimants in this respect. Unless it is clear from documents available to the claimant that a mistake has been made, a claimant should not be held liable. A claimant cannot be expected to carry out intricate investigations into the proper amounts of benefit payable. On the other hand, the duty to be mindful of the possibility of official error extends to ensuring that information has been acted on. Where a disclosure of information has been ineffective and a claimant ought to have realised this, s/he can be expected to disclose again.[61]

Although the above discussion offers some guidance to the proper approach to the test, it must always be borne in mind that all the facts of a case must be taken into account and looked at as a whole. The ultimate question will always be: has this particular claimant, taking into account his/her characteristics and knowledge and the information available to him/her, acted reasonably in all the circumstances?

---

55 *R(U) 1/73* para 16.
56 D Williams, 'Due care and diligence' (1995) 50 *Adviser* 15.
57 See *CSB 510/1987* para 5 in relation to failure to disclose under s71 (lawyers). See also *CS 30/1989 (social workers)*. AO *Guide*, para 12280.3 is wrong on this point.
58 *R(G) 2/72* para 9.
59 *R(P) 1/70* paras 6, 8. The *AO Guide*, para 12281 also seems wrong.
60 *R(S) 13/81* para 13.
61 *R(G) 4/91* para 16. In this way an overpayment may be recoverable under the test when it would not have been under s53.

CHAPTER 10
Challenging DSS decisions

The major area of concern for advisers and practitioners will be the method and practicalities of challenging decisions issued by the DSS. The law in relation to the recovery of general benefits is complex. The frequency of adjudication officer error, even simply on the basis that s/he did not have all the information before him/her, means that all decisions must be carefully scrutinised to examine the basis on which they were reached, and then the defendant must be asked all appropriate questions to determine whether the factual basis of the decision was a sound one.

This chapter sets out the procedure of a challenge to a decision, and gives practical suggestions for putting a client's case to both the adjudication authorities and the DSS.

The decision-making process
Referral to the adjudication officer

When a benefit officer believes that an overpayment has occurred, a request is made to an adjudication officer to examine all the evidence available and, if s/he thinks it appropriate, to review the existing decision(s) awarding benefit. After investigation s/he will then issue a decision that there has been an overpayment which is recoverable. At the same time a benefit officer will refer the case to the fraud section of the local office, if this is deemed appropriate.

When the adjudication officer makes a SSAA s71 decision, the defendant will be issued with a printed sheet containing the review and recovery decisions, a schedule showing how the overpayment was calculated and voluminous documentation setting out the defendant's rights of appeal.

Overpayments adjudication is a difficult task, and it appears that most, if not all, local offices have adjudication officers which specialise in this work. Specialisation, however, has proved to be no guarantee of excellence or even of competence, and the chief adjudication officer has been consistently critical of standards of overpayments adjudication, labelling it as a 'long-standing weak area'.[1] To be fair, it should be pointed out that the *AO Guide* is lamentably outdated in its coverage of the law and, in places, misleading.

The effect of promises and representations about recovery

Difficult problems of administrative law arise when a defendant is promised by an officer that there will not be recovery of an overpayment. The scope for holding the DSS to such promises will be quite limited.

Estoppel

Estoppel is a legal doctrine which, to put it simply, prevents a party from doing something that s/he has represented that will not be done, or from asserting a set of facts when the other party has acted on reliance that another set of facts exists. There has been controversy over whether an adjudication officer can be prevented by this doctrine from making a decision when a promise has been made that the decision will not be made, or from making a particular decision where it has been represented that a different decision will be made.

In *R(SB) 54/83*, the claimant was promised by an officer in an unemployment benefit office that the written disclosure made would be passed on to the DSS. On appeal to the commissioner, the claimant sought to argue that the adjudication officer was estopped by this promise from finding that the disclosure had not been so forwarded. The commissioner rejected the submission, holding that even if a sufficient representation had been made by the benefit officer, the adjudication officer could not be estopped from carrying out his/her statutory obligation to decide whether the overpayment was recoverable.[2]

---

1 *Report of the Chief Adjudication Officer 1994-5* (HMSO, 1995), p45. The report identified some problem with 89 per cent of all overpayment decisions relating to income support and 47 per cent of those relating to other benefits: pp43 and 44.
2 Para 15.

Ch 10 Challenging DSS decisions 159

This decision rests on the general principle of administrative law that a public body cannot be estopped from carrying out statutory duties.[3] This analysis will apply equally to a promise or representation made by an officer in the local office, or an adjudication officer, whether or not the latter is the same one before whom the case is placed for a recoverability decision.

EXAMPLE 10.1

A is interviewed by the local office about a suspected income support fraud. The interviewing officer tells him at the end of the interview that it is clear that he did not know that his wife was working and that he will not be prosecuted and no recovery of the income support will be sought. A then rings the local office a few days later to confirm this and is told that the case is before the adjudication officer, B. A first speaks to B's colleague, who tells him that B will simply reduce the existing award; B later confirms this to A. A is aggrieved to receive a decision that the overpayment is recoverable under SSAA s71. However, B was not prevented by any of the representations made to A from issuing the decision.

The situation may, however, be different in relation to actual recovery of the overpayment, where a local officer makes a promise in this way. The local officer will be deemed to be acting in the role of the Secretary of State. There is no statutory duty on the Secretary of State to seek recovery; there is merely a discretion to do so.

The courts have been reluctant to allow promises or representations to prevent a public body exercising its discretion. It is far from certain that estoppel can ever have this effect.[4] The present position seems to be that, if estoppel has any application at all, there are only two situations where it is effective.[5] The

---

3 *Birkdale District Electricity Supply Co Ltd v Southport Corporation* [1926] AC 355 at p364, PC; *Maritime Electric Co v General Dairies Ltd* [1937] AC 610, HL, cited in *R(SB) 54/83* para 15.
4 In *Goya v Attorney-General* (1984) *Times* 27 December, CA it was held that British authorities in India estopped the Secretary of State from denying that the applicant's children had British nationality. But the House of Lords appeared to be sceptical about the estoppel argument while upholding the decision on other grounds: [1985] 1 WLR 1003 at p1005.
5 *Western Fish Products Ltd v Penwith District Council* [1981] 2 All ER 204 at p219 to 221, CA

first, that procedural requirements may be waived, is not applicable here. The other situation is where there is a statutory power to delegate a function to officers and there are 'special circumstances' to justify the applicant in thinking that the officer had power to bind the authority.

The Secretary of State has statutory authority to employ DSS officers to discharge his/her duties. So where an officer makes such a representation in the course of his/her employment, the first of these two criteria is clearly met.[6] As to the other, the mere holding of the office is not enough. It may be possible to fulfil this criterion by arguing that there is 'some evidence of delegation of authority'[7] to DSS officers waiving the Secretary of State's right of recovery. This is in fact the case, such decisions being taken by senior managers in local offices. Certainly, the representation will have to be final in nature. An oral representation by an individual will not suffice. It is probable that nothing less than a letter on DSS notepaper undertaking not to seek recovery will suffice to estop the DSS.

However, the mere presence of those criteria does not suffice to raise an estoppel against the DSS. The Secretary of State will be entitled to act contrary to the representation unless the defendant can somehow show that s/he has acted to his/her detriment by relying on the representation.[8] The cases where this can be shown will be rare.

EXAMPLE 10.2

B is elderly and ill. The local office undertake not to enforce a right of recovery of income support overpaid on his move into a nursing home. B writes to them thanking them and informing them that, as a result of the DSS's decision, he has been able to give his £1,000 savings to his niece in gratitude for the care he has received from her. The local office then seeks to recover the income support. It is estopped from doing so.

The conclusion to draw is that there will be few, if any, situations in which the DSS can be estopped by promises not to recover.

6   *Re L(AC) (an infant)* [1971] 3 All ER 743, CA.
7   *Western Fish Products* (see n5 above) at p220h-j.
8   *Norfolk County Council v Secretary of State for the Environment* [1973] 1 WLR 1400 at p1405F-G, CA.

Legitimate expectation
A more fruitful ground of argument that the Secretary of State is bound by the actions of DSS officers may be that a legitimate expectation has been created by the 'express promise'[9] given on behalf of the DSS. This is a developing principle of administrative law and its precise extent is not clear. It has been most often used in cases where there has been a change of policy by some public body rather than a favourable decision in respect of a person which the authority later seeks to revoke or deprive the party the benefit of.

However, it has been said that 'English law has the definite beginnings of a general principle that public bodies should be held to their promises'.[10] It may be, therefore, that a defendant could seek to hold the DSS to a representation on these grounds. If the principle can be relied on, it is clear that the promise will have to be clear and unambiguous.[11] The defendant will also probably have to show some form of reliance in order to prevent the DSS changing its decision on giving the defendant proper notice and a chance to make representations.[12]

Requests for review

The approach of many advisers to challenging decisions of the adjudication officer is to write to the local office stating that the claimant wishes a review to be carried out and, if the decision is not reviewed, that the claimant should be treated as appealing to a tribunal. Whatever the merits of this practice in relation to other aspects of benefits adjudication, it must be avoided in challenging SSAA s71 decisions. The reason for this is the rule that a party seeking review of a decision must prove the grounds for that review.[13] If the adjudication officer refuses to review the

---

9 *Council of Civil Service Unions v Minister for the Civil Service* [1985] AC 374 at p401, HL.
10 Fordham, *Judicial Review Handbook* (Wiley Chancery Law Publishing, 1994), p251.
11 *R v Inland Revenue Commissioners ex p MFK* [1990] 1 WLR 1545 at pp1567, 1569 and 1575, CA.
12 *R v Jockey Club ex p RAM Racecourses* [1993] 2 All ER 225 at pp236 and 237, CA; *Lloyd v McMahon* [1987] AC 625 at pp696 and 714, HL; but see *Attorney-General of Hong Kong v Ng Yuen Shiu* [1983] 2 AC 629 at p635, PC.
13 *R(I) 3/75* para 9.

decision, then on an appeal against that refusal, the claimant must prove the grounds for that review. The burden of proof on the appeal is therefore reversed and the claimant is denied the use of the tactics relating thereto.

There are only two situations where it is appropriate to follow this procedure. The first is where the claimant is out of time for appealing (see below). The claimant gets a fresh right of appeal within three months of the decision on the review.[14] Even in these circumstances, it is better to try to get the appeal admitted late for special reasons. This course, however, has been rendered difficult by the new amendments to the Adjudication Regs (see pp163–164 below).

The other occasion where a review should be sought is in relation to an overpayment of a disability benefit.[15] This is because under the separate adjudication system for these benefits, a review must first be sought before an appeal can be made.[16]

Appeals to a tribunal

In relation to recovery of any benefit under any of the statutory provisions, defendant claimants have the right of appeal to a social security appeal tribunal.[17] The only situation where this does not apply is in relation to SSAA s71 recovery of disability benefits, where a disability question arises on the overpayment appeal. In such cases, which will be rare, a disability appeal tribunal will deal with all questions arising on the appeal.

EXAMPLE 10.3
C has been receiving disability living allowance. The DSS suggests that his claim has been fraudulent following an investigation by a local officer, during which C has allegedly been seen playing rugby. C claims that there has been a case of mistaken identity and that his disability is genuine. A disability appeal tribunal will hear C's appeal, because C's disability is in issue.

---

14 SSAA s28; Adjudication Regs Sch 2 para 4.
15 That is, disability living allowance, disability working allowance or attendance allowance.
16 SSAA ss30 and 33(1).
17 Ibid s22(1)(b). There is similar provision in s33(1)(b) in relation to disability living allowance, disability working allowance and attendance allowance.

Ch 10   Challenging DSS decisions   163

Other defendants have the same right of appeal as a claimant.[18] However, in relation to disability benefits where a disability question arises, there appears to be a hole in the statutory provisions. Only 'such other person as may be prescribed' besides the claimant has the right of appeal to a disability appeal tribunal.[19] The Adjudication Regs do not make provision for a defendant under s71 to challenge a decision in these circumstances and it therefore appears that, strictly speaking, such a defendant has no right of appeal to a tribunal and s/he must seek judicial review. Such cases will, however, be rare in the extreme.

Making the appeal

Time limits

A defendant has three months to appeal to a tribunal. That time begins to run from 'the date when notice of the decision was given to the appellant'.[20] A defendant is invariably notified by post and such notice is deemed to be given on the day that the decision was posted to the defendant.[21]

The very first thing that an adviser should check is, therefore, the date on which the decision was issued. A tribunal chairman has the power to admit the appeal late if there are 'special reasons',[22] but the draconian new amendments introduced in 1996 will drastically curb the previously liberal use by tribunal chairmen of this power. The defendant will have to satisfy three conditions:[23]

a) That there are 'reasonable prospects' that the appeal will be successful. The defendant ought to be entitled to the benefit of the doubt in all situations, and only hopeless appeals should be rejected on this ground.
b) It is 'in the interests of justice' that the appeal be admitted. This means that the chair will have to consider all the circumstances of the case, but the new regulations fetter his/

---

18 Ibid s22(5).
19 Ibid s33(1)(b).
20 Adjudication Regs Sch 2 paras 4 and 5.
21 Ibid reg 1(3)(b).
22 Ibid reg 3(3).
23 Ibid reg 3(3A)–(3D), added by the Social Security (Adjudication) and Child Support Amendment Regulations 1996 SI No 182, with effect from 28 February 1996.

her judgment considerably. It is not in the interests of justice to admit the appeal unless special reasons exist for the whole of the period from the expiry of the time limit until the appeal is made. The chair needs 'more cogent' reasons for a longer delay. The special reasons must be 'wholly exceptional' and 'of compelling weight'. In addition, ignorance of the law or time limits by the appellant or those acting for him/her, or any change in the law following a decision of a court or a commissioner cannot be taken into account.

c) The appeal must be made no more than six years after the decision is issued.[24]

Under the new regulations, it is absolutely imperative that the time limit is strictly complied with, because it seems likely that it will be very difficult to get late appeals admitted. A failure by an adviser to comply with a time limit would prima facie be negligent. Appeals must therefore be lodged well before the time limit. It is a good idea to send all appeals by recorded delivery post, so that service can be proved in the event of any dispute, and this should always be done if an appeal is being submitted within the last month.

Formulation of grounds

Although the regulations require that the appeal document 'shall contain particulars of the grounds on which it is made'[25] it has been held that this provision is directive, not mandatory, in nature.[26] The result is that it is possible to make a valid appeal simply by stating that it is desired to appeal. The 1996 amendments have not changed this principle. It is, however, necessary to identify the special reasons if the appeal is late and the decision under appeal. It can be difficult to comply with the latter because of the DSS's lamentable tendency to issue written decisions undated and without the appropriate reference codes. If faced with such a situation, the best course to take is to attach a copy of the decision to the grounds of appeal.

The material in the grounds will obviously depend on the nature of the defendant's version of events. A guide to conducting conferences with defendants appears at Appendix 3 to this book. One point always worth making, if it appears that a client needs

---

24 Adjudication Regs reg 3(3F).
25 Ibid reg 3(5).
26 *CSB 1182/1989* paras 5 and 11.

reassurance to this effect, is that criminal and recovery proceedings are entirely separate and just because the DSS is seeking recovery does not mean that a prosecution will occur.

The content of the grounds will depend on how the case is to be presented at the hearing. It is a good idea to separate out the claimant's version of the facts from the legal submission to be made. The best way to present the facts in a case is discussed at p170 below.

As to the legal submission, if the defendant is to appear without a representative, then obviously all submissions of law will have to be set out in full so that the defendant merely has to outline his/her version of the facts. On the other hand, some representatives prefer to present legal argument orally.

Whatever style is adopted, tribunals will appreciate neatly presented grounds. Ideally, they should be typed with all the points placed in separate, short, numbered paragraphs. Documents are easily lost and detached, so it is important to ensure that all documents are securely fastened. The typed grounds should be headed appropriately, with all the claimant's details on the first page for ease of reference.

Evidence

Overpayment appeals are arguably the cases before the tribunal in which the facts are most hotly disputed. A thorough, clear presentation of the defendant's version of the facts will be vital to the success of the appeal in the vast majority of cases.

The burden of proof

The general principle in relation to SSAA s71 recovery is that the burden of proof is on the DSS.[27] It must provide evidence to satisfy the adjudicating authorities that all the elements of a recoverability decision are made out. The defendant does not have to prove anything until such evidence is produced. There are only three exceptions to this rule:

a) *Where a defendant deliberately and unreasonably obstructs the obtaining of evidence.*[28] This principle should be narrowly confined to cases such as concealment of capital resources. It

---

27 *R(SB) 34/83* para 3; *R(SB) 6/85 (T)* paras 5 and 6.
28 *R(SB) 34/83* para 7.

should not apply to situations where a defendant declines to answer questions in interview. This is in accordance with a right not to incriminate oneself.

b) *Capital discovered in a claimant's estate after his/her death.* The DSS must prove the earliest date at which this was held and if there is no evidence of this, then the burden of proof has not been discharged. However, the estate must make 'every reasonable inquiry'.[29]

c) *Where a defendant has been convicted of a criminal offence in relation to the period of overpayment.* This has the effect of reversing the burden of proof, so the defendant must prove that the overpayment was not recoverable.[30] It ought to be noted that the converse does not apply and an acquittal of criminal charges will not have any relevance to the question of s71 liability. Convictions outside the period of overpayment will not have any relevance to the burden.

EXAMPLE 10.4

The DSS seeks recovery of D's income support over two periods, from 1989 to 1990 and from 1993 to 1995, on the grounds that his wife, E, was working full-time. Criminal charges are preferred against D in relation to both periods. D has a previous conviction for a similar offence in 1985. D is convicted in relation to the first but is acquitted by the magistrates in relation to the second charge, who accept his evidence that he did not know that E was working due to their estrangement. Before the tribunal, the burden of proof in relation to the first period lies on D, but in relation to the second period it lies on the DSS and neither of his convictions can affect this.

This cardinal principle is of special significance in appeals where disclosure is in issue (see pp76–78 above). However, it applies to all cases and tribunals often fail to apply the principle with the rigour it deserves. A defendant has the right to demand concrete proof of the parts of the DSS's case that s/he disputes, and advisers should always exercise this right in making an appeal. However, this right should be used sparingly. If a defendant

---

29 *R(SB) 34/83* paras 9 and 10, approved in *R(SB) 6/85 (T)* para 6.
30 *R(S) 2/80* para 13; *CSB 350/1983* para 5; *CSB 392/1985* para 12(1); *CSB 1269/1985* para 6.

admits that the benefit was paid, then to require proof of this will be onerous on the DSS and, more importantly, irritating to the tribunal. The DSS should only be put to proof on those matters substantially in issue. The model grounds of appeal in Appendix 2 below reflect this approach.

The DSS must produce all documentary and other evidence necessary for the foundation of its case.[31] If it fails to do this, then a tribunal ought to decide that it has failed to discharge its burden of proof and find in favour of the defendant. In reality, a tribunal is likely to grant an adjournment to enable the necessary proof to be gathered. However, there is a limit to the number of chances that the adjudication officer should be given and a repeated failure to provide the requisite material should not be condoned by repeated adjournments.

Once the adjudication officer has shown a prima facie case, then the defendant must rebut the evidence produced. The burden on the claimant (and initially on the DSS) is the civil standard of proof. The claimant must prove his/her case on the balance of probabilities, or to be more likely than not, rather than beyond a reasonable doubt.[32]

Though there is no authority for the point, a similar rule as to the burden of proof must also apply to other rights of recovery under statute. The DSS must demonstrate the basis of its claim before the claimant has to prove anything.

Documentary evidence

Ideally, all documents on which reliance is to be placed should be sent in with the grounds of appeal. This is not always possible, however, and is not mandatory. The Independent Tribunal Service requests that all documentation should have been sent in at least a week in advance of the hearing. If the papers are not all available at the time of making the appeal, it is better to wait until everything can be sent together. This minimises the chances of papers being misplaced, which frequently happens. For the same reason, originals of documents should not be sent in, at least not without keeping a copy. If more than a few pages of documents are submitted, then the pages should be numbered.

---

31 *CSB 615/1985* para 12.
32 *CS 234/1994* para 3. So the claimant's evidence need not be 'conclusive': *CSB 712/1985* para 9.

If it is proposed to rely on unreported commissioners' decisions, a copy of those should be sent in with the documents and, if not then at least a week before the hearing.

In their decisions, tribunals rarely bother to set out how an overpayment has been calculated but prefer to refer to the schedule furnished by the adjudication officer. If the defendant wishes to argue that an alternative amount should be substituted, it will be worthwhile taking the time to produce a separate schedule outlining the calculation. Busy tribunals will appreciate this because if the claimant raises contentions about the amount without providing an alternative calculation, it will fall to them to perform the task. It is more likely that they will simply refer the question to the adjudication officer. This may well lead to protracted disputes with the DSS.

The hearing

A tribunal consists of a legally qualified chair and two wing members. The latter are volunteers coming from a variety of backgrounds in the local community. As chairs are always at pains to emphasise at the outset of the hearing, the members of a tribunal have no connection with the DSS and will look at the defendant's case afresh. At the time of writing, tribunals are run by the Independent Tribunal Service (ITS). Once an appeal has been received by the DSS, it is forwarded to the ITS. A written submission on form AT2 is then prepared by an adjudication officer (usually a different one to the original officer). The ITS then compiles a bundle of the papers and sends a copy to all the parties involved.

Accompanying the bundle is a form requesting a list of convenient dates. Once these are returned, the tribunal clerk will fix an appropriate date. Experience shows that clerks are quite prepared to agree a specific date provided the local tribunal sits on that day and enough warning is given.

Preparation

The key to the best presentation of the defendant's case lies in preparation. Good preparation is carried out with as much time to spare before the hearing as possible. If the defendant is to have a representative, s/he should be given the case papers in plenty of time before the hearing.

If a defendant is to present his/her own case, there are means of helping him/her prepare. S/he should be told about the format of the hearing (see below) and reassured that the procedure is informal and that s/he will have a chance to put the points that need to be made. If possible, it will be useful to try to anticipate the kind of questions that s/he is likely to be asked by the tribunal and go through them. Tribunals will not blithely accept everything they are told at face value. Defendants must expect to be closely questioned where an appeal depends on the facts of the matter.

A representative must ensure that s/he arrives for the hearing with enough time for a discussion with the client (even if there has been a previous meeting). It is important to go through the format of the hearing with the client and run through the evidence one last time to deal with any last minute queries. This can often take a considerable amount of time and representatives should err on the side of caution in this respect in the amount of time they allow. If the tribunal calls the parties in and something vital has to be discussed, representatives should not hesitate to ask the clerk whether the tribunal would mind waiting for a few minutes. Tribunals do not usually object, provided the list of cases is not too crowded and other claimants will not have their hearings delayed.

Presentation of the case

The procedure at the hearing is entirely up to the chair, provided that both parties receive a fair hearing. Many chairs adopt an informal version of a civil trial, with the defendant giving evidence, followed by the presenting officer who appears on behalf of the DSS, and then the defendant responding to the DSS's case. Frequently, however, where the defendant is represented, the representative is allowed to elect how to proceed. The chair has to take a note of the evidence, so the case should proceed at an appropriate speed. Some chairs are very skilled at note-taking, others not. When the defendant is giving evidence, s/he should be reminded if s/he is going too quickly. The same applies to the representative making his/her submission.

All representatives, if they appear before tribunals frequently enough, will quickly form their own views on the best way to present a case. The author can only describe the technique that he feels most comfortable with. Other methods are just as valid. As stated above, the key to success is the most convincing presentation of the facts.

In the author's experience, tribunals generally prefer to hear the facts from the defendant rather than the representative if this is possible. There are several reasons for this. First, the defendant has first-hand experience of the facts and knows them better. There is nothing worse than a representative being continually corrected by his/her client. Secondly, reciting those matters about which the client has full knowledge is likely to make him/her feel at ease, which is less likely to be the case once s/he starts being questioned by the tribunal. Thirdly, this method is less likely to give the impression of a representative massaging the facts into a history that never really existed. The defendant is there to give the facts, the representative's job is to see that the tribunal has properly understood him/her and what the implications of those facts are.

This basic technique will often require variation with different cases and clients. Very nervous or inarticulate clients can often give excellent evidence with proper preparation, but some are not able to do so. Just as frequent are those who ramble. The key with the latter is to urge them to answer only the question that they are asked, and ask tightly focused questions throughout the giving of their evidence. Preparation will necessarily involve going through the client's evidence with him/her and forming a view as to how good a witness s/he will be.

There are some clients, however, who will not be able to give effective evidence, particularly in cases of extreme factual complexity; if this is the case, their evidence should be set out in a witness statement or in the grounds of appeal. The author feels that the disadvantage of this is that minor inconsistencies between the oral evidence and the written version before the tribunal are often seized upon and used to justify a finding that the defendant's evidence cannot be relied upon. It should be avoided where possible.

There is no requirement that a defendant's oral evidence should be corroborated, by documents or otherwise.[33] However, if such corroboration is available, this will be extremely useful. All documents should be discussed with the defendant before the case to ensure that the evidence is consistent, or if it is not, that there is an explanation for this. In some cases the claimant's case will directly contradict previous statements made by him/her.

---

33 CSB 615/1985 para 10(2).

While there is no reason why the claimant cannot raise a new case,[34] the inconsistency will have to be explained.

As to other witnesses, it is rare that someone will directly be able to support the defendant's version of events. However, indirect corroboration is sometimes available and will make a client's case far stronger. There are no rules of evidence in tribunals, whether relating to hearsay or otherwise, so evidence of conversations can be given as normal (see EXAMPLE 5.13 at p78 above). If a witness cannot appear at the tribunal to give oral evidence, a witness statement is better than nothing.

Careful consideration needs to be given to the content of any interviews by the DSS, which often feature heavily in SSAA s71 cases. The way in which many of these interviews are conducted is dealt with at p304 below. In the author's experience, tribunals are often alive to the fact that interviewees are frequently bludgeoned into making statements which do not reflect the truth of the matter simply by the lack of clarity and circularity inherent in some of the questioning. This, if not the aggressive attitude shown by many of the officers, should appear from the transcript of the interview. Interviewees are rarely given a free rein to tell their side of the story. If a client disputes the account of the interview or the facts that come out of his/her answers, then the interview must be dealt with and a full explanation given for any discrepancy. It should not be simply ignored but must be attacked head-on.

Presenting officers will often play little part in the hearing besides asking a few questions of the defendant. They may have nothing to add to the written submission placed before the tribunal. They can be useful, however, in helping with points of DSS procedure and practice in the local office.

After the evidence has been given, a submission should be made as to the effect of the facts that are applicable. This is not the time to repeat all the evidence, but the key points should be highlighted. Clear explanation should be given of the legal points that need to be made and the tribunal referred to all relevant authorities. The submission should be as succinct as possible.

---

34 In *CSB 392/1985* para 13 the commissioner made it clear that the doctrine of issue estoppel does not apply to social security law, and so the claimant could put forward a version of events inconsistent with that given in an affidavit in domestic violence proceedings.

After the hearing

When the hearing is finished, the parties retire and leave the tribunal to deliberate. The practice is that the tribunal announces the decision on the day where this is possible.[35] A representative should explain the result to the defendant.

If the appeal is unsuccessful, then when the written record of the tribunal hearing arrives between two and eight weeks later, the representative should consider whether any further steps can be taken on the client's behalf.

Obligations of the tribunal

The general obligation of a tribunal is to decide what the facts of the case are and then determine what the law is that applies to those facts. The tribunal has no discretion to disapply the law in any circumstances. If the defendant wishes recovery to be waived, then the proper course is to approach the local office (see pp178–181 below). However, a tribunal could be persuaded to make a recommendation that there are particularly compelling circumstances which the DSS should consider. It should only be asked to do this in conjunction with an appeal on the merits of recoverability. It would be improper to bring an appeal for this purpose alone, and would not be successful in any event.

General obligations

This section sets out in general form what a tribunal must do when giving its decision in writing.[36] The decision is not required to have the clarity of a High Court judge, but 'the minimum requirement must at least be that the claimant, looking at the decision should be able to discern on the face of it reasons why the evidence failed to satisfy the authority'.[37]

What this means, in practice, is that the tribunal must make sufficient findings of fact and give sufficient reasons for its decision on the form AT3, on which the written decision is printed.

Findings of fact must be conclusions on the evidence before the tribunal. It will not suffice to set out that evidence, at least where

---

35 ITS President's Practice Direction No 2 (16 July 1993). See Mesher, pp878 and 879.
36 Adjudication Regs reg 25(1).
37 *R(A) 1/72* para 8.

the evidence is disputed.³⁸ So it is not good enough simply to adopt the statement of facts in the adjudication officer's written submission, except where these are complete and undisputed.³⁹ Disputes of fact must be fully resolved. The tribunal must state which evidence is accepted and which is rejected.⁴⁰

The tribunal must give reasons in enough depth to enable the defendant to understand why it has reached the result that it did. It need not give chapter and verse of every aspect of the decision which is not in dispute.⁴¹ In relation to those matters which are in dispute, however, it must make clear whether evidence is rejected or accepted and why.⁴²

Obligations specific to overpayments cases

This section details what a tribunal must deal with in making a decision on an overpayment appeal. As a matter of law, a tribunal will not usually have to deal with absolutely every aspect of SSAA s71 in its decision, if some matters are accepted by both sides and not in dispute.⁴³ In particular, where the appeal concerns a case of failure to disclose, adjudication officers almost invariably quote the six-point test outlined in *R(SB) 54/83*,⁴⁴ but it is not an error of law for a tribunal not to deal with those aspects of the test which are not in contention.⁴⁵ However, it must be borne in mind that a tribunal has an inquisitive jurisdiction and it should call for evidence which can be obtained without undue effort and expense and which may help it to resolve an issue before it. So if DSS officers can give evidence on procedure or of the DSS's dealings with the defendant, and the chance to cross-examine such an officer will be helpful to the defendant, then the tribunal should give close consideration to adjourning to allow this to take place. If it declines to do so, it will err in law if it fails to give cogent reasons for not taking this course.⁴⁶

38 *R(SB) 42/84* para 6.
39 *CIS 393/1993* para 8; *CIS 402/1994* para 6.
40 *R(SB) 8/84 (T)* para 25.
41 *CS 234/1994* para 6.
42 *R(SB) 8/84 (T)* para 25; *CSB 1195/1984* para 7; *CIS 35/1990* para 4; *CSIS 50/1992* para 3(a); *CF 13/1992* para 7; *CSIS 37/1994* para 5.
43 *R(SB) 2/91* para 10; *CIS 584/1994* para 5.
44 Para 13.
45 *CSIS 51/1994* para 7.
46 *R(SB) 7/91* para 5. It is suggested that *CSB 99/1990* para 14 is wrongly decided on this point.

Likewise, where the existence of a document is asserted by one of the parties but the document is not immediately available, a tribunal ought not to decide a case adversely to that party without giving it an adjournment to produce it, if that document might make a difference to its decision.[47] A tribunal may not assume the existence or contents of a document which is not placed before it, at least where these are disputed.[48] Where the existence of a document is disputed, a tribunal may accept secondary evidence of it other than the document itself. Where the argument relates to the content of a standard document, such as a claim form or order book, a sample of the standard document used at the time will be evidence on which the tribunal can make a finding.[49]

Whatever the position in law, ideally a tribunal should attempt to deal comprehensively with the various elements of recoverability and Appendix 5 to this book gives a list of the matters that tribunals should consider and deal with in their decision.

A tribunal may substitute its own decision for that of the adjudication officer, and in particular may find an overpayment to be recoverable on the basis of misrepresentation where the adjudication officer based his/her decision on failure to disclose or vice versa. In both cases, however, a tribunal must give the defendant a proper chance to make submissions on the basis of the new decision proposed.[50]

The requirements of a tribunal decision in relation to each individual criterion of SSAA s71 recovery are considered below.

a) *Review and revision.* If the decision sent to the claimant, which should appear in the bundle of papers before the tribunal and is reproduced on the adjudication officer's submission on form AT2, contains a review decision and compliance with the requirements is not disputed by the defendant, then it is not an error of law for a tribunal not to refer to the fact that there has been a review.[51] If the tribunal

47 CU 47/1993 paras 12 to 16.
48 CP 20/1990 para 24(3) (contents of order book); CSB 18/1992 para 9 (wording on counterfoils).
49 CS 234/1994 para 7.
50 R(SB) 40/84 para 12; CSB 790/1988 para 8. CSB 942/1989 para 4 should not be interpreted as relaxing this requirement when the defendant is represented.
51 CSIS 62/1991 para 11, followed in CSIS 50/1992 para 7(a); CIS 137/1992 para 5; CIS 695/1992 para 11. CIS 584/1994 para 5 is too strict in insisting that this should be done.

is satisfied by other evidence that there has been a review, it should make clear findings of fact on that evidence.[52] If there is no or insufficient evidence of a review, a tribunal will err in law in not dealing with this point, even if it is not disputed by the claimant,[53] and even if there was a review decision which could have been found.[54]

b) *Misrepresentation.* Regardless of whether the claimant disputes the fact that there has been a misrepresentation, a tribunal must state exactly what fact has been misrepresented.[55] The date of the misrepresentation should be stated.[56] Where it is alleged by the defendant that a representation has been qualified by the surrounding circumstances, the tribunal must investigate the facts surrounding the making of the representation and make findings thereon.[57]

c) *Failure to disclose.* The fact not disclosed must be identified.[58] The fact that there has not been disclosure must be stated, and if the defendant has claimed that disclosure was made, full reasons must be given why the accepted evidence does not amount to disclosure.[59] There must be specific findings that the defendant knew or, where relevant, ought to have known, the fact[60] and that disclosure was reasonably to be expected.[61] Where, as in so many cases, the defendant disputes the latter factor, the tribunal must give proper reasons as to its view of the defendant's submission.

d) *Material fact.* Besides being identified, the tribunal must state, without necessarily referring to detailed regulations, why the fact affects the claimant's benefit.[62]

e) *Causation.* Even where it is not raised by the defendant, a tribunal must always state that the overpayment was 'in

---

52 CSIS 118/1990 para 4.
53 R(SB) 7/91 para 4; CIS 35/1990 para 8; CIS 312/1992 para 14.
54 CSIS 62/1991 para 11.
55 CSB 1195/1984 para 8; CIS 695/1992 para 10; CIS 583/1994 para 5; CIS 1209/1995 para 11.
56 CIS 583/1994 para 5.
57 R(SB) 18/85 para 10; R(SB) 2/91 para 12; CIS 389/1993 para 6.
58 CSB 1195/1984 para 9; CSSB 621/1988 para 8.
59 CSB 699/1986 para 3.
60 R(SB) 54/83 para 13(2).
61 R(SB) 54/83 para 13(3); R(SB) 40/84 para 11(2); CSB 1134/1985 para 4; CSB 790/1988 para 10; CS 234/1994 para 5.
62 CIS 514/1990 para 5.

consequence' of the defendant's breach of duty.[63] Where causation has been disputed, a tribunal must explain why it takes the view it does.

f) The amount of the overpayment must be stated in all cases,[64] as should the period of the overpayment.[65] Payment of the benefit can generally be assumed (see p125 above) if it is not put in issue by the defendant, but if this is done the adjudication officer must produce evidence of the amounts paid.[66] Where the adjudication officer has provided a schedule and the defendant does not dispute the amount, the tribunal should identify the schedule and record that it has been accepted.[67]

Where the amount is disputed or the tribunal does not accept the adjudication officer's schedule, a proper explanation of the calculation must be given.[68] It is an error of law not to consider an offset where one could be made,[69] though a tribunal need not consider the diminishing capital rule where the capital held by the claimant was so large that it could not make a difference.[70]

It is permissible for a tribunal to decide the merits of recoverability and leave the amount of the overpayment for agreement between the DSS and the defendant.[71] Such a decision is a final decision of a tribunal and can be appealed. However, the tribunal must make it clear that both parties have a right to refer the matter back to the same tribunal in default of agreement.[72] If a tribunal expresses itself to have adjourned, it has not made a final decision.[73]

g) The tribunal must state from whom the amount is recoverable.[73A]

63 *R(SB) 3/81* para 6; *R(SB) 40/84* para 11(1); *CSB 1195/1984* para 8; *CIS 584/1994* para 4.
64 *R(SB) 9/85* para 6; *CSSB 621/1988* para 8.
65 *CIS 545/1992* para 9(3).
66 *CS 366/1993* para 5.
67 *R(SB) 9/85* para 6; *CSB 1288/1985* para 7; *CSB 99/1990* paras 10 and 17; *CIS 173/1992* para 6; *CIS 734/1992* para 7(ii).
68 *R(SB) 9/85* para 6; *CSB 699/1986* para 3; *CSB 1272/1989* para 6; *CIS 583/1994* para 6.
69 *CIS 414/1992* para 13; *CSIS 8/1995* paras 8 and 14.
70 *CIS 674/1994* para 5.
71 *Riches v Secretary of State for Social Security* [1994] SLT 731 at p734H, Ct Sess (Inner House); *R(SB) 11/86* para 8; *R(SB) 15/87 (T)* para 23. *CSB 83/1991* para 8, which doubted the legitimacy of this useful power, must be regarded as overruled by *Riches*.
72 *CIS 645/1993* para 4.
73 *CSB 83/1991* para 8.
73A *CG 65/1989* para 5.

Challenging tribunal decisions

If the tribunal makes an error of law, either through not following the substantive law or through insufficiencies in its decision as outlined above, then the defendant has a right to appeal to a social security commissioner. An application for leave to appeal, stating the grounds, should be made to the chair of the tribunal within three months of the date that the written decision was sent to the parties.[74] If the chair refuses leave, the application can be renewed before the commissioner. A later application can be made direct to the commissioner if there are special reasons. It should be noted in relation to the latter course that at the time of writing the regulations have not been amended in 1996 as to the meaning of 'special reasons'.

If the defendant has been successful at the tribunal, then the DSS has a right of appeal, which it rarely exercises.

It cannot be over-emphasised that an appeal to the commissioner is only possible on a point of law. There is no appeal only on the grounds that the tribunal got the facts wrong. There are usually said to be five categories of error of law which will give a right of appeal to the commissioner:[75]

a) *A false proposition of law*: where the tribunal has misinterpreted the law in some way, eg, it may decide that there is a failure to disclose when the defendant did not know the material fact.

b) *No evidence*: if the DSS fails to produce evidence that no disclosure was made, when the defendant has asserted that one was made, but the tribunal decides against the defendant, that decision has been made unsupported by evidence.

c) *The findings as to the evidence were irrational*: it is often mistakenly thought that this heading allows dissatisfied appellants to attack findings of fact. It is a stiff test. It is not enough that the commissioner personally disagrees with the conclusion reached. It must be one that 'no person acting judicially and properly instructed as to the relevant law could have come to'.

d) *Breach of natural justice*: broadly, this means one of two things. First, where there is bias on the part of a tribunal. Commissioners are extremely reluctant to entertain appeals

---

74 Adjudication Regs Sch 2 para 5.
75 *R(I) 14/75* para 14; *R(A) 1/72* para 8.

on this ground and clear evidence of potential or actual partiality will be needed for a successful appeal.[75A] Secondly, both parties must be given a fair hearing. So if the tribunal refused to listen to a submission by the defendant's representative, there would be a breach under this hearing.

e) *Failure to state adequate reasons*: see above.

Appealing to the commissioners can be a long, drawn-out process due to the very heavy case-load. Many, perhaps even most, tribunal decisions are erroneous in law on some ground. It does not mean, however, that an appeal should be pursued. Advisers must give careful consideration to whether the appeal has any real ultimate prospect of success. If not, then all that is achieved is a delay of at least a year while the commissioner comes to a decision and a lot of wasted effort and public expense.

Commissioners will often not hold an oral hearing, particularly if the appeal relates only to adequacy of reasoning. The commissioner may determine the case or may remit it for another hearing. A further appeal on a point of law lies from the commissioner to the Court of Appeal or, in Scotland, to the Court of Session. At that point legal aid becomes available and specialist advice should be taken.

Requests to waive recovery

If an adviser concludes that an overpayment is recoverable or an attempt to challenge recoverability fails, then that is not necessarily the end of the matter. The DSS will not seek recovery of the requisite sum in every case. The government has made it clear that 'repayment may be waived depending on the circumstances of the case'.[76] In every case, therefore, consideration should be given to requesting the DSS to waive its right of recovery.

As stated previously, an adjudicating authority, be it an adjudication officer, a tribunal or a commissioner, has no power to waive recovery in individual circumstances.[77] Such decisions

---

75A *R v Gough* [1993] AC 646, HL, sets out the relevant principles.
76 Nicholas Scott MP, HC Written Answers, vol 150, col 683.
77 *R v Enniskillen Supplementary Benefits Appeal Tribunal ex p Department of Health and Social Security* [1980] NI 95 at p99F-G, QBD (NI); *R(SB)* 44/83 paras 4 and 6.

are entirely matters for the Secretary of State, or rather a DSS officer acting on his/her behalf. So a request to consider waiver should be addressed to whichever office is dealing with the claim (in the case of income support, the local office). It should be noted that where there has been a promise by the local office not to enforce recovery, this may give rise to an estoppel against enforcing a right to recover which may give a right to apply for judicial review (see pp158–160 below).

Advisers will need to take a number of matters into account when deciding whether to make such a request. It will be counter-productive to do this as a matter of routine with every case that an adviser deals with. A local office that receives letters from local advisers in relation to most of the overpayment cases with which it is dealing will be unlikely to give each request the serious consideration that it deserves. It is right that advisers should consider the position of future clients when deciding whether to act on behalf of a particular client. It must be borne in mind that officers are under continual pressure from the government to make savings in expenditure on benefits and administration and compelling circumstances will be required in order to persuade the DSS to accede to a request to waive recovery.

In making the application, it will be useful to have the assistance of the claimant's local councillor or MP. The latter can be particularly effective at bringing pressure to bear and can often help with other courses of action, such as recourse to the Parliamentary Commissioner for Administration.

It is not possible to draw up a comprehensive list of circumstances where an application should be made, but the following will be typical:

a) Where the DSS has saved money through not paying benefit to a third party. These will usually be cases where the claimant has been receiving money in respect of a third party who was part of his/her family for benefit purposes.

Example 10.5

F has been receiving income support in respect of his wife, G. They are estranged and live in different parts of the marital home, although F still gives money to G on a regular basis. The adjudication officer decides that they have not been living in the same household, and that F has only ever been entitled to income support as a single person. G has no income of her own and would have been entitled to income support as a single person had she claimed. A request should be made to waive recovery on the grounds that, had F and G both been receiving income support as single people rather than as a married couple, the DSS would have paid out more benefit than it did.

b) Where a claimant would have been entitled to a different benefit, which was not claimed. It is possible to offset entitlements to other benefits against the amount of an overpayment only in very limited circumstances (see pp134–135 above).

EXAMPLE 10.6
H is a single parent with four children. She has been receiving income support but does not make a disclosure to the DSS when she starts a low-paid, full-time job. The evidence is that H would have been entitled to an amount of family credit nearly as great as the overpayment of income support. The DSS should be asked to only seek recovery of the balance.

c) Where there has been an element of official error. A common official error, such as a failure by the Child Benefit Centre to inform the local office of child benefit entitlement, will probably not be seen as sufficient grounds for the Secretary of State to waive the right of recovery. However, where the claimant has been misinformed in some way by the DSS but is still liable under SSAA s71, it may be worth making a request.

d) Where there are compassionate grounds. This heading encompasses an almost infinite range of situations, such as personal tragedy, illness, lack of savings, total innocence in the breach of duty combined with other factors, recovery affecting innocent third parties and total inability to afford recovery. In the last-named circumstance, it will be useful to include a sketch of the claimant's budget to illustrate the huge difficulties that will result.

The application should be carefully drafted. In particular, standard form letters should be avoided, hence there is no sample letter in Appendix 2. It should be kept as brief as possible and give clear reasons why recovery should not be made. If there is documentary evidence relevant to the reasons given (see list above), this should be included in a summarised form. Careful consideration needs to be given to whether it is realistic to ask for the whole amount to be waived. A vague, over-optimistic application in relation to the whole award will usually be given short shrift, whereas cogent reasons given in relation to part of the overpayment ought to receive more serious consideration.

Many local offices are abominably bad at replying to letters and so a decision on the request should be pressed for. It will often be the case that a blanket refusal is made, without giving any reasons. If this occurs, a further letter requesting reasons for the decision should be sent. In extreme cases, it may be possible to challenge the decision to recover by way of judicial review (see pp185–187 below).

Recovery from third parties

There will be many cases under SSAA s71 where the DSS is entitled to recover from more than one person. Adjudication officers are supposed to determine whether the overpayment is recoverable from all possible defendants[78] but rarely do so. An exception was *CG 65/1989*, when it was decided that there could be recovery from the claimant and from two solicitors who had allegedly been appointed by the Secretary of State.

It is quite a frequent occurrence for defendants to be aggrieved about the conduct of some third party which has resulted in the overpayment. The question is whether anything can be done to place some legal liability on that third party.

The method of recovery

While there is no authority on the point, the author believes that it is possible to recover contribution from third parties by one of two means. Where the third party has knowingly made a false statement to the defendant, which directly results in the overpayment, it is possible for the defendant to sue the third

---

78 *CIS 332/1993* para 28.

party in the tort of deceit.[79] In practice, it will be very difficult to prove the necessary intention to deceive and that the overpayment was directly caused by the deceit. In other cases, use of the Civil Liability (Contribution) Act 1978 is possible. The right of contribution from a third party is defined as follows:

> ... any person liable in respect of any damage suffered by another person may recover contribution from any other person liable in respect of the same damage (whether jointly with him or otherwise).[80]

The overpayment is 'damage suffered by another person'. The right to recover under SSAA s71 is compensatory in nature,[81] and it therefore seems that the loss suffered by the Secretary of State in paying out too much money should come within this definition. The immediate problem comes in the requirement that the third party be 'liable' in respect of the loss. Liability for an overpayment does not arise automatically. It comes into being by the adjudication officer issuing a decision that a person should be liable. It is not possible for a public authority to bypass the statutory procedures when suing for recovery of an overpayment,[82] and so it will likewise not be permissible to directly seek contribution from a third party in the courts.

Before a defendant can seek contribution from a third party, therefore, the adjudicating authorities must have made a decision that the third party is liable. It is not possible to ask a tribunal to make a finding of liability on appeal by a defendant against a recoverability decision.[83] It would, in any case, be grossly unjust to the third party to find that s/he is liable without giving him/her notice or a chance to be heard. The adjudication officer must issue a fresh decision against the third party.

The proper course to take, therefore, is to write to the local office, contending that the adjudication officer has not issued a decision against all those liable and requiring the case to be referred back for further consideration, and giving full reasons for any refusal. If this course of action is declined, then an application for judicial review should be considered to force the

---

79 See, eg, *Winfield and Jolowicz on Tort* (14th edn, Sweet and Maxwell, 1994), pp281 to 290.
80 Civil Liability (Contribution) Act 1978 s1(1). The Act does not extend to Scotland: s10.
81 *R(SB) 2/92* para 13.
82 *Warwick District Council v Freeman* (1994) 27 HLR 616 at 619, CA.
83 *CIS 332/1993* para 28.

DSS to make the necessary decision. There would seem to be no objection to taking out such proceedings; the defendant has a clear interest in the outcome and should therefore have standing.

Once a decision on the third party's liability has been made, then contribution proceedings may be brought. The proceedings must be brought within two years of liability arising against the defendant.[84]

The criteria for recovery under the 1978 Act

Once it has been shown that the third party is jointly liable for the loss sustained by the Secretary of State. The apportionment of liability to the third party will be 'such as may be found by the court to be just and equitable having regard to the extent of that person's responsibility for the damage in question'.[85] The court will look at all the circumstances of the case and, in particular, where one of the parties is a claimant, will have regard to the receipt of the benefit by that claimant. It will be difficult for a claimant to argue that there should be contribution outside situations where the breach of duty by the third party was a substantial cause of the overpayment.

EXAMPLE 10.7

J received income support in respect of himself and his partner, I. She was working for her father, K, for eight hours a week at his nursing home. She increased her hours to 18 without telling J, keeping the money for herself. The DSS write to J to confirm I's hours and earnings. J asks I and she, worrying that she will not be able to keep the extra money, says that she is still working eight hours a week. J believes that she is visiting friends. K confirms to J in writing what her hours and earnings are and J duly fills in the form to this effect. When the true facts come to light, the adjudication officer issues a SSAA s71 decision against J. J can require the issuing of a decision against I and K, and can then sue them both for contribution and I in deceit.

---

84 Limitation Act 1980 s10.
85 Civil Liability (Contribution) Act 1978 s2(1).

Application to the court for relief by personal representatives

A personal representative is, in law, a trustee of the estate of the deceased. As such, the trustee is obliged to pay any debts owed by the estate, including recoverable benefits. If s/he fails to do so, s/he may be pursued personally under SSAA s71 or through the courts in an action for devastavit. Where a trustee is pursued for a breach of duty, in some circumstances s/he may apply to the court for relief.

> If it appears to the court that a trustee ... is or may be personally liable for any breach of trust ... but has acted honestly and reasonably, and ought fairly to be excused for the breach of trust and for omitting to obtain the directions of the court in the matter in which he committed such breach, then the court may relieve him either wholly or partly from personal liability for the same.[86-87]

The section can clearly be used if there is an action in devastavit but it is doubtful whether it can be used in cases of s71 liability. If the words 'breach of trust' are construed broadly, then it is possible that as the personal representative only comes under a duty to disclose by virtue of his/her status as a trustee, the s71 liability is a liability for a 'breach of trust'.

This jurisdiction will only need to be invoked where there is an innocent breach of duty, generally involving inaccurate information being supplied to the Secretary of State. The personal representative should, as soon as it is clear that recovery is being sought, apply to the county court by originating application (or the equivalent procedure in the Scottish sheriff court) invoking the jurisdiction to excuse him/her from the consequences of the breach of trust. Where a court action is brought, this can be by way of counterclaim.

The most important factor that the court will take into account is whether the personal representative has acted 'reasonably'.[88] That will depend on all the circumstances of the case. Generally speaking, if a personal representative made all reasonable enquiries into the deceased's assets, or complied, within his/her knowledge, with the duty to disclose to the Secretary of State, s/he should be entitled to the protection of the section. It has been held that where the DSS has not required the

---

86-87 Trustee Act 1925 s61.
88 *Perrins v Bellamy* [1898] 2 Ch 521, Ch D.

personal representative to furnish information, s/he will be excused liability for failing to advertise for creditors. However, the personal representative may have to pay over any sum taken as expenses under the estate.[89]

EXAMPLE 10.8
L is executor of her mother M's estate. M was claiming income support for many years before her death, and L produces a list of her modest assets at the request of the Secretary of State. Nothing happens until six months later, when clearing out the house, L discovers an old bank book of a dormant account containing £10,000. She writes to the local office to inform it but, due to an oversight, nothing is done. She then proceeds to distribute the money between the beneficiaries. The local office later asks for recovery of the overpayment due to capital resources from the estate and seeks recovery from L when she informs it that the money has been spent. L should be entitled to invoke the relief of the court.

Judicial review

Judicial review is a vast subject beyond the scope of this book.[90] Where it is thought that an application for judicial review may be appropriate, defendants should seek the advice of solicitors, and preferably a firm with experience in this area of the law. It cannot be over-emphasised that judicial review is a drastic step to take and careful thought is required as to whether it is appropriate.

It is important to bear in mind the general principle that judicial review will generally only lie where all other remedies have been exhausted.[91] So decisions of a tribunal that an overpayment is recoverable will not be susceptible to review. An appeal to the commissioner is the correct course of action.

89 *Secretary of State for Social Security v Blackie* [1975] CLY 3126, Liverpool CC.
90 Specialist works include Fordham, *Judicial Review Handbook* (Wiley Chancery Law Publishing, 1994); de Smith, Woolf and Jowell, *Judicial Review of Administrative Action* (5th edn, Sweet and Maxwell, 1995); Supperstone and Goldie, *Judicial Review* (Butterworths, 1992); and Manning, *Judicial Review Procedure* (LAG, 1995).
91 *R v Inland Revenue Commissioners ex p Preston* [1985] AC 835 at pp852 and 862, HL.

Procedure

Applying for judicial review involves a two-stage process. Leave to apply must first be sought by application to a High Court judge.[92] Notice of application must be made on form 86A, supported by an affidavit outlining the facts giving rise to the application. Many applications are considered on the basis of the papers alone. If the judge refuses leave on the basis of the papers, the applicant may then renew the application in open court. Alternatively, this may be done at the start.

If leave is granted, the application then proceeds to a substantive hearing where the DSS or other relevant public body will be represented.

There are strict time limits for bringing an application. These come in two forms. First, the applicant must make the application within three months of the decision under challenge unless there are good reasons for the delay.[93] Quite apart from that, leave to apply or any remedy may be refused if there is 'undue delay' in making the application.[94] It follows that advisers must ensure that clients obtain the correct advice quickly.

Review by the courts

There is separate discussion of possible grounds for judicial review in relation to specific topics elsewhere in this book, but a general outline of the law is given here.

Although the terminology in this area is fluid, it is traditionally said that an application for judicial review can be brought where a decision is flawed in one of three ways:[95]

a) *Illegality.* This ground will be appropriate where the public body has acted outside its powers or fails to exercise a jurisdiction which it possesses.
b) *Irrationality.* This is the most amorphous of the three grounds. The classical analysis gives four ways in which a decision can be irrational: where a body misdirects itself in law, where irrelevant matters are considered, where relevant

---

92 Supreme Court Act 1981 s31(3); RSC Ord 53 r3.
93 RSC Ord 53 r4(1).
94 Supreme Court Act 1981 s31(6).
95 *Council of Civil Service Unions v Minister for the Civil Service* [1985] AC 374 at pp410D-411B, 414E-H and 415B-C, HL

matters are not considered, and where the decision is one which the body could not reasonably have taken in the circumstances, duly appreciating its duties.[96] In more modern times it has encompassed a wide range of other matters such as abuse of power and irrational conclusions of fact.
c) *Procedural impropriety*. This ground will rarely be relevant in the present context. It includes matters such as failure to follow the correct procedure, bias and a failure to give a fair hearing.

As a rough rule of thumb, the courts are far more ready to accede to arguments under (a) and (c) than those based on irrationality. It is a general principle of judicial review that the court should not usually substitute its own judgment for that of the decision-maker.[97] It is not sufficient to show that a decision is wrong. It must be shown that no reasonable decision-maker could have reached it and the courts are ready to recognise that there may be legitimate differences of opinion in many matters.[98]

A wide range of remedies is available to an applicant for judicial review. In the present context, the remedy sought will most likely be a declaration of the applicant's rights or an order of certiorari to quash the decision in question.

---

96 *Associated Picture Houses Ltd v Wednesbury Corporation* [1948] 1 KB 223 at p229, CA.
97 See, eg, *In re Westminster City Council* [1986] AC 668 at p715G, HL.
98 Fordham, *Judicial Review Handbook* (Wiley Chancery Law Publishing, 1994), pp 324 to 326.

CHAPTER 11
Enforcement of recovery

This chapter outlines the system for repayment of sums due from the claimant and, where this fails, the two powers the Secretary of State is given to secure the recovery of benefits, by using the mechanisms of enforcement in the appropriate local courts and deducting sums from benefit being received by a claimant. It also deals with the controversial recovery from third parties to whom the DSS make direct payments.

Not all types of overpayment can be recovered by use of these powers. Overpayments under SSAA ss71 and 74, plus recovery of overpayments by credit transfer (see chapter 14 above) and of overpaid interim payments (see pp229–230) are those covered by the provisions.

Arrangements for payment

Few defendants will be in a position to comply with the request in the standard letter which accompanies an overpayment decision, which asks them to pay back what may be an enormous sum of money 'as soon as you can'. Many income support claimants will still be in receipt of benefit, and will be unable to make any payments other than by way of deduction from their benefit. This situation is dealt with below.

Where the defendant does not have a continuing claim for income support, the practice is to pass the question of repayment to the Central Recovery Group (CRG), when the existence and amount of a defendant's liability has been settled. The CRG is a division of the Benefits Agency set up specifically to enforce recovery of overpayments. The standard letter which is sent out when it begins to deal with the case is strongly worded, requiring immediate repayment on pain of court proceedings. However, a statement is made that 'reasonable instalments' will be acceptable.

An adviser faced with a worried defendant who is fearful of being taken to court should reassure the defendant that the policy of the CRG is generally less harsh than this letter might lead them to believe. There is plenty of scope for negotiation with the CRG about the scheme for repayment of the overpayment. It needs to be noted that the CRG is only concerned with enforcing payment of the amount that it has been instructed to recover. Thus, requests for the DSS to waive part or all of the amount recoverable should be addressed to the local office rather than the CRG (see pp179-181 below).

The starting point should always be to ascertain, first, how the defendant would ideally like to repay the amount, and then the maximum amount that s/he can practically afford to pay off weekly. If the defendant has any capital, then s/he should be asked whether s/he would be willing to use part or all of this towards paying off the debt. If s/he is not so willing, then a cogent reason will be necessary for retaining the money, particularly in cases of overpayment due to non-disclosure of capital resources.

Negotiations with the CRG, as with the local office, require realism. Where the overpayment is £10,000 and the defendant is an income support claimant whose partner has been working and earning £15,000 annually, the CRG is not going to be content with repayments of £1 a week. An adviser must counsel a defendant to expect the CRG to demand repayments commensurate with what can be afforded.

It is wise to make the CRG a positive offer, preferably with reasons why it is appropriate. Many of the factors mentioned in relation to negotiation with the DSS about waiving recovery will be relevant here (see pp179-181). Any financial commitments that the defendant has, and the effect on innocent parties such as the defendant's family are examples of matters that can be emphasised in the making of an offer.

Where the offer is not acceptable to the CRG, then it will be a good idea to ask it to state what it thinks is an appropriate scheme for repayment. In many cases the starting point for negotiations should be that it is simply not in the DSS's interests to force people into penury. No defendant should be forced below subsistence level by having to make repayments. No defendant should have his/her home placed in jeopardy. Where the defendant or his/her partner has an income from work, it can be pointed out that the CRG should not require repayment of such large sums that there is no incentive to work, contrary to the professed aims of the social security system.

In the last resort, where the CRG is completely intransigent and the scheme demanded is going to have a disastrous effect on the defendant's life, a threat to apply for judicial review should be considered. It may be argued that to fail to agree a level of repayment that is consistent with the aims and objectives of the benefits system is irrational.

Enforcement through the courts

The correct court for enforcement depends on whether the claimant 'resides' in the England and Wales jurisdiction or in Scotland. A claimant resides where s/he is living with some degree of permanence.[1]

If an order is to be enforced, the application must be made to the court within six years[2] of the cause of action arising. The question then becomes when a cause of action arises for these purposes.

There is no authority directly on the point but commissioners have suggested that the cause of action accrues when a final decision on the amount recoverable has been made by the adjudication authorities.[3] However, it has also been suggested[4] that the same rule applies as for enforcement of an arbitration award, where it has been held that the cause of action arises when the defendant refuses to pay the sum due under the award.[5]

It is submitted that the latter analysis cannot apply in the case of recovery of overpayments, since the basis of an action to enforce an arbitration award is a breach of a contractual term that the arbitration should be binding on the parties.[6] The Secretary of State's right to apply for the order stems from the

1 *Halsbury's Statutes* (Butterworths, 1992), vol 40, p872.
2 Limitation Act 1980 s7; Prescription and Limitation (Scotland) Act 1973 Sch 1 para 2(a).
3 CSB 1158/1982 para 9; R(A) 2/86 para 8; R(SB) 5/91 para 7.
4 *The County Court Practice 1996* (Butterworths, 1996) p353.
5 *Agromet Motoimport Ltd v Maulden Engineering Co (Beds) Ltd* [1985] 1 WLR 702, HC.
6 Ibid at pp772D to 773B.

Ch 11 Enforcement of recovery 191

decision of the adjudicating authorities that there is a right to recover the overpayment, and it is suggested that this is the date from which the limitation period starts to run.

If the claimant resides in England or Wales, then the overpayment 'shall be recoverable by execution issued from the county court or otherwise as if it were payable under an order of that court'.[7]

The specified procedure for enforcement of the award is set out as follows.[8] An application must be made on form N322A, certifying the amount that is due from the claimant and a 'copy of the award', which is presumably a copy of the final decision of the adjudicating authorities. The application must be made to the claimant's local court. The order will then be made by a court officer. If there is some irregularity in the course of the application, the correct course to take will be to apply on notice to the district judge to set aside the order.

Once the order has been made, the whole range of county court enforcement mechanisms becomes available to the DSS. Discussion of these is outside the scope of this work,[9] but such devices as attachment of earnings orders and enforcement by bailiffs are available.

Where the claimant is resident in Scotland, the overpayment is enforceable 'as an extract registered decree arbitral bearing a warrant for execution issued by the sheriff court of any sheriffdom in Scotland'.[10]

An alternative to the above procedures is just to bring an action for debt against the claimant. Such a claim must be brought within six years (five years in Scotland).[11]

Deduction from benefits

The Secretary of State is given the power by SSAA s71(8) to make regulations to provide for the recovery of overpayments by

---

7   SSAA s71(10)(a).
8   CCR Ord 25 r12.
9   See County Courts Act 1984 ss85 to 111 and *The County Court Practice 1996* (Butterworths, 1996) pp80–96 and 344–372 for the main provisions.
10 SSAA s71(10)(b).
11 Limitation Act 1980 s2; Prescription and Limitation (Scotland) Act 1973 s6 and Sch 1 para 1.

deductions from other benefits. The relevant provisions are in Overpayments Regs Part VII.

The scope of the provisions

There can be deduction from virtually all types of benefit.[12] Furthermore, if an overpayment relates to an income-related benefit[13] it can be recovered by deduction from any income-related benefit (not necessarily the same one) being received by the claimant's partner for as long as the couple remain a couple.[14] As this provision refers to 'an overpayment ... to one of a married or unmarried couple', it only applies to claimants and not to any third party who may be liable under SSAA s71.

Three problems arise in relation to the extent of the powers available. The first relates to the oddly-worded Overpayments Regs reg 16(3):

> Regulation 15 shall apply without limitation to any payment of arrears of benefit other than any arrears caused by the operation of regulation 37(1) of the Claims and Payments Regulations (suspension of payments).

Clearly, arrears caused by a suspension of benefit are to be treated differently from other arrears. It is not apparent why this should be so, since the withholding of arrears, however arising, will usually be one of the ways of enforcing recovery which is least painful to the claimant. Be that as it may, the distinction must be made and there are two possible ways of reading the regulation, depending on whether the words 'without limitation' are read as attached to the preceding or following words.

If the former construction is correct, then the words simply emphasise the word 'shall' as if there were commas at either end of the two words, and therefore the provisions can be applied to all arrears except those which result from a suspension of payment. A preference for the latter option could mean that arrears are to be paid 'without limitation' by reg 15, except those arising from a suspension.

On balance, the first possibility seems preferable as it seems to read more naturally. If the second construction had been intended, then one would have expected it to read: 'Regulation

---

12 Overpayments Regs reg 15(2).
13 That is, income support, family credit or disability working allowance.
14 SSAA s71(9); Overpayments Regs reg 17.

15 shall not apply to any payment ...'. However, the thinking behind the regulation is shrouded in mystery and the second option is certainly arguable.

The second issue stems from the fact that the system of recovery by deduction from other benefits was introduced by the Social Security Act 1986. The transitional regulations made under the Act, dealing with the phasing-in of the reforms, provided that the system could apply to overpayments arising before the system was introduced in 1987.[15] Previously, non-contributory benefits could only be recovered from non-contributory benefits.

Mr Britnell was aggrieved by this. He had been the subject of an overpayment decision relating to unemployment benefit in 1973. Only part of the amount had been recovered from payments of unemployment benefit before Mr Britnell's entitlement ran out and he began to receive supplementary benefit, from which there could be no recovery. In 1987, the Secretary of State began to deduct the outstanding sum from Mr Britnell's income support.

Judicial review proceedings were instituted to quash the Secretary of State's decision, with two arguments being deployed. The first contention was that the regulations offended against the principle that legislation should not be read retrospectively. This was rejected by the court at first instance, who held that the provision was procedural and did not affect the liability of Mr Britnell to repay.[16]

The first argument was not pursued further, but the second point, relating to whether there was power to make the regulation, was taken all the way to the House of Lords. The section giving power to make the regulation authorised the 'modification' of the Act for transitional purposes.[17] It was held that 'modification' of the Act could include an extension of the Act,[18] and that since the regulation would eventually become spent, even though that might take a long time, it was a transitional provision.[19]

---

15 Social Security (Payments on Account, Overpayments and Recovery) Regulations 1987 SI No 491 reg 20(2).
16 *R v Secretary of State for Social Security ex p Britnell* (1989) *Times* 27 January, DC.
17 SSA 1986 s89(1).
18 *R v Secretary of State for Social Security ex p Britnell* [1991] 1 WLR 198 at p203C, HL.
19 Ibid at p205A.

As far as claimants are concerned, therefore, their benefits can be deducted to repay overpayments dating from before 1987. However, there was no power to recover overpayments from benefits received by the claimant's partner before 1987. It is therefore suggested that a new obligation was created under the Overpayments Regs, and that they will not be enforceable as offending against the principle of non-retrospectivity, there being no retrospective effect specifically authorised by the 1986 Act.[20] If this is right, in any remaining case where recovery is sought from a claimant's partner in respect of overpayments decisions pre-dating the 1986 Act, such recovery is not permissible.

EXAMPLE 11.1

A was overpaid invalidity benefit between 1980 and 1986. An adjudication officer decided in 1986 that the overpayment was recoverable because A had not shown due care and diligence over the period of the overpayment. Due to an administrative error, no action was taken until 1990, when the DSS sought to recover the overpayment from income support being received by B, A's wife. No such recovery can be made.

The final point relates to the interaction of SSAA s71(8) with the insolvency legislation when a claimant is made bankrupt. In *R v Secretary of State for Social Security ex p Chapman*[21] the argument that Insolvency Act 1986 s285 operated to deny the DSS the right to operate s71(8), by forcing them to wait in line with the claimant's other creditors, was rejected. All that the Secretary of State was doing was withholding money due to the bankrupt claimant to offset against the debt owed by him, rather than seizing some of his property.[22]

---

20 Interpretation Act 1978 s16; *Plewa v Chief Adjudication Officer* [1995] AC 249 at pp259 and 260, HL.
21 (1996) *Times* 5 February, QBD. This application was heard with *ex parte Taylor* (see p228 below).
22 *Chapman* (official transcript, p20). It seems that the same rule will apply in Scotland following the allowing of the DSS's appeal in *Mulvey v Secretary of State for Social Security* [1996] SLT 267, Ct Sess (Inner House) (see pp228 below). *Chapman* is under appeal to the Court of Appeal and *Mulvey* to the House of Lords.

How much can be deducted?

The general rule is that the full amount of benefit may be deducted. There are two exceptions. The first is that for a 'specified benefit' a claimant is entitled to retain the princely sum of ten pence in each benefit week.[23] A 'specified benefit' refers to income support, together with other benefits that are paid in conjunction with it.[24-25]

Secondly, only a certain amount of income support to which the claimant is 'presently entitled' can be deducted. So arrears of income support will be treated as a 'specified benefit' as discussed above, but deduction from present entitlements is restricted.

There are two levels of maximum deduction, both the subject of unnecessarily complex formulae. The usual maximum deduction is £7.20, but currently a higher level applies to applies to those who have been convicted of an offence connected with their breach of duty, or have 'made a written statement after caution in admission of deception or fraud for the purpose of obtaining benefit'.[26] This latter part of the definition may be crucial. Such a statement is defined as being one in conformity with the relevant rules in England and Wales or one witnessed by two persons in Scotland.[27-28] The maximum weekly deduction at the higher level is currently £9.60.

It should also be borne in mind that these deductions from income support are 'subject to paragraphs 8 and 9 of Schedule 9 to the Claims and Payments Regulations'. Those provisions allow deductions from income support for fines, council tax and so on. Again, due to poor drafting, it is not absolutely clear whether the deductions under Overpayments Regs reg 16 are additional to those made for other reasons or can only be carried out to the extent that the deductions are less than the maximum deductions for recovery. The former must be the case as the formulae appear to be based on the absolute maximum amounts

---

23 Overpayments Regs reg 16(7).
24-25 Ibid reg 16(8).
26 Ibid reg 16(5).
27-28 Ibid reg 16(8). The relevant rules are the Codes of Practice under the Police and Criminal Evidence Act 1984 or the old Judge's Rules. The origins of such statements and whether they are likely to comply with the requirements are discussed further in the criminal context. See chapter 21 below.

that the DSS feels can be reasonably deducted from a claimant's income support.

Challenging decisions

It is not absolutely clear from the legislation, but a decision to deduct overpayments from other benefits appears to be a decision of the Secretary of State and not the adjudication officer. This conclusion is based on the fact that payability of benefits is a matter for the Secretary of State and other deductions are explicitly stated to be made by the adjudicating authorities. That being the case, there can be no appeal to a social security appeal tribunal and a decision to deduct can only be challenged by way of judicial review.

Before court proceedings are taken, however, persuasion should be tried. There is no reason why the Secretary of State should deduct the full amount allowable if there are compelling reasons why s/he should not. Further advice about such negotiation is given elsewhere (see pp179–181).

One possibly fertile area for argument before the courts concerns whether a statement admitting fraud is in conformity with the relevant rules and the higher rate of deduction should therefore be applied (see pp303–307).

Bypassing SSAA s71 by recovery from third parties

Recovery from mortgage lenders

The 'rent direct' system no longer exists, having been replaced with housing benefit, but it has a modern equivalent in the shape of the recovery of overpaid mortgage interest from mortgage lenders. With cuts in interest rates in recent years, there have been many cases of the DSS failing to act on a disclosure by a claimant of a decrease in the amount of interest payable.

Claimants in this position typically pay the minimum amount allowable towards the principal on their mortgage to keep up with repayments. When the lender repays the DSS, the claimants have suddenly found themselves in arrears on their mortgage repayments that they are in no position to meet and repossessions have resulted.[29]

The DSS has a statutory right to recover overpaid benefit from the

---

29 See *Guardian*, 18 February 1996.

lender in two circumstances. The first is where the claimant has ceased to be entitled to any benefit and the Secretary of State requests repayment within four weeks of the end of the claim.[30] The second requires three conditions to be met:

a) a reduction in the interest rate or the capital sum repayable;
b) a reduction in the applicable amount, following a review decision by an adjudication officer to reduce the level of housing costs to reflect the change in mortgage interest;
c) 'no corresponding reduction was made to the specified part': the latter words refer to the amount of mortgage interest payable as housing costs.

In *R v Secretary of State for Social Security ex p Golding*[31] it was argued that a retrospective recovery by the Secretary of State, purportedly made pursuant to this right, was unlawful. The DSS had failed to act on Mr Golding's disclosure, and later an adjudication officer reduced his applicable amount and the housing costs payable. The Secretary of State claimed to be entitled to recoup the overpayment made in the period of delay. It was argued that the final condition meant that the right to recover only arose when the adjudication officer did not, in the review decision, reduce the housing costs payable, whereon an overpayment arose due to the continuing interest payments reflecting the former amount of housing costs. Counsel for the Secretary of State asserted that it gave the minister the power to recover under retrospective reviews. Brooke J stated that he preferred the former construction and granted a declaration that recovery of the mortgage interest was unlawful in such circumstances.[32]

The Court of Appeal allowed the DSS's appeal, stating that the paragraph had to be given a purposive interpretation. Overpayments would inevitably arise when interest rates fell and so the paragraph had to be interpreted in such a way as to allow these overpayments to be recovered. In view of that, it was possible to say that a payment 'ought not to have been made'[33] even though it was correct at the time it was made in view of the subsisting award of benefit.[34]

It may still be possible, however, to ameliorate some of the worst

---

30 Claims and Payments Regs Sch 9A para 11(2)(b) and (3).
31 (1996) *Times* 13 March, QBD; (1996) unreported, 1 July, CA.
32 (1996) *Times* 13 March (official transcript, p14).
33 Claims and Payments Regs Sch 9A para 11(1).
34 (1996) unreported, 1 July (official transcript, pp16G to 17D, 20G to 21E and 32E-F), CA.

effects of the recovery of mortgage interest. The Court of Appeal expressed concern that the Secretary of State had not been requiring the lender to repay but had instead been offsetting the overpayment against current payments of mortgage interest. Counsel for the Secretary of State accepted it would be unlawful to do so where the practice of the lender effectively meant that the claimant's entitlement to mortgage interest was not being paid.[35] Sir Richard Scott V-C asserted 'that the use of set-off machinery to recoup overpayments is only permissible if it is accompanied by a credit to the beneficiary borrower's interest account with the lender of an amount equal to the set-off sum'.[36] Mr Golding was given liberty to further apply to the court if recovery of his overpayment had this effect. In view of this, judicial review must still be available to quash such set-off actions.

EXAMPLE 11.2

C's mortgage interest is £300 per month. Following a reduction in interest rates, and the failure of the DSS to act on C's disclosure of the reduction, an overpayment results. A review is carried out ten weeks later and interest payable over the ten weeks re-assessed at £250 per month. During the ten weeks, the building society has been paying the £50 surplus into C's capital account. When the overpayment is assessed, the Secretary of State then pays nothing for two weeks to offset the £500 overpayment. The result is that C's interest account is £500 in arrears. Unless the building society has procedures to transfer £500 from the capital to the interest accounts, the Secretary of State's actions are unlawful.

Recovery from other third parties

Income support payments are made to other third parties by way of deduction from a claimant's entitlement. Rent, fuel, and water charges are all payable directly in certain circumstances,[37] as are fines and council tax.[38] None of these payments are explicitly stated to be recoverable in the event of some overpayment. It is therefore suggested that any recovery from a third party in these cases would be unlawful.

---

35 Ibid pp34F to 35A.
36 Ibid p36E-F.
37 See Claims and Payments Regs Sch 9 for details.
38 Fines (Deductions from Income Support) Regulations 1992 SI No 2182; Council Tax (Deductions from Income Support) Regulations 1993 SI No 494.

Part II

Statutory recovery of general benefits: other rights

CHAPTER 12
Recovery of income-related benefits after late receipt of income

SSAA s74 contains important absolute rights of recovery in relation to income support or income-based jobseekers' allowance. It applies solely to those benefits (termed 'applicable benefits' in this chapter) and has been widely construed by the commissioners. Their approach is shown by the reporting of the controversial decision *R(IS) 14/94*, discussed below.

There are three distinct parts to s74, all of which have the same basic aim: to recover applicable benefit paid to a claimant because s/he had not received income due at the time s/he was receiving that benefit. The section is often used and advisers need to be aware of it to avoid falling into the trap of attacking it on its merits as if it were a s71 decision.

There is no requirement under s74 for the decision awarding applicable benefit to be reviewed and revised. Nor is the adjudication officer required to apply the provisions of the Overpayments Regs to make offsets from the amount of the overpayment. It has been held that no offsets are permissible under this section.[1]

It should also be noted that the three parts of s74 are not mutually exclusive. A source of income may result in recovery under more than one part. For example, late payment of other benefits may result in recovery under s74(1) or (2).

Late payments of prescribed income
Prescribed income generally
The first ground for recovery is that the claimant has received

1 *CSB 89/1990* para 4.

some form of 'prescribed income'[2] which should have been received at the time that applicable benefit was being received. The adjudication officer is required to treat that income as having been paid on the 'prescribed date' and work out the consequences for applicable benefit accordingly.

Clearly, the biggest potential for dispute under this section relates to the question of when the income should be taken into account. If the income is paid in relation to a specific period, then the first day of that period is the prescribed date.[3] If the income is not attributable to any period in particular, then the adjudication officer can select 'the day or the first day of the period to which it is fairly attributable'.[4] This gives the adjudication officer a fairly wide discretion, which can be the subject of appeal to a tribunal.

EXAMPLE 12.1

A receives income support from 25 February to 25 October. She is alienated from her family. Her grandmother sets up a trust fund for her in April to give her an income of £100 per month from 1 May. However, her family do not inform her of this. In September her grandmother dies, providing for an annual payment to A of £1,000 in her will. The will does not state on which dates the annuity is payable. In October A starts work, and in the following month she is reconciled with the family, who then hand over the accumulated monthly income. At the same time, probate of the will is granted.

The adjudication officer treats the monthly payments as having been made on the first day of each month. They would have been deducted in full from income support and so £600, being six months' payments, will be recoverable under SSAA s74. The adjudication officer then proceeds to treat the annuity of £1,000 as payable on the death of A's grandmother. It is possible for A to argue that the payment is not 'fairly attributable' to that date and should either be payable at the date of probate or at the start of each calendar year.

---

2 Defined by the Overpayments Regs reg 7(1) as any income which has to be taken into account under the Income Support (General) Regulations 1987 SI No 1967 Part V (and which will no doubt refer to the relevant regulations for jobseeker's allowance in due course).
3 Overpayments Regs reg 7(2)(a).
4 Ibid reg 7(2)(b).

A detailed discussion of what constitutes prescribed income is outside the scope of this work[5] but it should be noted that it will cover nearly all types of income. Consideration should, however, be given to the categories of exempt income[6] in each case.

Child support maintenance

There are special rules relating to maintenance under the Child Support Act 1991 due to the complex interaction between the child support and means-tested benefits systems. Maintenance is only recoverable for the period between the effective date of a child support assessment and the date that maintenance first becomes payable by direction of the Secretary of State.[7] There is always a delay between an application for maintenance and the first payments being made. However, once payments are being made, any overpayments of benefit are not recoverable under SSAA s74.

EXAMPLE 12.2

B, who is in receipt of income support, applies for a child support assessment on 1 February in relation to her sons, C and D, against E, the absent parent. The effective date of the assessment is 3 February, the date that it is received by the Child Support Centre. The assessment is made at £100 per week and E is required to make the first payment on 3 May. Due to a breakdown of communication E pays the first month's payment from that date and all the arrears directly to B instead of to the Child Support Agency. The arrears are recoverable from B under SSAA s74 but not the payment for May.

Unlike other types of prescribed income, the prescribed date for child support maintenance is the last day of the relevant

---

5 Part V is discussed in detail in Mesher, pp150 to 161.
6 Income Support (General) Regulations 1987 SI No 1967 Sch 9. These cover a wide range of payments from the commonplace, such as charitable payments and disability benefits, to the esoteric. See Mesher, pp314 to 328 for a discussion of Sch 9. The list is presented in a more comprehensible form in *National Welfare Benefits Handbook* (CPAG, 1996), pp343–345.
7 Overpayments Regs reg 7(1)(b). For details about how these dates are calculated see Jacobs and Douglas, *Child Support: the Legislation* (2nd edn, CPAG, 1995) pp208–211.

maintenance period.[8] A maintenance period is the interval (usually weekly) at which maintenance is paid. Where a part of a maintenance period is to be taken into account, the prescribed date is the last day of that part.[9]

> EXAMPLE 12.3
> As in EXAMPLE 12.2 above, except B starts a full-time job on 2 April. The maintenance period is one week and so the prescribed date in relation to the maintenance period beginning 3 February is 9 February, that in the week beginning 10 February is 16 February and so on until the week beginning 30 March. The prescribed date is 5 April, which is after income support ceases to be paid, so the maintenance received in that week cannot be recovered under SSAA s74. However, if E successfully applied for a review of the assessment on 2 April, then 1 April would be treated as the last day of the assessment. The maintenance received for the part-week between 30 March and 1 April would be treated as paid on 1 April, and would therefore be recoverable under s74.

Prescribed payments from public funds

SSAA s74(2) is aimed at recovery of benefits paid late to a claimant in relation to a period for which applicable benefit has already been received. Because virtually all benefits are deductible from applicable benefit, it is thought to be unfair to allow a claimant to have the full amount of back-dated benefit when, if that benefit had been paid timeously, s/he would have had it deducted from his/her applicable benefit. Therefore the amount of applicable benefit will be deducted from the arrears of benefit.

However, due to a defect in the drafting of the subsection, it may be possible to drastically limit its effect.

The mechanism

The adjudication officer must show the presence of two conditions to use the subsection to make recovery.

---

8   Overpayments Regs reg 7(3).
9   Ibid reg 7(4).

Payment made late

The first condition is that a prescribed payment which is to be made from public funds in the United Kingdom or another EU member state is not made by the prescribed date.[10]

'Prescribed payment' is defined very widely.[11] The subsection applies to virtually all benefits except grants, gratuities and widows' payments. In addition, it includes certain allowances paid for day release for training and instruction, and benefits paid by other member states of the EU.

It is not necessary for the prescribed payment to be made to the claimant. In *CSB 383/1988*, arrears of retirement pension were payable to the wife of a supplementary benefit claimant. As those arrears were a resource for supplementary benefits purposes, the DSS was entitled to withhold the arrears of retirement pension from the wife, even though she had not received the supplementary benefit.[12]

R(IS) 14/94 extended this principle to a case where the recipient of the prescribed benefit was not even a member of the claimant's family for income support purposes. Arrears of invalid care allowance became payable to the claimant's daughter, who was not living with the claimant. The claimant had been receiving a severe disability premium on her income support, which was not payable if invalid care allowance is 'in payment' to anyone for looking after the claimant.

An attractive argument was put to Commissioner Heggs that the operation of SSAA s74(2) should be restricted to cases where the recipient of the prescribed payment is the claimant or a member of the claimant's household. This was based on the fact that the prescribed date is that when the payments 'were to be taken into account'. As the invalid care allowance was not part of the resources of the claimant for income support purposes, it should be excluded from the definition of prescribed payments. The commissioner rejected this argument. She held that the words included a payment that an adjudication officer had to have regard to, rather than take into account for the purposes of calculating resources.[13] She also decided that the invalid care allowance was 'in payment' for the relevant income support

---

10 SSAA s74(2)(a).
11 Overpayments Regs reg 8(1).
12 Para 11.
13 Para 14.

weeks, because this phrase did not require that the payment was made at the time that it should have been.[14]

The decision has been the subject of criticism and it does seem unjust that a claimant should be required to account for payments made to another, leaving him/her with a reduced amount of income support without having previously received a corresponding benefit. The claimant appealed to the Court of Appeal but the appeal was compromised and directions issued to adjudication officers not to use s74 in these circumstances. The relevant legislation was also modified.[15]

Late payment of the prescribed payment

The second condition for operation of the subsection is that an applicable benefit is paid which would not have been paid if the prescribed payment had been made on the prescribed date. A number of points arise in relation to this condition.

First, in considering whether benefit 'would not have been paid' it must be assumed that the proper procedures would have been followed at the proper time. No account can be taken of the possibility of an error or omission by an adjudication officer, even if there is evidence that this would probably have occurred.[16]

Clearly, the question of what the 'prescribed date' is will be crucial and two further points arise out of its definition in the legislation, which is as follows:

> ... the date by which receipt of or entitlement to that benefit would have to be notified to the Secretary of State if it were to be taken into account in determining, whether on review or otherwise, the amount of or entitlement to income support.[17]

The most common use of s74(2) concerns late payments of a benefit. In these cases, when determining the amount recoverable it is important to bear in mind the need to match each instalment of the late benefit with the correct week of applicable benefit.[18] This is because different benefits are paid at different periods in advance or in arrears. This can lead to some very difficult problems of calculation.

14 Para 19.
15 See Mesher, p711 and Income Support (General) Regulations 1987 SI No 1967 Sch 2 para 13(3ZA).
16 *CIS 352/1990* para 7; *CIS 625/1991* paras 4 to 6.
17 Overpayments Regs reg 8(2).
18 *CSB 528/1983* paras 10 to 16, approved in *R(SB) 28/85* para 8 and *CIS 625/1991* para 6.

Finally, there is the potential defect in the legislation mentioned above. In many cases, the claimant will not merely have been paid the benefit late. S/he will also have been informed of his/her entitlement later than the date at which the arrears commence. A claimant is required to notify the Secretary of State of a change of circumstances 'as soon as reasonably practicable after its occurrence'.[19] S/he is not required to anticipate the change of circumstances.

The date is when the source of income 'would have to be notified' not when it 'would have had to have been notified had the claimant been aware of it'. It is therefore suggested that the prescribed date in these circumstances must be the date after the claimant becomes aware of his/her entitlement at which it is reasonably practicable for him/her to notify the Secretary of State. Awareness of the possibility of entitlement is not sufficient. Only when a claimant actually has a source of income is s/he required to declare receipt of it.

EXAMPLE 12.4

F has worked in England for two years, having previously lived for her whole life in Germany. In February she falls sick but has insufficient contributions for sickness benefit and so receives income support. In April she becomes aware of a possible entitlement to German invalidity benefit, which she applies for in May. In July her claim is adjudicated and she receives notification of entitlement. The overseas benefits section of the DSS receives the first instalment of F's benefit in September, backdated to April. The overseas benefit section is only entitled to retain that portion of the benefit from July under SSAA s74(2).

It should be noted, however, that there appears to be no reason why the outstanding amount of benefit should not be recoverable under s74(1) above.[20]

Recovery of benefits from other EU member states

Benefits from other member states of the EU are treated like any other prescribed payment under s74(2), but the interaction with EU law requires separate discussion.

19 Claims and Payments Regs reg 32(1).
20 CIS 501/1993 para 13.

208 Overpayments and Recovery Ch 12

By way of introduction, it should be made clear that under Regulations 1408/71/EEC and 574/72/EEC, where a citizen of the EU goes to another member state to seek work, s/he has a right to 'export' certain social security benefits to the new state of residence.[21] Where the new state has itself made payments in the form of 'assistance', it may request the authorities of the state of origin to withhold the appropriate amount from the payments of the benefit being exported under Regulation 574/72/EEC art 111(3). It is clear that income support is 'assistance' within the meaning of art 111(3).[22] In the United Kingdom this system is dealt with by the Overseas Benefit Directorate in Newcastle-upon-Tyne.

The benefits affected

The right of the member state under art 111(3) is enacted into domestic law by SSAA s74. An amount of foreign benefit is a 'prescribed payment' if it is:

> any payment of benefit under the legislation of any member State other than the United Kingdom concerning the branches of social security mentioned in Article 4(1) of Regulation (EEC) No. 1408/71 on the application of social security schemes to employed persons, to self-employed persons and to members of their families moving within the Community, whether or not the benefit has been acquired by virtue of the provisions of that Regulation.[23]

Article 4 is set out in full in Appendix 1. It clearly covers the vast majority of social security benefits, though not equivalents of income support and housing benefit,[24] which are unlikely to be exportable anyway. Moreover, the categories in art 4(1) have been broadly interpreted. For example, a minimum income payable to pensioners has been held to come within the category of an old-age pension.[25] However, there are four exceptions set out in art 4(4):

a) Social assistance. This has been very narrowly defined in EU law. It will cover many benefits which are only tenuously related to the categories in art 4(1).[26] It appears to be

---

21 A full summary of the provisions appears in *R(SB) 1/91* paras 7 to 8.
22 *CIS 501/1993* para 20.
23 Overpayments Regs reg 8(1)(g).
24 *Jackson and Cresswell v Chief Adjudication Officer* (joined cases C-63/91 and C-64/91) [1992] ECR I-4737, ECJ; *CIS 501/1993* para 21.
25 *Frilli v Belgium* (case 1/72) [1972] ECR 457, ECJ.
26 *Caisse Regionale d'Assurance Maladie de Lille v Palermo* (case 237/78) [1979] ECR 2729, ECJ.

confined mainly to discretionary assessments of need or personal circumstances.[27]
b) Medical assistance.
c) Benefit schemes for victims of war or its consequences. This will cover things such as war pensions, war widows' pensions and the schemes in Germany to compensate victims of Nazi persecution. It appears that the last category requires that the benefit be exclusively related to this purpose and not partially.[28] This was applied in *R(SB) 3/91*, where it was held that although some of the claimant's contributions which gave rise to his entitlement to German invalidity benefit were voluntary, under a scheme for those who had fled Nazi persecution and whose contribution record suffered as a result, the rest of his contributions were not made in this way and so the invalidity benefit did not come within the scope of art 4(4).[29]
d) Special schemes for civil servants.

The claimants covered

Regulation 1408/71/EEC covers workers, the self-employed, and their families and survivors. The first two categories are defined by art 1(a)(i) as 'any person who is insured, compulsorily or on an optional continued basis, for one or more of the contingencies' in art 4(1).

The category of 'employed persons' within the regulation has been interpreted to mean the same as 'worker' within the concept of freedom of movement in the EU. It is not therefore necessary to show that the claimant has worked in both member states. It is sufficient if s/he has worked in any member state of the EU.[30]

Moreover, the claimant need not be currently insured against one of the risks in art 4(1), nor against the particular risk in question. It is enough if s/he has been covered by a national scheme at some point, whatever its nature.[31]

---

27 *Fossi v Bundesknappschaft* (case 79/76) [1977] ECR 667, ECJ; *Tinelli v Berufsgenossenschaft der Chemischen Industrie* (case 144/78) [1979] ECR 757, ECJ.
28 *Vigier v Bundesversicherungsanstalt fur Angestellte* (case 70/80) [1981] ECR 229, ECJ.
29 Para 20(2).
30 *R(IS) 3/91* para 24.
31 *Hoekstra (nee Unger) v Bestuur der Bedrijfsvereniging voor Detailhandel en Ambachten* (case 75/63) [1964] ECR 177, ECJ.

The scope of the legislation

The right to recover foreign benefits under SSAA s74 has been widely interpreted. First, as is made clear by the definition above, the benefit does not itself have to be acquired under the regulation, provided that it falls within its scope.[32]

It does not matter what the purpose of the exported benefit is, provided it comes within the scope of art 4(1). In *R(SB) 1/91* the claimant argued that since his Belgian unemployment benefit was a benefit for him alone, only that proportion of supplementary benefit attributable to him, rather than the whole amount for him and his large family, should be deducted from the payments of Belgian benefit. This argument was rejected as there was no provision for 'dissecting' supplementary benefit.[33] As UK unemployment benefit is deducted in full from income support, the same must apply to foreign benefits.

A foreign benefit will also be looked at as a whole and will not be divided into its component parts. In *CIS 501/1993* part of the claimant's pension was a supplement raising it to a minimum level of income. It was held that this was still part of the old-age pension and came within the scope of art 4(1).[34]

Finally, in the unlikely event that a claimant receives benefit from another member state which relates to a period prior to 24 November 1980, the DSS is not permitted to recover that benefit pursuant to s74(2).[35]

Conversion into sterling

Payments of benefits from member states are likely to be made in the native currency, which must be converted into sterling to be dealt with under SSAA s74(2).[36] Overpayments Regs reg 10 provides that the sum taken into account under s74 will be the net sum after it is converted into sterling.[37] The regulation refers to where a payment 'is made' and so it appears that the whole

---

32 *R(IS) 3/91* para 19(5); *CIS 501/1993* para 13.
33 Para 11.
34 Para 20; *Caisse Regionale d'Assurance Maladie Rhone-Alpes v Gilletti* (joined cases 379 to 381/85 and 93/86) [1987] ECR 955, ECJ.
35 *R(SB) 28/85* para 7. This is the date that the Supplementary Benefits Act 1976 s12, the predecessor of SSAA s74, was amended to allow recovery from EU benefits.
36 SSAA s74(5).
37 Overpayments Regs reg 10, reversing *R(SB) 28/85* para 11 and *CSB 759/1982* para 19.

lump sum is converted at once rather than the periodical amounts converted at the exchange rate prevalent at the time each payment should have been made.[38]

A third party receiving benefit in respect of the claimant

SSAA s74(3) deals with the situation where a third party (described in the section as 'A') has received some benefit in respect of the claimant ('B'), who had been receiving income support. Three conditions must be fulfilled for its operation:

a) A is entitled to a 'prescribed benefit' in respect of B. Four benefits are prescribed:[39] child benefit, child's special allowance, guardians' allowance and any increase for a dependant (for example, that paid for recipients of invalidity benefit).
b) B received an applicable benefit or was part of the household of someone receiving an applicable benefit for the period for which A has become entitled.
c) The calculation of the applicable benefit does not take account of A's entitlement to benefit.

Section 74(3) envisages recovery from A by reducing the payments of arrears by the relevant amount. However, it is again important to be sure that the correct periods are used in the calculation.

EXAMPLE 12.5

G and H are separated and have two sons, I and J, who were living with H. H receives income support, including the relevant premiums for the boys, from June 1992 to January 1995. In June 1993 I left to live with G, who is self-employed but has been unable to work through illness. H disclosed I's departure to the DSS but this was not acted on, so the overpaid income support is not recoverable under SSAA s71. In June 1995 G claims sickness benefit for the period since January 1993 and his entitlement is backdated one year to June 1994 as he has shown good cause for his delay in claiming. He is awarded invalidity benefit with an increase for I for the year. The DSS wants to recover the whole of the overpaid income support child's premium from the arrears of increase payable in respect of I. However, it is only entitled to

---

38 Reversing *R(SB) 28/85* para 10.
39 Overpayments Regs reg 9.

> deduct the premium paid from June 1994 to January 1995 from the arrears. It cannot recover any excess income support paid to H for any period prior to that for which G is entitled to the increase.

Once the three conditions are met, then the abatement of the benefit is carried out 'at the discretion of the authority administering it'. This must mean, it is suggested, that the adjudication officer responsible for adjudicating A's benefit exercises the discretion and not the Secretary of State.

Enforcement

SSAA envisages that recovery of amounts falling under s74(2) or (3) will usually occur by abatement from the prescribed payment. This means that the relevant amount will be deducted from the prescribed payment before it is paid to the recipient.

However, this system sometimes does not work because the office administering the prescribed payment does not make the connection with the third party's receipt of an applicable benefit. This is what happened in *R(IS) 14/94*, where the arrears of invalid care allowance were paid to the claimant's daughter before the local office became aware of the situation. In these cases, recovery of an amount 'otherwise than by way of abatement' is possible from 'the person to whom it was paid' in the case of s74(2)[40] and 'the person to whom the prescribed benefit in question was paid' in other cases.[41]

In *R(IS) 14/94*, recovery was being sought from the claimant rather than her daughter under s74(2). Commissioner Heggs held that 'an amount' in s74(4)(a) could cover the overpayment of income support as well as the arrears of invalid care allowance, and as the claimant was 'the person to whom it was paid', the overpayment could be enforced against the claimant as well as her daughter.[42]

It is suggested that this wide interpretation is wrong. It is clear that if s74(2) stands alone, the overpayment is deducted from the arrears of invalid care allowance and that the amount cannot be

40 SSAA s74(4)(a).
41 Ibid s74(4)(b).
42 Para 15.

recovered from the income support claimant. Section 74(4) deals with the situation where this mechanism does not work: it refers to 'an amount which could have been recovered by abatement by virtue of subsection (2)'. The words 'an amount' ought to be interpreted consistently throughout s74(4), and 'an amount' could not have been recovered from the income support claimant by abatement under s74(2). The person to which 'an amount' was paid cannot therefore be the income support recipient, and so s74(4) cannot be applied against him/her.

To put it another way, the words 'an amount' must be read as 'an amount of the prescribed payment equivalent to the relevant amount as defined in subsection (2)(b)'. It is significant that in s74(4) the phrase 'the relevant amount' is not used, which corresponds to the amount of income support received under s74(2)(b). As against this, it must be conceded that if recovery was to be restricted to the person in receipt of the prescribed payment, one would have expected this to be made clear in s74(4)(a) as it is in s74(4)(b).

If the argument above is wrong and *R(IS) 14/94* was correctly decided, it is nevertheless clear from s74(4)(b) that there can be no recovery of amounts under s74(3) from B or from the member of B's family receiving an applicable benefit if the mechanism fails against A.

EXAMPLE **12.6**

In EXAMPLE 12.5 above, if the arrears of invalidity benefit increase are paid to G, there can be no enforcement under SSAA s74(4)(b) against H.

In the case of recovery under s74(2) of a payment from public funds in this country, it is provided that 'the authority responsible for making it may abate it by the relevant amount'. The use of the word 'may' appears to give the authority a discretion. Where the payment is another benefit, the responsible authority will be an adjudication officer, from whom an appeal will lie to a tribunal.

The normal methods of recovery under SSAA s71 are applicable to amounts sought under s74.[43] Thus there can be deduction from prescribed benefits and enforcement in the county court.

---

43 SSAA s71(8)(c)

Challenging decisions

An appeal will lie in the normal way to a social security appeal tribunal. It must be borne in mind that the merits of the situation will not generally be relevant. Recovery under s74 is an absolute right if the conditions are shown. It is not dependent on any breach of duty by the claimant.

However, the exercise of the express discretion in s74(3) and that implicit in s74(2)(a) by the adjudication officer will be subject to appeal to a tribunal. It is further suggested that the tribunal must reconsider the whole decision to exercise the discretion to enforce recovery. It can substitute its own decision if it disagrees with that of the adjudication officer. It does not have to be satisfied that the decision of the adjudication officer is unreasonable in a judicial review sense. It seems therefore that claimants can use these provisions to invoke arguments on the merits of recovery in their individual cases.

As elsewhere, there is the possibility of challenging the Secretary of State's decision to enforce recovery by judicial review in extreme cases.

CHAPTER 13
Payments under the severe hardship rule

In 1988, the government severely restricted the rights of most of those aged under 18 to receive income support. Previously, this category of claimants was treated in the same way as others. Since the changes, most claimants[1] under the age of 18 are only entitled to income support if the Secretary of State (or, rather, the Severe Hardship Unit acting on the minister's behalf) decides that the claimant will suffer severe hardship if s/he does not receive income support. A similar rule will apply to income-based jobseeker's allowance.

The hardship direction

In a case where it appears that the claimant will suffer severe hardship, the Secretary of State issues a direction to that effect.[2] This direction may be revoked by the Secretary of State at a later stage on one of three grounds, which will have the same meaning as the corresponding grounds for review of an adjudication officer's decision:[3]

a) there has been a change of circumstances;[4]

---

1 For those categories of persons under 18 who do not have to fulfil this criterion, see the Income Support (General) Regulations 1987 SI No 1967 reg 13A and Sch 1A.
2 Social Security Contributions and Benefits Act 1992 (SSCBA) s125(1); Jobseekers Act 1995 s16(1).
3 SSAA s25. See pp19–20 above for a full discussion of these grounds for a review.
4 SSCBA s125(3); Jobseekers Act 1995 s16(3)(a).

b) the direction was given in ignorance or under a mistake as to a material fact, and there is no severe hardship in light of the true facts;[5]
c) in the case of jobseeker's allowance, that training has been rejected without good cause.

The issuing of the direction and its revocation are decisions of the Secretary of State and so the adjudication officer cannot review these decisions under the normal procedure. Therefore it is not possible for the DSS to use SSAA s71 to recover an overpayment where the direction was issued or not revoked due to a breach of duty. This situation is dealt with under SSAA s71A for jobseeker's allowance and s 72 for income supoprt.

The content of the sections

The DSS does not have an absolute right to recover the overpaid income support in these cases. Recovery is dependent on a breach of duty. The wording of the sections is very similar to that of s71 when setting out the grounds for recovery.

The difference in the two sections lies in the fact that the existence of most of the requirements for recovery is certified by the Secretary of State rather than decided by the adjudication officer. The Secretary of State issues a certificate which is conclusive evidence[6] of the following matters:

a) The existence of a breach of duty.[7]
b) Who committed the breach of duty.[8] Although the section does not explicitly state that the overpayment can be recovered from persons other than the claimant, s72(7)[9] implicitly makes this clear.

Example 13.1
A is 16 years old. He runs away from home and complains to B, a social worker, that he was being abused by his parents. When A claims income support, B makes a statement to this effect to the

---

5   SSCBA s125(4); Jobseekers Act 1995 s16(3)(c).
6   SSAA ss71A(6) and 72(6).
7   Ibid ss71A(3) and 72(3).
8   Ibid ss71A(4)(a) and 72(4)(a).
9   Which makes SSAA s71(3) (overpayment recoverable from anyone committing breach of duty) applicable to recovery under the sections.

Severe Hardship Unit. This is subsequently found to be false. The DSS may proceed against B under SSAA s72 as well as A.

c) Whether the overpayment was made in consequence of the breach of duty.[10]

d) The period during which income support would not have been payable were it not for the breach of duty.[11]

The adjudication officer issues the decision that the overpayment is recoverable and is also responsible for calculation of the amount recoverable.[12]

Challenging SSAA s72 decisions

Appeals to a tribunal

Only two aspects of a s72 decision are subject to challenge before a tribunal, namely the existence and completeness of the Secretary of State's certificate and the amount of the overpayment. As to the former, it seems likely that the minister must make explicit reference to each of the elements of recovery which must be certified. If s/he fails to do this, recovery will not be possible.

EXAMPLE 13.2
A direction, made in February, that C will suffer severe hardship unless income support is paid, is revoked in October because she failed to disclose the fact that she got a job in July. The Secretary of State's certificate states that, 'C failed to disclose the material fact that she found employment in July and income support would not have been payable between then and October'. The adjudication officer issues a SSAA s72 decision seeking recovery from February. C can appeal to a tribunal on the grounds that (a) the Secretary of State has not certified that the overpayment was in consequence of her breach of duty; and (b) the amount of the overpayment is excessive, because recovery is only permissible from July.

10 SSAA ss71A(4)(b) and 72(4)(b).
11 Ibid ss71A(5) and 72(5).
12 As to calculation of the amount, the same rules apply as under SSAA s71: ss71A(7) and 72(7), applying s71(6). For a consideration of these rules, see chapter 8.

Judicial review

If a claimant wishes to challenge the content of the Secretary of State's certificate, then this must be by judicial review (see pp185–187 above on the grounds and procedure). In addition, if the Secretary of State cannot show any of the grounds for revoking the hardship direction, judicial review will lie to quash the decision to revoke.

In revoking the direction and considering the various elements which must be certified for recovery of the overpayment, the Secretary of State must presumably follow the law under SSAA s71 as set out previously in this work. A failure to do this will make the certificate susceptible to challenge on the ground of illegality.

> EXAMPLE 13.3
> D has been thrown out of the family home at the age of 17. Her great aunt has set up a complex trust fund which is the subject of litigation. D knows nothing of this trust. In February, when D applies for income support, the legal position is that D has no rights under the trust, but in July the Court of Appeal rules that D is a beneficiary under the trust. D is not aware of this until the family solicitor contacts her in September. The Secretary of State revokes his direction on the grounds of change of circumstances, and certifies that an overpayment has occurred due to D's failure to disclose her rights under the trust. D can apply for judicial review on the ground of illegality that: (a) a court decision changing the interpretation of the law from what had previously been understood does not amount to a change of circumstances; and (b) as she knew nothing of the trust, there is no 'failure' to disclose.

Enforcement

A severe hardship overpayment is recoverable by execution through the county court as under s71.[13] However, it is not possible to recover a s72 overpayment by deduction from other benefits, because s71(8) does not refer to an overpayment under

---

13 SSAA ss71A(7) and 72(7), referring to s71(10).

either s71A or s72 as being one of the overpayments recoverable under that subsection

> **EXAMPLE 13.4**
> E failed to disclose an award of disability living allowance while he was the subject of a SSAA s125 direction. The DSS is not allowed to recover the overpayment by deduction from his benefit.

CHAPTER 14
Overpayments by credit transfer

An absolute right to recovery is embodied in Overpayments Regs reg 11. It aims to deal with the situation where a claimant has been overpaid directly into his/her bank account.

What must be made clear at the outset is that, although recovery is possible under reg 11 without showing a breach of duty by the claimant, those who have their benefit paid in this way do not lose the protection of SSAA s71 in the normal case. Instead this regulation only allows recovery of overpayments which are 'materially due'[1] to the credit transfer arrangements. Thus, it is chiefly aimed at circumstances where, due to an official error, a claimant is paid more than s/he is entitled to. As will appear below, the regulation is defective and presents difficulties for the DSS. However, there can be recoverability under s71 provided a breach of duty can be shown.

Recoverability under reg 11 is a decision made by the adjudicating authorities, not the Secretary of State. There are four conditions that must be present before the Secretary of State has the absolute right to recovery.

The four conditions
Revision of the determination
The reason why the legislation appears not to achieve its aim lies in the first condition for recoverability. The enabling legislation giving the Secretary of State the power to make Overpayments Regs reg 11 is SSAA s71(4). Section 71(5) reads, in so far as material, as follows:

1   Overpayments Regs reg 11(2)(a).

> Except where regulations otherwise prescribe, an amount shall not be recoverable under ... regulations under subsection (4) above unless –
> (a) the determination in pursuance of which it was paid has been ... revised on a review ...

Clearly, therefore, just as with recovery under s71(1), review and revision of the claimant's award of benefit is a necessary precondition for recovery under reg 11.[2] The problem is that reg 11 is primarily aimed at cases where the determination on the claim is correct, but the wrong amount has been paid due to official error. Where the determination is correct, none of the conditions for review and revision (see pp19–20 above) will be met and it will therefore not be possible to revise the determination.

It is not possible to use Overpayments Regs reg 12 to dispense with the requirement for review and revision. That regulation only applies 'where the fact and circumstances of the misrepresentation or non-disclosure do not provide a basis for reviewing and revising the award'. As such, it is clearly only relevant to recovery based on a breach of duty under s71 and has no application to reg 11.

A possible option for the DSS is to argue that the excess paid to the claimant was not paid 'in pursuance of' the award at all because only the amount of the award can be paid 'in pursuance of' the award. This argument is based on one of the possible constructions of s71(5) considered in *CS 102/1993*.[3] If this argument is correct, then it would seem that s71(5) has no application to these cases, because as far as the extra amount is concerned, there is no 'entitlement' at all to review.

There are three objections to this argument. First, it is thoroughly artificial. The payment made into the claimant's account is one sum: it is not divided into two sums, one being the correct amount and the other being the incorrect excess. Either the whole payment is made 'in pursuance of' the award or none of it is.

The second objection is linked to the first. *CS 102/1993* was concerned with a case where a payment had been made after the claimant's entitlement had been revised and terminated, rather than revised and reduced. It is much more tenable to argue that

---

2 See, eg, *R(SB) 7/91* para 7 and other authorities discussed at pp21–33 above.
3 Para 15.

an amount is not paid 'in pursuance of' an award when there is no award at all than it is when there is an award, but for a lower amount than that paid.

Finally, Commissioner Rowland stated in *CS 102/1993* that he preferred to construe those words 'very loosely so that it is enough that the person ... operating the direct credit system is doing so in purported compliance with the determination'.[4] Applying this to the case currently under discussion, an amount in excess of the award is paid in purported compliance with that award. Accordingly it is suggested that if this argument is put forward, it should be rejected.

EXAMPLE 14.1

A claims income support. She is single without dependants. Her entitlement is correctly determined by the adjudication officer at £50 per week, and appears as such on the letter sent to her. Due to a computer defect, however, twice as much income support as she is entitled to is transferred into her bank account. Recovery under Overpayments Regs reg 11 is not possible, as there are no grounds for the adjudication officer to revise A's entitlement.

It seems therefore that the only cases in which this condition can be fulfilled are where the claimant's award has been revised and lowered but the revision does not come into effect until after further payments have been made by credit transfer at the higher rate. This, however, raises questions of whether the overpayment is 'materially due' to the arrangements (see below).

A payment in 'excess of entitlement'

Naturally, there must be an overpayment for the regulation to operate. This requirement goes beyond that, however. The 'entitlement' of the claimant at any given time will be whatever amount is awarded by the adjudication officer. If an award is too high due to the adjudication officer's error, then the claimant is still 'entitled' to the higher amount and to all monies paid under the award until such time as the award is reviewed and revised. This condition further reinforces the first condition above, that

---

4 Paras 15 and 16.

The Secretary of State's certificate

The third condition is that the Secretary of State certifies that the excess payment is 'materially due' to the credit transfer arrangements. It is this condition that prevents the DSS using the regulation as a way of circumventing the requirements of SSAA s71.

The use of the word 'materially' suggests that it is not necessary for the credit transfer arrangements to be the sole cause of the overpayment. It would suffice for it to be a significant factor. On the other hand, the Secretary of State would have to be satisfied that the system was a material factor in relation to each penny of the amount sought to be recovered. Thus if part of an overpayment is caused by an error in the adjudication officer's calculations and part is caused by problems with the credit transfer arrangements, the Secretary of State may only certify the latter as being recoverable under Overpayments Regs reg 11. It must also be borne in mind that the same regulations as to calculation of the amounts owing apply to reg 11 recovery as under s71 recovery.[5]

It must be borne in mind that it has only been possible for income support to be payable by credit transfer since April 1993. Where recovery of income support is sought, it is therefore necessary to check that the payments in question do not pre-date this period.

Notice of the regulation given to the claimant

The final requirement is that 'notice of the effect which this regulation would have, in the event of an overpayment, was given in writing to the beneficiary, or to a person acting for him, before he agreed to the arrangement'.[6]

The standard procedure by which this is fulfilled has varied over time and between benefits, but recently has always required the signing of a particular form following the issue of a notice outlining the effect of Overpayments Regs reg 11. It should be noted that as the regulation only requires notice to be given,

---

5 SSAA s71(6). See chapter 8 for a detailed consideration of these rules.
6 Overpayments Regs reg 11(2)(b).

there need be no proof of the signing of the form. In the event of recovery being sought for periods prior to 6 April 1987, the requirements are slightly different,[7] in that a specific statement is required that the claimant has read and understood that payment would be required in these circumstances.

Challenging decisions

Appeals to a tribunal

Because recoverability under Overpayments Regs reg 11 is stated to be a matter for 'the adjudicating authority', it follows that a challenge to a decision on the basis that one of the conditions for recoverability is not met will be by appeal to a social security appeal tribunal. The exception is the Secretary of State's issue of the certificate. A challenge before a tribunal is only possible on the grounds that no such certificate has been issued. Once it is shown that the certificate exists, the tribunal cannot consider the merits of the Secretary of State's action and the claimant must consider judicial review.

As the burden of proof of showing all the elements of SSAA s71 recovery generally rests on the DSS (see pp165–167 above), it seems logical that the same rule should prevail here.[8]

EXAMPLE 14.2

The adjudication officer decides that an overpayment is recoverable from B under Overpayments Regs reg 11. B claims that: (a) he was never issued with the form informing him of the implications of the regulation; (b) the review was not carried out properly; and (c) in any case, he never received the payment in question. The adjudication officer will have to provide specific proof that all these elements are met.

---

7 Ibid reg 11(3).
8 *AO Guide*, paras 12207 to 12210, gives examples of the evidence which could be relied on by an adjudication officer to prove that the claimant has had the regulation drawn to his/her attention.

Judicial review

The merits of the decision of the Secretary of State to issue the certificate stating that the overpayment is related to the credit transfer system are subject to judicial review if the claimant can demonstrate any of the usual grounds (see pp185–187 above).

> EXAMPLE **14.3**
> C financed her business with a second mortgage on her house. The business collapsed and C claims income support. She receives housing costs which are paid by credit transfer rather than direct to the mortgage lender. The adjudication officer mistakenly allows interest on both mortgages. The DSS wants to recover the overpayment, but there has been no breach of duty by C and so recovery under SSAA s71 is not possible. The Secretary of State issues a certificate stating that the overpayment is related to the credit transfer system, although there is no evidence of this. C may seek to have the minister's decision quashed by order of certiorari on the ground of irrationality.

In extreme cases a challenge to the Secretary of State's decision to enforce the right to recovery may also be possible.

Request for non-enforcement

As with all types of recovery, an attempt can be made to persuade the Secretary of State not to pursue his/her right of recovery (see pp178–181 above).

Enforcement

The same mechanisms for enforcing recovery under SSAA s71 are available for recovery under Overpayments Regs reg 11. Therefore, deduction from other benefits[9] and by execution in the county court[10] are both possible.

---

9 SSAA s71(8)(b). See pp192–196 above.
10 Ibid s71(10). See p191 above

CHAPTER 15
Miscellaneous rights of recovery

This chapter deals briefly with other rights of recovery of benefit which advisers can expect to deal with, albeit rarely; awareness of their existence and an outline knowledge of the form they take is important.

Recovery of social fund payments

There is an absolute right to recover repayable social fund loans under SSAA s78. The people from whom recovery can be made are defined in s78(3) as:

a) The recipient of the award or the person 'for the benefit of whom it was made', if this is different.
b) The partner of one of these people, apparently regardless of whether they were living together at the time that the loan was made.
c) '... a person who is liable to maintain the person by or on behalf of whom the application for the award was made or any person in relation to whose needs the award was made.' The rules for liability to maintain are discussed at pp230-231 below.

Repayable loans

The power to determine whether a social fund loan is repayable is given to a social fund officer[1] but since an officer is obliged to follow the directions of the Secretary of State,[2] the power

1 SSCBA s139(3).
2 Ibid s140(2).

effectively lies with the latter. It is, however, clear from the above provision that an officer can only order the repayment of those items over which s/he has jurisdiction. These do not include either maternity or funeral expenses.[3] Under the current Social Fund Directions, a community care grant is not repayable, but the two types of loan are.[4]

Such a loan 'shall be repayable upon such terms and conditions as before the award is paid the Secretary of State notifies to the person by or on behalf of whom the application for it is made'.[5] This wording strongly suggests that notification is mandatory and if the Secretary of State fails to make such notification, the loan is not repayable. As the Secretary of State will be purporting to recover the loan, the correct remedy is judicial review. If recovery through the courts is attempted, the unlawful nature of such recovery can be raised as a defence.[6]

Maternity and funeral expenses

There is no provision for recovery of maternity expenses in normal circumstances, although there can be SSAA s71 recovery if a breach of duty is shown.[7] Funeral expenses, on the other hand, are recoverable in all cases from the estate in the same way that a personal representative can deduct them.[8] The recovery takes priority over all other debts of the estate in both England and Scotland.[9]

The decision to recover a funeral payment is for the Secretary of State and no appeal to a tribunal lies against the decision.[10] Again, the proper course is judicial review proceedings or defending a court action.

---

3 This is because by SSCBA s139(1) the officer only has jurisdiction over payments under s138(1)(b). These items are payable under s138(1)(a).
4 Direction 6.
5 SSCBA s139(4).
6 *Wandsworth Borough Council v Winder* [1985] AC 461, HL; *Warwick District Council v Freeman* (1994) 27 HLR 616, CA.
7 SSAA s71(11)(e).
8 Ibid s78(4).
9 *R(SB) 18/84* paras 8 and 10 respectively.
10 *CIS 616/1990* para 10.

Method of recovery

The usual method of recovery from recipients of a social fund loan will be by way of deductions from benefit. Virtually any benefit can be the subject of a deduction, with the notable exception of disability living allowance.[11]

A recent battle in the courts has concerned the power of the Secretary of State to make deductions under this provision after a claimant has been made bankrupt in England and Wales or sequestrated in Scotland. At the time of writing, the DSS has been victorious in both jurisdictions. Taking Scotland first, in *Mulvey v Secretary of State for Social Security*[12] it was initially decided that SSAA s78 had to be read in the context of the general law of sequestration and that it would give the Secretary of State an unfair advantage over other creditors to allow him/her to make deductions from the applicant's income support. The DSS's appeal was allowed, it being decided that s78 operated outside the general law relating to sequestration and therefore took priority.[13] The claimant is appealing to the House of Lords.

In England, Keene J came to the same conclusion in *R v Secretary of State for Social Security ex p Taylor*.[14] There it was decided that the provisions of the Insolvency Act 1986 did not operate to exclude s78.[15] Furthermore, the Secretary of State was not enforcing his right of recovery against the claimant's property, as there was only entitlement to the net amount of benefit received.[16] This latter conclusion is clearly wrong as it fails to recognise the distinction between entitlement to and payment of benefit. The adjudication officer determines the claimant's entitlement. The Secretary of State is then required by law to pay it, unless s/he has some statutory right to make a deduction. The claimant was granted leave to appeal.

---

11 SSAA s78(2); Social Fund (Recovery by Deductions from Benefits) Regulations 1988 SI No 35 reg 3.
12 1995 SC 102, Ct Sess (Outer House). See A Walker, 'Reclaiming social fund loans from bankrupts' (1994) 218 *SCOLAG* 184 for an interesting description of the background to the case.
13 (1995) *Times* 24 November (1995) 227 *SCOLAG* 177, Ct Sess (Inner House).
14 (1996) *Times* 5 February, QBD.
15 *Taylor* (official transcript, p20).
16 Ibid p18.

The right to recover from benefits is 'without prejudice' to other rights of recovery and so the Secretary of State could bring court proceedings, although s/he cannot use the procedures of enforcement available under SSAA s71 (see pp190–191 above).

Recovery of interim payments

The DSS has become progressively less willing in recent years to make interim payments to claimants, and its power to make them has recently been reduced, and so the power to recover them may be less significant than previously. The rights to recover interim payments can be discussed under three headings. It should be noted that although the decision to make interim payments is exclusively for the Secretary of State, some of the decision-making powers are given to the adjudication officer and will therefore attract statutory rights of appeal to a tribunal.

One important proviso is that the claimant must have been given notice at the time the interim payment was made of the effect of the recovery provisions if the payment proves to be excessive.[17] A failure to do so will render the overpayment irrecoverable, and it will be for the DSS to prove that the notice was issued in the event of any dispute. Payments arising out of late receipt of maintenance and certain interim payments of disability living allowance are the only situations where notice of the recovery provisions is not required.[18]

Interim payments made due to late receipt of maintenance

The first situation covered by these provisions is where an interim payment of income support is made because the claimant has not been paid certain types of maintenance by a former partner. There are two means of recovery in such cases:

a) Withholding of arrears of child support maintenance by the Secretary of State.[19]
b) Where a final decision on entitlement to a claim cannot be made immediately and the adjudication officer determines

---

17 Overpayments Regs reg 2(2).
18 Ibid reg 2(3) and (4).
19 Ibid reg 3(b).

that the interim payment was an overpayment.[20] The amount of the overpayment is determined according to the same rules as for recovery under SSAA s71 (see chapter 8 above) and recovery is also by the same means (see chapter 11 above).[21]

Offsetting interim payments

Where an award of benefit is made following an interim payment, the adjudication officer is required to offset the amount from the award of benefit.[22] If this is not done, the Secretary of State can reduce the payments made on that award or any subsequent award of the same benefit.[23] These powers will be used only where the award exceeds the amount of the interim payment or it is likely to be a successful means of recovery.

Determination of overpaid interim payments

An adjudication officer can determine that an interim overpayment is recoverable in other situations. It is necessary that there has been no award of benefit, or an entitlement less than the interim payment, following a determination or withdrawal of the claim, or a failure to complete a valid claim.[24] Such overpayments are again calculated and recovered according to the powers in relation to SSAA s71 cases.

Recovery on the grounds of failure to maintain

The importance of the provisions for the Secretary of State to take action against those who fail to fulfil obligations to maintain people who claim income support are somewhat diminished following the introduction of the Child Support Act 1991, but nevertheless it remains a spectre hanging over broken relationships where one partner is likely to have to rely on benefit.[25] The aim

---

20 Ibid reg 4(3)(c).
21 Ibid reg 4(2).
22 Ibid reg 3(a)(i).
23 Ibid reg 3(a)(ii).
24 Ibid reg 4(3).
25 See Street, *Money and Family Breakdown* (2nd edn, LAG, 1994) for details of the scheme in this context.

Ch 15 Miscellaneous rights of recovery   231

of the scheme is to prevent the DSS incurring expense which should be borne by the liable person.

A person ('the liable person') is liable for the maintenance of his/her spouse and natural children, whether the couple were married at the time of the birth of the children or not. An undertaking to maintain an immigrant also makes a person liable for these purposes.[26] The Secretary of State is given two powers to reduce the DSS's outlay on those who should be maintained within this definition:

a) An application to the magistrates' court in England or Wales or to the sheriff court in Scotland for a maintenance order against the liable person.[27] On such application, the court will award such maintenance as it considers appropriate. In so far as the amounts paid correspond to income support paid to the maintained person, the Secretary of State receives the payments. The balance is received by the maintained person. It is no bar to the Secretary of State taking proceedings that the maintained partner has agreed not to claim maintenance[28] or that there is a consent order to this effect, in exchange for the transfer of the matrimonial home.[29] If the maintained person comes off income support, the order is transferred to him/her.

b) Enforcement of an existing order.[30] The Secretary of State is given all the rights of the parent in whose favour the order is made. The payments under the order must be made to the parent, but the DSS can then adjust the parent's income support and recover benefit under SSAA s74 if appropriate (see chapter 12 above).

Recovery of income support paid after a trade dispute

The normal rules about entitlement to income support are drastically modified if the claimant is involved in a trade dispute so as to reduce the entitlement of strikers to well below subsistence level.[31] A

---

26 SSAA s78(6).
27 Ibid s106.
28 *National Assistance Board v Parkes* [1955] 2 QB 506, CA.
29 *Hulley v Thompson* [1981] 1 WLR 519, CA.
30 SSAA s108.
31 SSCBA s126.

purported incentive to return to work is provided by a provision that when the striker returns to work, s/he is entitled to income support under almost normal principles for 15 days after his/her return.[32] That money is then recovered from the wages paid by the employer.[33]

The decision to make this deduction is a decision of the adjudication officer and can be challenged on appeal to a tribunal.

---

32 Ibid s127.
33 Overpayments Regs regs 18 to 29.

CHAPTER 16

Recovery from compensation payments

This chapter examines three ways in which benefits can be recouped from different types of compensation payment received by a claimant. Knowledge of these provisions is perhaps less important for lay advisers than it is for those who are legally qualified, who need proper knowledge of when these provisions apply so as to properly advise their clients in the course of litigation. Failure to be aware of the implications of this legislation may result in advice given to clients having severe financial consequences for them.

The Compensation Recovery Scheme

The Social Security Act 1989 (SSA) introduced new provisions for the recovery of benefits from defendants to personal injury claims. The legislation, as will appear below, is extremely widely drawn and has caused great controversy, with over 50 parliamentary questions concerning the scheme since its introduction and a number of MPs raising cases of constituents who have been effectively denied proper compensation for serious injuries by its operation.

The Secretary of State recently announced that the DSS was examining how the scheme was working in practice and would consider reform,[1] but until action is taken the provisions remain a considerable complication for both plaintiffs and defendants in considering how a personal injury action can be compromised. It has, however, become a considerable weapon in the hands of

1 Department of Social Security, *Press Release 96/26*, 14 February 1996.

the latter in forcing plaintiffs to accept settlements of the maximum exempt payment of £2,500, which often bears no relation to the true value of their claims. Following the Court of Appeal's suggestion that the recoverable benefits can be awarded as a head of special damages,[2] it should now be possible to avoid this injustice. Nevertheless, there will still be situations which raise problems where the DSS is seeking to claw back more than it is entitled to and legal representatives will need to take the proper steps to protect their clients' interests.

Procedure

A specialist wing of the Benefits Agency, the Compensation Recovery Unit (CRU), administers the scheme. A heavy administrative burden potentially lies on the defendant, or in reality the relevant insurance company ('the compensator'), on the plaintiff ('the victim') and on the plaintiff's employer, particularly on the former.[3]

The procedure varies slightly in different cases, but the basic principles are always applicable. It is essential to carry out all form-filling within the maximum time period allowed. For the victim, all the incentive that should be required in this respect is that the compensator is forbidden to pay out any compensation until the CRU has calculated the benefit recoverable.[4]

a) When the victim first seeks compensation (not when proceedings are issued) the compensator notifies the CRU on form CRU 1 of the victim's details. This must be done in all cases, whether or not it is thought that the victim has been receiving benefit. This must be done within 14 days.[5]

b) The CRU acknowledges receipt, sends a CRU 4 to the compensator and informs the victim of his/her involvement.

c) When it is ready to make a payment of compensation, the compensator applies for a certificate of total benefit ('the certificate') on form CRU 4. This contains the victim's details and a calculation of all the benefit which the Secretary

---

2 *Hassall and Pether v Secretary of State for Social Security* [1995] 1 WLR 821 at pp818H to 819C, CA. See pp246–247 below.
3 SSAA s94.
4 Ibid s84(7).
5 Social Security (Recoupment) Regulations 1990 SI No 322 (hereafter the 'Recoupment Regs') regs 5 and 8(1)(a).

of State claims to have been paid in consequence of the accident, injury or disease giving rise to the claim. A certificate remains in force for a period set out on its face. After that date expires, the compensator may apply for a new certificate or the CRU may issue one of its own volition.[6]

d) The CRU acknowledges receipt of the request for a certificate 'as soon as reasonably practicable'.[7] This is so that the compensator knows when the time limit for the provision of the certificate starts to run.

e) The CRU must provide the certificate within four weeks of the date that the request is received.[8] If it fails to do so, the compensator's liability to repay recoupable benefit becomes unenforceable unless the Secretary of State has removed the effect of the section due to problems with normal means of communication.[9]

f) When the amount of the compensation has been settled, the compensator deducts the amount shown on the certificate, pays it to the Secretary of State within 14 days and gives the victim a certificate of deduction certifying the amount deducted from the compensation payment.[10]

Application of the provisions

The scheme introduced by the SSA 1989 only applies to compensation payments made after 3 September 1990 in relation to accidents or injuries occurring after 1 January 1989 or diseases which result in a claim for benefit after the latter date.[11]

The scheme bites on 'a compensation payment ... in consequence of an accident, injury or disease' suffered by the victim. The deduction is the amount of any 'relevant benefits' paid 'during the

---

6 SSAA s84.
7 Recoupment Regs reg 10.
8 SSAA s95(1)(a). From 27 April 1995, a period of three months was substituted pursuant to the power in s96(4) to substitute a different time period: Social Security (Recoupment) (Prolongation of Period for Furnishing of Certificate of Total Benefit) Order 1995 SI No 1152. Such orders have to be renewed every three months and this does not seem to have been done.
9 Ibid s96.
10 Ibid ss84(1) and 83.
11 Ibid s81(7). For older injuries and payments under the limit of £2,500 the old law will apply: see Kemp and Kemp, *The Quantum of Damages* (looseleaf, Sweet and Maxwell) paras 10-055ff.

relevant period' and which are 'in respect of that accident, injury or disease'.[12] The meaning of these terms will be considered in term.

'Compensation payment'

In deciding whether a payment comes within the scope of the scheme, the DSS will have to show that two criteria are met.[13-14] Subject to these rules, the legislation bites on 'any payment'. It has consistently been held that this means that there can be recovery, not just from such portion of the compensation such as loss of earnings which has already been partially compensated by the award of benefit, but also over a period where loss of earnings has not been compensated, and from compensation for pain, suffering and loss of amenity.[15] This has probably been the source of greatest grievance to victims.

a) The payment is made 'to or in respect of the victim in consequence of the accident, injury or disease in question'. The phrase 'in respect of' relates to the situation where a claim is made by personal representatives on behalf of a deceased victim. Benefits received by the deceased are recoverable under the scheme. It should be noted, however, that this is not true of claims by the victim's relatives under the Fatal Accidents Act 1976, which are exempt payments.[16] There must be a clear causal link between the accident and the compensation payment.

EXAMPLE 16.1

A Ltd employs B. B claims compensation for an injury at work but does not eventually pursue his claim, even though A is liable. B is forced by his injuries to be on long-term sick leave and is eventually made redundant. He is paid incapacity benefit and pursues an unfair dismissal claim against A, which is successful. Although the benefit is clearly paid as a consequence of B's injuries, the compensation for unfair dismissal is not. The facts of B's redundancy and unfair dismissal claim break the link between the compensation payment and the injury.

---

12 SSAA s82(1)(a).
13-14 Ibid s81(1).
15 *CCR 1/1993* para 8: 'it covers economic and non-economic loss'. This wide definition was approved in *Hassall and Pether v Secretary of State for Social Security* [1995] 1 WLR 812 at p817E, CA, and followed in *CCR 2/1993* para 6; *CCR 5/1993* para 4.
16 SSAA s81(3)(c).

b) The payment must be made 'by or on behalf' of the defendant who is liable, or under a 'compensation scheme for motor accidents'. The latter refers to payments by the Motor Insurers' Bureau where responsible drivers are not identifiable.

The scheme applies to awards made by an order of the court, whether by consent or following judgment, and to settlements agreed before trial. In the latter case, care must be taken by those advising plaintiffs that it is clearly understood by all parties whether the agreed sum includes or excludes the amount to be paid to the CRU. Any misunderstanding between the parties will rebound to the disadvantage of the plaintiff, since the compensator will still be obliged to deduct the amount on the certificate.[17]

There are special rules dealing with different types of payment. Situations where there is more than one compensator are dealt with by requiring the CRU to reduce the amount recoverable from one compensator by amounts paid by other compensators. The latter then acquire rights of contribution from the former, so there is no advantage in delaying in the hope that the other compensators will pick up the bill.[18]

Structured settlements, under which periodical payments are made to a victim, sometimes in addition to a lump sum, are dealt with by requiring a single payment to the Secretary of State when the periodical payments start.[19]

Where a compensator makes a payment into court, there is no liability to pay recoverable benefits until there is payment out to the victim. The compensator may include or exclude the recoverable benefits from the payment in. The 'relevant period' will end on the day of the payment in if it is accepted within 21 days, otherwise it runs to the day of acceptance.[20]

Exempt payments

Advisers need to be aware of the categories of exempt payments, to which the scheme does not apply. By far the most significant is a 'small payment', where the amount or total amounts paid to the victim is £2,500 or less.[21] This figure refers to the gross amount of compensation and not the net amount after the

---

17 *Rees v West Glamorgan County Council* [1994] PIQR P37, CA.
18 SSAA ss86 and 87.
19 Ibid s88.
20 Ibid s93.
21 Ibid s85; Recoupment Regs reg 3.

compensator has deducted the sum recoverable by the Secretary of State.[22]

There is a large number of other exemptions of varying degrees of importance.[23] Payments under various statutory schemes such as criminal injuries compensation and vaccine damage payments are exempt. Redundancy payments are exempt if they are deducted from the compensation payment. Others include various special payments by trusts for haemophiliacs and contractual sick pay. Advisers should refer to the legislation and familiarise themselves with the categories.

The 'relevant benefits'

Virtually all types of benefit, contributory and non-contributory, means-tested and not, are covered by the scheme.[24] It includes payments of income support together with other benefits.[25] In *CCR 158/1995* it was argued that only benefit paid to the claimant for his family and not income support housing costs paid to the claimant's mortgagee was affected. This argument was rejected.[26] If more than one payment is made in respect of a benefit, all the payments will be covered.

Either the whole benefit paid to the claimant is recoverable or none of it is. All that is required is that the benefit is 'paid to or for the victim'. So it is not possible to argue that only the proportion of income support paid to the victim and not those amounts in respect of his/her family can be recovered, as the benefit is paid to the victim.[27] The same principle will apply to increases in contributory benefits paid for dependants. However, this wording does offer a way round the provisions for some income support claimants with partners. The solution is for the partner to claim instead of the victim. The benefit is not then paid to the victim, and because one amount is paid for the couple, no part of the benefit is paid 'for' the victim either. If the partner claims a contributory benefit, however, an increase will be paid 'for' the victim and will be recoverable.

---

22 CCR 5/1993 para 6.
23 SSAA s81(4); Recoupment Regs reg 4.
24 The full list appears in Recoupment Regs reg 2(1).
25 Ibid reg 2(2), confirmed in *CCR 158/1995* para 5.
26 Para 5.
27 CCR 1/1993 para 11, upheld in *Hassall and Pether v Secretary of State for Social Security* [1995] 1 WLR 812 at p818F, CA.

Example 16.2
C has been in receipt of long-term incapacity benefit while her husband D was working. He suffers an accident at work and C claims income support for the family and also an increase to her incapacity benefit in respect of D and their children. When the CRU issues a certificate in respect of D, it can only include the increase of incapacity benefit in respect of him. None of the income support is recoverable.

There can be no fraction of the benefit recovered where the payment of the benefit is only partly caused by the accident.[28] Neither can there be any reduction where there has been contributory negligence by the victim. There are special provisions to deal with the situation where there is more than one compensator.

However, payments made to a victim are only recoverable if they constitute 'benefit'. Thus if a victim is paid in excess of the award of benefit made to him/her, the excess payments are not 'benefit' and should therefore not be included in the certificate. There is no reason why compensators should have to subsidise errors by the DSS.[29]

The 'relevant period'
Benefits paid over a maximum of five years are recoverable. This period runs from the accident or injury, or from the first time a relevant benefit is claimed in respect of a disease. The period ends on the date that the compensation payment is made.

Causation: 'in respect of'
It is not sufficient that the benefit is paid following the accident, injury or disease. The benefit must be paid 'in respect of' the victim's ailment. This phrase means the same as the phrase 'in consequence of' which links the compensation payment with the health problems and is used in SSAA s97, which gives the right

---

28 CCR 4/1993 para 5.
29 Rowland, *Medical and Disability Appeal Tribunals: the legislation* (2nd edn, Sweet and Maxwell, 1995) (hereafter referred to as 'Rowland'), p158 It is suggested that *CS 102/1993* para 13, which holds that such payments may be recoverable under s71 (see p21 above), is not authority for the contrary.

of appeal.[30] A number of appeals have dealt with the issue of whether the benefit was paid 'in respect of' the victim's ailment, and this will continue to be the source of most disputes concerning decisions by the CRU.

One question that arose at the time that the legislation was introduced was the effect of the claimant being in receipt of benefits before the accident. In a number of appeals it was argued that benefit subsequently received was not paid 'in respect of the accident' because the victim would have been receiving benefit anyway. The argument was decisively rejected in *Hassall and Pether v Secretary of State for Social Security*.[31] Mr Hassall had been in receipt of unemployment benefit and income support prior to the accident and sickness benefit, invalidity benefit and income support thereafter. Mr Pether received income support both before and afterwards. However, in their appeals, Commissioner Rice pointed out that the basis on which they had been receiving the income support had changed.[32] Because they were incapable of work by virtue of their injuries, they were not required to make themselves available for employment as a condition of receiving benefit. The income support was paid as a consequence not of their unemployment, but of their incapacity and hence 'in respect of' the accidents that they had suffered. The Court of Appeal approved this decision emphatically, Henry LJ stating that 'no other construction was possible'.[33]

If, however, the victim continues to receive income support as an unemployed person, benefit continues to be paid 'in consequence' of the lack of employment rather than the relevant ailment.

Two commissioners have offered further guidance on the meaning of 'in consequence of'. In *CCR 2/1994* the victim had suffered the relevant accident in March 1989. She claimed income support and was paid this as incapable of work until July 1991, when she ceased to submit medical certificates and signed on as unemployed. However, a medical appeal tribunal had decided that she was capable of work from January 1991. Commissioner Heggs decided that benefit from July 1991 was

---

30 CCR 3/1993 *para D*.
31 [1995] 1 WLR 812, CA.
32 CCR 1/1993 para 10; CCR 2/1993 para 6.
33 [1995] 1 WLR 812 at p818B-C, CA.

Ch 16 Recovery from compensation payments   241

paid because of the victim's unemployment and not due to her incapacity and hence should not be recoverable.[34]

However, the commissioner then decided that the benefit from January to July 1991 was properly included in the certificate. She stated that whether the victim is actually incapacitated as a result of the accident is irrelevant. The important thing is that benefit was claimed and awarded on the basis that the victim had an injury connected with the accident.[35] The only solution for compensators in this situation is to seek a review of the decision as from the date that the victim was no longer incapacitated under SSAA s26 and hence no longer fulfilled the conditions of entitlement.[36-37]

In *CCR 5336/1995*, Commissioner Rowland was faced with the problem of a claimant whose incapacity could have arisen out of an unrelated stomach disorder as well as a shoulder injury sustained in the accident. He pointed out that it was not sufficient to show that the relevant accident had caused some disability. It would be necessary to show that the victim was incapable of work, by reason at least in part of the injury sustained in the accident. He clearly set out how recoverability of sickness, invalidity and incapacity benefit has to be approached where there is more than one possible cause of incapacity.

> The effect of *Hassall* is that, if a claimant is rendered permanently incapable of work by an accident and then suffers from an unrelated illness which would have rendered him incapable of work even if the accident had not occurred, the claimant is still to be regarded as incapable of work in consequence of the accident. Similarly, a claimant is to be regarded as incapable of work in consequence of an accident if neither the accident nor an unrelated illness would individually have rendered him incapable of work but where their combined effect does so. However, where, in consequence of an accident, a claimant suffers disablement which is not in itself incapacitating and then suffers from an unrelated illness which would, by itself, have rendered him incapable of work, it cannot be said that the relevant accident is an effective cause of the incapacity. In such a case, the claimant's incapacity is solely due to the unrelated illness.[38]

The commissioner also considered the significance of the medical certificates signed by the claimant's doctor. Where only one

34 Para 15.
35 Para 19.
36-37 Claims and Payments Regs reg 17(4).
38 Para 9.

condition was mentioned, that should prima facie be taken to be the reason why an adjudication officer awarded benefit. However, where more than one condition was mentioned, it could not be assumed that both those conditions were effective causes of the incapacity and it would be necessary to look at medical evidence as to which condition was causing the incapacity or whether both did.[39]

There is no authority on what happens where there is a cause of incapacity which pre-dates the accident. It is suggested that if that cause of incapacity would have been permanent even without the intervention of the accident, then benefit will not have been paid 'in consequence' of the accident even if it has aggravated the pre-existing condition or if a separate injury has been sustained which would have rendered the victim incapable of work of itself. If, however, the existing cause of incapacity was only temporary, then a date must be identified at which that condition would no longer have caused the claimant to be incapacitated. Benefit was paid 'in consequence' of the accident from that date onwards.

Slightly different considerations may apply to industrial injuries benefits where there is a pre-existing ailment. If the impact of the accident is minor, and a new assessment of disability increases the percentage of disablement but not by a sufficient amount to take the victim into a higher bracket for the amount of benefit received, it would seem that the benefit would not have been paid in consequence of the accident because exactly the same amount of benefit would have been paid in any case.

EXAMPLE 16.3

E and F are injured in a car accident. E was receiving incapacity benefit at the time of the accident on the basis of the 'own occupation' test, the stated cause of incapacity being chronic back pain. This back pain originated in an industrial accident for which there is an assessment of 12 per cent disability, for which E is receiving disablement benefit and reduced earnings allowance. The back condition is aggravated by the accident, so that E can pass the 'all work' test and his assessment of disability is increased to 30 per cent. It appears that E would not have passed the 'all work' test on the basis of the original ailment. Incapacity benefit is recoverable from the time that E would have had the 'all work'

---

39 Para 12.

> test applied to him. However, the disablement benefit is not recoupable, because E receives the same amount of benefit on 30 per cent disability as he did on a 22 per cent assessment. F is a lifeguard. She suffers chronic knee injuries and is likewise awarded incapacity benefit on the basis of the 'own occupation' test, but would have been capable of sedentary work. Three months later, she is unlucky enough to be run down by a car and her legs are amputated. Only the first three months' benefit is recoverable by the Compensation Recovery Unit. Subsequent benefit is paid 'in respect of' the second accident and not the initial injury.

Appeals and reviews

Powers of review

SSAA s97 gives the Secretary of State the power to review a certificate on the grounds either that the certificate was issued in ignorance or on of the basis of a mistake as to a material fact, or a mistake has occurred in its preparation.

The certificate may be confirmed or varied, but importantly the amount of total benefit recoverable may not be increased. The Secretary of State may treat an appeal as an application for review.[40]

Rights of appeal

A compensator, a victim or the intended recipient of the compensation (eg, the personal representative of a deceased victim) may appeal against the contents of a certificate on the grounds that either an 'amount, rate or period' is wrong or benefit paid 'otherwise than in consequence' of the ailment has been included.[41] The Secretary of State has no right of appeal and can only review the certificate as discussed above.

On receipt of the appeal, the Secretary of State will refer it to the appropriate tribunal (see below). However, this should only be done if the appellant's grounds of appeal clearly show an appeal on one of the two statutory grounds.[42] If neither is referred to, the Secretary of State should consider that an

---

40 Recoupment Regs reg 13.
41 SSAA s98(1).
42 *CSCR 2/1994* para 11.

unrepresented appellant may not be able to express a grievance with clarity and should use the power to seek further particulars of the appeal before dismissing it out of hand.[43]

The burden of proof that benefits should be included within the certificate and that all details are correct lies on the Secretary of State.[44]

Procedure and hearings

There is no right of appeal until the claim for compensation has been 'disposed of' and the Secretary of State has paid the amount on the certificate.[45] Once that has been done, however, the appellant must appeal within three months in writing to the CRU, making clear the ground relied on.[46] Careful consideration must be given by the Independent Tribunal Service as to where the case should be listed, when the various parties are resident in different places. An appeal should not be automatically listed near where the victim lives, but consideration should be given to which parties are materially interested in the outcome. So if a compensator is appealing, it should ask for the case to be heard at a convenient location.[47]

The procedure for dealing with the case depends on the question arising. If a 'medical question' is involved in the appeal, the case will first be referred to a medical appeal tribunal.[48] A 'medical question' is one on the cause of an ailment or the length of time the victim was suffering.[49] In deciding the question, the tribunal must 'take into account' a court decision relating to the issue.[50] It is very clear from that wording that although the court's view of the question is a very weighty matter to consider, it does not bind the tribunal and it may depart from the court's opinion if it sees fit.

Unlike the procedure in relation to other parts of its jurisdiction, the medical appeal tribunal can only decide the medical question

---

43 Recoupment Regs reg 11(7).
44 *CCR 2/1993* para 7. Note however that in *CCR 3/1993* the commissioner described this issue as 'misleading' and urged tribunals simply to deal with the issues and evidence before it.
45 SSAA s98(2). This includes a payment of provisional damages: s98(3).
46 Recoupment Regs reg 11. This time can be extended if there are 'special reasons'.
47 *CSCR 1/1994* para 8.
48 SSAA s98(5).
49 Ibid s98(12).
50 Ibid s98(6).

and does not decide other issues arising on the appeal.[51] These other issues will be dealt with by a social security appeal tribunal after any medical questions have been dealt with. The conclusions of the medical appeal tribunal on the medical questions bind the social security appeal tribunal.

Although the legislation states that questions as to an 'amount, rate or period' in the certificate are referred to the social security appeal tribunal, it is clear that an appeal also lies in relation to the causation of the payment of benefit.[52] This may involve the tribunal in considering medical matters which do not come within the definition of 'medical question'. If a medical appeal tribunal has expressed an opinion on these matters, it has acted outside its jurisdiction and the social security appeal tribunal must determine the facts for itself.[53]

EXAMPLE 16.4

G suffers a bad back injury in a car accident. On the way to the hospital, the ambulance is also involved in an accident, following which G complains of a twisting of his spine. It is not clear which accident causes an aggravation of asymptomatic back trouble. The insurers of the car driver appeal on the basis that the benefit was not payable in consequence of the first accident and, in the alternative, that the back trouble would have incapacitated G within three years anyway. A medical appeal tribunal decides that G's injury was caused by the initial car crash and not by the incident involving the ambulance. The case is then referred to the social security appeal tribunal, which must decide after which period of time the degenerative back disorder would have created incapacity. This is not a medical question because it is concerned with the length of time that benefit was paid in consequence of the injury, not with the length of time for which the injury was suffered. The injury itself is continuing.

When the social security appeal tribunal has made its decision, it must then decide whether the certificate should be confirmed or varied. The tribunal may increase the amount recoverable, including by adding a new benefit to the certificate, even though

---

51 *CSCR 1/1994* para 7.
52 *CCR 2/1994* para 13; *CSCR 1/1995* para 13 and 14.
53 *CCR 4/1993* para 6.

this cannot be done on review.[54] The Secretary of State may then issue a new certificate if necessary.[55] There is a further appeal on a point of law to a commissioner.[56]

The fact that a tribunal has power to increase a certificate on appeal means that victims must consider carefully their position before exercising their rights of appeal. The certificate must be examined to see whether the CRU has missed anything.

Enforcement

If a certificate is varied on appeal, the recipient of the compensation or the Secretary of State must make the appropriate payment to adjust the entitlements of the parties appropriately. A sum can be recovered from a recipient as if it were a SSAA s71 overpayment.[57]

Where a compensator fails to pay the amount to the Secretary of State, it is recoverable through the county court (sheriff court in Scotland) in the same way as a SSAA s71 overpayment.[58] It is also specified that joint compensators are jointly and severally liable for the recouped sum, so that if one fails to pay anything, the Secretary of State can recover the full amount from the other.

The solution

Most of the grievances caused by the potentially harsh operation of the provisions so as to deny victims proper compensation for their injuries can now probably be alleviated. In *Hassall and Pether v Secretary of State for Social Security*,[59] the Court of Appeal examined the scheme of the legislation in some detail to examine whether it was unfair to victims. Henry LJ concluded that it was not. As the scheme did not affect the calculation of damages, the solution

---

54 *CCR 4/1993* para 18, follwed in *CSCR 1/1995* paras 18 to 22. Note that in the latter case the commissioner pointed out that a tribunal may only reconsider questions referred to it by the Secretary of State. A tribunal cannot consider the question of its own volition: para 22.
55 SSAA s98(8) and (9).
56 Ibid s98(11). The legislation leaves the precise scope of the commissioner's powers on appeal uncertain. In *CSCR 1/1994* para 8 the commissioner stated that he would imply all the powers that were not explicitly given that a commissioner would normally exercise.
57 SSAA s99. See pp 192–196 above for this method of recovery.
58 SSAA s100. See p191 above for discussion of this method of recovery.
59 [1995] 1 WLR 812, CA.

to the hardship suffered by victims was to claim the recoupable benefits as a head of special damages.[60] Reliance was placed on a dictum of Dillon LJ before the introduction of the new legislation:

> If English statute law provided that welfare benefits payable to a person in respect of injuries in an accident should be recovered from him by the welfare authorities, if and to the extent that he recovered damages from anyone else for the same injuries, I cannot conceive that the English courts would require the welfare benefits to be deducted in the assessment of the amount of damages payable to the injured person.[61]

This statement, however, does not quite fit in with the scheme, because the benefit is recoverable not from 'him', the victim, but from the compensator. A partial explanation lies in Henry LJ's observation that the new legislation aimed to prevent the state subsidising the compensator as had been the case under the old legislation.[62] There will be some cases, however, in which victims will be overcompensated by effectively receiving benefit and lost wages for the same period of time. On the other hand, these injustices are small compared with those suffered by some plaintiffs who recovered no or trifling compensation for serious injuries, before the solution to the problem was made clear by the Court of Appeal in *Hassall and Pether*.

One question that arises from the legislation is the meaning of SSAA s81(5) which reads as follows:

> Except as provided by any other enactment, in the assessment of damages in respect of an accident, injury or disease the amount of any relevant benefits paid or likely to be paid shall be disregarded.

This subsection was not referred to in *Hassall and Pether* and on one reading it might be argued that it prevents the recoverable benefit being claimed as a head of special damages, by requiring it to be ignored in the 'assessment'. In fact, the provision is intended to have the opposite effect. It prevents the court deducting the benefits received from the award of special damages

---

60 Ibid at pp817 and 819A-C. This part of the decision was followed in *Donnelly v McCoy* (1995) 9 BNIL 20, QBD (NI).
61 *Berriello v Felixstowe Dock and Railway Co* [1989] 1 WLR 695 at p700, CA, cited by Henry LJ in *Hassall and Pether* (see n59 above) at p819D.
62 *Hassall and Pether* (see n59 above) at p817, CA.

made to the plaintiff, as had been permissible under the old law to a limited extent.[63]

Recovery from compensation under employment protection legislation

Scope

The Employment Protection (Consolidation) Act 1978 provides for recovery from an employer of unemployment benefit and income support paid to employees following an award by an industrial tribunal.[64]

The scope of the scheme is considerably more narrow than the Compensation Recovery Scheme, for a number of reasons. First, it only applies to an 'award' made by a tribunal.[65] It does not apply to a settlement made between the parties. Secondly, only unemployment benefit and income support are recoverable under the provisions and no other benefits.[66] This is a particularly important point to remember in the common case of an employee unfairly dismissed due to incapability due to illness, who has been receiving incapacity benefit or its predecessors. That benefit will not be recoverable.

A third restriction is that recoupment cannot usually bite on the whole award to the employee. Only a 'prescribed element' can be affected. For unfair dismissal awards and many others, this is so much of the compensatory award as is referable to the employee's loss of wages up to the conclusion of the proceedings.[67]

---

63 Kemp and Kemp, *The Quantum of Damages* (looseleaf, Sweet and Maxwell) paras 10-044-6. The subsection must be seen as a response to the decision in *Hodgson v Trapp* [1989] AC 807, HL. But see *Mitchell v Department of the Environment* (1996) 3 BNIL 15, QBD(NI), in which the former construction was preferred and *Hassall and Pether* not followed. *Donnelly* (see n60 above) was not cited.
64 s132.
65 Ibid s132(2)(a); Employment Protection (Recoupment of Unemployment Benefit and Supplementary Benefit) Regulations 1977 SI No 674 (hereafter the EP Recoupment Regs) reg 3(1).
66 Employment Protection (Consolidation) Act 1978 s132(2)(a). Note, however, that other benefits may be deducted from a compensatory award: *Puglia v C James & Sons* [1996] IRLR 70, EAT, at pp74 and 75.
67 EP Recoupment Regs reg 3(1)(a), including a remedies hearing or appeal: *Mason v Wimpey Waste Management Ltd* [1982] IRLR 454, EAT, at p455.

Fourthly, the scheme does not apply to all types of award under the 1978 Act. Most importantly, it does not apply to redundancy payments. There are special rules relating to protective awards where union members are being victimised.[68]

Procedure

The industrial tribunal must initiate the recoupment process when it is 'satisfied' that the employee has been receiving benefit. It cannot assume that this is the case,[69] though the fact of receipt of one of the two benefits is sufficient. Consideration of the amount received is for the DSS. The following is the process specified:

a) The tribunal assesses the award without regard to the benefit (ie, without making any deductions). It then sets out the award, the prescribed element, the period over which the prescribed element has been awarded, and the difference between the total award and the prescribed element. Where there is contributory fault or some other deduction, the prescribed element must be reduced by a like amount.[70] This will be so even in the rare cases where a reduction is applied only to the basic award for unfair dismissal and not the compensatory award.

> **EXAMPLE 16.5**
> H is unfairly dismissed by her employer. She is awarded £500 basic award and £2,500 compensatory award, including £1,000 loss of wages. The tribunal decides that it will reduce her basic award by half to reflect her conduct in confusing the employer in relation to whether she would accept an offer of redundancy, but will leave the compensatory award untouched. The prescribed element is £500, as it must also be reduced by half.

b) The award is stayed (or sisted in Scotland) to the extent of the prescribed element.
c) The secretary of the tribunals informs the Secretary of State that the award has been made and the amounts specified by the tribunal.[71]

---

68 Ibid regs 3(1)(b), 6 and 7.
69 Ibid reg 5(8).
70 Ibid reg 5(1), (3) and (2) respectively. See *Mason* (n67 above) at p455.
71 Ibid reg 5(5).

d) The Secretary of State serves a recoupment notice on the employer, who must pay the amount of the prescribed element or the amount of benefit, whichever is the less. The notice, to be valid, must be served within 21 days of the hearing or nine days of the promulgation of the tribunal's written decision, whichever is the later. The amount is recoverable as a debt.[72]

Appeals

Only an employee has the right to appeal. The procedure is that an adjudication officer first looks at the decision and makes any adjustments deemed appropriate. If the employee is still dissatisfied, there is a right of appeal to a social security appeal tribunal, which follows its normal procedure.[73]

Recovery from criminal injuries compensation

There is no formal recovery process from awards made by the Criminal Injuries Compensation Board, or now by the new Criminal Injuries Compensation Authority set up under the Criminal Injuries Compensation Act 1995. Instead, benefits are taken into account when the award is initially assessed.

Under the old scheme, in assessing compensation, the Board will deduct all benefits received by the applicant.[74] It is not necessary to show any link between the injury and the payment of benefit. It is not quite clear to which benefits this rule extends but it would seem logical for there to be consistency between recovery by CRU and those benefits offset by the Board.[75]

The position is slightly different under the new system, which took effect on 1 April 1996. The rule is that benefits are only to be deducted where the award is not based on one of the tariff figures specified in the scheme.[76]

---

72 Ibid reg 9(1), (2), (6) and (9).
73 Ibid regs 11(1) and (2) and 12(2).
74 Criminal Injuries Compensation Scheme 1990 para 19(a).
75 D Greer, *Criminal Injuries Compensation* (Sweet and Maxwell, 1991), para 4.69.
76 Criminal Injuries Compensation Scheme 1995 para 45(a).

Part III

Statutory recovery of housing benefit and council tax benefit

CHAPTER 17
The rules for recovery

This chapter and chapters 18 and 19 deal with the distinct rules and procedures relating to the recovery of overpaid housing benefit and council tax benefit by the local authority that paid it. It is frequently forgotten by advisers that the system for recovery of these benefits is completely distinct from that under SSAA s71. The adjudicating authorities have no power to deal with housing and council tax benefit overpayments[1] and any attempt to contest recoverability under that system will fall on stony ground.

The criteria for recoverability are much easier to meet than those under s71, and there is little guidance from the courts on the subject, since the only authoritative decisions relating to those benefits are cases where judicial review proceedings have been brought. The scope for legal niceties is considerably reduced and much more depends on persuasion and presentation of particular cases.

The system for recovery is governed by regulations.[2] The criteria for the two benefits are similar, though not identical, and it will be made clear in this book where there are divergences in the rules. For council tax benefit the term 'excess benefit' is used rather than 'overpayment', but the latter term will be used to mean both an overpayment of housing benefit and excess council tax benefit unless otherwise stated.

---

1 If authority were needed: *CSB 1288/1985* para 8; *CSB 1134/1988* para 6.
2 Housing Benefit (General) Regulations 1987 SI No 1971 (hereafter the HB Regs) Part XIII and Council Tax Benefit (General) Regulations 1992 SI No 1814 (hereafter the CTB Regs) Part XI, made under SSAA ss75 and 76 respectively.

Conditions for recovery

Definition of overpayment

The basic definition of an overpayment of these benefits is 'any amount which has been paid by way of housing benefit and to which there was no entitlement under these Regulations (whether on initial determination or as subsequently revised on review or further review)...'.[3] It is clear, therefore, that this covers situations where there was an entitlement at the time that the benefit was paid but which is subsequently reviewed when the local authority discovers the true situation.

The majority of cases will be caught by the above formulation. However, additional situations are brought within the definitions for both benefits. In the case of housing benefit, a payment on account made to a claimant in advance of a final determination being made on a claim.[4] For council tax benefit, the definition includes benefit which should not have been paid in view of a subsequent reduction, discounting or substitution of the council tax which the claimant is liable to pay under certain enactments.[5] However, where a local authority revokes a modification that it has made to the criteria for certain benefits,[6] the entitlement during the period of modification will not change, and so there is no overpayment.

EXAMPLE 17.1

A receives a war disablement pension. His council tax bill for one financial year is set at £400 and A receives the appropriate amount of council tax benefit. The local authority has modified the rules for benefit to disregard the pension received by A for the purposes of calculating council tax benefit. Subsequently the council tax is reduced to £350 for that year and the council revokes the modification in partial compensation. Even though A was entitled to benefit on the basis of a £400 bill at the time it was paid, it is deemed to be an overpayment of excess benefit under CTB Regs reg 83(b). However, it cannot review the benefit received by A as though the modification had never been made.

---

3 HB Regs reg 98; CTB Regs reg 83.
4 HB Regs reg 98.
5 CTB Regs reg 83(a) and (b).
6 This power is given by SSAA s134(8) in relation to housing benefit and s139(6) in relation to council tax benefit.

Who can recover?

The local authority which paid the recoverable overpayment has the sole right of recovery.[7] It should therefore be noted that the Secretary of State has no right to seek recovery, even though central government provides the bulk of funding for the two benefits through subsidy to the local authority. The Secretary of State instead exerts indirect pressure on local authorities to seek recovery by penalising those that fail to do so through the system for determining subsidies.

It must also be remembered that the local authority paying the benefit is not necessarily the authority within the boundaries of which the claimant is living. There is provision for local authorities to make arrangements to deal with benefits on behalf of each other.[8] This power is frequently used by local authorities who own housing estates within the boundaries of other authorities, which is common in London.

From whom can there be recovery?

In any case, an overpayment can be recovered from 'the claimant or the person to whom the overpayment was made'.[9] It should be noted that the latter category will only include a landlord when the claimant has elected for housing benefit to be paid direct to a landlord. Housing benefit is not the equivalent of rent, it is simply a payment to a claimant that s/he can use to discharge a liability to pay rent.[10] There can therefore be no recovery from a landlord unless there is direct payment, even where benefit is paid directly into the claimant's bank account and there is a direct debit to pay the landlord.

Where a landlord is the direct recipient of the rent allowance, the payment of benefit discharges the claimant's obligation to pay rent. If the overpayment is subsequently recovered from the landlord, this does not give rise to a rent liability on the part of the tenant.[11] The significance of this is that a landlord from whom housing benefit has been recovered cannot then seek

---

7 HB Regs reg 100; CTB Regs reg 85.
8 SSAA s134(5) (housing benefit) and s139(5) (council tax benefit).
9 HB Regs reg 101(1)(b); CTB Regs reg 86(1).
10 *DPP v Huskinson* (1988) 20 HLR 562 at p565, DC.
11 *R v London Borough of Haringey ex p Ayub* (1992) 25 HLR 566 at p576, QBD.

possession of the property from the claimant on the grounds of rent arrears. A civil action for debt or deceit may lie, but there are no arrears of rent.

Recovery of housing benefit from other persons can only occur when the following requirement is fulfilled:

> ... where the overpayment was in consequence of a misrepresentation or failure to disclose a material fact (in either case whether fraudulent or otherwise) by or on behalf of the claimant or any other person to whom a payment of housing benefit may be made, the person who misrepresented or failed to disclose that material fact.[12]

This is for all practical purposes identical to SSAA s71, and it is suggested that the legal tests for a breach of duty will be the same. The duty of disclosure is said by the regulations to exist when the recipient of benefit knows or ought reasonably to know that benefit entitlement might be affected.[13] There is no equivalent provision for recovery of council tax benefit.

When is an overpayment recoverable?

In contrast to recovery under SSAA s71, the general rule is that any overpayment of housing or council tax benefit is recoverable.[14] The only overpayments that are not recoverable are those where the defendant can show the existence of the three criteria which make up the exception to this general rule.

However, it must be borne in mind that there are certain overpayments to which the exception does not apply and hence will always be recoverable:

a) Rent rebate in respect of periods after the date of a review which gave rise to the overpayment.[15] Rent rebate is usually paid in advance and this provision prevents claimants in receipt of rent allowance being in a worse position than those getting a rent rebate on the rent payable to the local authority.

EXAMPLE 17.2

B is a local authority tenant and receives a rent rebate of one-half of his eligible rent. The authority's system is to credit the rent

---

12 HB Regs reg 101(1)(a).
13 Ibid reg 75; CTB Regs reg 65.
14 HB Regs reg 99(1); CTB Regs reg 84(1).
15 HB Regs reg 99(4).

> rebate to B's rent account every four weeks in advance. B tells the local authority that he has been awarded sickness benefit, but no review is carried out until half-way through the four-week period. B had no way of knowing that the mistake had been made. The excess rebate for the third and fourth weeks will be recoverable regardless of the existence of the exception. However, the authority cannot recover the rebate for the first two weeks if the three criteria that make up the exception are shown.

b) Council tax benefit which has been credited for dates after a review, in a similar way to rent rebate as outlined above.[16]
c) Overpayments of council tax benefit consequent upon a reduction in the council tax bill for that year (see p254 above).

The exception: official error

The first criterion that must be shown if recoverability is to be avoided is that the overpayment was caused by official error.[17] This is defined as follows:

> ... a mistake made or something done or omitted to be done by the appropriate authority or by an officer or person acting for that authority or by an officer of the Department of Social Security or the Department of Employment acting as such ...[18]

On the face of it, this is quite a wide definition. There is surprisingly little case-law on what kinds of situations come within it. It is clear that negligence or even carelessness is not necessary. Even if an authority makes a mistake which it could not possibly have avoided making, it still falls within this definition.[19] If a benefit officer gets the law wrong, even through following incorrect guidance by the DSS, there will be an official error. It is suggested that the definition is sufficiently wide to cover incorrect advice from an officer 'acting as such' (though the defendant may fall foul of the other criteria in this situation). However, it could only be said that something is 'omitted to be done' if there is some breach of procedure by the officer. There would be no omission in this sense if the officer fails to do

---
16 CTB Regs reg 84(5).
17 HB Regs reg 99(2); CTB Regs reg 84(2).
18 HB Regs reg 99(3); CTB Regs reg 84(3).
19 *R v Liverpool City Council ex p Griffiths* (1990) 22 HLR 312 at p315, DC.

something that s/he could not reasonably be expected to do. Some support for this proposition comes from the fact that there is no official error where a claim form for housing benefit does not specifically request a particular piece of information which may be relevant.[20]

EXAMPLE 17.3
C is overpaid housing benefit after she finds that she had a capital resource of which she was not aware and hence had not disclosed to the local authority. She cannot argue that the authority has made an official error through failing to make a complete investigation into her financial circumstances, because the authority is entitled to rely on the information supplied by the claimant, in the absence of something which would put them on enquiry.

The reference to the Departments of Social Security and Employment makes it clear that the local authority is fixed with the mistakes of officers in these Departments. So there is an official error whenever there is a breakdown in the procedures for the Departments to pass relevant information to local authorities, such as an income support and housing benefit recipient leaving the rented accommodation for which rent allowance is being paid.[21] Likewise, if there is a mistaken award of income support and the local authority awards benefit in reliance thereon, there is an official error for the whole period that income support is paid. This is true even if the award of income support is subsequently revised and in theory even if it is subsequently recovered under SSAA s71.

EXAMPLE 17.4
D receives income support and housing benefit. She gives birth to a child. She discloses a claim for, but not the receipt of, child benefit. The Child Benefit Centre fails to inform the local office dealing with income support. She makes an innocent misrepresentation when signing her order book slip for income

---

20 *R v Housing Benefit Review Board of the London Borough of Islington ex p de Grey and Hornby* (1992) unreported, 11 February, DC.
21 *Warwick District Council v Freeman* (1994) 27 HLR 616 at p621, CA.

support each week. The failure of the Child Benefit Centre does not absolve D from SSAA s71 recovery. However, it is an official error for the purposes of whether any overpaid housing benefit is recoverable.

The exception: no material contribution to the error

Once it has been shown that the overpayment in question was caused by official error, the next step is to show that 'the claimant, a person acting on his behalf or any other person to whom the payment is made did not cause or materially contribute to that mistake, act or omission'.[22]

Clearly, it is not necessary that the person in question was the sole cause of the official error. It is sufficient if part of the blame must be laid at his/her door. On the other hand, it must be borne in mind that the role of the person at fault must be significant; there must be some real link between something that person did or omitted to do and the official error. If looking at the situation as a whole, the error was overwhelmingly due to the actions of the official, then the person did not 'materially' contribute towards the error. The other point that must be made is that the act or omission of the person at fault must have caused the official error, not the overpayment.

EXAMPLE 17.5

E's niece, F, rents a room in E's rented flat. Both are in receipt of income support and housing benefit. E informs the DSS about her income from F, and F tells both the DSS and the local authority. E does not inform the local authority about her receipt of income, believing that it will take the appropriate action by applying the appropriate procedures following E's disclosure to the DSS and F informing the local authority. Neither procedure is properly implemented. Even though it can be said that E contributed towards the overpayment by not making a separate disclosure herself, the relevant official error was the failure to operate the procedures and E did everything appropriate to allow these procedures to be operated.

22 HB Regs reg 99(2); CTB Regs reg 84(2).

The final question is whether the defendant must have materially contributed towards the official error or whether it is sufficient that any one of 'the claimant or a person acting on his behalf or any other person to whom the payment is made' can be so blamed. In *Warwick District Council v Freeman*[23] the tenant claimed housing benefit in May and gave notice to quit in October. The same day that he was informed, the defendant landlord informed the local authority that the tenant had given one month's notice. Benefit was stopped from November. It later transpired that the tenant, unknown to the landlord, had left the property in August. The local authority sought to recover the overpayment from the landlord.

The Court of Appeal decided that although the landlord, being 'any other person to whom the payment is made', had not contributed to the official error, the tenant as 'the claimant' had done. It was not necessary that the defendant should be the person contributing to the official error. Hale J came to this conclusion because it was not 'expressly said that it can only be recovered from a person who himself or herself contributed to the error. Hence it must be sufficient if any one of those people contributed.'[24]

It is suggested that this conclusion is wrong. It is first erroneous on policy grounds. The policy of recovery in relation to housing and council tax benefit is that an overpayment should be recoverable from anyone receiving the payment unless there is an official error for which the defendant is blameless. The landlord in *Freeman* had no way of knowing that his tenant had left the property. A landlord cannot be expected to keep abreast of a tenant's circumstances. To require him/her to do otherwise encourages intrusion by landlords into the lives of their tenants.

Secondly, given the undesirable consequences of the decision, it is suggested that it is legally dubious. It was not necessary for it to be 'expressly provided' that the defendant must be the person contributing to the official error for the Court of Appeal to come to this conclusion. As the consequences of the decision are unpalatable, it is legitimate to have regard to the principles of statutory interpretation to determine whether the wide or narrow interpretation should be adopted. It is submitted that the regulations should be interpreted according to the doctrine of

23 (1994) 27 HLR 616, CA.
24 Ibid at 621.

reddendo singula singularis (reading each with each). As discussed above at pp255 to 256, an overpayment may be recovered from 'the claimant', a person acting 'on behalf of the claimant' or 'any other person to whom a payment of ... benefit may be made'. Under the doctrine, the words 'the claimant' must be read with the same words in the regulation dealing with recoverability, the words 'any other person to whom a payment of ... benefit may be made' with the words in the earlier regulation and so on. This would mean that it must be the defendant who materially contributed to the omission.

Accordingly, it is contended that this part of the decision in *Freeman* introduced an unjustified extension of the right to recover and potentially places a crippling burden on landlords. Since the Court of Appeal was dealing primarily with the issue of the local authority's failure to comply with the statutory procedure regarding recovery, it is arguable that this part of the decision is obiter. It would have to be regarded as highly persuasive, however, by review boards and county courts.

The exception: not reasonable to realise there was an overpayment
The final criterion that must be shown to make an overpayment non-recoverable is that 'the claimant or a person acting on his behalf or any other person to whom the payment is made could not, at the time of receipt of the payment, or of any notice relating to that payment reasonably have been expected to realise that it was an overpayment'.[25]

It was decided in *Freeman* that the person who could reasonably have realised that there was an overpayment need not be the defendant.[26] According to *Freeman* it was enough that the tenant could reasonably have realised that she was not entitled to housing benefit as she had left the rented property, even though the defendant landlord was ignorant of this fact.

Another authority on the wording of the paragraph is more favourable to defendants. In *R v Liverpool City Council ex p Griffiths*[27] the local authority was unable to implement changes to regulations made in 1988 before they came into effect and decided to make estimated payments instead. All claimants were made aware that their benefit had been calculated on an estimated

---

25 HB Regs reg 99(2); CTB Regs reg 84(2).
26 (1994) 27 HLR 616 at p621, CA.
27 (1990) 22 HLR 312, DC.

basis and that it was likely that they would be receiving either too much or too little benefit. Mrs Griffiths' benefit changed very little. It was held that the fact that she knew that she might be receiving an overpayment was not enough. It was necessary that she could reasonably know that the benefit was actually an overpayment, and she could not be expected to carry out the complex calculations herself. Accordingly the overpayment was not recoverable.[28]

This analysis can be applied to many situations. A claimant cannot be expected to understand the detailed workings of the system or how much a particular change in circumstances will result in a change in the amount of benefit being received. Moreover, it is suggested that the wording of the regulation means that the personal circumstances of the defendant are to be taken into account when deciding whether s/he could reasonably have known that there was an overpayment.

EXAMPLE 17.6
G is unemployed and receiving housing benefit. She knows little about the housing benefit system and has difficulty in reading. At the same time, G's father, H, moves in with her and G starts a job for ten hours per week. Both these changes are disclosed to the local authority, but due to official error only the effect of H being a non-dependant is taken into account and not G's job. G receives a notice informing her that her benefit has been halved by 'the change of circumstances'. In view of G's lack of knowledge and the fact that the notice does not refer to which change has been taken into account, it is not reasonable to expect her to realise that there is an overpayment.

Some of the authorities on whether there is a 'failure' to disclose under SSAA s71 (see pp79–91 above) may be relevant in these circumstances. So if a piece of information is not requested in the information supplied to the defendant, or the defendant receives advice from an appropriate source that a fact is irrelevant to the calculation of housing benefit, then it is not reasonable for them to anticipate an overpayment. Where there is no disclosure of a change of circumstances and it is reasonable for the defendant to think there ought to be disclosure and that the matter not

---

28 Ibid at p317.

disclosed may be relevant, it must be reasonable for him/her to think that there is an overpayment.

As with the concept of a continuing obligation to disclose (see pp61–65 above), it will be vital to determine at exactly what point the claimant could reasonably have expected that s/he was being overpaid. This is particularly relevant in the very common situations where a claimant discloses a change of circumstances to the DSS but not to the local authority, and where disclosure is made to the local authority but no action is taken. The defendant can reasonably expect a certain amount of time to elapse before it realises that the claimant is being overpaid. Some of the criteria which may be relevant for determining this period are discussed at pp64–65 above. Once that period is elapsed, the overpayment will be recoverable from the time of the next payment of benefit.

EXAMPLE 17.7

I comes off unemployment benefit when he starts working full-time. He informs the local authority which is paying housing benefit, but it fails to stop payment. I does not inform it again for two months. Most of this overpayment will be recoverable as I ought to have realised that he was being overpaid much more quickly. A review board decides that he should have realised as soon as he next looked at his bank balance, ten days after the first overpaid instalment of benefit. The first two instalments of overpaid benefit are not recoverable, because it is only at the time of the third instalment that I could be reasonably expected to know that he was being overpaid.

EXAMPLE 17.8

J is a landlord with several tenants on housing benefit. One of his tenants, K, informs him that he is about to start work and that he will inform the relevant authorities. K does so but dies three months after starting work. The benefit was being paid directly to J and so K had no way of knowing that there was an overpayment. The local authority pursues J for recovery of the overpayment. The evidence is that J received a notice some six weeks after K started work which made it clear that J was still receiving housing benefit in respect of K. All payments made after the receipt of that notice will be recoverable, but not those beforehand.

Calculating the amount

The method of calculation is considerably more simple than that under SSAA s71. However, it is suggested that the three-stage process suggested in chapter 8 above is a good way to approach the process of calculation:

a) calculate the total benefit paid to the claimant under the original decision;
b) deduct any part of that total benefit which is not recoverable, giving what will be called the 'gross overpayment';
c) deduct any offsets allowable, giving the 'net overpayment', which is the amount properly recoverable.

Calculating the gross overpayment

The first two steps involve the deduction of the amount to which the claimant is entitled following the review of the claimant's entitlement from the amount paid. This follows from the definition of an overpayment as an amount to which there was 'no entitlement' following the review (see p254 above).

> EXAMPLE 17.9
> L mistakenly wrote on his housing benefit claim form that his rent was £80 per week when the true figure was £60. Although he has been overpaid, he was entitled to benefit of £60 per week. The gross overpayment will therefore be £20 for each week of the overpayment period.

Offsets

The diminishing capital rule

Three types of offset from the amount of an overpayment are allowable. The first is a deduction under the diminishing capital rule. This applies where there has been an overpayment for at least 13 weeks ('the overpayment period') and the overpayment is due to a person having capital in excess of the limits and that capital having been misrepresented or not disclosed.[29] Counting

---

29 HB Regs reg 103(1); CTB Regs reg 89(1). It must be borne in mind that at the time of writing, the upper limits for capital were £16,000 and not £8,000 as for income support: HB Regs reg 37; CTB Regs reg 28.

from the beginning of the overpayment period, at 13-week intervals the capital shall be treated as reduced by the amount of benefit which would not have been allowed in the previous 13 weeks. It is not possible to make reductions over any period other than 13 weeks.[30]

EXAMPLE 17.10

M failed to disclose the contents of his bank account, in which he holds £17,460. He received housing benefit of £85 per week. The overpayment period was 80 weeks. The offset under the diminishing capital rule is calculated as follows:

Weeks 1 to 13: No entitlement.
Amount of benefit not entitled to: 13 × 85 = £1,105.
Deemed capital after period: 17,460 − 1,105 = £16,355

Weeks 14 to 26: No entitlement.
Amount of benefit not entitled to: 13 × 85 = £1,105.
Deemed capital after period: 16,335 − 1,105 = £15,250.

Weeks 27 to 39: Tariff income under reg 45: (15,250 − 3,000) / 250 = £49.
Entitlement: 85 − 49 = £36.
Amount of benefit entitled to: 13 × 36 = £468.
Amount of benefit not entitled to: 13 × 49 = £637.
Deemed capital after period: 15,250 − 637 = £14,883.

Weeks 40 to 63: Tariff income under reg 45: (14,883 − 3,000) / 250 = £48 (rounded up).
Entitlement: 85 − 48 = £37.
Amount of benefit entitled to: 13 × 37 = £481.
Amount of benefit not entitled to: 13 × 48 = £624.
Deemed capital after period: 14,883 − 624 = £14,259.

Weeks 64 to 77: Tariff income under reg 45: (14,259 − 3,000) / 250 = £46 (rounded up).
Entitlement: 85 − 46 = £39.
Amount of benefit entitled to: 13 × 39 = £509.
Amount of benefit not entitled to: 13 × 46 = £598.
Deemed capital after period: 14,259 − 598 = £13,661.

Weeks 78 to 80: No further reduction in deemed capital allowed as period is less than 13 weeks.
Entitlement: £39.
Amount of benefit entitled to: 3 × 39 = £117.

---

30 HB Regs reg 103(2); CTB Regs reg 89(2).

> Offset allowed due to diminishing capital rule is sum of amounts of benefit entitled to in each period: 468 + 481 + 509 + 117 = £1,575.

Lesser amounts allowable

The second type of allowable offset is any 'lesser amount [which] was properly allowable in respect of the whole or part of the overpayment period'.[31] It has been suggested that the phrase 'the overpayment period' has to be interpreted in the same way as in the regulation allowing for the diminished capital rule, so that this rule cannot apply to any overpayment period of less than 13 weeks.[32] Parliament cannot have intended that where there is an overpayment of 12 weeks the defendant should have to repay all the benefit received, but that a defendant required to repay 13 weeks of benefit can reduce the amount by what s/he ought to have received.

In any case, it is suggested that this reduction will already have been carried out in the process of determining the gross overpayment. Therefore, it will be important not to allow an offset under this heading as well.

However, this regulation is not otiose because it also allows additional amounts of housing benefit rent allowance which on a review can be offset from the amount. So if, eg, the local authority is persuaded that its decision to reduce an unreasonably high rent or if the eligible rent was wrong, then the extra amount to which the claimant would have been entitled may be offset from the amount.

> EXAMPLE 17.11
> N's rent is £70 per week. The local authority refuses to pay the full amount of rent, claiming that it is unreasonable, and allows £50 per week. N does not seek advice about this. The authority later discovers that N has been working part-time and earning £50 per week. After allowing the £15 disregard, £35 of earnings per week is counted as income and has therefore been overpaid every week. N appeals to the review board and successfully argues that the deduction should not have been made. There will

---

31 HB Regs reg 104(a); CTB Regs 90(a).
32 Findlay and Ward, *CPAG's Housing Benefit and Council Tax Benefit Legislation* (7th edn, CPAG, 1994), p248.

therefore be an offset of £20 per week from the amount of the overpayment.

Reduction for payments in excess of obligations

The final allowable offset concerns the situation where a claimant has paid more in relation to his/her obligation than required. The situation is different for each of the benefits:

a) *Housing benefit*: the claimant has paid more rent or rates than legally obliged in any case.[33] This only applies to rent or rates rebate and not to rent allowance. The reason for the offset is that rent and rates rebates are paid direct to the authority in any case, so if the claimant had paid too much rent or rates to the local authority, the authority would simply have been paying itself too much money and has sustained no loss.

b) *Council tax benefit*: the claimant has paid more council tax than legally obliged.[34]

The regulations state that these amounts 'may' be deducted (unlike those relating to lesser amounts payable which 'shall' be deducted). It appears that the local authority has a discretion over whether or not they should be deducted, though it is suggested that a convincing reason will be needed before the local authority declines to do so. It does not seem fair that it should effectively pay itself too much money and then recoup the same amount from a defendant.

As with the regulations relating to lesser amounts payable, the offset is stated to be potentially applicable throughout an 'overpayment period' but it is suggested for the reasons given at p266 above that this does not require a 13-week period to become operable, as is the case with the diminishing capital rule. The term 'overpayment period' in these regulations simply means the whole of the period during which an overpayment was made.

---

33 HB Regs reg 104(b).
34 CTB Regs reg 90(b).

CHAPTER 18
Challenging local authority decisions

A different approach is required when challenging decisions to recover housing and council tax benefit. Those cases which depend on legal argument and the interpretation of the regulations will be relatively few compared with recovery of general benefits under SSAA s71. Far more frequently, a defendant will wish to contest the appropriateness of recovery in the particular case. In order for a client's case to be put persuasively, it is important for advisers to be aware of local policy and practice and which factors commonly influence the thinking of the local authority.

When representing a defendant in the process of reviewing decisions to recover, the demanding time limits must be carefully observed. The time limits are honoured far more in the breach than in the observance by authorities: they are more in the nature of targets as the authority may extend them if it is not 'reasonably practicable' to comply. However, some authorities apply the provisions far more strictly in relation to defendants than they do to themselves.

It follows that, although the limits can be extended for 'special reasons' at the instance of the authority or on application by a defendant,[1] it is risky to rely on the local authority looking favourably on an individual case. Once an authority or a review board has decided to refuse to extend time, it is not possible to seek review of the refusal.[2] Defendants and their advisers should therefore take great care to ensure timely despatch of all notices requesting reviews. Care must also be taken with the contents of letters requesting appeal and review. What is being requested must be clearly stated, and grounds stated in sufficient detail for the authority to be in no doubt of the issues raised.

1 HB Regs reg 78(3) and (4); CTB Regs reg 68(3) and (4).
2 HB Regs reg 78(5); CTB Regs reg 68(5).

Ch 18 Challenging local authority decisions   269

It is important to remember the rules regarding posted notices. A notice posted to the authority is not deemed to be received until it is actually received at the designated office, while a notice to a claimant is deemed to be received by a defendant on the day that it is posted.[3] Experience shows that local authorities lose correspondence with depressing regularity and it is essential that receipt by the authority of a notice can be proven by sending correspondence by recorded delivery post.

There are four stages to the process of challenge to a decision by a local authority to recover:

a) the initial determination by the authority that an overpayment of housing or council tax benefit is recoverable and should be recovered;
b) the review by the authority of its initial determinations;
c) further review by the review board;
d) an application for judicial review.

There are two other possibilities open to defendants for challenging authority decisions. Where there has been some clerical error, an application may be made for it to be corrected.[4] The other option is to seek to set aside a determination on certain restricted grounds. In practice, this will only be of relevance before review boards and the subject is therefore dealt with at p278 below.

The initial determination by the authority

An important distinction between SSAA s71 recovery and recovery of housing and council tax benefit is that the same agency determines both recoverability of benefit and whether recovery should actually be made. It is important that the authority does not confuse the two facets of its decision and assume that it will recover simply on the basis that an overpayment is recoverable.

Authorities are exhorted by the DSS to keep the decision-making process on recoverability and recovery distinct,[5] but very often make this fundamental mistake. If they fail to

---

3   HB Regs reg 78(1) and (2); CTB Regs reg 68(1) and (2). There is therefore no room for the presumption in the Interpretation Act 1978 s7 that a notice is received two days after it is sent.
4   HB Regs reg 85; CTB Regs reg 74.
5   *Housing Benefit General Manual* (looseleaf, HMSO), para A7.23.

consider the merits of recovery as a separate question, then this is one ground upon which judicial review may be considered at a later stage (see p271 below). The authority is also required to follow the formal provisions on notice of its determination (see pp272–273 below).

Since an overpayment is defined for these purposes as being an excess 'as subsequently determined',[6] it follows that there must be a review of the previous determinations on entitlement before an overpayment can arise. If this is not done, it is suggested that similar consequences will follow as to an absence of a review in SSAA s71 recovery (see pp21–33 above).

Very often, a defendant will not know that the authority is seeking to make recovery until s/he is notified of the initial determination. However, where this is not the case, there may be instances in which a pre-emptive strike against the merits of recovery will be a good idea where it is anticipated that recovery will be sought. For example, if a defendant is interviewed by officers investigating a suspected case of fraud, then s/he will have an idea of the substance of the allegations and what the answer to them will be. Likewise, if s/he has just informed the authority of a retrospective change of circumstances but it will cause hardship to the defendant for recovery to be made, it may be useful to outline these grounds for non-recovery before the initial determination is made.

There are, however, two reasons why caution is necessary. First, the very act of making a request in writing not to recover may break the bureaucratic inertia which frequently means that authorities overlook cases in which there may be recovery. An officer may, as a result of the request, look at the defendant's case and decide that there should be recovery notwithstanding the defendant's reasons, when otherwise the case would probably never have been examined at all. Unless it is clear that a recovery determination is likely to be made, therefore, and the local authority is reasonably efficient, this course of action ought not to be taken.

Secondly, it is important to be wary of tying the defendant down to a particular case at an early stage, since an authority will not be impressed with additions to the case put by a defendant at a later stage in the proceedings, and still less so with alterations thereto. Advisers must carefully consider the case being put

6 HB Regs reg 98(1); CTB Regs reg 83.

forward by a defendant and whether it is likely to be the whole case that s/he wishes to put at a later stage. If documentary evidence supporting the defendant's case is expected to become available but cannot be sent at this initial stage, it is probably better to wait until it can all be put before the authority.

The determination as to recoverability

This part of its determination will involve the authority applying the rules discussed in chapter 17.

The determination to recover

It cannot be over-emphasised that the authority is not obliged to recover a recoverable overpayment. It has a discretion over whether recovery should be made. In some cases, it must also decide from whom recovery should be sought. A failure to exercise discretion or to exercise it in a judicial, reasonable manner will render the determination vulnerable to judicial review. An authority will need to be able to justify departing from the DSS's advice on recovery.[7]

It has been questioned whether a wrong use of discretion can be challenged through the review process or whether the defendant must immediately seek judicial review. The authorities seem to suggest that this is possible.[8] It makes sense that a dispute should be dealt with through the review process where at all possible, and where the issue is over the use of the discretion on the facts of the particular case, rather than any legal principle, the review process is a far better means of resolving the conflict. Judicial review is designed to deal with disputes of law, not fact.

EXAMPLE **18.1**
A suffers from agoraphobia. His wife, B, is housebound and they have no telephone. When A receives notification that he is to

---

7 For example, the advice that the DSS should consider carefully whether recovery from a dead claimant's estate is appropriate: *Housing Benefit General Manual* (looseleaf, HMSO), para A7.45.
8 *R v London Borough of Brent ex p Kalibala* (1991) unreported, 17 June, CA; Findlay and Ward, *CPAG's Housing Benefit and Council Tax Benefit Legislation* (CPAG, 1994), p242.

receive his old-age pension, they fail to inform the local authority, their problems compounded by the death of their daughter in a car accident. The authority decides to exercise its discretion to recover. Before judicial review will lie, A and B must go through the review process as their case for a favourable use of discretion relates to matters of fact rather than an attack on the local authority's policy.

The statement of the determination

Once an authority has decided that an overpayment is recoverable and that it intends to recover, it is then required to issue a written determination to 'any person affected' by the decision. This will always include the claimant, and if the defendant is somebody else, s/he must also receive such a written determination.[9] If recovery is sought from a landlord, then clearly for these purposes s/he is a 'person affected'.[10]

The statement must contain the following information:[11]

a) The fact that there has been an overpayment.
b) The reason why the overpayment is recoverable. This, it is suggested, must include a statement that the previous award has been reviewed, the grounds for review and the new entitlement on review.
c) The amount of the overpayment.
d) A description of how the amount of the overpayment was calculated.
e) The benefit weeks affected by the determination.
f) In the case of housing benefit where recovery is to be made by deductions from rent allowance or rent rebate, the fact and amount of those deductions. In the case of council tax benefit, the intended method of recovery, be that by payment by the defendant, addition to his/her council tax bill or deduction from other benefits.

If a statement is not issued or it does not contain the requisite information, then the determination is invalid and of no effect.[12]

9 HB Regs reg 77(1); CTB Regs reg 67(1).
10 *Warwick District Council v Freeman* (1994) 27 HLR 616 at p621, CA.
11 HB Regs Sch 6 para 14; CTB Regs Sch 6 para 16.
12 *R v Housing Benefit Review Board ex p Thomas* [1991] COD 335 at p336, QBD; *Warwick District Council v Freeman* (1994) 27 HLR 616 at pp619 and 620, CA.

Where the issue of a statement is in dispute, it is suggested that it will be for the authority to produce some proof that the statement was issued. However, if a decision is invalid on these grounds, it is suggested that the local authority can go on to make a fresh determination that there has been an overpayment, unless the final decision specifically states that the overpayment has not been recoverable. In short, the same analysis will apply as for a failure to review under SSAA s71 (see pp21–33 above).

> EXAMPLE 18.2
> C did not disclose an award of invalidity benefit to the local authority. The overpayment determinations for housing and council tax benefit are issued, but omit to state the amount recoverable. On review, the review board states, as to the housing benefit overpayment, that, 'the decision that housing benefit is recoverable is invalid because the notice requirements have not been followed'. As to the council tax benefit, it states that, 'the excess benefit is not recoverable'. Although the local authority may issue a fresh determination in relation to housing benefit, this is not possible in relation to council tax benefit, because the review board has made a final decision that the overpayment is not recoverable. The authority must seek judicial review of the review board's decision.

It must also follow from the required content of the statement that it is not possible for an authority to make a decision that there will be recovery at some later stage after determining recoverability. They must be made at the same time or not at all.

Review by the local authority

When a defendant has received the statement of the determination that the authority is to seek recovery, the first step in challenging the determination is to apply for a review of this decision. This must be done within six weeks of the date of notification of the determination.[13] This is a compulsory step, and there is no

---

13 HB Regs reg 79(2); CTB Regs reg 69(2). Para 4 of both regulations excludes time when a statement of the reasons for the decision is being sought.

prejudice to a defendant in seeking a review as there is under SSAA s71 (see pp161-162 above). Moreover, it should not be seen as a formality preceding an application for a review board. Benefit officers tend to be more amenable to well-reasoned argument than adjudication officers.

Review is triggered by 'a person' seeking a fresh look at the determination in question, and it has been held that this means the same as 'a person affected' and will therefore include a landlord in the context of overpayments.[14]

In order to review a determination, the authority will have to show the existence of one of three grounds.

A relevant change of circumstances

A review on the grounds of change of circumstances takes effect from the date that the change is effective. There are complex rules for determining this date, but generally speaking the first benefit week after the change will be the day the change affects benefit entitlement.[15]

An important deficiency in the regulations was exposed in *R v Middlesborough Borough Council ex p Holmes*.[16] The claimant had received a backdated payment of industrial injuries benefit covering a two-year period of housing benefit entitlement. On receiving the payment, he informed the local authority who revised the determinations awarding benefit on the ground of a change of circumstances. It was held that the regulations only authorised them to take the change into account from the date that the claimant informed them of the change.

The result of this decision was that whenever a claimant was awarded backdated benefit, s/he would be able to keep housing benefit to which s/he would not otherwise have been entitled. The DSS quickly amended the regulations to add a paragraph dealing specifically with backdated benefit.[17] However, the amendments are not retrospective and only have effect from 6 March 1995.[18] So the decision in *Holmes* will still govern all back payments prior to that date. The DSS has apparently issued

14 *Warwick District Council v Freeman* (1994) 27 HLR 616 at p620, CA.
15 HB Regs regs 79(3)(a) and 68; CTB Regs regs 69(3)(a) and 59.
16 (1995) unreported, 15 February, QBD, noted (1995) 50 *Adviser* 23.
17 Housing Benefit and Council Tax Benefit (Amendment) Regulations 1995 SI No 511, adding HB Regs reg 68(7); CTB Regs reg 59(9).
18 See reg 4 of the 1995 Amendment Regulations (n17 above).

advice suggesting that such overpayments can be recovered on the ground of mistake of law. This is misconceived. The reason why the benefit should not have been received was because in relation to that period, the claimant had income which should have been taken into account. This is a mistake of fact, not of law. It is not the entitlement of the claimant to the benefit which gives rise to the overpayment, but rather the payment of benefit pursuant to that entitlement. The fact of payment is just that: a fact.

> **EXAMPLE 18.3**
> D receives housing benefit from January 1994 to January 1996. In the latter month, D receives three years of invalidity benefit, following a lengthy appeal involving a hearing before the commissioner. The authority can only revise the determination awarding housing benefit from 6 March 1995 on the grounds of change of circumstances.

It must be borne in mind that *Holmes* only applies in cases of backdated entitlement to other social security benefits. The regulations before the 1995 amendments clearly covered other income received in respect of an earlier period,[19] and the regulations preceding the present ones clearly authorised a retrospective revision, the presumption against retrospectivity not arising in these circumstances.[20]

Ignorance of or mistake as to a material fact

Under this ground for review, it is suggested that a 'material fact' has the same meaning as in SSAA s25, namely a fact that required serious consideration by the authority in awarding benefit.[21] It is also suggested that the problem in *Holmes* cannot be avoided by reviewing on this ground, because it is necessary that the fact existed at the time of the decision under review.[22]

This will usually be the appropriate ground of review to apply for when a defendant seeks a review of a determination that there

---

19 HB Regs reg 68(6); CTB Regs reg 59(8).
20 *R v Stockton-on-Tees Borough Council ex p Smith* [1988] RVR 38 at p40, QBD.
21 *Saker v Secretary of State for Social Services* (1988) (appendix to *R(I) 2/88*), CA.
22 See *CIS 650/1991* paras 13 to 16 on reviews under SSAA s25.

Mistake of law

This ground will rarely, if ever, be relevant to recovery of overpayments. It ought to be noted that there can be no review of a determination of a review board on this ground.[23]

Further review by a review board

If the defendant is dissatisfied with the result of the review, whether or not the initial determination was changed on the review, s/he may then go on, within four weeks of receiving the review decision, to give reasons why there should be a further review of the determination.[24] This review will be heard by a review board comprising a varying number of councillors from the local authority.[25] If the same matter arises in relation to housing benefit, council tax benefit or the old community charge benefit, the same review board can hear all the reviews together.

An authority is required to hold an oral hearing of a review board. There has been a lamentable tendency for some local authorities to deny claimants the right to a hearing. The regulations are quite explicit; a review board 'shall hold an oral hearing'.[26] It is not held at the option of one of the parties. A threat to apply for judicial review should suffice to persuade an authority to comply with the requirements.

The hearing before the review board

The chair of a review board will not usually be legally qualified, but receives assistance from a solicitor employed by the local authority, whose role during the proceedings is rather like that

---

23 HB Regs reg 79(1)(c); CTB Regs reg 69(1)(c).
24 HB Regs reg 81; CTB Regs reg 70.
25 HB Regs and CTB Regs Sch 7.
26 HB Regs reg 82(1); CTB Regs reg 70(1).

of a magistrates' clerk. The solicitor remains with the review board during its deliberations.

The proceedings tend to be more formal than those of social security appeal tribunals. A government leaflet sets out recommended procedure for review boards, and many follow this to the letter. A housing benefit officer has the first and last say in the hearing, and questions from the appellant, the review board and the authority's solicitor precede the claimant's evidence. Where the issue in the case concerns whether there was an official error, full opportunity should be taken to cross-examine the housing benefit officer on proper procedures.

The review board schedule will often be demanding, and hearings are frequently held in the evening when the members will be keen to get home. It is therefore important to keep submissions to the board as succinct as possible. The interest of boards in legal submissions varies, and most tend to focus on the facts and what they perceive to be the essential justice of the case.

However, brevity should not be put at the expense of presenting a defendant's case properly. Where oral evidence is required, this too should be kept as brief as possible. Where a defendant has a tendency to stray from the essential points, it will often be worth putting his/her evidence in the form of a statement to be placed before the board.

The obligations of the review board

Certain obligations of the board arise from the regulations.[27] In making its decision, the review board is obliged to confirm or revise the determination of the authority. It must exercise all duties, powers and discretion open to the authority in the process. The chair of the board must record the decision and the reasons in writing. This requirement is mandatory and cannot be delegated to a clerk.[28] The written decision must then be sent to the claimant within seven days.

The obligation to give reasons must be fulfilled in the same way as for a social security appeal tribunal. While the board need not show the standard of reasoning of a judge, it must at least deal with all the matters raised by the defendant and allow

---

27 HB Regs reg 83; CTB Regs reg 72.
28 *R v Solihull Metropolitan Borough Council Housing Benefit Review Board ex p Simpson* [1994] COD 225, QBD.

a party to see why the case has been decided against him/her. Moreover, a board is required to investigate the case for itself and if neither the authority nor a defendant takes a point, it is obliged to raise the matter itself and give both parties an adequate chance to deal with it.[29] In addition, a board, comprising councillors of the authority, will have to take care not to appear biased towards the council and thereby breach the rules of natural justice.

If a defendant is still not satisfied with the decision of the review board, an application may be made to set the decision aside if a document was not in front of a party, a party or their representative was not present, or 'the interests of justice so require'.[30] This procedure is only for dealing with procedural defects and not simply because the party is dissatisfied with the result. If an application to set aside is inappropriate, the only remaining course is judicial review proceedings.

Judicial review

A defendant may raise new points of law on judicial review proceedings that were not raised earlier in the review process.[31] Consideration of judicial review is given at pp185–187 above, but the following points need emphasising.

First, the above process must be fully exhausted before an application for judicial review is made. This includes instances where, if the view taken at p271 on the nature of jurisdiction as to the determination to recover is correct, the application solely relates to an unlawful exercise of discretion.

In considering its discretion to recover, the authority must consider each case on its own merits. Rigid policies are not permissible. Nor is it legitimate for an authority to follow a widespread practice of other local authorities without consideration of the facts of the individual case.[32] It is legitimate for an authority to take the implications of its decision for its

---

29 *R v London Borough of Sutton Housing Benefit Review Board ex p Keegan* (1992) 27 HLR 92 at p100, QBD.
30 HB Regs reg 86; CTB Regs reg 75.
31 *R v Housing Benefit Review Board ex p Thomas* [1991] COD 335, QBD.
32 *R v London Borough of Haringey ex p Ayub* (1992) 25 HLR 566 at p576, DC.

finances into account,[33] but it cannot use this to justify a blanket policy.

While the court will deal with errors of law (whether substantive or failures to comply with procedure) matters of fact are for the review board, and the court will not be prepared to review findings of fact made by the board unless there is no evidence to support them. The same applies to the use of the discretion to recover an overpayment. Unless the authority has not followed its policy, the court is unlikely to interfere with the review board's decision. In effect, judicial review of a review board's decision is effectively an appeal on grounds of error of law, with the difference that the court is not obliged to give the defendant the relief sought if it is not just in all the circumstances to do so. Thus, the court might decline to grant relief where the merits of the case are clear and the error of law is a mere technicality.

Finally, the strict time limits for judicial review must be borne in mind, and defendants should be urged by lay advisers to seek help from solicitors with all possible speed.

Contribution proceedings

It is suggested that the right to bring contribution proceedings against other potential defendants will only arise in the same circumstances as for SSAA s71 recovery (see pp183–185 above). The fact that the local authority decides both whether an overpayment is recoverable and whether it should be recovered makes no difference, because other potential defendants must receive proper notice of a determination before it is recoverable. Only the local authority can issue such a notice.

---

33 *R v Housing Benefit Review Board of the London Borough of Brent ex p Connery* (1989) 22 HLR 40 at p44, DC.

CHAPTER 19
Enforcement of recovery

This chapter deals with the mechanism for repayment of an overpayment of housing benefit or council tax benefit and with the means available to secure payment where it is not forthcoming from the defendant.

The system for repayment

It is difficult to give general advice about how local authorities will require repayment to be made, as practice appears to vary widely. Much of the advice given at pp188–190 about negotiating a scheme for repayment with the DSS will also apply to overpayments of housing benefit and council tax benefit.

However, it should be noted that many local authorities show far less zeal in their pursuit of defendants than is the case with the DSS, due to inefficiency and bureaucratic inertia. It is probably therefore good advice for a defendant to wait for the local authority to chase him/her before entering into such negotiations, rather than initiating discussions as with the Central Recovery Group.

Requests to waive recovery

Again, many of the tactics for requesting the DSS not to recover general benefits outlined at pp178–181 above will apply when dealing with local authorities. It will be helpful to have the assistance of the defendant's local councillor or MP if possible. Local authorities vary even more widely in their practice on enforcement than the DSS.

Enforcement through the courts

There is no equivalent provision to SSAA s71(10) to allow the local authority to enforce the overpayment through the local court without bringing a separate action.[1] If the authority wishes to use the court mechanisms, therefore, it will be necessary to bring an action for a debt owing.

The local authority is not, however, entitled to proceed in the county court without first making a determination in the normal way.[2] If it does so, then not only will it be barred from recovering at all because it has not followed the correct procedure, but the defendant will be entitled to raise the issue of recoverability in the county court proceedings.[3] If a county court judge determines that an overpayment is not recoverable, then that decision will be final, the doctrine of *res judicata* applying. There is no power to review a decision of a judge under the regulations discussed in chapter 17.

An important question will be when the limitation period expires for such an action. For a debt action the limitation period is six years in England and Wales, and five years in Scotland.[4] It is suggested that, unlike the situation with benefits recoverable under the SSAA (see pp15–16 above), this time runs from the date that the overpayment occurs and not the date of a review carried out by the local authority or the date that the overpayment is discovered. This is because the local authority itself and not a third party (namely, the adjudication officer) determines that there is a right to recovery of the benefit. The review, if there is any, can be seen as a mere internal procedure and not the event that gives rise to the debt.

EXAMPLE 18.1
A is overpaid income support of £5,000 and housing benefit of £3,000 between January 1987 and January 1991. In January 1995 the DSS reviews entitlement to income support and the local

---

1 CTB Regs reg 88 does not have this effect, because the statutory wording is not in the correct form for this purpose. Reg 88 simply confirms the availability of an action for a debt.
2 *Warwick District Council v Freeman* (1994) 27 HLR 616 at p620, CA.
3 Ibid at pp619 and 620.
4 Limitation Act 1980 s2; Prescription and Limitation (Scotland) Act 1973 s6 and Sch 1 para 1(d).

> authority does likewise in relation to housing benefit. As A is working, both agencies have to resort to court action to recover the overpayments. The six-year limitation period for use of the county court powers to recover income support only starts to run in January 1995 and so the full amount can be recovered, but A can raise the defence of limitation to the debt action in relation to the period up until January 1989.

A local authority is not permitted to use remedies available in the courts without the benefit of an appropriate court order. This general principle can be drawn from *R v London Borough of Haringey ex p Ayub*.[5] The applicant was a landlord with many tenants in receipt of housing benefit from the local authority, most of which was paid directly to him. When the authority discovered that overpayments had been made, it purported to deduct them from the regular payments it was making to him.

Before the divisional court, the authority claimed, first, that it was entitled to garnish (ie, seize the money paid to the debtor by a third party) the debt owed to the landlord by the claimants. Alternatively, the authority could set the overpayments off against the monies payable to the landlord. Both these arguments failed as there was no authority of the court that the authority should be so entitled and in any case it would be impossible to tell which tenants had their benefit held back and which had it paid.[6]

Deduction from benefits

Deductions from the same benefit

A local authority is entitled to deduct an overpayment of housing benefit from housing benefit in payment to the claimant.[7] In the case of council tax benefit, the same effect is achieved by an addition to the defendant's council tax bill.[8] Deductions may also be made from benefit being received by the claimant's partner, provided that the couple 'were members of the same

---

5 (1992) 25 HLR 566, DC.
6 Ibid at p576.
7 HB Regs reg 102.
8 CTB Regs reg 87(2)(b).

household both at the time of the overpayment and when the deduction is made'.⁹

There is no limit specified for the deductions, and this will be a matter for negotiation with the local authority.

Deductions from other benefits

The local authority may also request the Secretary of State to deduct an overpayment from any other benefits the defendant may be receiving. Deduction can be made from any benefit under the SSCBA, except guardian's allowance,[10] or from any benefits from other member states.[11]

Again, no maximum amount for deductions is specified and where there is deduction from income support the Secretary of State will presumably apply the maximum amounts deductible from income support where the DSS is recovering benefit (see pp195–196 above).

---

9 HB Regs reg 101(2); CTB Regs reg 86(2).
10 HB Regs reg 105(1)(a) and (b); CTB Regs reg 91(1)(a).
11 HB Regs reg 105(1)(c); CTB Regs reg 91(1)(b). See pp208–209 above for a discussion of what these benefits are.

Part IV

Recovery under common law

CHAPTER 20
Recovery through the courts

When enacting the legislation that provides for the recovery of benefits, parliament could have chosen to make an overpayment recoverable in all cases where a claimant received too much benefit. It did not do so. Instead it provided that benefit should only be recovered if the DSS or the local authority could show the existence of certain criteria. Parliament clearly took the view that certain types of overpayment should not be recoverable (particularly, eg, in the case where the sole cause of the overpayment was official error).

However, the statutes and regulations that govern recoverability do not exist in a legal vacuum. The common law has long provided for recovery of money paid over to somebody by mistake. Both the DSS and the local authorities have sought to rely on these common law rules to recover benefit in cases where it is clear that they cannot recover the overpayment under the statutory tests. Though no central statistics are kept on the amount of benefit recovered in this way,[1] anecdotal evidence suggests that it represents a significant weapon in the hands of the DSS or local authority. There have been cases where a threat of legal action has been sufficient to persuade a claimant to repay the benefit without seeking legal advice. There are also instances where a letter before action has been sent to claimants without suggesting that they seek legal advice. It is not surprising that many of those on the receiving end of such sharp practice yield without a fight.

The possibility of recovery being sought under common law is therefore something of which advisers need to be aware. Lay advisers will have to refer clients under this threat to solicitors. As a claimant will be pursued through the courts, there will be

1 HC Written Answers, vol 168, col 363.

entitlement to legal aid provided that the claimant fulfils the normal criteria. It is all the more important that claims to recover under the common law are firmly resisted, because if the analysis presented here is correct, such recovery is not possible at all.

In this chapter, 'the plaintiff' will be used as shorthand for the DSS or the authority seeking to use the common law to recover an overpayment.

The basis of recovery: conversion

The first cause of action which has been used by those seeking recovery is to claim that the claimant is liable in the tort of conversion. The argument runs as follows.[2] The money was paid to the claimant in mistake and therefore s/he can acquire no legal title to it. Therefore, there is an obligation on the claimant to return the money to its rightful owner on demand, and a failure to comply with such a demand will amount to conversion and a right of action in the courts.

Unfortunately for the prospective plaintiff, this overlooks one of the most basic limitations of the tort of conversion. Conversion is a tort relating to interference with property and there is long-standing authority that no action will lie where the tortfeasor is retaining money rather than other forms of property.[3] Any attempt to recover an overpayment by suing in conversion is therefore fundamentally misconceived.

The basis of recovery: restitution

The other cause of action that has been relied on is to claim that the claimant is liable to make restitution of the sum overpaid. This possibility requires a rather more detailed analysis.

The aim of the law of restitution is to prevent the unjust enrichment of a defendant who has received monies to which

2 See (1993) 119 *Welfare Rights Bulletin* 17.
3 *Orton v Butler* (1822) 5 B & Ald 652; *Foster v Green* (1862) 7 H & N 881; Street (ed), *Clerk and Lindsell on Torts* (17th edn, Sweet and Maxwell, 1995), para 13-44. It is possible to recover money which is seen as property rather than currency, such as collectors' coins and treasure, but it seems unlikely than any claimant will receive his/her social security benefit in such a form.

s/he is not entitled.[4] However, the cause of action is currently rather more restricted than this broad statement of principle might suggest. In order to establish the right of recovery, the entity pursuing the claimant will have to show that:

a) money was paid over to the defendant;
b) the money was paid over as a result of a mistake; and
c) the mistake was one of fact rather than of law.

The claimant will then still be able to evade liability by taking advantage of one of a number of defences available to him/her.

Money was paid over

A court will be much more rigorous about requiring the pursuing agency to prove the basis of its claim for restitution than tribunals and review boards generally. This will mean that, if it has not been formally admitted, it must be proved that the amount of benefit which is being sought tallies with that which actually was paid over.

Standards of record-keeping both by the DSS and local authorities tend to be low, and the practice of routine destruction of old documents will often make it difficult to prove that the benefit was received. The task of proof may be made easier by the admissibility of computer records of payment provided that certain conditions are met and certified by a responsible person as existing.[5] Nevertheless, those instructed by claimants from whom restitution is being sought are entitled to require specific proof of the payments in question having been made. The court should be slow to infer that the payments were made as alleged without specific proof, particularly where non-means-tested benefits are concerned. In the case of income-related benefits, the court will be entitled to make this inference on the grounds that the claimant would have no other means of living.

A second point is that recovery of overpayments through restitution is only possible from the recipient of the benefit. It is therefore not possible to pursue any third parties through the common law who have never received any payment of benefit.

---

4 Goff and Jones, *The Law of Restitution* (4th edn, Sweet and Maxwell, 1994), pp12 to 16.
5 Civil Evidence Act 1968 s5.

Money was paid over as a result of a mistake

Where benefits are concerned, the plaintiff will have to show that the benefit in question was paid over as a result of some identifiable mistake on its part. If the plaintiff was not labouring under any mistake, then there can be no restitution. This means, eg, that if there is an award in the claimant's favour for the amount paid, the plaintiff cannot rely on the mistake of the fact that more benefit was paid than the claimant should have been receiving. As long as there is a valid (though erroneous) award of benefit, then there is no mistake in paying the amount of that award. It seems likely that it is not possible to say retrospectively that there was a mistake by reviewing the award.[6]

The main issue that arises in relation to this criterion is what happens when one officer or section of the relevant entity is aware of the true state of affairs, but the officer or section responsible for the payment is not.

It is clear that when an agent of the plaintiff pays the plaintiff's money to the defendant as the result of some mistake of the agent, the plaintiff can recover the money in restitution. This is true even where the plaintiff or some other agent of the plaintiff's is aware of the true situation.[7] Questions then arise as to whether an individual officer can be said to be an agent of an office, and whether an office is in turn an agent of the plaintiff, or whether they must be seen as an integrated whole. It seems likely that a court would interpret the concept fairly loosely in this context. It is suggested that an office must be seen as a whole, so that if one officer is aware of the true state of affairs but another is mistaken, the mistake cannot be relied upon. On the other hand, if one office is aware of the truth, another office is not fixed with its knowledge.

EXAMPLE 20.1

A is in receipt of income support and child benefit. Her son leaves home at the age of 16. A rings the Child Benefit Centre and speaks to an officer who fails to pass his records to the relevant officer for action. For good measure, the officer then informs A that he

---

6 *R v Secretary of State for Social Security ex p Golding* (1996) *Times* 13 March (official transcript, pp19 and 20), QBD.
7 *Anglo-Scottish Beet Sugar Corporation Ltd v Spalding UDC* [1937] 2 KB 607, CA.

> will inform the local office for her and she need not bother, thus rendering SSAA s71 recovery of the income support impossible. As the Child Benefit Centre is aware of the true situation, recovery of the overpaid child benefit by restitution is not possible. However, the local office paying income support is not fixed with the knowledge of the Child Benefit Centre.

In particular, where the unemployment benefit office is aware of the true state of affairs but the local office paying income support is not, recovery of overpaid income support by restitution is not precluded, even though the unemployment benefit office is the agent of the local office following the established authorities under SSAA s71 (see pp72–75 above), and the local office is not fixed with this knowledge.

> EXAMPLE 20.2
> B informs the unemployment benefit office that he has started work, but the local DSS office is not informed. Recovery of the resulting income support overpayment may be sought in restitution.

Recovery in restitution is not precluded by the fact that the defendant is also labouring under the mistake. In addition, actual knowledge of the material circumstance by the plaintiff must be demonstrated before it can be said that the plaintiff is not acting under a mistake. Even if the plaintiff is negligent in not being aware of the mistake, this does not prevent the money being sought.[8]

Mistake of fact rather than law

Historically the courts only allowed restitution where the plaintiff paid the money as a result of a mistake of fact rather than one of law. This was as a result of the general principle that 'every man must be taken to be cognisant of the law; otherwise there is no saying to what extent the excuse of ignorance might not be carried. It would be used in almost every case'.[9]

---

8 *Kelly v Solari* (1841) 9 M & W 54 at p59, Exch.
9 *Bilbie v Lumley* (1802) 2 East 469 at p472.

There is more recent authority, however, that suggests that the distinction may be breaking down somewhat. It is suggested by Goff and Jones (see p289, n4 above) that recovery should only be precluded 'where the money has been paid over in settlement of an honest claim'. This has been said to be 'beyond argument'.[10] A 'claim', it is suggested, means something wider than a threat to sue someone.[11] If this is right, it ought to include a claim for social security benefit made in good faith.

> ... certainty in commerce and public transactions ... is an essential element of the well-being of the community. The narrower rule applicable to mistake of law as compared to that applicable to mistake of fact springs from the need for this security and the consequential freedom from disruptive undoing of past concluded transactions.[12]

The chief relevance of the distinction in this context is that it has been held that the amount of benefit that a claimant is entitled to in particular circumstances is a question of law rather than one of fact.[13] So if a mistake is made in calculating the claimant's benefit, it seems that restitution will not be available.

EXAMPLE 20.3

C claims income support. He has a mortgage, half of which was used to set up his business which has recently collapsed. The adjudication officer knows this but mistakenly allows the whole of the mortgage as eligible housing costs. The excess will not be recoverable in restitution.

Defences

As seen above, the circumstances in which a claim for restitution is available are already severely restricted. Further constraints are provided by the defences discussed below.

---

10 *Sawyer and Vincent v Window Brace Ltd* [1943] 1 KB 32 at p34, HC.
11 *William Whiteley v R* (1909) 26 TLR 19 (request for the Inland Revenue to give a licence to employ people); *Sharp Brothers & Knight v Chant* [1917] 1 KB 771 (demand by a landlord for increased rent).
12 *Hydro-Electric Commission of the Township of Nepean v Ontario Hydro* (1982) 132 DLR (3rd) 193 at p243, Canadian Supreme Court.
13 *Jones v Chief Adjudication Officer* [1994] 1 WLR 62 at p69C, CA; *CS 102/ 1993* para 11.

Recovery against statutory policy

The courts will not permit recovery in restitution if to do so would frustrate the policy of a statute or some common law principle.[14] In *Chief Adjudication Officer v Sherriff*[15] the Court of Appeal assumed that recovery was available in restitution but without the benefit of argument and the view cannot be said to be authoritative. It may therefore be argued that for the DSS to seek recovery in restitution of amounts which are not recoverable under SSAA Part III offends the policy behind the statute.[16] The conditions for recovery set out in the Act and the regulations made thereunder are not merely the policy of government, which is subject to change; they have been formulated by parliament to reflect what was thought to be a reasonable balance between the interests of public finance and the financial security of the defendant. To allow circumvention of these safeguards by claiming in restitution is surely contrary to this policy.[17]

There are at least three points that can be made in support of this principle. First, the old principle that it is presumed that a statute intended to leave the common law and equity unaffected has been said by commentators to be 'discredited'.[18]

> ... the true rule for interpreting statutes which may affect the rules of common law and equity ... is to consider whether the statutory provision is repugnant to the former substantive or adjective law, or whether it merely operates to strengthen the former law by giving more effectual remedies.[19]

SSAA s71 clearly affects the substantive rights of the claimant and of the DSS. The changes in the law it enacted were not merely procedural in nature and were not merely providing a new remedy.[20] The same is true of the other rights of recovery enacted under SSAA Part III. It is doubtful whether recovery under the statutory provisions is more 'effectual', in the sense

---

14 *R Leslie Ltd v Sheill* [1914] 3 KB 607, HC; *Orakpo v Manson Investments Ltd* [1978] AC 95, HL.
15 (1995) *Times* 10 May (official transcript, pp9 and 11), CA.
16 Compare *Liverpool Corporation v Hope* [1938] 1 KB 751, CA, at p754.
17 Rowland, p147.
18 *Bennion on Statutory Interpretation* (2nd edn, Butterworths, 1992), pp563 and 564.
19 *Craies on Statute Law* (7th edn, Sweet and Maxwell, 1971), p343.
20 *Plewa v Chief Adjudication Officer* [1995] 1 AC 249, HL; contrast *R v Secretary of State for Social Security ex p Britnell* [1991] 1 WLR 189, HL.

that when all the irrecoverable administrative costs are weighed up against the more effective court procedures of enforcement, it does not seem likely that recovery under Part III is significantly cheaper or quicker. What would be the point of parliament enacting complex legislation with stringent criteria for the recoverability of benefit if the DSS could simply ignore it?

Secondly, recovery under the common law violates the integrity of the social security decision-making process. In *Jones v Department of Employment*[21] it was held that no action in negligence lay against an adjudication officer for loss suffered when a decision was wrongly issued adversely to the claimant. One of the reasons given for this conclusion was that such an action offended against the principle of finality under SSAA s60. The statutory scheme states that a decision of an adjudicating authority is final unless the decision is reviewed or appealed in accordance with the legislation. It is suggested that recovery in restitution is a 'challenge to its finality, by a route other than that provided by the statutory provisions themselves'.[22]

It could be said that the argument could be met by an adjudication officer reviewing the decisions to award benefit and then the DSS seeking recovery of the surplus in restitution. One answer to this is that the payments of which recovery is sought must have been made under a mistake of fact (see pp290–292 above); the other is that SSAA s71 clearly envisages a separate right of appeal for a defendant against a decision to recover. Nothing in the Overpayments Act alters this fact and the point was repeatedly emphasised by the government in debating the Act.

Thirdly, in *Warwick District Council v Freeman*[23] (discussed at p260 above), the defendant landlord was able to use the defence available to him under public law which would normally have been resolved through the review process.[24] He was able to argue, as a defence to an action for a debt, that the overpayment arose out of an official error for which he was not responsible and could not have realised. Similarly, therefore, if the DSS

---

21 [1989] QB 1, CA.
22 Ibid at pp19C-D and 25A-B.
23 (1994) 27 HLR 616, CA.
24 Applying *Wandsworth Borough Council v Winder* [1985] AC 461, HL; *Roy v Kensington and Chelsea and Westminster Family Practitioner Committee* [1992] 1 AC 624, HL.

brings a claim in restitution when there can be no recovery under SSAA s71, there would appear to be a good defence that there was no misrepresentation or failure to disclose, that if there was then the breach of duty did not cause the overpayment and so on.

It may also be possible to seek to attack the DSS's proceedings by alleging that the Secretary of State, by seeking to rely on the common law, is frustrating the legislative purpose of s71.[25] Such an act would be *ultra vires* the powers of the Secretary of State and, if so, it should be possible to obtain an injunction to stay the action.

If this line of argument is correct, then it must follow that it is of universal application and there is no recovery in restitution whatever the circumstances.

Res judicata

If the plaintiff fails in one claim for restitution, it cannot bring a second case to claim the same money. However, the failure to secure recovery in tribunal proceedings will not of itself prevent the plaintiff bringing a claim for restitution. This is because the issues before the tribunal and the court are different, though they may be based on the same subject matter.

Estoppel

There is a general rule that estoppel cannot operate when it would prevent the plaintiff from carrying out its public duty.[26] However, there is no public duty on the Secretary of State to recover overpaid benefit. There is merely a right to do so and it is suggested that it is possible for estoppel to operate to prevent recovery in restitution.

Three conditions must be met before the defence can be used:

a) The plaintiff made a representation of fact which led the defendant to believe that s/he was entitled to treat the money as his/her own. In this context, where the claimant has been sent a letter outlining the award, that will normally be the relevant representation. It seems probable, however, that the sum on a girocheque or in an order book could not amount

---

25 *Padfield v Minister of Agriculture Fisheries and Food* [1968] AC 997 at pp1030B-D, 1032G to 1033A, 1054G and 1060G, HL.
26 *Halsbury's Laws of England* (4th edn, Butterworths, 1984), vol 16, para 1043. See further pp158–160 above.

to such a representation, particularly if it is different to the one contained in the letter.
b) The defendant changed his/her position in reliance on the representation. This is further discussed below in relation to the separate defence of change of position.
c) The mistaken payment was not primarily the fault of the defendant.[27] This will not be difficult for the defendant to show in most cases. Even where the defendant was well aware that a mistake had been made and said nothing, it does not seem likely that it will displace the mistake as the primary cause of the overpayment.

Change of position

The House of Lords has recently recognised that the defendant will have a defence where the defendant has changed his/her position as a result of the payment being made, without necessarily having to demonstrate the other ingredients of estoppel.[28]

A number of limitations were placed on the availability of the defence. It is not available where the defendant is acting in bad faith, particularly where he is aware of the mistake and takes no steps to correct the plaintiff's misapprehension. A plaintiff may seek to establish this in cross-examination. Nor is it available when the defendant is a wrongdoer in some other way. It must be 'inequitable in all the circumstances'[29] to require the defendant to make restitution.

It is suggested that many claimants will be able to demonstrate a change of position by showing a change in their standard of living. In one case the defendant, who had been paid full- and half-pay while on sick leave for longer than he was entitled to under the terms of his contract of employment, was able to point to the purchase of a suit and a car and a forbearance to claim benefit as proof of a change in lifestyle. It was held that this amounted to a change of position.[30] This is so even though a change of position is narrowly defined:

> ... the mere fact that the defendant has spent the money, in whole or in part, does not of itself render it inequitable that he should be

---

27 *Larner v London County Council* [1949] 2 KB 683 at p689, CA.
28 *Lipkin Gorman v Karpnale Ltd* [1991] 2 AC 548 at pp579 and 580, HL.
29 Ibid at p580F.
30 *Avon County Council v Howlett* [1983] 1 WLR 605 at pp621 and 622, CA.

called upon to repay, because the expenditure might in any event have been incurred by him in the ordinary course of things.[31]

Although the overpayment made to a claimant may not be a large increase in his/her income, it should be possible for a court to understand that for claimants of benefit, particularly income support and other means-tested benefits, even a small increase in the amount s/he is receiving can make an enormous difference to the quality of his/her life.

It may be difficult to prove that items have been bought which would not have been if the claimant was not receiving the extra benefit, though the court may be prepared to infer this by common sense in many cases.[32] Ideally what is required is specific proof of increased expenditure. This need not relate to specific items or commitments, but could be part of overall outgoings, provided it seems likely that they are related to the claimant's increased income.

EXAMPLE 20.4

D is a single parent on income support with two children and a part-time job. Her benefit is paid directly into her bank account. When she writes to the local office to tell it that her hours have been reduced, her benefit is re-assessed as though she had left the job. As a result she is receiving excess benefit of £20 per week. D is in the habit of paying for her weekly shopping with an automatic debit card. Her bank statements clearly show that for those weeks where she was receiving more benefit, she spent an average of £12 more on the weekly shop. This is sufficient to establish a change of position.

Limitation

If a claim for restitution is open to the plaintiff, the limitation period for starting a court action runs from the date of the payment.[33] The limitation period is six years in England and

---

31 *Lipkin Gorman v Karpnale Ltd* [1991] 2 AC 548 at p580G, HL.
32 *Goff and Jones, The Law of Restitution* (4th edn, Sweet and Maxwell, 1994), p745.
33 *Re Diplock* [1948] Ch 465 at p514, CA.

Wales and five years in Scotland.[34] Each payment should be seen distinctly rather than as a lump sum paid in instalments. Therefore, if the limitation period has expired in relation to some of the payments but not in relation to others, the defence of limitation will bar recovery of the former.

---

34 Limitation Act 1980 s5; Prescription and Limitation (Scotland) Act 1973 s6 and Sch 1 para 1(b).

Part V

Overpayments and criminal law

CHAPTER 21
The process of investigation

Most people would agree that it is important to prevent the current widespread abuse of the social security system. Such abuse tarnishes the vast majority of claimants who claim and receive payments completely honestly, and gives rise to understandable anger among taxpayers. However, it may be argued that the present government sees social security fraud as being a far more significant problem than it is. There is no doubt that very large sums of money can be involved, but the loss to public funds from revenue fraud and tax evasion is far greater than that from frauds on the DSS and local authorities, but the former has not received the same attention as the latter.

Some schemes to reduce fraud are put into effect by the recruitment of more fraud officers and toughening of prosecution policy, while others come to nothing. The result of this political stance by the government has undoubtedly been to put greater pressure on those involved in investigating fraud to get results. This in turn may have led to corners being cut and injustices in the investigative process. This chapter on the criminal law aspects of overpayment of benefits therefore focuses on the process and how it works.

Mechanisms for detection of fraud

Most, if not all, local DSS and housing benefit offices have specialist fraud units. The detection of dishonesty is undoubtedly a specialised skill, but there is a danger that officers perpetually dealing with the small minority of dishonest claimants will lack the proper perspective and will see their duty as extracting admissions of fraud rather than investigating cases objectively. Most cases investigated by fraud officers are referred to them by other sections of the DSS, but there have been widespread reports of fraud sections taking initiatives and investigating a set of claimants at random. It is not clear how often this is still done.

Claims can be referred to the fraud section for any number of reasons. Anonymous informants are a frequent occurrence. Some officers report suspicious circumstances such as claimants writing down inconsistent information on forms or arriving to sign on with a partner when they are receiving benefit as a single person. Probably, however, most cases of fraud come to light through cross-checks carried out by the DSS or local authority or when acting on information disclosed by a claimant. Once there is a suspicion that the claim may be tainted, officers are instructed to refer the claim to the fraud section. That section then receives the case papers and investigates.

Claimants will usually be interviewed, but before that is done some attempt will be made to obtain evidence of their activities to put to them. Officers have very wide powers to make investigations and obtain information. This includes entry onto premises where people are employed or employment agencies, and the questioning of people there.[1] They are not police, however, and they do not have the powers of the police. So officers visiting a claimant's house have no right to enter to investigate without obtaining a search warrant and the assistance of the police, unless the claimant gives them permission.

There is a criminal sanction for refusing to co-operate with investigations, if somebody 'intentionally delays or obstructs an inspector in the exercise of any power under this Act' or 'refuses or neglects to answer any question or to furnish any information or to produce any document when required to do so under this Act'.[2] These sanctions will be of limited use against claimants, unless the prosecuting authority can point to some specific power under the SSAA which the officer was exercising when requiring the claimant to provide the information. In most situations, the only relevant power will be the general power 'to exercise such other powers as may be necessary for carrying the Acts into effect'.[3] This offence is mainly designed for use against companies that fail to provide information necessary for assessing

---

1 SSAA s110(2).
2 Ibid s111(1).
3 Ibid s110(2)(d).

national insurance contributions and similar situations and is unlikely to be used against claimants.

Interviews

Once the fraud officers are satisfied that there is some evidence of fraud, the claimant will be interviewed and the allegations put to them. Naturally, an admission by the claimant of fraud is some of the best evidence against him/her for prosecution purposes, and it also allows a higher rate of deduction from income support to recover an overpayment, even when there has been no prosecution (see p195 above). Fraud officers are frequently subject to criticism for an overly aggressive approach to claimants. Their questioning technique is often poor, some questions are long, rambling and difficult to understand. Little allowance appears to be made for language difficulties and claimants who do not understand the questions that are asked are often accused of being deliberately obstructive. Claimants are not given a proper opportunity of explaining their version of events. Few have had the benefit of legal advice before the interview, and virtually none have an adviser present with them.

The DSS's practice is for two officers to be present. One carries out the questioning, while the other writes down a transcript of the interview. While the author is not aware of any systematic study of the subject, if the interview transcripts are typical, it seems likely that many interviews will not comply with the requirements of the Police and Criminal Evidence Act 1984 for being admissible in evidence. There is no doubt that fraud officers will be bound by the Codes of Practice under that Act as they are persons 'other than police officers who are charged with the duty of investigating offences or charging offenders'.[4] The word 'duty' connotes 'any type of legal duty, whether imposed by statute or by the common law or by contract'.[5]

The interviewee's right of silence has now been substantially restricted by the Criminal Justice and Public Order Act 1994.

---

4 Police and Criminal Evidence Act 1984 s67(9).
5 *Joy v Federation Against Copyright Theft Ltd* [1993] Crim LR 588, DC. DSS officers were specifically held to be subject to the codes in *Department of Health and Social Security v McKee* (1995) 6 BNIL 17, CC(NI).

Under that Act,⁶ such adverse inferences may be drawn 'as appear proper' if a suspect does not mention facts under questioning or on being charged which s/he later relies on in the course of his/her defence.⁷ A conviction cannot be based solely on an omission to mention facts.⁸ The restriction does not simply apply to cases where the interviewee refuses to answer any questions at all; it applies wherever the interviewee does not mention the relevant facts, though they may well have answered other questions. It seems clear that adverse inferences may only be drawn when the interviewee puts forward a positive case at trial and not when the prosecution is simply put to proof.⁹ The interviewee must also have been aware of the facts at the time of the interview.

EXAMPLE 21.1

A is paid income support by order book. She informs the DSS that she has started working and the DSS asks her to return her order book. She asks her husband, B, to return the book but unknown to A he retains it and cashes four weeks' worth of orders. When the DSS writes to A again, B tells her that he returned the book. A is interviewed and denies cashing the order book slips. B later admits to A what he has done. When the couple are charged jointly, the prosecution cannot rely on A's failure to tell the interviewer about what B did as she was unaware of this at the time.

Code C

The code governing interviews with suspects is Police and Criminal Evidence Act 1984 Code C, 'Code of Practice for the Detention, Treatment and Questioning of Persons by Police Officers'. The relevant contents are as follows:

---

6 Section 34. This section came into force from 10 April 1995: Criminal Justice and Public Order Act 1994 (Commencement No 6) Order 1995 SI No 721. The prosecution cannot rely on the section in relation to any interview taking place before that date: s34(6).
7 Ibid s34(1) and (3).
8 Ibid s38(3).
9 *Blackstone's Criminal Practice 1996* (Blackstone's, 1996), para F19.4.

a) The interviewee has a right to consult with his/her solicitor or other legal adviser. It must be noted in the interview that s/he has been reminded of the right to free legal advice. 'No attempt should be made to dissuade the suspect from obtaining legal advice',[10] so no adverse inferences should be drawn from the interviewee stopping the interview to visit the local law centre or similar.

b) The interviewee must be told that s/he is free to leave and s/he must be cautioned in the appropriate words or words to the same effect. If s/he does not appear to understand the caution it must be explained to him/her.[11] The new recommended form of caution, following the abolition of the absolute right to silence under the Criminal Justice and Public Order Act 1994, is:

> You do not have say anything. But it may harm your defence if you do not mention when questioned something which you later rely on in court. Anything you do say may be given in evidence.

c) There must be no 'oppression' of the interviewee. In particular, there must be no 'threats' as to the action that will be taken if s/he answers or refuses to answer any question, unless the interviewee asks what will happen.[12]

EXAMPLE 21.2

C is a single parent with two young children. She is interviewed by fraud officers on suspicion of claiming benefit while working. One of her children is sick and is being cared for by a neighbour during the interview. She refuses to answer any questions, stating that she wishes to take legal advice first. The officers tell her that if she refuses to answer questions, they will be forced to assume her guilt and prosecute her. In order to get home in time, she admits to fraud. The officers' behaviour renders the confession inadmissible as evidence.

---

d) Once the interviewer takes the view that there is enough evidence for a conviction, the interview must be brought to

---

10 Code C paras 6.1, 11.2 and 6.4 respectively.
11 Ibid paras 10.2, 10.1 and Note for Guidance 10C.
12 Ibid para 11.3.

an end, but the interviewee must be asked if there is anything further s/he wishes to say.[13] It is arguable that if the interviewee is not allowed to give his/her account at this stage, then Code C has been breached.

e) An accurate record of the interview must be kept, which may either be verbatim or a fair summary. All appropriate comments must be recorded, including those made outside the time of the interview.[14] The interviewee must have the opportunity to read the record and correct any inaccuracies.[15]

f) A mentally disordered or handicapped person is not to be interviewed without an 'appropriate adult' being present.[16] There is to be no interview where the interviewee has difficulty understanding English and there is no-one available to speak his/her language, unless the interviewee does not want an interpreter.[17]

g) Where the interviewee wishes to write down a statement, s/he must be allowed to write down what s/he wants without any prompting. If the officer writes down such a statement, s/he must write down the interviewee's exact words and give him/her an opportunity to correct them. The interviewee must state that the statement is made of his/her own free will.[18]

Exclusion of interview material at trial

Under the Police and Criminal Evidence Act 1984 (PACE), there are a number of provisions for excluding evidence. Only an outline guide can be given here to these important provisions and the mass of related case-law.[19] For present purposes, two of the provisions are particularly important:

---

13 Ibid para 11.5.
14 Ibid paras 11.5 and 11.13.
15 Ibid para 11.10.
16 Ibid para 11.14. The term 'appropriate adult' derives from the Police and Criminal Evidence Act 1984 and means a responsible relative or professional person.
17 Ibid para 13.2.
18 Ibid Annex D.
19 See, eg, *Archbold's Criminal Pleading, Evidence and Practice* (44th edn, Sweet & Maxwell, 1995), paras 15-290ff; *Blackstone's Criminal Practice 1996* (Blackstone's, 1996), F2.10-19.

a) A confession must be excluded if it was obtained by oppression or is otherwise unreliable.[20]
b) Any evidence may, in the judge's discretion, be excluded if it would have 'such an adverse effect on the fairness of the proceedings that the court ought not to admit it'.[21]

The latter provision will usually be used to exclude interview evidence obtained in breach of Code C. The mere fact that the code has been breached will not suffice to exclude evidence under PACE s78.[22] Even a plain breach will not be sufficient unless there has been some prejudice to the accused.[23] It appears that the court must decide whether the nature of the breach makes it 'significant and substantial'.[24] If the interviewer is acting in bad faith, eg, by lying or deliberately taking advantage of some vulnerability of the accused to obtain a confession, then exclusion is much more likely,[25] but bad faith is not a prerequisite for exclusion.[26] It is a matter of fact and degree in each case.

Advising those under investigation

Advisers must provide reassurance to those under investigation. Many claimants who have committed innocent breaches of duty or even who are victims of official error will find themselves under investigation with the same vigour as seasoned criminals and will be distressed at the allegations. Lay advisers should bear in mind that where criminal proceedings are pending legal aid will be readily available and clients should be referred to solicitors.

Unfortunately, many clients only seem to take advice after an interview, perhaps because they are often not told outright that they are under investigation until the interview. Those who do take earlier advice should be urged to have someone with them at the interview, if it is not possible to provide professional help. That person should take a note of what is said. Failing that, the

---

20 Police and Criminal Evidence Act 1984 s76.
21 Ibid s78.
22 *R v Delaney* (1989) 88 Cr App R 338 at p341, CA; *R v Parris* (1989) 89 Cr App R 68 at p72, CA.
23 *R v Canale* [1990] 2 All ER 187 at p189f, CA.
24 *R v Keenan* [1990] 2 QB 54 at p69F-H, CA.
25 *R v Allardice* (1988) 87 Cr App R 380 at p386, CA.
26 *R v Samuel* [1988] QB 621 at p630D, CA.

client should take such a note. Transcripts of interviews are frequently disputed, and this procedure should help the client establish his/her version of the facts.

Following the abolition of the absolute right to silence (see p304 above), if a client has a positive defence to put forward, it is essential that s/he makes that clear when interviewed. The questioning practices of officers have already been mentioned, but claimants should attempt to remain calm and insist on putting forward their version of events.

When a claimant is under investigation, there may often be a suspension of his/her benefit. Suspicion of, or even a conviction for fraud, is no grounds for removing a client's benefit unless there is 'a question' as to his/her entitlement.[27] Once the true facts are known and the claimant has a prima facie entitlement to benefit, it should be restored. Unfortunately the DSS is often slow to do this. Suspension of benefit is a Secretary of State decision and a threat to apply for judicial review should be made in such cases. Where the adjudication officer has reviewed the award unjustifiably this should be appealed, and where there is no entitlement on the review a fresh claim should also be put in by the claimant.

---

27 Claims and Payments Regs 1987 reg 37.

CHAPTER 22
Prosecution of offences

Prosecution practice

After a decline in the mid-1980s, the number of those prosecuted for obtaining benefit to which they were not entitled has increased. This has coincided with the present government using benefit fraud as a convenient political bugbear with continued promises of harsh crackdowns. Many of these avowals have amounted to empty rhetoric, but there has been a steady increase in the number of staff employed in the combating of benefit fraud.

As a general rule of thumb, a defendant is unlikely to be prosecuted where the amount involved is very small. The government has said that there will not be a prosecution when the amount involved is under £50. It is understood that normal practice is to take into account any notional benefit entitlement of the claimant when making a decision on whether to prosecute. However, it is dangerous to seek to give firm guidance on practice, as the propensity to prosecute varies widely between different local offices. In particular, it has been said that local offices will be more ready to prosecute particular types of fraud which are prevalent in the areas under their jurisdiction.[1] Local authorities differ in their practices to an even greater degree. Advisers may find it profitable to analyse the circumstances of clients who are prosecuted in an attempt to ascertain the local practice.

The volume of offences prosecuted is considerable and preparation by prosecuting authorities anticipating a guilty plea is minimal. Testing the prosecution's evidence on each element

1   *R v Stewart* [1987] 2 All ER 383 at p384h, CA.

of the offence where a defendant is pleading not guilty is, therefore, good practice.

The vast majority of offenders are dealt with in the magistrates' court. Of the two principal offences under which social security fraud is punished, the lesser offence of making a false statement to obtain benefit will always be tried summarily. Certain DSS and local authority officers will have a right of audience before magistrates for the prosecution of cases. Where a defendant is charged with the more serious offence of obtaining property by deception (see pp314–315 below), s/he should still be dealt with by way of summary trial unless the justices consider that their sentencing powers are insufficient and there has been organised fraud on a large scale or substantial frauds carried out over a long period of time.[2]

The offences

There are a large number of offences that can be committed by those who are dishonest in their dealings with the DSS. This section will centre on a typical situation faced by advisers, that of a claimant who is accused of making deliberate misrepresentations to obtain benefit. Two offences call for consideration.

Making a false representation in obtaining benefit

As a rule of thumb, less serious cases will be dealt with by prosecuting for this offence which is specific to the social security system. It is defined thus:

> If a person for the purpose of obtaining any benefit or other payment under the legislation to which section 110 above applies whether for himself or some other person, or for any other purpose connected with that legislation –
> (a) makes a statement or representation which he knows to be false; or
> (b) produces or furnishes, or knowingly causes or knowingly allows to be produced or furnished, any document or information which he knows to be false in a material particular,
> he shall be guilty of an offence.[3]

---

2 *Practice Note (Mode of Trial: Guidelines)* (1995) unreported, reproduced in *Blackstone's Criminal Practice 1996* (Blackstone, 1996), pp997 to 999.
3 SSAA s112(1). An identical offence is created by Jobseekers Act 1995 s34(1).

The first point is that anybody making a false statement or connected with the production of a false document can be convicted, not just a claimant. In addition, this offence can be committed by a body corporate. Moreover, if it is attributable to deliberate conduct or neglect by a particular person or officer within that body corporate, s/he can be prosecuted personally in addition to the company.[4]

EXAMPLE 22.1

A is claiming invalid care allowance. His employer, B Ltd, is requested to produce a statement of his earnings. A persuades his manager, C, to state his earnings as being lower than they really are. C orders his secretary, D, to complete the DSS's form to this effect. D protests but complies with the request. A and C are guilty of causing the false statement to be produced under SSAA s112(1)(b). D is guilty of making a false statement under SSAA s112(1)(a). B Ltd can be prosecuted under either paragraph.

It must be proved that the statement was false at the time that it was made. In relation to s112(1)(b), it is suggested that the meaning of the phrase 'material particular' is the same as that of a 'material fact' for the purposes of SSAA s71 (see chapter 6 above), except that the statement can probably be one of law as well as one of fact. A literally true statement may be false if it omits vital information that gives a different meaning to the representation.[5]

Moore v Branton[6] made clear that the defendant must have known of the falsity of the statement at that time. If a defendant 'shuts his/her eyes' to the true facts, s/he will be deemed to have knowledge of its falsity. This must be proved by the prosecution,[7] and this element of the offence will be the battleground in the vast majority of cases where the defendant pleads not guilty. This will usually be done by proving that the defendant must have had certain information in his/her possession at the time. If the defendant was working and states that s/he was not, then this

---

4 SSAA s115.
5 *R v Birshirgian* [1936] 1 All ER 586 at p594, CCA.
6 (1974) 118 SJ 40, DC.
7 *Gaumont British Distributors Ltd v Henry* [1939] 2 KB 711 at pp719 and 723, DC.

will be simple. But there will be cases, eg, where the defendant had capital resources which were not declared, in which it will be less simple for the Crown to prove this element of the offence.

The defendant's representative must fully test whatever evidence is brought to satisfy this requirement. This will particularly be the case where the false representation relied on by the prosecution is said to be a declaration in an order book or elsewhere, and a previously valid claim has become fraudulent due to a change of circumstances. The prosecution will have to prove that the defendant knew that s/he had reported all material facts or that there was no entitlement. It will not be sufficient that the defendant was uncertain of whether something might be relevant and did not ask for assistance. A mere failure to make enquiries does not fix a defendant with knowledge.[8]

In such cases, unless there is some admission by the defendant that s/he knew that the representation was false, then the prosecution will have to prove that it is not credible that the defendant did not know of the falsity. Critical here will be the instructions given to the claimant, especially in the notes to the order book or wherever the declaration is made. If the instructions are at all ambiguous, then it will be extremely difficult for the prosecution to prove that the defendant had the requisite knowledge. It will also be possible to look at personal characteristics of the defendant. Someone suffering from an illness rendering it difficult for him/her to understand instructions may not have the requisite degree of knowledge that a healthy person in his/her position would have.

EXAMPLE 22.2
E is in receipt of sickness benefit. He is semi-literate and mentally ill. He is offered a part-time job as a cleaner. He cannot understand the declaration that he signs each week that tells him to report changes of circumstances. A friend tells E that only full-time work disentitles a person to sickness benefit. His lack of understanding and the misleading advice from his friend are strong proof that he did not know that he was making a false statement.

---

8 *Taylor's Central Garages (Exeter) Ltd v Roper* (1951) 115 JP 445 at pp449 and 450, DC.

It is not necessary to show that the defendant intended to obtain benefit as the result of the of the false statement. All that needs to be shown is that the statement was connected in some way with a benefit claim. So in *Barrass v Reeve*[9] the defendant was not able to absolve himself by claiming that his misrepresentation as to his capacity for work was only intended to deceive his employer and that he had given no thought to the effect on the DSS. The defendant in *Clear v Smith*[10] claimed that his work for his family while in receipt of supplementary benefit was not remunerated and therefore he did not regard it as work affecting his benefit. Likewise, the fact that he knew that he had made a false statement was sufficient.

It is suggested that these cases were wrongly decided. The phrase 'for the purpose of obtaining ...' would seem to connote that the defendant should be aiming to obtain benefit by means of his/her false statement. The interpretation given to the section in *Barrass* and *Clear* unduly widens the scope of the offence and criminalises those who unthinkingly (and hence recklessly) make a statement as a result of which benefit is paid. There have been cases where illiterate defendants have been pressurised into signing forms by their partners, the contents of which they do not understand, leading to prosecution. It may be right that such actions should attract SSAA s71 recoverability but imposing a criminal sanction is harsh.

The phrase 'obtaining any benefit' is not restricted to the award of benefit by an adjudication officer. In *Tolfree v Florence*[11] the statement was true at the time that the DSS made the award but later became false as a result of a change of circumstances. The claimant knew this while signing on for benefit. It was held that the claimant was 'obtaining' benefit when he signed his order book at the post office and thereby committed the offence. The DSS is not required to prove the commission of the offence on a particular date or the place where

---

9 [1981] 1 WLR 408 at p413, DC.
10 [1981] 1 WLR 399 at p406, DC. These two cases distinguish *Moore v Branton* (1974) 118 SJ 40, DC, on the basis that the defendant's statement was not, on the evidence, false. Some ambiguous statements in *Moore* about the defendant's intention to secure benefit were expressly disclaimed to be authority for that point by the court in *Reeve* (see n9 above) and *Clear*. See also *Department of Social Security v Barr* [1996] 5 CL 674, QBD.
11 [1971] 1 WLR 141 at p144, DC.

it was committed.[12] Nor is it necessary that an adjudication officer has reviewed the award of benefit.[13]

The offence is triable summarily only.[14] The maximum penalty is a fine on level 5 or three months' imprisonment.

Obtaining property by deception

More serious cases of fraud will be dealt with by charging the defendant with the general offence of obtaining property by deception. This offence is committed by a 'person who by any deception dishonestly obtains property belonging to another, with the intention of permanently depriving the other of it'.[15] 'Property' includes money and intangibles such as giro cheques.[16]

Normally, for this offence to be committed, there must be specific proof that the deception operated on the mind of the deceived person at the time that the payment was made. Potentially, this would require the post office clerk or the computer operator making the payment to give evidence that s/he was so deceived. However, it has been held that where a declaration could not have been honestly signed and payment could not conceivably been made without the declaration being made, evidence from such witnesses need not be called.[17] This radically reduces the importance of this requirement in the context of social security fraud.

On the other hand, there must be specific proof that the property was obtained by the defendant. This element in the offence will be particularly important where the defendant denies having received any benefit. In *Bogdal v Hall*[18] the prosecution presented the claim forms which falsely stated that the defendant was unemployed, together with evidence of the processing of claims and issuing of giro cheques. It was held that this was insufficient proof of the obtaining of the benefit. There had to be evidence that would prove beyond reasonable doubt that the defendant had received the money. The divisional court

---

12 *Department of Social Security v Cooper* (1994) 158 JPN 354, DC.
13 *Department of Social Security v Lally* [1989] Crim LR 648, DC.
14 SSAA s122(2).
15 Theft Act 1968 s15.
16 Ibid ss4(1) and 34.
17 *Etim v Hatfield* [1975] Crim LR 234, DC; *R v Lambie* [1982] AC 449 at p461D-E, HL.
18 [1987] Crim LR 500, DC.

suggested that 'cogent' evidence of posting might suffice. Evidence that the money entered the defendant's bank account will also suffice to show an obtaining, which includes control of the property in question.

The question of dishonesty must be considered separately from the other elements of the offence. In many cases, it will simply be inferred from the fact of the deception that the defendant was dishonest. However, there will be situations in which the requirement of dishonesty becomes a live issue. It must be proved that the defendant's actions would have been seen as dishonest by 'reasonable and honest people' and that the defendant must have realised that his/her actions did not meet that standard of behaviour.[19] Where the defendant believed that the false statement was honestly made in claiming a right to benefit, and a reasonable person would take that view, there is no dishonesty.

EXAMPLE 22.3

F spent a year claiming supplementary benefit in the 1970s while doing voluntary work for an employment charity. He was allowed benefit on a discretionary basis, as he was contributing to the employment of others. F returns to this work after an absence of many years and omits to mention his work on his income support claim form. He has a belief that there is no need to do so, as he had previously been allowed benefit. F has committed no offence, provided that the court accepts that a reasonable person could have acted in the same way. The prosecution could seek to rebut this by pointing to the contents of the instructions given to F and question whether it is reasonable for him to assume that the rules for benefit entitlement remain the same.

This offence is triable either way.[20] The maximum penalty is one of ten years' imprisonment. Where the offence is tried summarily, the longest period of imprisonment is six months and the statutory maximum fine applies.

---

19 *R v Ghosh* [1982] QB 1053 at p1064D–G, CA.
20 Magistrates' Courts Act 1980 s17 and Sch 1 para 28.

Sentencing

The available options

A full discussion of the powers of the courts and the criteria by which they must be exercised when sentencing is outside the scope of this book and only a few points of specific relevance to social security fraud are discussed here.

Simply to cover the reported cases on appropriate sentencing in this area would give a misleading impression that benefit frauds will almost invariably attract sentences of imprisonment. In fact, the vast majority of defendants are dealt with by non-custodial means, particularly in view of the criteria laid down in the guideline case of *R v Stewart*.[21] The case makes the important point that deterrence has no place in sentencing for this type of offence. Before determining the penalty, the Court of Appeal in *Stewart* urged sentencers to consider the possibility of the DSS pursuing recovery through other means. The prosecution must have information available about this, and also about the amount of the overpayment made.

When imposing financial penalties, a court must exercise caution. Most defendants will have few or no resources to meet such a penalty. A court must take into account the means of an offender when imposing a fine.[22] The ability of others, such as members of the defendant's family, to pay the fine should be ignored.[23]

It is clear that it is proper to impose a compensation order in favour of the DSS for an appropriate amount, as there has been 'loss' to the DSS in terms of the benefit wrongly paid out.[24] The Court of Appeal has stated that such orders can be made, subject to the normal rule that they must be realistic in terms, which 'will usually only be the case when the defendant is in work'.[25] It is wrong to impose a compensation order in anticipation of a defendant finding work in the future.[26]

---

21 [1987] 2 All ER 383, CA.
22 Criminal Justice Act 1991 s18(1).
23 *R v Curtis* (1984) 6 Cr App R (S) 250, CA; *R v Charambous* (1984) 6 Cr App R (S) 389, CA.
24 Powers of Criminal Courts Act 1973 s33. The observations of Commissioner Henty in *CIS 683/1994* para 5 are wrong.
25 *R v Stewart* [1987] 2 All ER 383 at p386h, CA.
26 *R v Diggles* (1988) *Times* 6 July, CA.

Alternatively, on a conviction for obtaining property by deception, a restitution order may be made compelling the defendant to reimburse the DSS with the money.[27]

The sentencing criteria

The starting point

The Magistrates' Association Sentencing Guidelines suggest that the starting point when determining sentence should be a community sentence. On this point, *Stewart* is instructive. Lane LCJ referred to the statistics of sentencing in the magistrates' courts, which showed that only one in 40 defendants were sentenced to immediate terms of imprisonment. The court felt that 'a suspended sentence or (especially) a community service order may be an ideal form of punishment in many of these cases'.[28]

There has been a marked and welcome trend away from using immediate sentences of imprisonment on first conviction. Cases pre-dating *Stewart* must be treated with extreme caution. In particular, cases like *R v Goldstraw*,[29] where the Court of Appeal decided that three months' imprisonment was appropriate for a defendant with no previous convictions, whose business would be disrupted and who had received an overpayment of less than £250, would certainly not attract a custodial sentence today.

One criticism that could be made of sentencing practice in this area today is the overuse of financial penalties. The financial dire straits that most defendants are in make such penalties a crippling burden. There is therefore plenty of scope to argue that a community penalty is more appropriate than imprisonment, particularly for a first offence, and many claimants are in the best position to fulfil the requirements of such a sentence. Nevertheless, the courts treat social security fraud as serious offences of dishonesty. According to the statistics recited in *Stewart*, virtually all offenders will receive financial or community penalties.

The criteria: more serious offences

These criteria are taken from the authorities and from the Magistrates' Association Guidelines, but other factors are listed where relevant:

---

27 Theft Act 1968 s28.
28 [1987] 2 All ER 383 at p386f, CA.
29 [1981] Crim LR 728, CA. Compare *R v Breeze* (1993) 15 Cr App R (S) 94, CA.

a) Where the defendant commits an offence on bail.
b) The offences are committed over a long period of time and large amounts of money are involved.[30]
c) Planning and organisation are involved in the fraud. These cases are explicitly identified in *Stewart* as being the most serious.[31] Multiple claims and the use of false identities[32] and documentation[33] will both be seen in a very dim light.
d) The offence is committed by a group.
e) A failure to respond to previous sentences.
f) Previous convictions for similar offences.

The criteria: less serious offences

a) Where the defendant is ignorant of regulations. The maxim that ignorance of the law is no defence applies in this sphere as much as anywhere else, but a genuine misunderstanding of the extent of a defendant's obligations should be a relevant factor.
b) Offences of omission. It seems to be common sense that a defendant who does not inform the DSS of a change of circumstances ought to be less culpable than one who sets out to deliberately make false statements.[34]
c) Voluntary repayment of the amounts overpaid or any part thereof, or other efforts to make recompense.
d) Benefit spent on household necessities rather than luxuries.[35]
e) Difficult personal circumstances. The effect on the defendant's family life was held to be particularly important in *R v Mills*.[36]
f) Cases where the defendant pleads guilty. The usual discount must be given for a plea.
g) Where the defendant would have had entitlement to some benefit other than that wrongly obtained. Although this

---

30 *R v Rae* (1987) 9 Cr App R (S) 523; *R v Weild* (1993) 15 Cr App R (S) 585, CA.
31 [1987] 2 All ER 383j-384a, CA.
32 *R v Adams* (1985) 7 Cr App R (S) 411; *R v McDonagh* (1989) 11 Cr App R (S) 94.
33 See, in particular, *R v Rae* (1987) 9 Cr App R (S) 523, CA.
34 *R v Stewart* [1987] 2 All ER 383 at 386d, CA.
35 *R v Olusoji* (1993) 15 Cr App R (S) 356, CA.
36 (1987) 9 Cr App R (S) 3, CA. This criterion has its limits as an exculpatory factor: *R v Tucker* (1993) 15 Cr App R (S) 349, CA.

should be drawn to the attention of the court by the prosecution, those representing defendants should not count on this and should always be prepared to justify their assertion to the court.

Application of the criteria

Stewart envisages that elaborate, persistent frauds will attract over two years' imprisonment.[37] More straightforward cases involving less than £10,000 will not usually require a sentence of more than a year.

The crucial question is where the line of a custodial sentence being the only justifiable sentence is crossed. The answer seems to be that for a first-time offender, a moderate overpayment over a few months does not call for a custodial sentence,[38] while for those with poor records, prison will be justified where anything larger than a few hundred pounds is overpaid.[39] It is suggested that, all other things being equal, to impose a prison sentence on a defendant who does not step over whichever of those lines is applicable would be wrong in principle.

---

37 [1987] 2 All ER 383 at p385j, CA.
38 *R v Graham* (1988) 10 Cr App R (S) 352, CA; *R v Miah* (1989) 11 Cr App R (S) 163, CA.
39 *R v Breeze* (1993) 15 Cr App R (S) 94, CA.

Appendices

APPENDIX 1
Extracts from legislation

Social Security Administration Act 1992

Note: it is assumed that the Jobseekers Act 1995 is fully in force.

Review of decisions
25. – (1) Subject to the following provisions of this section, any decision under this Act of an adjudication officer, a social security appeal tribunal or a Commissioner (other than a decision relating to an attendance allowance, a disability living allowance or a disability working allowance) may be reviewed at any time by an adjudication officer or, on a reference by an adjudication officer, by a social security appeal tribunal, if –
(a) the officer or tribunal is satisfied that the decision was given in ignorance of, or was based on a mistake as to, some material fact; or
(b) there has been any relevant change of circumstances since the decision was given; or
(c) it is anticipated that a relevant change of circumstances will so occur; or
(d) the decision was based on a decision of a question which under or by virtue of this Act falls to be determined otherwise than by an adjudication officer, and the decision of that question is revised; or
(e) the decision falls to be reviewed under section 25A(4) or (5) of the Contributions and Benefits Act.
  (2) Any decision of an adjudication officer (other than a decision relating to an attendance allowance, a disability living allowance or a disability working allowance) may be reviewed, upon the ground that it was erroneous in point of law, by an adjudication officer or, on a reference from an adjudication officer, by a social security appeal tribunal.

Overpayments – general

Note: *words in square brackets are repealed, and those in italics are inserted, by the Overpayments Act. The former apply to a recoverability decision issued before 24 July 1996, the latter to a decision after that date.*

71. – (1) Where it is determined that, whether fraudulently or otherwise, any person has misrepresented, or failed to disclose, any material fact and in consequence of the misrepresentation or failure –

(a) a payment has been made in respect of a benefit to which this section applies; or

(b) any sum recoverable by or on behalf of the Secretary of State in connection with any such payment has not been recovered,

the Secretary of State shall be entitled to recover the amount of any payment which he would not have made or any sum which he would have received but for the misrepresentation or failure to disclose.

(2) [Where any such determination as is referred to in subsection (1) above is made on an appeal or review, there shall also be determined in the course of the appeal or review the question whether any, and if so what, amount is recoverable under that subsection by the Secretary of State.]

(2) Where any such determination as is referred to in subsection (1) above is made, the person making the determination shall –

(a) determine whether any, and if so what, amount is recoverable under that subsection by the Secretary of State, and

(b) specify the period during which that amount was paid to the person concerned.

(3) An amount recoverable under subsection (1) above is in all cases recoverable from the person who misrepresented the fact or failed to disclose it.

(4) In relation to cases where payments of benefit to which this section applies have been credited to a bank account or other account under arrangements made with the agreement of the beneficiary or a person acting for him, circumstances may be prescribed in which the Secretary of State is to be entitled to recover any amount paid in excess of entitlement; but any such regulations shall not apply in relation to any payment unless before he agreed to the arrangements such notice of the effect of the regulations as may be prescribed was given in such manner as may be prescribed to the beneficiary or to a person acting for him.

(5) Except where regulations otherwise provide, an amount shall not be recoverable under [subsection (1) above or] regulations under subsection (4) above unless –

(a) the determination in pursuance of which it was paid has been reversed or varied on an appeal or revised on a review; and

(b) it has been determined on the appeal or review that the amount is so recoverable.

(5A) Except where regulations otherwise provide, an amount shall not be recoverable under subsection (1) above unless the determination in

pursuance of which it was paid has been reversed or varied on an appeal or revised on a review.

(6) Regulations may provide –
(a) that amounts recoverable under subsection (1) above or regulations under subsection (4) above shall be calculated or estimated in such manner and on such basis as may be prescribed;
(b) for treating any amount paid to any person under an award which it is subsequently determined was not payable –
  (i) as properly paid; or
  (ii) as paid on account of a payment which it is determined should be or should have been made,
  and for reducing or withholding any arrears payable by virtue of the subsequent determination;
(c) for treating any amount paid to one person in respect of another as properly paid for any period for which it is not payable in cases where in consequence of a subsequent determination –
  (i) the other person is himself entitled to a payment for that period; or
  (ii) a third person is entitled in priority to the payee to a payment for that period in respect of the other person,
  and for reducing or withholding any arrears payable for that period by virtue of the subsequent determination.

(7) Circumstances may be prescribed in which a payment on account by virtue of section 5(1)(r) above may be recovered to the extent that it exceeds entitlement.

(8) Where any amount paid is recoverable under –
(a) subsection (1) above;
(b) regulations under subsection (4) or (7) above; or
(c) section 74 below,
it may, without prejudice to any other method of recovery, be recovered by deduction from prescribed benefits.

(9) Where any amount paid in respect of a married or unmarried couple is recoverable as mentioned in subsection (8) above, it may, without prejudice to any other method of recovery, be recovered, in such circumstances as may be prescribed, by deduction from prescribed benefits payable to either of them.

(10) Any amount recoverable under the provisions mentioned in subsection (8) above –
(a) if the person from whom it is recoverable resides in England and Wales and the county court so orders, shall be recoverable by execution issued from the county court or otherwise as if it were payable under an order of that court; and
(b) if he resides in Scotland, shall be enforced in like manner as an extract registered decree arbitral bearing a warrant for execution issued by the sheriff court of any sheriffdom in Scotland.

(11) This section applies to the following benefits –
(a) benefits as defined in section 122 of the Contributions and Benefits Act;
(aa) subject to section 71A below, a jobseeker's allowance;
(b) subject to section 72 below, income support;
(c) family credit;
(d) disability working allowance;
(e) any social fund payments such as are mentioned in section 138(1)(a) or (2) of the Contributions and Benefits Act; and
(f) child benefit.

Recovery of jobseeker's allowance: severe hardship cases
71A.—(1) Where –
(a) a severe hardship direction is revoked; and
(b) it is determined by an adjudication officer that –
   (i) whether fraudulently or otherwise, any person has misrepresented, or failed to disclose, any material fact; and
   (ii) in consequence of the failure or misrepresentation, payment of a jobseeker's allowance has been made during the relevant period to the person to whom the direction related, an adjudication officer may determine that the Secretary of State is entitled to recover the amount of the payment.

(2) In this section –
"severe hardship direction" means a direction given under section 16 of the Jobseekers Act 1995; and
"the relevant period" means –
(a) if the revocation is under section 16(3)(a) of that Act, the period beginning with the date of the change of circumstances and ending with the date of the revocation; and
(b) if the revocation is under section 16(3)(b) or (c) of that Act, the period during which the direction was in force.

(3) Where a severe hardship direction is revoked, the Secretary of State may certify whether there has been misrepresentation of a material fact or failure to disclose a material fact.

(4) If the Secretary of State certifies that there has been such misrepresentation or failure to disclose, he may certify –
(a) who made the misrepresentation or failed to make the disclosure; and
(b) whether or not a payment of jobseeker's allowance has been made in consequence of the misrepresentation or failure.

(5) If the Secretary of State certifies that a payment has been made, he may certify the period during which a jobseeker's allowance would not have been paid but for the misrepresentation of failure to disclose.

(6) A certificate under this section shall be conclusive as to any matter certified.

(7) Subsections (3) and (6) to (10) of section 71 above apply to a

jobseeker's allowance recoverable under subsection (1) above as they apply to a jobseeker's allowance recoverable under subsection 71(1) above.

(8) The other provisions of section 71 above do not apply to a jobseeker's allowance recoverable under subsection (1) above.

Special provision as to recovery of income support
72. – (1) Where –
(a) a direction under section 125(1) of the Contributions and Benefits Act is revoked; and
(b) it is determined by an adjudication officer that, whether fraudulently or otherwise, any person has misrepresented, or failed to disclose, any material fact and in consequence of the misrepresentation or failure a payment of income support has been made during the relevant period to the person to whom the direction related,
an adjudication officer may determine that the Secretary of State shall be entitled to recover the amount of the payment.

(2) In subsection (1) above "the relevant period" means –
(a) if the revocation is under subsection (3) of section 125 of the Contributions and Benefits Act, the period beginning with the date of the change of circumstances and ending with the date of the revocation; and
(b) if the revocation is under subsection (4) of that section, the period during which the direction was in force.

(3) Where a direction under section 125(1) of the Contributions and Benefits Act is revoked, the Secretary of State may certify whether there has been misrepresentation of a material fact or failure to disclose a material fact.

(4) If he certifies that there has been such misrepresentation or failure to disclose, he may also certify –
(a) who made the misrepresentation or failed to make the disclosure; and
(b) whether or not a payment of income support has been made in consequence of the misrepresentation or failure.

(5) If he certifies that a payment has been made, he may certify the period during which income support would not have been paid but for the misrepresentation or failure to disclose.

(6) A certificate under this section shall be conclusive for the purposes of this section as to any matter certified.

(7) Section 71(3) and (6) to (11) above apply to income support recoverable under subsection (1) above as they apply to income support recoverable under section 71(1) above.

(8) The other provisions of section 71 above do not apply to income support recoverable under subsection (1) above.

Income support and other payments

74. – (1) Where –

(a) a payment by way of prescribed income is made after the date which is the prescribed date in relation to the payment; and

(b) it is determined that an amount which has been paid by way of income support or an income-based jobseeker's allowance would not have paid if the payment had been made on the prescribed date,

the Secretary of State shall be entitled to recover that amount from the person to whom it was paid.

(2) Where –

(a) a prescribed payment which apart from this subsection falls to be made from public funds in the United Kingdom or under the law of any other member State is not made on or before the date which is the prescribed date in relation to the payment; and

(b) it is determined that an amount ("the relevant amount") has been paid by way of income support or an income-based jobseeker's allowance that would not have been paid if the payment mentioned in paragraph (a) above had been made on the prescribed date,

then –

    (i) in the case of a payment from public funds in the United Kingdom, the authority responsible for making it may state it by the relevant amount; and

    (ii) in the case of any other payment, the Secretary of State shall be entitled to receive the relevant amount out of the payment.

(3) Where –

(a) a person (in this subsection referred to as A) is entitled to any prescribed benefit for any period in respect of another person (in this subsection referred to as B); and

(b) either –

    (i) B has received income support or an income-based jobseeker's allowance for that period; or

    (ii) B was, during that period, a member of the same family as some person other than A who received income support or an income-based jobseeker's allowance for that period; and

(c) the amount of the income support or an income-based jobseeker's allowance has been determined on the basis that A has not made payments for the maintenance of B at a rate equal to or exceeding the amount of the prescribed benefit,

the amount of the prescribed benefit may, at the discretion of the authority administering it, be abated by the amount by which the amounts paid by way of income support or an income-based jobseeker's allowance exceed what it is determined that they would have been had A, at the time the amount of the income support or an income-support jobseeker's allowance was determined, been making payments for the maintenance of B at a rate equal to the amount of the prescribed benefit.

(4) Where an amount could have been recovered by abatement by virtue of subsection (2) or (3) above but has not been so recovered, the Secretary of State may recover it otherwise than by way of abatement –
(a) in the case of an amount which could have been recovered by virtue of subsection (2) above, from the person to whom it was paid; and
(b) in the case of an amount which could have been recovered by virtue of subsection (3) above, from the person to whom the prescribed benefit in question was paid.
(5) Where a payment is made in a currency other than sterling, its value in sterling shall be determined for the purposes of this section in accordance with regulations.

Recovery of social fund awards
78. – (1) A social fund award which is repayable shall be recoverable by the Secretary of State.
(2) Without prejudice to any other method of recovery, the Secretary of State may recover an award by deduction from prescribed benefits.
(3) The Secretary of State may recover an award –
(a) from the person to or for the benefit of whom it was made;
(b) where that person is a member of a married or unmarried couple, from the other member of the couple;
(c) from a person who is liable to maintain the person by or on behalf of whom the application for the award was made or any person in relation to whose needs the award was made.
(4) Payments to meet funeral expenses may in all cases be recovered, as if they were funeral expenses, out of the estate of the deceased, and (subject to section 71 above) by no other means.
(5) In this section –
"married couple" means a man and woman who are married to each other and are members of the same household;
"unmarried couple" means a man and a woman who are not married to each other but are living together as husband and wife otherwise than in circumstances prescribed under section 132 of the Contributions and Benefits Act.
(6) For the purposes of this section –
(a) a man shall be liable to maintain his wife and any children of whom he is the father; and
(b) a woman shall be liable to maintain her husband and any children of whom she is the mother;
(c) a person shall be liable to maintain another person throughout any period in respect of which the first-mentioned person has, on or after 23rd May 1980 (the date of the passing of the Social Security Act 1980) and either alone or jointly with a further person, given an undertaking in writing in pursuance of immigration rules within the meaning of the Immigration Act 1971 to be responsible for the maintenance and

accommodation of the other person; and

(d) "child" includes a person who has attained the age of 16 but not the age of 19 and in respect of whom either parent, or some person acting in place of either parent, is receiving income support or an income-based jobseeker's allowance.

(7) Any reference in subsection (6) above to children of whom the man or the woman is the father or mother shall be construed in accordance with section 1 of the Family Law Reform Act 1987.

(8) Subsection (7) above does not apply in Scotland, and in the application of subsection (6) above to Scotland any reference to children of whom the man or the woman is the father or the mother shall be construed as a reference to any such children whether or not their parents have ever been married to one another.

(9) A document bearing a certificate which –

(a) is signed by a person authorised in that behalf by the Secretary of State; and

(b) states that the document apart from the certificate is, or is a copy of, such an undertaking as is mentioned in subsection (6)(c) above,

shall be conclusive of the undertaking in question for the purposes of this section; and a certificate purporting to be so signed shall be deemed to be so signed until the contrary is proved.

Interpretation of Part IV

81. – (1) In this Part of this Act –

...

"compensation payment" means any payment failing to be made (whether voluntarily, or in pursuance of a court order or an agreement, or otherwise) –

(a) to or in respect of the victim in consequence of the accident, injury or disease in question, and

(b) either –
   (i) by or on behalf of a person who is, or is alleged to be, liable to any extent in respect of that accident, injury or disease; or
   (ii) in pursuance of a compensation scheme for motor accidents, but does not include benefit or an exempt payment or so much of any payment as is referable to costs incurred by any person;

...

"compensator", "victim" and "intended recipient" shall be construed in accordance with section 82(1) below;

...

"relevant period" means –

(a) in the case of a disease, the period of 5 years beginning with the date on which the victim first claims a relevant benefit in consequence of the disease; or

(b) in any other case, the period of 5 years immediately following the day on which the accident or injury in question occurred; but where before the end of that period the compensator makes a compensation payment in final discharge of any claim made by or in respect of the victim and arising out of the accident, injury or disease, the relevant period shall end on the date on which that payment is made;

...

(3) For the purposes of this Part of this Act the following are the "exempt payments" –

(a) any small payment, as defined in section 85 below;
(b) any payment made to or for the victim under section 35 of the Powers of Criminal Courts Act 1973 or section 58 of the Criminal Justice (Scotland) Act 1980;
(c) any payment to the extent that it is made –
   (i) in consequence of an action under the Fatal Accidents Act 1976; or
   (ii) in circumstances where, had an action been brought, it would have been brought under that Act;
(d) any payment to the extent that it is made in respect of a liability arising by virtue of section 1 of the Damages (Scotland) Act 1976;
(e) without prejudice to section 6(4) of the Vaccine Damage Payments Act 1979 (which provides for the deduction of any such payment in the assessment of any award of damages), any payment made under that Act to or in respect of the victim;
(f) any award of compensation made to or in respect of the victim by the Criminal Injuries Compensation Board under section III of the Criminal Justice Act 1988;
(g) any payment made in the exercise of a discretion out of property held subject to a trust in a case where no more than 50 per cent. by value of the capital contributed to the trust was directly or indirectly provided by persons who are, or are alleged to be, liable in respect of –
   (i) the accident, injury or disease suffered by the victim in question; or
   (ii) the same or any connected accident, injury or disease suffered by another;
(h) any payment made out of property held for the purposes of any prescribed trust (whether the payment also falls within paragraph (g) above or not);
(i) any payment made to the victim by an insurance company within the meaning of the Insurance Companies Act 1982 under the terms of any contract of insurance entered into between the victim and the company before –
   (i) the date on which the victim first claims a relevant benefit in consequence of the disease in question; or
   (ii) the occurrence of the accident or injury in question;

(j) any redundancy payment failing to be taken into account in the assessment of damages in respect of an accident, injury or disease.

(4) Regulations may provide that any prescribed payment shall be an exempt payment for the purposes of this Part of this Act.

(5) Except as provided by any other enactment, in the assessment of damages in respect of an accident, injury or disease the amount of any relevant benefits paid or likely to be paid shall be disregarded.

...

(7) This Part of this Act shall apply in relation to any compensation payment made on or after 3rd September 1990 (the date of the coming into force of section 22 of the Social Security Act 1989 which, with Schedule 4 to that Act, made provision corresponding to that made by this Part) to the extent that it is made in respect of –

(a) an accident or injury occurring on or after 1st January 1989; or

(b) a disease, if the victim's first claim for a relevant benefit in consequence of the disease is made on or after that date.

Recovery of sums equivalent to benefit from compensation payments in respect of accidents, injuries and diseases

82. – (1) A person ("the compensator") making a compensation payment, whether on behalf of himself or another, in consequence of an accident, injury or disease suffered by any one person ("the victim") shall not do so until the Secretary of State has furnished him with a certificate of total benefit and shall then –

(a) deduct from the payment an amount, determined in accordance with the certificate of total benefit, equal to the gross amount of any relevant benefits paid or likely to be paid to or for the victim during the relevant period in respect of that accident, injury or disease;

(b) pay to the Secretary of State an amount equal to that which is required to be so deducted; and

(c) furnish the person to whom the compensation payment is or, apart from this section, would have been made ("the intended recipient") with a certificate of deduction.

(2) Any right of the intended recipient to receive the compensation payment in question shall be regarded as satisfied to the extent of the amount certified in the certificate of deduction.

Overpaid benefits

91. – In any case where –

(a) during the relevant period, there has, in respect of the accident, injury or disease, been paid to or for the victim any relevant benefit to which he was not entitled ("the overpaid benefit"), and

(b) the amount of the relevant payment is such that, after taking account of the rest of the total benefit, there remains an amount which represents the whole or any part of the overpaid benefit, then, notwithstanding anything in section 71 above or any regulations under that section or section 53 of the 1986 Act, the receipt by the Secretary of State of the relevant payment shall be treated as the recovery of the whole or, as the case may be, that part of the overpaid benefit.

False representations for obtaining benefit etc
112. – (1) If a person for the purpose of obtaining any benefit or other payment under legislation to which section 110 above applies whether for himself or some other person or for any other purpose connected with that legislation –
(a) makes a statement or representation which he knows to be false; or
(b) produces or furnishes, or knowingly causes or knowingly allows to be produced or furnished, any document or information which he knows to be false in a material particular,
he shall be guilty of an offence.
(2) A person guilty of an offence under subsection (1) above shall be liable to summary conviction to a fine not exceeding level 5 on the standard scale, or to imprisonment for a term not exceeding 3 months, or to both.

Social Security Act 1975

Effect of adjudication on payment and recovery
119. – (1) Where benefit is or has been paid in pursuance of a decision which is reversed or varied on appeal, or is revised on a review, then, subject to subsection (2) below, the decision given on the appeal or review shall require repayment to the Secretary of State of any benefit which was paid in pursuance of the original decision to the extent to which it –
(a) would not have been payable if the decision on the appeal or review had been given in the first instance; and
(b) is not directed to be treated as paid on account of the benefit awarded by the decision on appeal or review, or as having been properly paid.
(2) A decision given on appeal or review shall not require repayment of benefit paid in pursuance of the original decision in any case where it is shown to the satisfaction of the person or tribunal determining the appeal or review that in the obtaining and receipt of the benefit the beneficiary, and any person acting for him, has throughout used due care and diligence to avoid overpayment.
(2A) Where, in pursuance of a decision, an amount of benefit was paid which would not have been paid if the facts established for the purpose of any subsequent decision by an insurance officer, local tribunal or Commissioner had been known and –
(a) the subsequent decision is given in relation to the same benefit but is not given on an appeal against or a review of the earlier decision; and

(b) the circumstances are not such as to enable the earlier decision to be reviewed;

the subsequent decision shall require repayment of that amount (except so much of it as is directed by the decision to be treated as having been properly paid) unless it is shown to the satisfaction of the insurance officer, tribunal or Commissioner that in the obtaining and receipt of the benefit the beneficiary, and any person acting for him, has throughout used due care and diligence to avoid overpayment.

Social Security (Claims and Payments) Regulations 1987 SI No 1986

Information to be given when obtaining payment of benefit

32. – (1) Every beneficiary and every person by whom or on whose behalf sums payable by way of benefit are receivable shall furnish in such manner and at such times as the Secretary of State may determine such certificates and other documents and such information or facts affecting the right to benefit or to its receipt as the Secretary of State may require (either as a condition on which any sum or sums shall be receivable or otherwise), and in particular shall notify the Secretary of State of any change of circumstances which he might reasonably be expected to know might affect the right to benefit, or to its receipt, as soon as reasonably practicable after its occurrence, by giving notice in writing (unless the Secretary of State determines in any particular case to accept notice given otherwise than in writing) or any such change to the appropriate office.

Schedule 9A
Recovery of sums wrongly paid

11. – (1) Where sums have been paid to a qualifying lender under regulation 34A which ought not to have been paid for one or both of the reasons mentioned in sub-paragraph (2) of this paragraph, the qualifying lender shall, at the request of the Secretary of State, repay the sum overpaid.

(2) The reasons referred to in sub-paragraph (1) of this paragraph are –

(a) that –
 (i) the rate at which the borrower pays mortgage interest has been reduced or the amount outstanding on the loan has been reduced, and
 (ii) as a result of this reduction the applicable amount of the relevant beneficiary has also been reduced, but
 (iii) no corresponding reduction was made to the specified part; or
(b) subject to paragraph (3), that the relevant beneficiary has ceased to be entitled to any relevant benefits.

(3) A qualifying lender shall only repay sums which ought not to have been paid for the reason mentioned in sub-paragraph (2)(b) of this paragraph if the Secretary of State has requested that lender to repay the sums within a period of 4 weeks starting with the last day on which the relevant beneficiary was entitled to any relevant benefits.

Social Security (Payments on Accounts, Overpayments and Recovery) Regulations 1988 SI No 664

Offsetting prior payment against subsequent award

5. – (1) Subject to regulation 6 (exception from offset of recoverable overpayment), any sum paid in respect of a period covered by a subsequent determination in any of the cases set out in paragraph (2) shall be offset against arrears of entitlement under the subsequent determination and, except to the extent that the sum exceeds the arrears, shall be treated as properly paid on account of them.

(2) Paragraph (1) applies in the following cases:

Case 1: Payment under an award which is revised, reversed or varied
Where a person has been paid a sum by way of benefit under an award which is subsequently varied on appeal or revised on a review.

Case 2: Award or payment of benefit in lieu
Where a person has been paid a sum by way of benefit under the original award and it is subsequently determined, on review or appeal, that another benefit should be awarded or is payable in lieu of the first.

Case 3: Child benefit and severe disablement allowance
Where either –
(a) a person has been awarded and paid child benefit for a period in respect of which severe disablement allowance is subsequently determined to be payable to the child concerned; or
(b) severe disablement allowance is awarded and paid for a period in respect of which child benefit is subsequently awarded to someone else, the child concerned in the subsequent determination being the beneficiary of the original award.

Case 4: Increase of benefit for dependant
Where a person has been paid a sum by way of an increase in respect of a dependent person under the original award and it is subsequently determined that that other person is entitled to benefit for that period, or that a third person is entitled to the increase for that period in priority to the beneficiary of the original award.

Case 5: Increase of benefit of partner
Where a person has been paid a sum by way of an increase in respect of a partner (as defined in regulation 2 of the Income Support

Regulations) and it is subsequently determined that that other person is entitled for that period.

(3) Where an amount has been deducted under regulation 13(b) (sums to be deducted in calculating recoverable amounts) an equivalent sum shall be offset against any arrears of entitlement of that person under a subsequent award of income support for the period to which the deducted amount relates.

(4) Where child benefit which has been paid under an award in favour of a person (the original beneficiary) is subsequently awarded to someone else for any week, the benefit shall nevertheless be treated as properly paid if it was received by someone other than the original beneficiary, who –

(a) either had the child living with him or was contributing towards the cost of providing for the child at a weekly rate which was not less than the weekly rate under the original award, and
(b) could have been entitled to child benefit in respect of that child for that week had a claim been made in time.

(5) Any amount which is treated, under paragraph (4), as properly paid shall be deducted from the amount payable to the beneficiary under the subsequent award.

Exception from offset of recoverable overpayment
6. – No amount may be offset under regulation 5(1) which has been determined to be a recoverable overpayment for the purposes of section 71(1) of the Social Security Administration Act 1992.

Recovery of overpayments by automated or other direct credit transfer
11. – (1) Where it is determined by the adjudicating authority, that a payment in excess of entitlement has been credited to a bank or other account under an arrangement for automated or other direct credit transfer made in accordance with regulation 21 of the Claims and Payments Regulations and that the conditions prescribed by paragraph (2) are satisfied, the excess, or the specified part of it to which the Secretary of State's certificate relates, shall be recoverable under this regulation.

(2) The prescribed conditions for recoverability under paragraph (1) are as follows: –
(a) the Secretary of State has certified that the payment in excess of entitlement, or a specified part of it, is materially due to the arrangement for payments to be made by automated or other direct credit transfer; and
(b) notice of the effect which this regulation would have, in the event of an overpayment, was given in writing to the beneficiary, or to a person acting for him, before he agreed to the arrangement.

(3) Where the arrangement was agreed to before 6th April 1987 the condition prescribed by paragraph 2(b) need not be satisfied in any

App 1 Extracts from legislation 337

case where the application for benefit to be paid by automated or other direct credit transfer contained a statement, or was accompanied by a written statement made by the applicant, which complied with the provisions of regulation 16A(3)(b) and (8) of the Social Security (Claims and Payments) Regulations 1979 or, as the case may be, regulation 7(2)(b) and (6) of the Child Benefit (Claims and Payments) Regulations 1984.

Circumstances in which determination need not be revised
12. – Section 71(5) of the Social Security Administration Act 1992 (recoverability dependent on reversal, variation or revision of determination) shall not apply where the fact and circumstances of the misrepresentation or non-disclosure do not provide a basis for reviewing and revising the determination under which payment was made.

Sums to be deducted in calculating recoverable amounts
13. – In calculating the amounts recoverable under section 71(1) of the Social Security Administration Act 1992 or regulation 11, where there has been an overpayment of benefit, the adjudicating authority shall deduct
(a) any amount which has been offset under Part III;
(b) any additional amount of income support which was not payable under the original, or any other determination, but which should have been determined to be payable –
   (i) on the basis of the claim as presented to the adjudicating authority, or
   (ii) on the basis of the claim as it would have appeared had the misrepresentation or non-disclosure been remedied before the determination;
but no other deduction shall be made in respect of any other entitlement to benefit which may be, or might have been, determined to exist.

Quarterly diminution of capital resources
14. – (1) For the purposes of section 71(1) of the Social Security Administration Act 1992, where income support, family credit or disability working allowance has been overpaid in consequence of a misrepresentation as to the capital a claimant possesses or a failure to disclose their existence, the adjudicating authority shall treat that capital as having been reduced at the end of each quarter from the start of the overpayment period by the amount overpaid by way of income support, family credit of disability working allowance within that quarter.

(2) Capital shall not be treated as reduced over any period other than a quarter or in any circumstances other than those for which paragraph (1) provides.

(3) In this regulation –
"a quarter" means a period of 13 weeks starting with the first day on

which the overpayment period began and ending on the 90th consecutive day thereafter;

"overpayment period" is a period during which income support, family credit or disability working allowance is overpaid in consequence of a misrepresentation as to capital or a failure to disclose its existence.

Social Security (Recoupment) Regulations 1990 SI No 322

Small payments

3. – (1) A person shall be exempted from liability to make the relevant deduction or the relevant payment where the amount of the compensation payment in question, or the aggregate amount of 2 or more connected compensation payments, does not exceed £2,500.

(2) Where an amount has been deducted and paid to the Secretary of State which, by virtue of paragraph (1), ought not to have been so deducted and paid, the Secretary of State –
(a) Where he is satisfied that the whole of the amount ought to have been paid to the intended recipient, shall pay the whole of that amount to that person; or
(b) Where he is not so satisfied, shall either pay the whole of the amount to the compensator or pay to the compensator that part of the amount which he would have been entitled to retain and to the intended recipient that part which he would have been entitled to receive had the amount not been so deducted and paid.

Exempt payments

4. The following payments shall be exempt payments for the purposes of Part IV of the Social Security Administration Act 1992 –
(a) any payment made out of property held for the purpose of the charitable trust called the Macfarlane Trust and established partly out of funds provided by the Secretary of State to the Haemophilia Society for the relief of poverty or distress among those suffering from haemophilia;
(b) any compensation payment made by British Coal in accordance with the NCB Pneumoconiosis Compensation Scheme set out in the Schedule to an agreement made on the 13th September 1974 between the National Coal Board, the National Union of Mine Workers, the National Association of Colliery Overmen Deputies and Shot-firers and the British Association of Colliery Management;
(c) any payment made to the victim in respect of sensorineural hearing loss where the loss is less than 50db in one or both ears; and
(d) any contractual amount paid to an employee by an employer of his in respect of a day of incapacity for work;

(e) any payment made from the Macfarlane (Special Payments) Trust established on January 29, 1990 partly out of funds provided by the Secretary of State, for the benefit of certain persons suffering from haemophilia; and
(ee) any payment made from the Macfarlane (Special Payments) (No. 2) Trust established on 3rd May 1991 partly out of funds provided by the Secretary of State for the benefit of certain persons suffering from haemophilia and other beneficiaries;
(f) any payment made under the National Health Service (Injury Benefits) Regulations 1974 or the National Health Service (Scotland) (Injury Benefits) Regulations 1974;
(g) any payment made by or on behalf of the Secretary of State for the benefit of persons eligible for payment in accordance with the provisions of a scheme established by him on April 24, 1992 or, in Scotland, on April 10, 1992;
(h) any payment made from the Eileen Trust established on 29th March 1993 out of funds provided by the Secretary of State for the benefit of persons eligible for payment in accordance with its provisions.

Housing Benefit (General) Regulations 1987 SI No 1971

Note: the Council Tax Benefit (General) Regulations 1992 SI No 1814 are in substantially similar form.

Meaning of overpayment
98. – In this Part "overpayment" means any amount which has been paid by way of housing benefit and to which there was no entitlement under these Regulations (whether on initial determination or as subsequently revised on review or further review) and includes any amount paid on account under regulation 91 which is in excess of the entitlement to housing benefit as subsequently determined.

Recoverable overpayments
99. – (1) Any overpayment, except one to which paragraph (2) applies, shall be recoverable.
 (2) Subject to paragraph (4) this paragraph applies to an overpayment caused by an official error where the claimant or a person acting on his behalf or any other person to whom the payment is made could not, at the time of receipt of the payment, or of any notice relating to that payment reasonably have been expected to realise that it was an overpayment.
 (3) In paragraph (2), "overpayment caused by official error" means an overpayment caused by a mistake made or something done or omitted to be done by the appropriate authority or by an officer or person acting for that authority or by an officer of the Department of

Social Security or the Department of Employment acting as such where the claimant, a person acting on his behalf or any other person to whom the payment is made did not cause or materially contribute to that mistake, act or omission.

(4) Where in consequence of an official error, a person has been awarded rent rebate to which he was not entitled or which exceeded the benefit to which he was entitled, upon the award being reviewed any overpayment of benefit, which remains credited to him by the appropriate authority in respect of a period after the date of the review, shall be recoverable.

Person by whom recovery may be made
100. – The authority which paid the recoverable overpayment may recover it.

Person from whom recovery may be sought
101. – (1) Subject to paragraph (2) a recoverable overpayment shall be recoverable from either –
(a) where the overpayment was in consequence of a misrepresentation or failure to disclose a material fact (in either case whether fraudulent or otherwise) by or on behalf of the claimant or any other person to whom a payment of housing benefit may be made, the person who misrepresented or failed to disclose that material fact; or
(b) in any case, the claimant or the person to whom the overpayment was made.

(2) Where a recoverable overpayment is made to a claimant who has one or more partners, recovery of the overpayment may be made by deduction from any housing benefit payable to a partner, provided that the claimant and that partner were members of the same household both at the time of the overpayment and when the deduction is made.

Method of recovery
102. – Without prejudice to any other method of recovery, an authority may recover any recoverable overpayment from any person referred to in regulation 101 by deduction from any housing benefit to which that person is entitled or, where it is unable to do so, may request the Secretary of State to recover the overpayment from the benefits prescribed in regulation 105, in accordance with the provisions of that regulation.

Diminution of capital
103. – (1) Where in the case of a recoverable overpayment, in consequence of a misrepresentation or failure to disclose a material fact (in either case whether fraudulent or otherwise) as to a person's

capital, or an error, other than one to which regulation 99(2) (effect of official error) refers, as to the amount of a person's capital, the overpayment was in respect of a period ("the overpayment period") of more than 13 benefit weeks, the appropriate authority shall, for the purpose only of calculating the amount of that overpayment –
(a) at the end of the first 13 weeks of the overpayment period, treat the amount of that capital as having been reduced by the amount of housing benefit overpaid during those 13 weeks;
(b) at the end of each subsequent period of 13 benefit weeks, if any, of the overpayment period, treat the amount of that capital as having been further reduced by the amount of housing benefit overpaid during the immediately preceding 13 benefit weeks.

(2) Capital shall not be treated as reduced over any period other than 13 benefit weeks or in any circumstances other than those for which paragraph (1) provides.

Sums to be deducted in calculating recoverable overpayments
104. – In calculating the amount of a recoverable overpayment, the appropriate authority –
(a) if it determines that a lesser amount was properly payable in respect of the whole or part of the overpayment period, shall deduct that amount;
(b) in the case of a rent or rate rebate only, may deduct so much of any payment by way of rent or, as the case may be, rates in respect of the overpayment period which exceeds the amount, if any, which the claimant was liable to pay for that period under the original erroneous determination.

Recovery of overpayments from prescribed benefits
105. – (1) For the purposes of section 29(7) of the Act (recovery of overpaid housing benefit by deduction from other benefits), the benefits prescribed by this regulation are –
(a) any benefit under the Social Security Act, except guardian's allowance;
(b) income support family credit or disability working allowance under Part II of the Act;
(c) any benefit payable under the legislation of any member State other than the United Kingdom concerning the branches of social security mentioned in Article 4(1) of Regulation (EEC) No. 1408/71 on the application of social security schemes to employed persons, to self-employed persons and to members of their families moving within the Community, whether or not the benefit has been acquired by virtue of the provisions of that Regulation;
(d) [*Repealed.*]
(2) [*Repealed.*]
(3) Where the Secretary of State is satisfied that –
(a) a recoverable overpayment of housing benefit has been made, in consequence of a misrepresentation of or failure to disclose a material

fact (in either case whether fraudulently or otherwise), by or on behalf of a claimant or any other person to whom a payment of housing benefit has been made; and

(b) the person who misrepresented that fact or failed to disclose it is receiving a sufficient amount of one of more of the benefits prescribed in paragraph (1) to enable deductions to be made for the recovery of the overpayment,

he shall, if requested to do so by an authority under regulation 102, recover the overpayment by deduction from any of those benefits.

Regulation 1408/71/EEC

Article 4
1. This Regulation shall apply to all legislation concerning the following branches of social security:
(a) sickness and maternity benefits;
(b) invalidity benefits, including those intended for the maintenance or improvement of earning capacity;
(c) old-age benefits;
(d) survivor's benefits;
(e) benefits in respect of accidents at work and occupational diseases;
(f) death grants;
(g) unemployment benefits;
(h) family benefits.

2. This Regulation shall apply to all general and special social security schemes, whether contributory or non-contributory, and to schemes concerning the liability of an employer or shipowner in respect of the benefits referred to in paragraph (1).

2a. This Regulation shall also apply to special non-contributory benefits which are provided under a legislation or schemes other than those referred to in paragraph 1 or excluded by virtue of paragraph 4, where such benefits are intended:
(a) either to provide supplementary, substitute or ancillary cover against the risks covered by the branches of social security referred to in paragraph 1(a) to (h), or
(b) solely as specific protection for the disabled.

2b. This Regulation shall not apply to the provisions in the legislation of a Member State concerning special non-contributory benefits, referred to in Annex II, Section III, the validity of which is confined to part of its territory.

APPENDIX 2
Precedents

This appendix contains precedents which, it is hoped, will prove helpful to advisers drafting grounds of appeal and other documents required in the more common types of overpayment cases. Like all precedents, advisers should beware copying them verbatim without carefully considering the facts of the case with which they are dealing.

Several of the precedents relate to the examples in the text. Readers should refer to the relevant example for the facts of the case.

The precedents are intended to be cumulative, so that if there is more than one ground of challenge, one precedent can simply be added to another. When dealing with statutory rights of appeal, the following information should always be put in the grounds of appeal for ease of reference:

– Full name, address and telephone number of the defendant.
– National insurance number and claim number (if any) of the defendant, and of the claimant, if not the same person.
– Name, address, telephone and fax numbers of any representative and the organisation, if any, to which s/he is attached.
– Full details of the decision under challenge, including the date it was given, by whom it was made and a summary of what it decides. It is a good idea to append a photocopy if possible.

SSAA s71

1 No review: EXAMPLE 3.2

1 It is a condition precedent of liability under Social Security Administration Act 1992 s71 that the decision or decision to award benefit are 'reversed on appeal or revised on a review': s71(5)(a). There has been no relevant appeal in this case.
2 The decision to recover the overpayment does not revise the decision in February to award income support. The decision is therefore invalid: *R(SB) 7/91* para 4.
3 Alternatively, if there has been a review of the February decision,

the adjudication officer is put to proof that the decision was made and of its contents. If the adjudication officer is unable to prove the existence of the review decision, the decision to recover is invalid: CSSB 316/1989 para 11.

2 *Defective review:* EXAMPLE *3.4 (income support decision)*
1 [Precedent 1 paragraph 1]
2 The review of the decision dated 1 February is invalid. Any review decision accompanying a decision to recover under Social Security Administration Act 1992 s71 must specifically state the fact that the overpayment is recoverable and the amount recoverable: s71(2) and (5).
3 The tribunal has no power to correct the defects in the review decision: *CIS 312/1992* para 17; *CSSB 540/1989* para 14.

3 Misrepresentation: qualification by other documents
1 The claimant admits that the amount of capital specified in the claim form for income support completed in February was incorrect. The claimant forgot that a further account was held at the X Building Society. It is also admitted that the account had £3,000 in it at the time that income support was claimed.
2 The claimant realised her mistake the day after sending the claim form to the Belfast office. That same day, she wrote a letter to the Belfast office, giving her address and national insurance number, asking that the account be taken into account. The claimant thereby represented that the contents of the letter should be taken into account when considering her claim. The representation in the claim form as to the amount of capital should therefore be regarded as qualified by the contents of the letter. Accordingly there was no misrepresentation: *R(SB) 2/91* para 10; *CSB 348/1990* para 4.

4 Misrepresentation: qualification by previous disclosure: agency of UBO: EXAMPLE *7.11*
1 The claimant admits signing the declarations on form UB 24 every fortnight that he had done no work. There was no misrepresentation made, because on the day that he was employed by X Ltd he visited the unemployment benefit office and informed an officer that he was starting employment for ten hours per week, earning £60. The officer made a note of the information.
2 The claimant reasonably believed that the information had not been overlooked in view of the fact that the officer made a note of the information. Accordingly the written representations were qualified by the disclosure made to the officer: *CS 130/1992* paras 15 and 16.
3 Further, disclosure to the officer at the UBO must be treated as equivalent to disclosure to the office administering income support, because the claimant was required to make himself available for

work and make a concurrent claim for unemployment benefit: *R(SB) 2/91* para 11; *CIS 389/1993* para 7.
4 Alternatively, it was reasonable for the claimant to assume that the information about his job would be passed to the relevant DSS office, because the officer took a note of the information and did not tell him to inform the DSS office: *CSB 906/1985* para 6; *R(SB) 54/83* para 17.

5 Misrepresentation: reliance on declaration: lack of knowledge
1 The claimant initially completed a claim form for sickness benefit with dependency addition in January, when his partner was not working. He made no misrepresentation on the claim form.
2 The adjudication officer claims that the claimant misrepresented that there had been no change of circumstances in completing form Med 3. The declaration on the form must be interpreted in such a way that the claimant only represents that the information given is true and complete to his knowledge: *CIS 674/1994* para 14; *Franklin v Chief Adjudication Officer* (1995) *Times* 29 December, CA. The claimant did not know that his partner was working until June, when he disclosed the fact immediately. He therefore made no misrepresentation on form Med 3.

6 Failure to disclose: disclosure to correct office: no continuing duty: EXAMPLE 5.11
1 The claimant disclosed the fact that he was starting a new job by handing his completed UB 40 form to an officer at the local unemployment benefit office.
2 [Precedent 4 paragraphs 3 and 4]
3 The claimant had accordingly made an adequate disclosure and there was no duty on him to make any further disclosure to the DSS: *R(SB) 15/87* para 19; *CSB 1397/1985* paras 9 and 10; *CIS 668/1994* para 6.

7 Failure to disclose: disclosure not reasonably to be expected: reliance on advice from officer: continuing duty to disclose: EXAMPLE 5.5
1 The claimant admits that she did not disclose receipt of child benefit to the local office administering income support. She was told by the Child Benefit Centre that the information would be passed on by them. Due to the contradictory advice given, further disclosure to the local office was not reasonably to be expected: *R(SB) 3/81* para 7; *CIS 584/1994* para 11.
2 Alternatively, it was not reasonable to expect the claimant to realise that she was being overpaid income support until she received a bank statement five weeks after the award of child benefit. The overpayment of income support is not recoverable during that five-week period: *CSSB 621/1988* para 8.

8 Failure to disclose: disclosure not reasonably to be expected: advance disclosure: EXAMPLE 5.18

1 The claimant informed the DSS by letter in March that she was leaving the country. She enclosed a photocopy of her air ticket and thereby showed a 'settled intention' to leave the country in June. Further disclosure of the change of circumstances was not reasonably to be expected: *CS 130/1992* para 18; *CS 234/1994* para 4.
2 Accordingly there was no 'failure' to disclose: *R(SB) 21/82* para 4(2).

9 Failure to disclose: burden of proof: disclosure by post

1 The claimant disclosed the fact that she had begun to live together with her partner by writing to the local DSS office. The letter was posted on 1 October.
2 By the Interpretation Act 1978 s7, it is presumed that a posted document was delivered in the normal course of post if an Act 'authorises or requires' such a document to be posted. The claimant contends that the letter containing disclosures as to the material fact that she had started to live with her partner was a document authorised to be served by post for the following reasons:
   (a) It has been held that a claim form is a document authorised to be served by post within the scope of the section: *CSIS 48/1992* para 8. Like a completed claim form, the letter to the local office contained information which the claimant placed before the adjudication officer for her entitlement to benefit to be worked out.
   (b) The Social Security (Claims and Payments) Regulations 1987 reg 32(1) requires notice of a change of circumstances in writing, and therefore envisages that a document containing such notice can be served by post. That regulation is made under the Social Security Administration Act 1992 s5(h)–(j), which allow regulations to require information to be 'furnished'. Those sections authorise the posting of notices of changes of circumstances for the purpose of the Interpretation Act 1978.
   (c) On claiming benefit, the claimant was given pre-paid envelopes which she was instructed to use to report changes of circumstances and told that further envelopes were available at the post office. She was thereby authorised by the DSS to inform the local office of changes by post.
3 Accordingly, it is presumed that the local office received the letter a few days after it was posted. It is for the adjudication officer to prove that the letter was not received.

10 Failure to disclose: burden of proof

1 The claimant orally disclosed the fact that he was starting work to

an officer in the unemployment benefit office on 15 December. The name of the officer in question was Mr Smith.
2 The adjudication officer must prove that it is more likely than not that no disclosure was made: *CSB 347/1983* para 10, followed in *R(SB) 10/85* para 7. The claimant requires the Department of Employment to make Mr Smith available at the hearing for cross-examination: *CSB 1195/1984* para 10.

11 Causation: knowledge of DSS

1 The claimant concedes that the overpayment of income support is recoverable from 10 March to 20 May. On 21 May the Child Benefit Centre informed the local office of the increased child benefit entitlement.
2 From that date the local office was aware of the material fact and any further overpayment of income support was not 'in consequence' of the claimant's failure to disclose the increased child benefit: *R(SB) 15/87* para 30; *CIS 159/1990* para 4; *CSB 712/1985* para 6.

12 Causation: intervention of third party: EXAMPLE 7.9

1 The claimant is reliant on her next-door neighbour, K, to help her with household tasks. K is not the claimant's appointee under the Social Security (Claims and Payments) Regulations 1987 reg 33, but she has often passed information to the DSS on the claimant's behalf.
2 On 6 July the claimant became aware of the inheritance from her late brother. She did not know what effect this would have on her benefit and asked K to tell the DSS about this. K promised to do so, but failed. She later told the claimant that she had told the DSS.
3 In *CIS 395/1992* para 10, it was held that the criminal conduct of the claimant's husband was the only cause of the overpayment. The claimant submits that the carelessness of K and her misleading of the claimant was a new intervening act which broke the chain of causation of the overpayment, and that it was reasonable for the claimant to rely on K. The overpayment is therefore not recoverable as it was not 'in consequence' of the claimant's failure to disclose.

13 Amount of overpayment: not 'in consequence' of breach of duty: EXAMPLE 8.3

1 The claimant disputes the amount of the overpayment given in the schedule attached to the adjudication officer's decision. It is conceded that the claimant was overpaid £5 per week from April to June as a result of a mistake made in filling in the income support claim form.
2 However, from June, the claimant's wife increased her earnings to £60 per week and did not inform the claimant of this. Due to the claimant's lack of knowledge, no misrepresentation was made on

form UB 24, as he only represented that he had disclosed all facts known to him: *CIS 393/1993* para 7; *Franklin v Chief Adjudication Officer* (1995) *Times* 29 December, CA.

3 Accordingly, only £5 of the overpayment is recoverable from June, because only that amount was made 'in consequence' of a misrepresentation, namely, that made on the claim form. The rest of the overpayment was caused by the failure of the claimant's wife to inform him of her earnings.

14 Amount of overpayment: reduction in separate review: EXAMPLE *8.5*

1 The claimant asks that the tribunal incorporates a separate review into the decision to review his entitlement. On 15 August 1993, his granddaughter, I, came to England to live with him whilst she studied. She was his dependent for income support purposes and hence the claimant was entitled to receive the following premiums for her care: child aged 16 to 18, family and lone parent. She left England on 20 July 1993.

2 The claimant never requested a review between those dates to reflect this additional entitlement on the grounds of ignorance of a material fact: Social Security Administration Act 1992 s25(1)(a). The claimant asks that the review be carried out now and the additional benefit which ought to have been paid should be offset against the amount of the overpayment.

3 The Social Security Adjudication Regulations 1995 reg 57 does not prevent the claimant's entitlement being taken into account now. It only imposes a 12-month limit on the payment of income support and not on the claimant's entitlement. It is therefore possible to take the claimant's entitlement to extra benefit into account when working out the amount of benefit which ought to have been paid: *R(SB) 11/86* para 15.

Recovery of benefit paid before 1987

15 Due care and diligence

1 For the period prior to April 1987, the claimant submits that the overpayment of dependency addition to invalidity benefit is not recoverable. For payments prior to 6 April 1987, the tribunal must apply the test of whether the claimant has used 'due care and diligence' to avoid an overpayment: Social Security Act 1975 s119.

2 The test as to whether a claimant has shown due care and diligence is a subjective one, and the claimant submits that due care and diligence was shown for the following reasons:
  (a) The claimant and his wife are both in poor health and have no family in the United Kingdom. The claimant is housebound and his wife has only a limited ability to walk. They have no

telephone.
(b) Both the claimant and his wife are illiterate and have little understanding of the benefits system. Thus, their inability to understand official documents or the requirements of disclosure must be taken into account: *R(U) 7/64* para 7; *R(U) 6/70* para 13.
(c) When the claimant's wife started her job, she sought advice from an adviser at the cultural centre. She was told that she would have to tell the DSS about the information. She went to the local office and attempted to communicate with an officer, who was a young man. The officer appeared to make notes and said 'yes' at the end of the conversation. The claimant's wife, whose English is poor, took that to mean that she had been understood.
3 In view of the inability of the claimant and his wife to appreciate the significance of her job for the dependency increase, they could only be expected to do everything in their power to communicate the fact of the job to the DSS. In so far as it is necessary to show due care and diligence on the part of the claimant's wife as well as the claimant, this is shown by her efforts to disclose: *R(U) 7/64* para 8; *R(A) 1/79* para 8.

SSAA s74

16 Section 74(1): discretion as to prescribed date: EXAMPLE *13.1*
1 The claimant submits that the adjudication officer was wrong in selecting the date of her grandmother's death as the date to which the payment of the annuity was 'fairly attributable': Social Security (Payments on Account, Overpayments and Recovery) Regulations 1988 reg 7(2)(b).
2 The tribunal does not have to be satisfied that the adjudication officer erred in law in the exercise of his discretion. The right of appeal to a social security appeal tribunal under the Social Security Administration Act 1992 s22 is not confined to a point of law only. The tribunal must exercise the discretion afresh, unfettered by consideration of the adjudication officer's decision.
3 It was wrong to select the date of the grandmother's death because the money could not have been available for the use of the claimant until the time that probate of her grandmother's will was granted at the earliest. Furthermore, the will gave the executors an unfettered discretion as to the time that the annuity was payable. Accordingly, the claimant contends that the appropriate date for the annuity to be taken into account was:
(a) The date on which the executors decided that the annuity should be paid to the claimant, namely 1 January, because the

claimant had no means of compelling the exercise of the discretion by the executors at any time.
(b) Alternatively, the date on which probate of the will was granted.

17 Section 74(2): 'prescribed date': date of knowledge: EXAMPLE *13.4*
1 The Secretary of State is only entitled to receive overpaid income support under the Social Security Administration Act 1992 s74(2)(b) if benefit would not have been paid if the German invalidity benefit had not been paid on the 'prescribed date'. The 'prescribed date' is defined as 'the date by which receipt of or entitlement to that benefit would have to be notified to the Secretary of State'.
2 The receipt of German invalidity benefit is a change of circumstances. The time at which a change of circumstances must be notified is 'as soon as reasonably practicable after its occurrence': Social Security (Claims and Payments) Regulations reg 32(1). The 'prescribed date' in relation to the receipt of German invalidity benefit is therefore July, when the claimant was informed by the German authorities of her entitlement to benefit. German invalidity benefit can only be taken into account in so far as it is referable to the period following that date.

Overpayments by credit transfer

18 No grounds for review: EXAMPLE *14.1*
1 The Social Security (Payments on Account, Overpayments and Recovery) Regulations 1988 reg 11 is made under the Social Security Administration Act 1992 s71(4). There can therefore be no amount recoverable under the regulation unless 'the determination in pursuance of which it was paid has been reversed or varied on appeal or revised on a review': s71(5)(a).
2 The benefit was paid under a determination of the adjudication officer that the claimant was entitled to benefit of £50. Following the alleged review by the adjudication officer, the claimant's entitlement at all material times is £50. The determination has not therefore been 'reversed or varied' and there can be no recovery under reg 11.

Compensation recovery

19 Benefit not paid 'in consequence' of injury: EXAMPLE *16.3*
1 Before the relevant accident, the victim, E, was suffering from chronic back pain and was in receipt of incapacity benefit with back pain as the stated cause of incapacity.
2 It is conceded that the relevant accident caused an aggravation of the victim's back pain, but the victim will rely on the medical report

of Ms Jones, consultant orthopaedic surgeon, to show that her back condition was already so severe prior to the accident that the victim would have met the 'all work' test even had the accident not occurred.
3 There is therefore no causal link between the relevant accident and the payment of benefit, and the benefit is therefore not recoverable by the CRU: *CCR 5336/1995* para 9.

Housing benefit and council tax benefit

20 *Official error: overpayment not recoverable:* EXAMPLE 17.6

1 The claimant contends that the overpayment of housing benefit is not recoverable, because it was 'caused by an official error where the claimant or a person acting on his behalf or any other person to whom the payment is made could not, at the time of receipt of payment, or of any notice relating to that payment, reasonably have been expected to realise that there was an overpayment': Housing Benefit (General) Regulations 1987 reg 99(2).
2 The claimant disclosed both the fact that she was starting work and that her father, H, was moving in with her to the DSS and the local authority. There were two official errors:
   (a) The local authority failed to consider the effect of the claimant starting work at the time that it recalculated benefit to take account of H's presence.
   (b) The DSS failed to follow the correct procedures to keep the local authority informed of changes which might affect the claimant's entitlement to housing benefit.
3 The official errors were not contributed to in any way by the claimant, as she provided full information orally to all the officers concerned about the two changes of circumstances.
4 The claimant could not have realised that there was an overpayment at the time that she received notification of the payments. She expected that there would be a reduction in her benefit as a result of the two changes but she could not be expected to know how much the reduction was to be. The letter from the local authority did not specify the changes that had been taken into account and she reasonably assumed that both changes had been taken into account on the review.

21 *Amount of overpayment: diminishing capital: surplus council tax paid*

1 The claimant challenges the amount of council tax benefit which the local authority is seeking to recover. The amount of which recovery is sought is £300.
2 The claimant's council tax bill was reduced from £800 to £650 for the relevant year. The claimant has overpaid £150 and claims to be

entitled to offset the £150 difference against the overpayment: Council Tax Benefit (General) Regulations 1992 reg 90(b).
3 Secondly, the officer calculating the overpayment has failed to have regard to the diminishing capital principle embodied in reg 89 of the 1992 Regulations. The attached table shows that the claimant's capital would have reduced below the £16,000 limit during the period of the overpayment and there would therefore have been some entitlement to benefit for that period. This amounts to £100.
4 Taking the two offsets into account, the true amount of the overpayment is £50.

Court proceedings

(Note: precedents 22 and 23 will require modification, according to the basis on which the Particulars of Claim is drafted. Normal headings will be used for all pleadings.)

22 Defence to claim for recovery of benefit in restitution: EXAMPLE 20.4
1 It is admitted that the Defendant was in receipt of income support, but no admissions are made as to the amount of benefit paid or the periods over which the same was paid and the Plaintiff is put to strict proof of the same.
2 It is admitted that on 1 February, an adjudication officer conducted a review of the Defendant's entitlement to income support pursuant to the Social Security Administration Act 1992 s25. It is further admitted that the said officer issued a revised decision stating that the claimant's entitlement to income support had been based on a mistake as to a material fact, and that excess income support amounting to £800 had been paid to the Defendant. It is averred that the said officer issued no decision pursuant to s71 of the said Act or pursuant to any other legislation providing that the Secretary of State had the right to recover the said excess income support.
3 It is denied that the Plaintiff is entitled to recover the said or any excess income support as alleged or at all. Without prejudice to the generality of the denial, the Defendant will rely on the matters set out hereinafter.
4 If (which is not admitted) the alleged or any excess income support was paid to the claimant, the same was paid pursuant to the awards of the adjudication officer following the Defendant's claim for income support and not as a result of any mistake by the Plaintiff, its servants or agents.
5 Further or in the alternative, it is denied that the Plaintiff has any cause of action based on money had and received. It is averred that the Plaintiff's right to recover overpaid income support is exclusively governed by the statutory scheme in Part III of the 1992 Act and

secondary legislation made thereunder.
6 Further or in the further alternative, if (which is denied) the Plaintiff has a cause of action against the Defendant for money had and received, it would be inequitable to require the Defendant to make restitution of the amount claimed by the Plaintiff or any amount. The Defendant will rely on the following matters:
   (a) The Defendant was entirely innocent of any wrongdoing or breach of duty in relation to the overpayment of income support. The same was caused wholly by an error on the part of the Plaintiff's servants or agents. The Defendant is not familiar with the rules for the calculation of income support and assumed that the Plaintiff's servants or agents had correctly calculated her entitlement.
   (b) At all material times, the Defendant was a single mother with two young children. She was in the habit of budgeting carefully according to the wages she earned and the amounts of income support paid into her bank account by the Plaintiff.
   (c) As a result of representations made by the Plaintiff, its servants or agents, in letters dated 8 August and 10 November, the Defendant was induced to believe that she was entitled to £50 income support and planned her expenditure accordingly. Between 10 August and 31 January, the Defendant spent an average of £12 more on her weekly expenditure than she had done prior to 10 August and an average of £10 more than she did in February and March.
7 By reason of the matters pleaded in paragraph 6, it is averred that the Plaintiff is estopped from recovering the amount sought or any amount by reason of the detrimental reliance of the Defendant on the Plaintiff's representations as to her entitlement.
8 Alternatively to the averment pleaded in paragraph 7, it would be inequitable to require the Defendant to make restitution of the amount sought or any amount in view of her change of position.
9 In the premises, it is denied that the Plaintiff is entitled to recover the amount alleged or any amount.

23 Defence to claim for recovery of housing benefit: failure to give proper notice
1 It is admitted that the Defendant owns the said house and that the same was let to Mr Smith between the dates alleged. It is further admitted that the rent payable on the said house was as alleged in the Particulars of Claim and that Mr Smith was in receipt of housing benefit during the period that Mr Smith was the Defendant's tenant, but no admissions are made as to the amounts of such housing benefit or as to the periods over which it was paid.
2 It is admitted that the Defendant sent a letter as alleged in the

Particulars of Claim purporting to be a determination that the alleged amount of housing benefit was a recoverable overpayment and that the same was recoverable from the Defendant. It is averred that the same is void and of no effect in law.

3 Further or in the alternative, it is not admitted that the amount sought or any part thereof was in excess of Mr Smith's entitlement to housing benefit and/or was an overpayment within the meaning of the Housing Benefit (General) Regulations 1987 reg 98.

4 Further or in the further alternative, if (which is not admitted) the amount sought or any part thereof is an overpayment of housing benefit as aforesaid, it is specifically denied that the amount sought or any part thereof is recoverable from the Defendant. The Plaintiff is put to strict proof of the matters put in issue by this paragraph and the one preceding.

5 In the premises, it is denied that the amount sought or any amount is owing as a debt to the Plaintiff by the Defendant and it is denied that the Plaintiff is entitled to the relief sought or any relief.

24 Particulars of claim: indemnity from third party and claim in deceit:
EXAMPLE *10.7*

(Note: the First Defendant is the partner, I, and the Second Defendant is the father, K.)

1 From approximately 1988 until September 1994 the First Defendant and the Plaintiff cohabited at various addresses with the First Defendant's two children by a previous relationship. The Second Defendant is the First Defendant's father and the sole owner of a nursing home known as 'The Reaper', 1 New Street, Trumpton.

2 From approximately 1992 the Plaintiff was in receipt of income support for himself, the First Defendant and the children. In or about March 1993 the First Defendant was employed by the Second Defendant as an assistant at the said nursing home for 8 hours per week at a weekly wage of £50. The First Defendant informed the Plaintiff of this, and the Plaintiff, in accordance with his statutory duty under the Social Security (Claims and Payments) Regulations 1987 reg 32(1), informed the Department of Social Security ('the Department') about this change of circumstances.

3 As a result of the disclosure by the Plaintiff, the Department made enquiries of the Second Defendant as to the level of the First Defendant's earnings and then duly recalculated the Plaintiff's entitlement to income support.

4 In May 1994, the Department wrote to the Plaintiff enquiring whether the First Defendant had changed her hours of work or her earnings, and asking for copies of recent wageslips. The Plaintiff asked the First Defendant whether she was earning more money or working more hours. She replied that she was still working for 8 hours per week and earning £50. On the First Defendant's request, the

Second Defendant provided the Plaintiff with handwritten wageslips which confirmed the details provided by the First Defendant.

5   Further, it is alleged that by failing to inform the Plaintiff of the change in her circumstances when she was under a duty to do so, the First Defendant represented to the Plaintiff at all times from December 1993 that she was still working 8 hours per week and earning £50.

6   The representations made by the Defendants were in fact false, in that from about December 1993 the First Defendant agreed to and did work 18 hours per week at the said nursing home, earning £125 per week.

7   The Defendants and each of them made the said representations fraudulently, in that they knew that the said representations were false, or made the said representations and each of them recklessly, not caring whether they were true or false. Further the Defendants and each of them made the said representations and each of them in the intention that the Plaintiff should rely thereon.

8   In reliance on the representations made by the Defendants, the Plaintiff represented in writing to the Department that there had been no change in the First Defendant's circumstances and forwarded the said wageslips to the Department. Further, in reliance on that representation by the Plaintiff, the Department continued to pay income support to the Plaintiff.

9   By reason of the matters aforesaid, the Plaintiff has suffered loss and damage.

PARTICULARS OF LOSS AND DAMAGE

(1) On or about 7 September 1994, the First Defendant informed the Plaintiff that she had been working 18 hours per week since December 1993. The Plaintiff informed the Department of this on the following day.

(2) As a result of the disclosure by the Plaintiff, on 25 October 1994 the Department reviewed the Plaintiff's entitlement to income support. The revised decision was that the Plaintiff was not entitled to any income support. On the same date, the Department issued a decision pursuant to the Social Security Administration Act 1992 s71 that £3,500 of income support ('the overpayment') had been overpaid and was recoverable from the claimant. On 30 March 1995 a social security appeal tribunal dismissed the Plaintiff's appeal against the latter decision.

(3) On or about December 1994, the Plaintiff obtained employment as a security guard. He has been paying the overpayment back at the rate of £40 per week.

(4) Had the Defendants or either of them told the Plaintiff of the

First Defendant's change of circumstances in December 1993, the Plaintiff would have immediately informed the Department, as a result of which the overpayment would not have been made and the Plaintiff would not have incurred liability to the Department.

(5) Alternatively to (4), had the Defendants or either of them told the Plaintiff at some date after December 1993, a proportion of the overpayment would not have been made and the Plaintiff's liability to the Department would have been reduced.

(6) It is averred by the Plaintiff that the First Defendant spent the extra money she earned herself, without using any of it for the benefit of the Plaintiff or her children. It is further averred that had the Defendants or either of them told the Plaintiff of the First Defendant's increased earnings in or after December 1993, then all or part of the increase would have been used for the family budget.

10 Alternatively, on 13 May 1996, following representations by the Plaintiff, the Department issued decisions pursuant to s71 of the 1992 Act stating that the First and Second Defendants were liable to repay the overpayment. By letter dated 29 May, the Department indicated that it would not exercise its discretion to recover part of the overpayment from the Defendants or either of them. It is averred that the Defendants and each of them are liable to the Department in respect of the same damage in respect of which the Plaintiff is liable. It is further averred that the Plaintiff is entitled to an indemnity and/or a contribution from the Defendants and each of them in respect of the liability incurred by him.

11 Further, the Plaintiff claims interest pursuant to the County Courts Act 1984 s69 on the amount found to be due to the Plaintiff at such rate and for such period as the Court thinks fit.

AND THE PLAINTIFF CLAIMS:

(1) Damages for deceit.
(2) Further or alternatively to (1), an indemnity or contribution pursuant to the Civil Liability (Contribution) Act 1978 s1 in such amount as the Court may find to be just and equitable.
(3) The aforesaid interest pursuant to the County Courts Act 1984 s69 to be assessed.

APPENDIX 3
Checklist for conferences with defendants

1 Obtain a copy of the decision on which the client needs advice. Check the following details:
   – Under which piece of legislation is it made?
   – On what grounds is recovery of the overpayment sought?
   – Establish the date of decision and calculate the dates on which time limits for appealing, seeking review, etc, expire.
   – What amount is sought to be recovered?
   – Have the procedural requirements as to the decision been met?
2 Establish from the client what steps s/he has taken, if any.
3 Ask the client why s/he opposes the decision and if specific grounds of challenge are mentioned consider those first.
4 Using the relevant parts of this book as a guide, carefully consider each criterion for recoverability and whether it has been shown, and whether the claimant has grounds for challenging the decision on the basis of each criterion.
5 Consider possible sources of evidence to support the claimant's assertions in relation to each ground of challenge. Discuss both documentary and oral evidence, and ensure that the claimant gathers together all documents and seeks help from possible witnesses at the earliest possible stage.
6 Consider the amount claimed and check the calculations by the recovering authority. If possible, recalculate the amount using Appendix 4 as a guide.
7 Advise the client on the prospects of a successful challenge to the recoverability of the overpayment.
8 Consider how the mechanics of recovery will affect the client. Explain how the process of recovery works and enquire into the client's ability to repay. Attempt to work out an appropriate scheme for repayment. Consider the possibility of a challenge to the decision to recover.
9 Obtain the client's written authorisation to take necessary steps on his/her behalf, if appropriate.

10 If so instructed, draft grounds of appeal or application for review. Ensure that these are lodged as soon as possible, and in any event well before the expiry of the time limit.

APPENDIX 4
Checklists for calculating amounts of overpayments

Note: in this appendix, 'D' is used as shorthand for 'defendant'.

SSAA s71 overpayments

1 Calculate the total amount of benefit paid under the relevant decisions. It is possible to get this information from the written decisions issued to the claimant. If these have not been retained, ask the DSS for details. Consider other evidence if the defendant contests the amount that has been paid.
2 Calculate how much, if any, of the benefit was paid in consequence of any breach of duty.
   – Where D made disclosure, and the ground is failure to disclose, or where the ground is misrepresentation and the disclosure vitiates later misrepresentations, later benefit is not recoverable.
   – If benefit was paid after the local office became aware of the material fact relevant to D's benefit, later benefit is not recoverable.
   – If benefit was paid after some other intervening event which rendered the breach of duty of no effect, later benefit is not recoverable.
   – Elements of awards paid due to official error are not recoverable.
3 Apply any offsets that are appropriate in D's case.
   – The full amount of benefit to which D is entitled after the review decisions are implemented.
   – Any additional benefit to which D becomes entitled following an external review for which D is able to demonstrate the grounds.
   – Any additional benefit which should have been awarded on the basis of the claim as presented.
   – Any additional benefit which would have been awarded had the breach of duty not been committed.

- Apply the diminishing capital rule if appropriate.
- Other offsets under the Overpayments Regulations reg 5.
4 Ensure that there is no double counting, in view of the reductions made by steps 2 and 3.
5 If the DSS is recovering from another source, deduct the amount which will be recovered from that source due to the danger of double recovery.
6 Check whether D would have been entitled to some other benefit over the relevant period. If not possible to treat D's claim as being for that benefit, consider application for extra-statutory offset.

SSAA s74 overpayments

General points

1 Check that D admits that the benefit was actually received. If this is denied, examine the evidence available.
2 If benefit is not recoverable under one subsection, it may be held on appeal to be recoverable under another, provided that D is given adequate opportunity to consider the new case.

Note: All references to regulations are to the Income Support (General) Regulations 1987 as amended.

Section 74(1): prescribed income

1 Check that the income received by D is in fact prescribed income, within the scope of Part V of the Regulations.
2 Where the income is child support maintenance:
   - Ascertain the effective date of the relevant assessment and the date that maintenance became payable.
   - Ensure that no benefit outside that period is being recovered.
   - Consider the treatment of the payments under regs 60A to 60D.
3 Where the income is some other type of income, is it paid in respect of a specific period?
4 If 'yes' to 3, it is treated as paid on the first day of that period. Work out the consequences for income support under Part V if it had been paid on that day.
5 If 'no' to 3, it is treated as paid on the date to which it is fairly attributable. Ascertain that date, and work out the consequences as in 4.

Section 74(2): payments from public funds

1 Check that the payment which is alleged to have been made late is a prescribed payment.
2 Check that the payment was in fact made late and that income support would not have been paid if the payment had not been made late.
3 Ascertain the date at which receipt of the payment ought to have

App 4 Checklists for calculating amounts of overpayments 361

been notified by the claimant, which will be when D became aware of his/her entitlement.
4   Match up the payment, or each part of it, with the benefit week in which it is paid under reg 31(1)(b), and apply Part V to ascertain the effects on income support.

Section 74(3): payments to third parties
1   Check the period for which the three conditions are met.
    - A becomes entitled to child benefit, child's special allowance, guardian's allowance or an increase to a benefit in respect of B.
    - B received income support or was part of the family of C, who received income support.
    - The income support entitlement does not take account of the entitlement to benefit of A.
2   Match up the payment, or each part of it, with the benefit week in which it is paid under reg 31(1)(b), and apply Part V to ascertain the effects on income support.
3   Consider whether it is right that the discretion should be exercised to withhold arrears of benefit from A.

Housing benefit and council tax benefit overpayments

1   Calculate the total amount of benefit paid under the various decisions (see step 1 for s71 overpayments).
2   Calculate how much benefit is not recoverable because it was a non-exempt payment made due to an official error which was not contributed to and could not have been noticed by a relevant person.
3   Apply any offsets that are appropriate in D's case.
    - In excess capital cases, apply the diminishing capital rule.
    - Deduct any lesser amount of benefit allowed on the review decision.
    - Where the claimant has 'paid' too much rent rebate or council tax.
4   Ensure that there is no double counting, in view of the reductions made by steps 2 and 3.
5   If the authority is recovering from another source, deduct the amount which will be recovered from that source due to the danger of double recovery.

APPENDIX 5

Guide to decision-making by appellate bodies

This appendix is intended as an aid for tribunals and review boards dealing with appeals. A failure to follow each stage religiously will not necessarily make a decision erroneous in law, particularly where an issue has not been contested by the defendant. The detailed requirements of a tribunal decision are dealt with at pp172–176 above, and those for a review board at pp277–278. At all stages, tribunals and review boards should try to make clear findings of fact and refer to those findings of fact in reaching each conclusion.

Note: throughout this appendix, 'D' is used as shorthand for 'defendant'.

SSAA s71 appeals

Review
1 Is there a review decision in the AT2 or another document before the tribunal?
2 Is there clear evidence in the documents before the tribunal that a review was carried out and what the terms of the decision were?
3 If 'no' to 1 and 2, the recoverability decision is invalid.
4 Does the decision revise all relevant decisions awarding benefit and state the amount of the overpayment?
5 If 'no' to 4, the recoverability decision is invalid. If 'yes' to 4 the recoverability decision is valid.
6 Ensure that the review decision states the amounts and periods of entitlement under the revised decision, and that the grounds for review are properly set out.

Misrepresentation cases
1 What is the statement relied on by the DSS?
2 What is the evidence that the statement was made by D? Was it in fact made?

App 5 Guide to decision-making by appellate bodies

3 If 'no' to 2, there is no misrepresentation.
4 If 'yes' to 2, is the statement false, having regard to the context in which it was made?
5 If 'yes' to 4, there has been a misrepresentation.
6 If 'no' to 4, there is no misrepresentation. Consider whether there may have been failure to disclose, ensuring that D has a fair chance to deal with this case.

Failure to disclose cases

1 Was D under a duty to disclose? Why?
2 If 'no' to 1, there is no failure to disclose.
3 If 'yes' to 1, did D make a disclosure?
4 If 'yes' to 3, was the disclosure sufficient?
5 If 'yes' to 4, there is no failure to disclose.
6 If 'no' to 2 or 3, did D do everything that could reasonably be expected of him/her?
7 If 'no' to 6, there is a failure to disclose.
8 If 'yes' to 6, there is no failure to disclose. Consider whether there may have been misrepresentation, ensuring that D has a fair chance to deal with this case.

Material fact

1 What does the DSS allege the material fact to be?
2 Is it a fact?
3 Is it a primary fact?
4 Is it material to the claimant's benefit entitlement or to the payment of benefit?
5 If 'yes' to 2, 3 and 4, the breach of duty relates to a material fact.
6 If 'no' to 2, 3 or 4, consider whether there is a material fact which could found recovery, ensuring that D has a fair chance to make representations on the point, that there is a breach of duty relating to that fact, and that the some amount of benefit was paid in consequence of the breach of duty relating to that fact.

Causation

1 Did the relevant DSS office, or its agent, ever become aware of the falsity of the material fact?
2 If 'yes' to 1, the overpayment is not recoverable after that time.
3 If 'no' to 1 and the breach of duty alleged is a misrepresentation, was there any previous disclosure?
4 If 'yes' to 3, can this vitiate the effect of the misrepresentation?
5 If 'yes' to 4, the overpayment is not recoverable from the time of the disclosure.
6 If 'no' to 3 or 4, was there some intervening event between the breach of duty and each subsequent payment that may also have caused the overpayment?

7 If 'yes' to 6, was the breach of duty still a sufficiently significant cause of the overpayment, notwithstanding the intervening event?
8 If 'no' to 7, the overpayment is not recoverable from the time of the intervening event.
9 If 'yes' to 7, causation is established.

Amount

1 Is payment of the benefit in dispute?
2 If 'no' to 1, does the tribunal accept the calculations on the AT2 schedule?
3 If 'yes' to 2, identify the schedule and state that it is accepted.
4 If 'yes' to 1 or 'no' to 2, can the tribunal practically do the recalculation itself at the hearing, being fair to both parties?
5 If 'no' to 4, make a final decision on the principle and periods of recoverability and remit the question of the amount for the agreement of the parties, with the right to return to the tribunal should agreement not be reached.
6 If 'yes' to 4, use Appendix 4 to recalculate the amount.

Housing benefit or council tax benefit review board

1 Was a statement of the authority's determination, containing the correct information, served on D and the claimant (if not D)?
2 If 'yes' to 1, are the authority's stated grounds for reviewing the awards of benefit valid?
3 If 'no' to 2, does the authority have valid grounds for review, and has the claimant had an adequate chance to make representations about those grounds?
4 If 'no' to 1 or 3, the decision to recover is invalid.
5 If 'yes' to 2 or 3, is the overpayment in those categories which are always recoverable? If 'yes', state why and go to 14.
6 If 'no' to 5, was there any official error in relation to the claim?
7 If 'yes' to 6, consider who or what was responsible, what the mistake was and what the effect of the mistake was. Did the official error cause the overpayment?
8 If 'yes' to 7, did the claimant, a person acting on his/her behalf, or a person to whom the payment was made cause or contribute to that official error?
9 If 'yes' to 8, the overpayment is recoverable. State who caused or contributed to the official error, in what way and why his/her conduct was material and go to 14.
10 If 'no' to 8, could the claimant, a person acting on his/her behalf, or a person to whom the payment was made have reasonably realised that there was an overpayment?

11 If 'yes' to 10, at least some of the overpayment is recoverable. State who should have noticed the overpayment and why. Consider the date that s/he should have realised that there was an overpayment. The overpayment is recoverable from then.
12 If 'no' to 10, the overpayment is not recoverable.
13 If 'no' to 6 and 7, the overpayment is recoverable.
14 Consider the amount of the overpayment according to Appendix 4 and adjust appropriately if it is inaccurate.
15 Is it right that the authority should exercise its discretion not to recover the amount?
16 If 'no' to 15, should it exercise its discretion to recover a reduced amount?
17 If 'no' to 16, state the decision to recover in the appropriate sum. If D has requested the exercise of the discretion, give full reasons for declining to do so.
18 If 'yes' to 15 or 16, give full reasons for the decision and state the sum (if any) to be recovered from D.

Index

Abolished benefits
   recovery under s71, 8
Action for debt, 191
Adjudication officer
   referral to, 157-158
Advising those under investigation, 307-308
Age addition
   retirement pension, to, recovery under s71, 8
Appeal
   compensation payments, recovery from, 243-246, 250
   guide to decision-making by appellate bodies, 363-366
   review and revision requirement, rectification of,
      appellate body seised of issue, 29-30
      Commissioner, position of, 30-31
      generally, 26-29
      reversing award on appeal, 30
      varying award on appeal, 30
   tribunal, to. *See* Social security appeal tribunal
Appointees
   disclosure, duty of, 59-60
   recovery under s71 from, 11-12
Arrangements for payment, 188-190
Attendance allowance
   recovery under s71, 8
Beliefs
   relevant material fact, as, 95-96
Breach of duty
   causal link, requirement of, 108-109
   committed before 6 April 1987, 142-143

Breach of duty – *contd*
   operative cause, as,
      DSS, acts and omissions of, 111-115
      generally, 109-111
      misrepresentations and previous disclosures, 118-123
      third parties, acts and omissions of, 115-118
Calculating amount owed
   extra-statutory offsets, applying for, 140-141
   generally, 124-125
   method of calculating amount,
      calculate benefit paid, 125-127
      deduct allowable offsets, 128
      deduct elements which are not recoverable, 127-128
      generally, 125
   offsets allowed under statute,
      diminishing capital rule, 137-138
      double recovery, prevention of, 139-140
      generally, 128
      original claim, offsets based on, 135-137
      other benefits, offsets of, 138
      other offsets under reg 5, 133-135
      review, offsets in course of, 128-133
Capital
   diminishing capital rule, 137-138
Causal link. *See* General benefits, statutory recovery of
Challenging decisions
   credit transfer, overpayments by, 224-225

Challenging decisions – *contd*
  DSS. *See* Department of Social Security (DSS)
  deduction from benefits, 196
  income support, recovery of, 214
  local authority. *See* Local authority
  tribunal, of, 177-178
Changes of circumstances
  written statement of, 35
Checklists
  conferences with defendants, 358-359
  overpayments, calculating amounts of, 360-362
Child benefit
  recovery under s71, 8
  wrong person, paid to, 135
Child Support Agency
  disclosure to, 75
Child support maintenance
  late receipt of income, recovery after, 203-204
Child's special allowance
  recovery under s71, 8
Claim form
  declaration, 44-45
Claimants
  disclosure, duty of, 57-59
  irrelevance of disclosure by, 89
  recovery under s71 from, 10-11
Cohabitation
  relevant material fact relating to, 98
Cold weather payments
  recovery under s71, 8
Commissioner
  review and revision requirement, rectification of, 30-31
Common law
  courts, recovery through,
    basis of recovery, 288-298
    generally, 287-288
  non est factum, 52-54
Communication
  DSS failures of, 113-114
Compensation payments
  Compensation Recovery Scheme,
    appeal, rights of, 243-246
    application of provisions, 235-243

Compensation payments – *contd*
  compensation Recovery Scheme – *contd*
    causation, 239-243
    enforcement, 246
    exempt payments, 237-238
    generally, 233-234
    procedure, 234-235
    relevant benefits, 238-239
    relevant period, 239
    review, powers of, 243
    solution, 246-247
  criminal injuries compensation, recovery from, 250
  employment protection legislation, recovery under,
    appeals, 250
    procedure, 248-249
    scope, 248
  precedent, 351-352
  recovery from, 233
Conditions for recovery
  basic definition, 9
Conferences with defendants
  checklist for, 358-359
Contribution proceedings, 279
Contributory benefits
  increases to, recovery under s71, 8
  recovery under s71, 8
Conversion
  common law, recovery under, 288
Council tax benefit
  challenging local authority decisions,
    contribution proceedings, 279
    further review by review board, 276-278
    generally, 268-269
    initial determination by authority, 269-273
    judicial review, 278-279
    review by local authority, 273-276
  enforcement of recovery,
    courts, through, 281-282
    deduction from benefits, 282-283
    generally, 280
    requests to waive recovery, 280

Council tax benefit – *contd*
  enforcement of recovery – *contd*
    system for repayment, 280
    precedents, 352-353
    rules for recovery,
      calculating amount, 264-267
      conditions for recovery, 254-263
      generally, 253
County court
  execution through, 191
Court of Protection receiver
  disclosure, duty of, 59-60
  recovery under s71 from, 13
Courts
  common law, recovery under,
    basis of, 288-298
    conversion, 288
    generally, 287-288
    restitution, 288-298
  council tax benefit, enforcement
    of recovery of, 281-282
  county court, execution through,
    191
  debt, action for, 191
  enforcement through, 190-191
  housing benefit, enforcement of
    recovery of, 281-282
  judicial review, 186-187
  personal representative, application
    for relief by, 184-185
  precedents, 353-357
  sheriff court, execution through,
    191
Credit transfer, overpayments by. *See*
  Overpayments
Criminal injuries compensation
  recovery from, 250
Debt
  action for, 191
  See also Enforcement of recovery
Deception
  obtaining property by, 314-315
Decisions of DSS. *See* Department of
  Social Security
Declaration
  claim form, 44-45
  order book, 42-44
  UB 24, 45-47
Deduction from benefits
  amount of deduction, 195-196

Deduction from benefits – *contd*
  challenging decisions, 196
  generally, 192
  scope of provisions, 192-194
Defective review, 23-25
Defences
  restitution. *See* Restitution
Defendant
  personal characteristics of,
    failure to disclose, 89-91
  lack of knowledge of, 84
Department of Social Security (DSS)
  acts and omissions of,
    communication, failures of,
      113-114
    generally, 111-112
    investigations, failure to carry
      out, 114-115
    knowledge of material facts,
      failure to act on, 112-113
  budget, 1
  challenging decisions of,
    adjudication officer, referral to,
      157-158
    appeal to tribunal, 162-176
    decision-making process, 157-
      161
    estoppel, 158-160
    generally, 157
    judicial review, 185-187
    legitimate expectation, 161
    personal representative,
      application to court for
      relief by, 184-185
    promises, effect of, 158-161
    representations about recovery,
      158-161
    request to waive recovery,
      178-181
    review, request for, 161-162
    third party, recovery from,
      181-183
    tribunal decision, challenge to,
      177-178
  communication, failures of, 113-
    114
  financial impact of overpayments,
    1
  investigations, failure to carry out,
    114-115

Department of Social Security (DSS)
  – *contd*
  knowledge of material fact,
    failure to act on, 112-113
    failure to disclose, 65-66
  reliance on advice from, 85-87
  total overpaid benefits recovered
    in 1993/94, 1
Diminishing capital rule, 137-138
Disability living allowance
  recovery under s71, 8
Disability working allowance
  recovery under s71, 8
Disablement pension
  recovery under s71, 8
Disclosure
  continuing duty of,
    circumstances where there is,
      62-64
    consequence of, 64-65
    generally, 61-62
  duty of,
    appointees, 59-60
    claimants, 57-59
    generally, 57
    other defendants, 59-61
    other people assisting
      claimants, 59-60
    other third parties, 61
    personal representatives, 60-61
    receivers, 59-60
  failure to disclose. *See* Failure to
    disclose
  intention, of, 87-88
  meaning, 66-67
  nature of,
    disclosure, meaning, 66-67
    place of disclosure, 69-76
    proving disclosure, 76-79
    who can make disclosure, 68-69
  oral, 78
  other offices, to, 75-76
  place of,
    other offices, 75-76
    post offices, 76
    relevant office, 69-72
    unemployment benefit office,
      72-75
  post, by, 79
  post office, to, 76

Disclosure – *contd*
  proving,
    generally, 76-78
    oral disclosure, 78
    post, disclosure by, 79
  reasonable expectation of,
    DSS, reliance on advice from,
      85-87
    generally, 84-85
    intention, disclosure of, 87-88
    irrelevance of disclosure by
      claimant, 89
    matters of public knowledge,
      88-89
    other experts, reliance on
      advice from, 87
    personal characteristics of
      defendant, 89-91
  relevant office, to, 69-72
  unemployment benefit office, to,
    72-75
  who can make, 68-69
Double recovery
  prevention of, 139-140
Due care and diligence test
  nature of,
    generally, 151
    peripheral matters, 151-153
    statutory language, 153-156
  payment before 6 April 1987,
    recovery of,
    decision-making process, 150-
      151
    generally, 149-150
    nature of test, 151-156
Employment protection legislation
  compensation under, recovery
    from, 248-250
Enforcement of recovery
  arrangements for payment, 188-190
  compensation payments, 246
  council tax benefit, relating to,
    courts, through, 281-282
    deduction from benefits, 282-283
    generally, 280
    requests to waive recovery, 280
    system for repayment, 280
  courts, through, 190-191
  credit transfer, overpayments by,
    225

Enforcement of recovery – *contd*
  deduction from benefits, 192-196
  generally, 188
  housing benefit, relating to,
    courts, through, 281-282
    deduction from benefits, 282-283
    generally, 280
    requests to waive recovery, 280
    system for repayment, 280
  income support, 212-213
  mortgage lender, recovery from, 197-198
  severe hardship rule, payments of income support to 16- and 17-year olds under, 218-219
  third party, recovery from, 196-198
Estoppel
  promises, effect of, 158-160
  representations about recovery, 158-160
  restitution, recovery in, 295-296
European Convention of Human Rights
  possessions, right to enjoy, 7n
European Union (EU)
  recovery of benefits from other member states, 207-211
Evidence
  appeal to tribunal,
    burden of proof, 165-167
    documentary evidence, 167-168
    generally, 165
  secondary, review and revision requirement and, 25-26
Execution
  county court, through, 191
  sheriff court, through, 191
Expectations
  relevant material fact, as, 96-97
Experts
  reliance on advice from, 87
  See also Department of Social Security
Extra-statutory offsets
  applying for, 140-141
Extracts from legislation, 323-343
Failure to disclose
  continuing duty,
    circumstances where there is, 62-64

Failure to disclose – *contd*
    consequence of, 64-65
    generally, 61-62
  DSS,
    knowledge of material fact by, 65-66
    reliance on advice from, 85-87
  duty of disclosure,
    appointees, 59-60
    claimants, 57-59
    continuing duty, 61-65
    generally, 57
    knowledge of material fact by DSS, 65-66
    other defendants, 59-61
    other people assisting claimants, 59-60
    other third parties, 61
    personal representatives, 60-61
    receivers, 59-60
  establishing, 56
  generally, 56
  knowledge of material fact by DSS, 65-66
  material fact,
    DSS knowledge of, 65-66
    lack of knowledge of, 80-83
    proving lack of knowledge, 83-84
  nature of disclosure,
    disclosure, meaning, 66-67
    place of disclosure, 69-76
    proving disclosure, 76-79
    who can make disclosure, 68-69
  requirement of,
    generally, 79-80
    lack of knowledge of material fact, 80-83
    proving lack of knowledge, 83-84
    whether disclosure was reasonably to be expected, 84-91
  tribunal, obligations of, 175
Failure to maintain
  recovery on grounds of, 230-231
False representation made in obtaining benefit, 310-314
Family
  entitlement to benefit in member's own right, increases to benefit where, 135

Index 371

Family credit
  recovery under s71, 8
Family income supplement
  payment before 6 April 1987,
    recovery of, 149
Form UB 24
  declaration, 45-47
Fraud
  mechanisms for detection of, 301-303
Fraudulent breach of duty
  recovery under s71, 15
Funeral expenses
  recovery of, 227
  recovery under s71, 8
General benefits, statutory recovery of
  breach of duty. *See* Breach of duty
  calculating amount owed,
    extra-statutory offsets,
      applying for, 140-141
    generally, 124-125
    method of calculation, 125-128
    offsets allowed under statute, 128-140
  causal link, requirement of,
    analysis in *Duggan*, 106-107
    basic principles, 105-109
    breach of duty as one of causes, 108-109
    DSS, acts and omissions of, 111-115
    generally, 102-105
    misrepresentations and previous disclosures, 118-123
    operative cause, breach of duty as, 109-123
    third parties, acts and omissions of, 115-118
    tribunal, obligations of, 175-176
  challenging DSS decisions,
    appeals to tribunal, 162-176
    challenging tribunal decisions, 177-178
    decision-making process, 157-161
    generally, 157
    judicial review, 185-187
    personal representative, application to court for relief by, 184-185

General benefits, statutory recovery of – *contd*
  challenging DSS decisions – *contd*
    request to waive recovery, 178-181
    requests for review, 161-162
    third party, recovery from, 181-183
  enforcement of recovery,
    arrangements for payment, 188-190
    courts, through, 190-191
    deduction from benefits, 192-196
    generally, 188
    mortgage lender, recovery from, 197-198
    third party, recovery from, 196-198
  failure to disclose,
    duty of disclosure, 57-66
    generally, 56
    nature of disclosure, 66-79
    requirement of failure, 79-91
    tribunal, obligations of, 175
  income support. *See* Income support
  material fact. *See* relevant material fact, *below*
  misrepresentation,
    content of representation, 37-49
    definition, 35-37
    generally, 34-35
    personal factors, relevance of, 49-55
    tribunal, obligations of, 175
  overpayments. *See* Overpayments
  payments made before 6 April 1987,
    due care and diligence test, recovery under, 149-156
    family income supplement, recovery of, 149
    generally, 8, 142-143
    non-retrospectivity of SSA 1986 s53, 143-147
    supplementary benefit, recovery of, 148
  recovery from 'any person',
    appointees, 11-12

General benefits, statutory recovery of – *contd*
  recovery from 'any person' – *contd*
    claimants, 10-11
    Court of Protection receivers, 13
    generally, 10
    other third parties, 14
    personal representatives, 14
  relevant material fact,
    generally, 92-93
    materiality, 99-101
    need for fact, 93-97
    primary and secondary fact, 97-99
    tribunal, obligations of, 175
  review and revision requirement,
    exceptions to requirement, 20-21
    failure to comply with requirement, 21-33
    generally, 17-18
    nature of, 18-19
    process of review, 19-20
    tribunal, obligations of, 174-175
  structure and scope of SSAA s71,
    applicability of s71, 7-9
    conditions for recovery, 9
    full list of benefits recovered, 8
    objective of s71, 7
    precedents, 344-349
    recovery from 'any person', 10-14
    right to recover, 7
    time at which benefit was paid, 8
    time limits, 15-16
    whether fraudulently or otherwise, 15
  time limits, 15-16
  whether fraudulently or otherwise, 15
Graduated retirement benefit
  recovery under s71, 8
Guardian's allowance
  recovery under s71, 8
Hearing. *See* Social security appeal tribunal
Household
  relevant material fact relating to, 99
Housing benefit
  challenging local authority decisions, contribution proceedings, 279

Housing benefit – *contd*
  challenging local authority decisions – *contd*
    further review by review board, 276-278
    generally, 268-269
    initial determination by authority, 269-273
    judicial review, 278-279
    review by local authority, 273-276
  enforcement of recovery,
    courts, through, 281-282
    deduction from benefits, 282-283
    generally, 280
    requests to waive recovery, 280
    system for repayment, 280
  precedents, 352-353
  rules for recovery,
    calculating amount, 264-267
    conditions for recovery, 254-263
    generally, 253
Illegality
  judicial review, 186
Incapability
  misrepresentation, effect on, 51-55
Incapacity
  misrepresentation, effect on,
    generally, 51
    no knowledge of representation, 51-52
    non est factum, 52-54
    proof of incapacity, 54-55
  proof of, 54-55
Incapacity benefit
  recovery under s71, 8
Incapacity for work
  relevant material fact relating to, 97-98
Income support
  late receipt of income, recovery after,
    challenging decisions, 214
    child support maintenance, 203-204
    enforcement, 212-213
    generally, 201
    prescribed income generally, 201-203

Index 373

Income support – *contd*
  late receipt of income, recovery after – *contd*
    public funds, prescribed payments from, 204-211
    third party receiving benefit, 211-212
  recovery under s71, 8
  severe hardship rule, payments to 16- and 17-year olds under, 215-219
  trade dispute, paid after, recovery of, 231-232
Industrial injuries benefits
  recovery under s71, 8
Innocent breach of duty
  recovery under s71, 15
Intentions
  disclosure of, 87-88
  relevant material fact, as, 96-97
Interim payments
  late receipt of maintenance, made due to, 229-230
  offsetting, 230
  overpaid, determination of, 230
  recovery of, 229-230
Interview
  Code C, 304-306
  investigation, process of, 303-307
  trial, exclusion of material at, 306-307
Invalid care allowance
  recovery under s71, 8
Invalidity
  review and revision requirement, effect on, 31-32
Invalidity pension and allowance
  recovery under s71, 8
Investigation
  DSS failure to carry out, 114-115
  overpayments,
    advising those under, 307-308
    fraud, mechanisms for detection of, 301-303
    generally, 301
    interviews, 303-307
Irrationality
  judicial review, 186-187
Judicial review
  challenging DSS decisions, 185-187

Judicial review – *contd*
  council tax benefit, recovery of, 278-279
  courts, review by, 186-187
  credit transfer, overpayments by, 225
  housing benefit, recovery of, 278-279
  illegality, 186
  irrationality, 186-187
  procedural impropriety, 187
  procedure, 186
  severe hardship rule, payments of income support to 16- and 17-year olds under, 218
Legitimate expectation
  promises, effect of, 161
  representations about recovery, 161
Local authority
  challenging decisions of,
    contribution proceedings, 279
    further review by review board, 276-278
    generally, 268-269
    initial determination by authority, 269-273
    judicial review, 278-279
    review by local authority, 273-276
  council tax benefit. *See* Council tax benefit
  housing benefit. *See* Housing benefit
Maintenance
  child support, 203-204
  failure to maintain, recovery on grounds of, 230-231
  late receipt of, interim payments made due to, 229-230
Making false representation in obtaining benefit, 310-314
Material fact
  DSS knowledge of,
    failure to act on, 112-113
    failure to disclose, 65-66
  lack of knowledge of,
    failure to disclose and, 80-83
    level of knowledge required, 81-83
    personal factors, relating to, 50

Material fact – *contd*
  lack of knowledge of – *contd*
    proving, 83-84
  lack of understanding of
    materiality, 51
  misrepresentation. *See*
    Misrepresentation
  need for fact,
    expectations not facts, 96-97
    fact not law, 93-95
    intentions not facts, 96-97
    opinions and beliefs not facts,
      95-96
  primary and secondary fact,
    cohabitation, 98
    generally, 97
    household, 99
    incapacity for work, 97-98
    other secondary facts, 99
  relevant,
    generally, 92-93
    materiality, 99-101
    need for fact, 93-97
    primary and secondary fact,
      97-99
  tribunal, obligations of, 175
  whether represented, 37
Maternity expenses
  recovery of, 227
  recovery under s71, 8
Means-tested benefits
  recovery under s71, 8
Misrepresentation
  actual statement which is untrue,
    existence of, 35, 36
  content of representation,
    analysis of general
      representation, 40-47
    construing representation, 37-40
    generally, 37
    material fact, whether
      represented, 37
    relying on general
      misrepresentation, 47-49
  definition, 35-37
  generally, 34-35
  personal factors, relevance of,
    generally, 49
    incapability, 51-55
    incapacity, 51-55

Misrepresentation – *contd*
  personal factors, relevance of –
    contd
    material fact, lack of
      knowledge of, 50
    materiality, lack of
      understanding of, 51
  previous disclosure, and,
    earlier disclosure suffices, 120-
      123
    effect of previous disclosure,
      118-120
    generally, 118
  tribunal, obligations of, 175
  written representation, reliance
    on, 35
Mobility allowance
  recovery under s71, 8
Mortgage lender
  recovery from, 197-198
Negligent breach of duty
  recovery under s71, 15
Non est factum
  common law doctrine, 52-54
Non-contributory benefits
  increases to, recovery under s71, 8
  recovery under s71, 8
Non-enforcement
  request for, 225
Obtaining property by deception,
  314-315
Offences. *See* Prosecution of offences
Offsets
  allowable, deduction of, 128
  council tax benefit, recovery of,
    264-266
  diminishing capital rule, 137-138
  double recovery, prevention of,
    139-140
  extra-statutory, applying for,
    140-141
  housing benefit, recovery of, 264-
    266
  interim payments, 230
  original claim, based on, 135-137
  other benefits, of, 138
  other offsets under reg 5, 133-135
  review, in course of,
    generally, 128
    inherent power, 128-130

Index 375

Offsets – *contd*
  review, in course of – *contd*
    Overpayments Regs, under, 130
    scope of review, 130-133
  statute, allowed under,
    diminishing capital rule, 137-138
    double recovery, prevention of, 139-140
    generally, 128
    original claim, offsets based on, 135-137
    other benefits, offsets of, 138
    other offsets under reg 5, 133-135
    review, offsets in course of, 128-133
One parent benefit
  recovery under s71, 8
Opinions
  relevant material fact, as, 95-96
Oral disclosure
  proof of, 78
Order book
  declaration, 42-44
Overpayments
  checklists for calculating amounts of, 360-362
  council tax benefit. *See* Council tax benefit
  credit transfer, by,
    appeal to tribunal, 224
    challenging decisions, 224-225
    enforcement, 225
    four conditions, 220-224
    generally, 220
    judicial review, 225
    non-enforcement, request for, 225
    notice of regulation given to claimant, 223-224
    payment in excess of entitlement, 222-223
    precedent, 351
    revision of determination, 220-222
    Secretary of State's certificate, 223
  generally, 1-3
  housing benefit. *See* Housing benefit

Overpayments – *contd*
  investigation, process of,
    advising those under investigation, 307-308
    fraud, mechanisms for detection of, 301-303
    generally, 301
    interviews, 303-307
  meaning, 254
  overpaid interim payments, determination of, 230
  tribunal, obligations of, 173-176
Payments
  arrangements for, 188-190
  benefits paid before 6 April 1987,
    due care and diligence test, recovery of benefits under, 149-156
    family income supplement, recovery of, 149
    generally, 8, 142-143
    non-retrospectivity of SSA 1986 s53, 143-147
    precedents, 349-350
    supplementary benefit, recovery of, 148
Personal factors
  misrepresentation, effect on. *See* Misrepresentation
  personal characteristics of defendant,
    failure to disclose, 89-91
    lack of knowledge of, 84
Personal representative
  application to court for relief by, 184-185
  disclosure, duty of, 60-61
  recovery under s71 from, 14
Post
  proof of disclosure by, 79
Post office
  disclosure to counter clerk in, 76
Precedents, 344-357
Presentation of case
  tribunal, to, 169-171
Primary fact. *See* Material fact
Procedural impropriety
  judicial review, 187

Promises
  challenging DSS decisions,
    estoppel, 158-160
    generally, 158
    legitimate expectation, 161
Proof
  appeal to tribunal, relating to, 165-167
  disclosure, of,
    generally, 76-78
    oral disclosure, 78
    post, disclosure by, 79
  incapacity, of, 54-55
  lack of knowledge, of,
    generally, 83-84
    personal characteristics of defendant, 84
  misrepresentation alleged, of, 35
Property
  obtained by deception, 314-315
Prosecution of offences
  deception, obtaining property by, 314-315
  making false representation in obtaining benefit, 310-314
  practice, 309-310
  sentencing,
    application of criteria, 319
    available options, 316-317
    criteria, 317-319
    less serious offences, 318-319
    more serious offences, 317-318
    starting point, 317
Public funds
  prescribed payments from, late payment of, 204-207
Public interest
  recovery of money wrongfully paid over, 7
Public knowledge, matters of
  reasonable expectation of disclosure, 88-89
Receiver. *See* Court of Protection receiver
Recovery
  compensation payments, from. *See* Compensation payments
  conditions for, 9
  double, prevention of, 139-140

Recovery – *contd*
  enforcement. *See* Enforcement of recovery
  from 'any person',
    appointees, 11-12
    claimants, 10-11
    Court of Protection receivers, 13
    generally, 10
    other third parties, 14
    personal representatives, 14
  general benefits, of. *See* General benefits, statutory recovery of
  generally, 1-3
  misrepresentation, effect of. *See* Misrepresentation
  representations about,
    estoppel, 158-160
    generally, 158
    legitimate expectation, 161
  requests to waive, 178-181
  third party, from, 181-183
Reduced earnings allowance
  recovery under s71, 8
Relevant material fact. *See* Material fact
Representation
  construing,
    context of representation, 39-40
    generally, 37
    precise wording, 38
  content of,
    analysis of general representation, 40-47
    construing representation, 37-40
    material fact, 37
    reliance on general representation, 47-49
  context of, 39-40
  general,
    analysis of, 40-47
    claim form declaration, 44-45
    med 3 declaration, 47
    order book declaration, 42-44
    power to rely on, 47-49
    UB 24 declaration, 45-47
  no knowledge of, 51-52
  precise wording of, 38
  written, reliance on, 35
Representations about recovery
  estoppel, 158-160

Index 377

Representations about recovery
– *contd*
  generally, 158
  legitimate expectation, 161
Requests to waive recovery, 178-181
Res judicata, 295
Restitution
  common law, recovery under, 288-298
  defences,
    change of position, 296-297
    estoppel, 295-296
    generally, 292
    limitation, 297-298
    res judicata, 295
    statutory policy, recovery against, 293-295
  money was paid over,
    generally, 289
    mistake , as result of, 290-291
    mistake of fact rather than law, 291-292
Retirement allowance
  recovery under s71, 8
Retirement benefit
  graduated, recovery under s71, 8
Retirement pension
  age addition to, recovery under s71, 8
  recovery under s71, 8
Review
  board, further review by,
    generally, 276
    hearing, 276-277
    obligations of board, 277-278
  compensation payments, recovery from, 243
  local authority, by,
    further review by review board, 276-278
    generally, 273-274
    material fact, ignorance of or mistake as to, 275-276
    mistake of law, 276
    relevant change of circumstances, 274-275
  offsets in course of,
    generally, 128
    inherent power, 128-130
    Overpayments Regs, under, 130

Review – *contd*
  offsets in course of – *contd*
    scope of review, 130-133
  requests for, 161-162
  revision requirement. *See* Review and revision requirement
  scope of, 130-133
Review and revision requirement
  exceptions to, 20-21
  failure to comply with,
    conclusions, 32-33
    defective review, 23-25
    generally, 21-22
    invalidity, consequences of, 31-32
    no review, 22-23
    rectification on appeal, 26-31
    secondary evidence, 25-26
  generally, 17-18
  nature of, 18-19
  process of review, 19-20
  tribunal, obligations of, 174-175
Scotland
  sheriff court, execution through, 191
Secondary evidence
  review and revision requirement, failure to comply with, 25-26
Secondary fact. *See* Material fact
Sentencing. *See* Prosecution of offences
Severe disablement allowance
  recovery under s71, 8
Sheriff court
  execution through, 191
Sickness benefit
  recovery under s71, 8
Social fund payments
  recovery of,
    funeral expenses, 227
    generally, 226
    maternity expenses, 227
    method of recovery, 228-229
    repayable loans, 226-227
  recovery under s71, 8
Social security appeal tribunal
  appeal to,
    burden of proof, 165-167
    documentary evidence, 167-168
    evidence, 165

Social security appeal tribunal – *contd*
  appeal to – *contd*
    formulation of grounds, 164-165
    generally, 162-163
    making appeal, 163-168
    time limits, 163-164
  challenging decisions of, 177-178
  credit transfer, overpayments by, 224
  hearing,
    after, 172
    generally, 168
    preparation, 168-169
    presentation of case, 169-171
  obligations of,
    general obligations, 172-173
    generally, 172
    overpayments case, specific to, 173-176
  severe hardship rule, payments of income support under, 217
Statutory recovery
  general benefits, of. *See* General benefits, statutory recovery of
Supplementary benefit
  payment before 6 April 1987, recovery of, 148
Third party
  acts and omissions of, 115-118
  bypassing SSAA s71 by recovery from, 196-198
  disclosure, duty of, 61

Third party – *contd*
  receiving benefit in respect of claimant, recovery of income support, 211-212
  recovery from,
    criteria for recovery, 183
    generally, 181
    method of recovery, 181-183
    recovery under s71 from, 14
Time limits
  appeal to tribunal, 163-164
  recovery under s71, 15-16
  restitution, recovery in, 297-298
Trade dispute
  recovery of income support paid after, 231-232
Tribunal. *See* Social security appeal tribunal
Unemployment benefit
  recovery under s71, 8
Unemployment benefit office (UBO)
  disclosure to, 72-75
Widow's payment
  recovery under s71, 8
Widow's pension
  recovery under s71, 8
Widowed mother's allowance
  recovery under s71, 8
Young person
  severe hardship rule, payments of income support to 16- and 17-year-olds under, 215-219